Get the eBook FREE!

(PDF, ePub, Kindle, and liveBook all included)

We believe that once you buy a book from us, you should be able to read it in any format we have available. To get electronic versions of this book at no additional cost to you, purchase and then register this book at the Manning website.

Go to https://www.manning.com/freebook and follow the instructions to complete your pBook registration.

That's it!
Thanks from Manning!

Logs and Telemetry

Logs and Telemetry

USING FLUENT BIT, KUBERNETES, STREAMING, AND MORE

PHIL WILKINS

FOREWORD BY EDUARDO SILVA PEREIRA

MANNING

SHELTER ISLAND

For online information and ordering of this and other Manning books, please visit
www.manning.com. The publisher offers discounts on this book when ordered in quantity.
For more information, please contact

> Special Sales Department
> Manning Publications Co.
> 20 Baldwin Road
> PO Box 761
> Shelter Island, NY 11964
> Email: orders@manning.com

Manning Publications Co.
20 Baldwin Road
PO Box 761
Shelter Island, NY 11964

Development editor:	Katie Sposato Johnson
Technical editor:	Karthik Gaekwad
Review editor:	Dunja Nikitović
Production editor:	Kathy Rossland
Copy editor:	Keir Simpson
Proofreader:	Katie Tennant
Technical proofreader:	Braydon Kain
Typesetter:	Dennis Dalinnik
Cover designer:	Marija Tudor

ISBN: 9781633437470
Printed in the United States of America

To my wife, Catherine, and our boys, Christopher and Aaron

brief contents

contents

foreword

The art of translating signals from applications and system services to insights on performance and system health is a difficult task, especially when the data comes from different sources and in different formats. Although the industry is trying to evolve and create standards to solve this problem for the long term, the short-term result is that we have to deal with several protocols and data structures to enable end users to perform meaningful analysis. In parallel, data volume is a constant challenge for companies as they see year-over-year data growth. The growth in data volume directly affects user experience. The more data there is to process, the slower the analysis gets.

When I started Fluent Bit in early 2015, little did I know that this lightweight agent, created for Embedded Linux at that time, would rule the logging world in what we now call cloud-native environments. Its ability to adapt to different protocols, pluggable architecture, and continuous focus for almost 10 years on performance (low memory, low CPU, and high throughput) has positioned it as the default solution for cloud providers such as Amazon, Google, Microsoft, and Oracle.

Fluent Bit started as a sibling of the Fluentd project. But with the industry's intensive migration to microservices and new ways of deploying workloads in orchestrated containers, the need arose for a more performant solution than Fluentd. Fluent Bit was built to enable companies building for Kubernetes and containers to scale and manage high volumes of data, making it the new preferred choice of the ecosystem. At this writing, Fluent Bit has been deployed more than 14 billion times from public repositories, not counting the number of cloud providers, which exceeds that.

Behind the project scenes, Fluent Bit isn't a one-person job. Hundreds of individuals and companies continuously contribute to improving it by writing code and documentation, maintaining distribution channels, and speaking at events. Phil Wilkins, the author of this book, is an active member of the Fluent community who has been at the center of the evolution of telemetry, data pipelines, and observability in general.

In this book, Phil concentrates on the Fluent concepts in a way that's easy to consume and learn for those who want to migrate from Fluentd. He walks the reader through the steps to implement Fluent Bit, from simple telemetry pipelines to advanced use cases. Readers will find great insights about the internals, such as buffering, routing, and threading, as well as the capability to handle other signal types, such as metrics and traces. He also provides details on using the upcoming industry protocol standards, such as OpenTelemetry.

In summary, this book distills nearly a decade's worth of innovation and development in Fluent Bit technology. It provides practical guidance on addressing modern challenges in observability, particularly in distributed systems like Kubernetes. I hope you enjoy this content as much as I did.

May the telemetry force be with you.

—EDUARDO SILVA PEREIRA
Fluent Bit creator and maintainer

preface

The idea of writing about Fluent Bit first came up around 2021. At the time, I was writing a book on Fluentd for Manning (*Logging in Action*), and I'd talked with Eduardo Silva Pereira, the creator of Fluent Bit, and Anurag Gupta, the leader of Fluentd. Extending *Logging in Action* wasn't a practical option, and I wasn't sure I could make the case for a dedicated book. I could see the trend toward OpenTelemetry and its influence on technology direction, but the standards weren't yet stable, and I assumed that Fluentd would lead the charge in engaging with the OpenTelemetry Protocol (OTLP) standard. But Eduardo and Anurag had already picked up on the trends accelerating the adoption of Fluent Bit. They saw the continued adoption of native binaries in the Kubernetes space getting more compact and providing faster performance. (After all, at scale, saving even 5% of your compute effort yields dividends.)

By early 2023, I'd forgotten how much time writing a book takes and could see clearly that Fluent Bit was gaining a lot of momentum. I also understood better how a new book could differ from and complement *Logging in Action*.

Now that the book is written, it's related to what came before but entirely freestanding and independent, like Fluentd and Fluent Bit—independent and complementary. I think that the book's timing is working out well. Fluent Bit v3 is out without breaking changes from v2. In many respects, v1.9 and v2 introduced the key foundation to support users' needs as OpenTelemetry matured, the standards became stable, and Fluent Bit is now in the mainstream. Innovations in observability are coming in the form of eBPF (extended Berkeley Packet Filter), which Fluent Bit will be more than capable of handling.

The book starts with the basics and addresses all the important features of v2 and v3. Features that are only available in v3 are identified. But Fluent Bit's configuration doesn't have any breaking changes, so while not all features and configuration options will be available, the principles explained in this book will still hold true for versions before v2. Therefore, if you work in an organization that's very cautious about moving up to recent releases, this book will still help. If you're new to the Fluent projects, this book is the place to start your learning journey.

acknowledgments

This book is my second with Manning and with some of the same team. The writing process took longer than we expected. But I hope you'll agree that the Manning editorial team's prodding and encouragement means this book will deliver for you. I want to thank everyone at Manning, particularly development editor Katie Sposato Johnson, acquisitions editor Andrew Waldron, and technical editor Karthik Gaekwad, who have been with me throughout this adventure.

Anurag Gupta and Eduardo Silva Pereira, the founders of Calyptia, who have been at the forefront of Fluentd and Fluent Bit for many years, took time to share their insights and support. Eduardo, who started the Fluent Bit project, also kindly gave his time to write the foreword, for which I'm very grateful. Calyptia employs many Fluent Bit committers, and I'd like to particularly acknowledge fellow Brit Patrick Stephens at Chronosphere, who helped hugely and with whom I've collaborated on conference presentations about Fluent Bit.

In writing this book, I had the support of volunteer reviewers and MEAP readers, some of whom come from the active Fluent Bit community. Their feedback provided great help and insight. Not every suggestion made it into the book, but I'm thinking about building on them in other ways, such as blog posts and DZone articles. I'd like to single out Braydon Kains for his contributions as a reviewer; he took the time to share his insights into the OpenTelemetry community and offered ideas on how to make running all the book's scenarios as easy as possible.

To all the reviewers—Abhay Paroha, Ajay Lotan Thakur, Amar Mani, Andres Sacco, Arpit Singh, Arun Pandiyan Perumal, Atul S. Khot, Ayisha Tabbassum, Braydon

Kains, Conor Redmond, Curtis Bates, Eduardo Silva Pereira, Frans Oilinki, Glen Yu, Harsha Patil, Harshavardhan Nerella, James Liu, Jerome Meyer, John Guthrie, Jonathan Blair, José Lecaros Cisterna, Kerry E. Koitzsch, Kosmas Chatzimichalis, Leonardo Taccari, Magnus Therning, Mario-Leander Reimer, Monojit Banerjee, Narayanan Seshan, Nico de Wet, Nikhil Kumar, Patrick Stephens, Pradeep Chintale, Prashant Dwivedi, Raymond Cheung, Samson Hailu, Sau Fai Fong, Simeon Leyzerzon, Sudeep Batra, Victor Declerk, and Vladislav Bilay—thank you, your suggestions helped make this book better.

Publishing a book involves more than engineering and writing. Often, help of other kinds is needed. That help has come from Manning, of course, but also from Calyptia and its parent organization, Chronosphere. Thank you all.

My journey as an author wouldn't have started without support and encouragement over the years. Those involved in my journey to becoming an Oracle Ace Director (think Java Rock Star or Microsoft MVP for Oracle Integration and Cloud) have been central to this journey. Many thanks to my friends and colleagues, past and present, at Oracle.

Last and most important, this book would never have happened without the support and understanding of my wife, Catherine, and our two sons, Christopher and Aaron, when I've spent evenings and weekends at the computer rather than in their company. All my love to you.

about this book

Logs and Telemetry is for anyone involved in the practical tasks of developing, configuring, and running IT solutions. One of the most dominant uses of Fluent Bit is in the Kubernetes ecosystem, so the book gives a great deal of consideration to Kubernetes and containers. But don't be fooled; like many cloud-native technologies, it applies to traditional IT environments, so the book looks at features that support them. Modern monitoring doesn't separate infrastructure monitoring, application logging, and operational performance metrics. We have a technology that could be used in a DevOps or platform engineering context, as well as old-school organizations that separate infrastructure and application responsibilities.

Within the world of Kubernetes, there are probably as many opinions on what is involved in Kubernetes monitoring as there are flavors of Kubernetes. This book looks at all the major Kubernetes features available at this writing, but don't expect it to be a comprehensive guide on, say, building Helm charts for Fluent Bit. (For that, read a book about Helm first and then read this book. This will give you an understanding of how to package Fluent Bit, which is no different from any other application.) More of us work with prepackaged Kubernetes stacks than build Kubernetes environments from scratch. These configurations are opinionated, so if you know how they're configured, this book will equip you with the understanding to capture those metrics, logs, and traces. In its most basic form, Kubernetes is a clever and highly configurable application process running on a configurable OS. Keeping this in mind and seeing a lot of Fluent Bit's standard features will help you. Much of the book runs things locally to make it easy to see what's going on. We don't want the Kubernetes experience to be an impediment to grasping what you can do with Fluent Bit.

Developers and operationally involved people will benefit from the book, but so will architects. We'll reveal the art of the possible and show how Fluent Bit can simplify the IT landscape to make the most of the latest thinking on observability.

How this book is organized: A road map

This book was written to partner with *Logging in Action*, but as with all the best sequels, you don't have to have read the first book to enjoy and benefit from the second. *Logging in Action* addresses some architectural and design considerations that apply equally to Fluent Bit and Fluentd, and the products are interoperable.

This book is made up of 3 parts in 11 chapters. Part 1 sets out the big ideas:

- Chapter 1 introduces Fluent Bit's ideas and background and addresses its relationship with the wider observability and application ecosystem. We explore the industry trends accelerating and driving the growth in Fluent Bit adoption.
- Chapter 2 takes us through configuring and running Fluent Bit. We run a simple configuration that every developer implements: "Hello, World."

Part 2 takes us from "Hello, World" to seeing and using Fluent Bit's core capabilities, which enable us to solve many of our needs:

- Chapter 3 is our first deep look at Fluent Bit and the features we'll need in the real world. To do anything, we need data in the form of logs, traces, and metrics, so chapter 3 examines the most common sources.
- Containers and Kubernetes are, first and foremost, sources of events and enrichment data for Fluent Bit, so chapter 4 covers both. In addition, the chapter touches on filters, which chapter 7 revisits in depth.
- We need to put event data (logs, metrics, and traces) somewhere. Chapter 5 looks at how to output metrics, traces, and logs.
- Events may be partially or completely unstructured, but without structure, it is difficult to get any meaning from them. In chapter 6, we parse events. We can use parsers in several ways, from formatting to converting strings and handling encoded characters.
- Chapter 7 takes us from parsers to filters. Now that we can extract meaning from our events, we need to impose order and structure on them, enrich them with additional context, and manipulate them so that they're routed or excluded correctly.

Part 3 takes on advanced options:

- Chapter 8 tackles stream processing with Fluent Bit. We use stream processors to derive meaningful new data using SQL-based syntax and work with multiple events in a time series.

- Chapter 9 looks at Fluent Bit's processor capability to incorporate custom logic within input and output plugin configuration. Eventually, we'll encounter a situation where we must build a proper plugin. To prepare, we need to examine the different options for building custom plugins.
- Chapter 10 turns the concept of custom plugins into reality and examines how plugins interact with Fluent Bit's core as we walk through building our own input and output plugins.
- Chapter 11 shows how Fluent Bit can be applied to an enterprise use case. We will explore how Fluent Bit could help an organization without undue disruption.

Appendixes have been provided to cover the setup of third-party building blocks we need to allow us to exercise Fluent Bit. They also provide details of additional reference information and insights:

- Appendix A provides details on setting up the tools and services needed to run the exercises in this book.
- Appendix B lists many additional resources and reference tables.
- Appendix C provides an overview of the differences between Fluent Bit and Fluentd.

About the code

This book contains many examples of Fluent Bit's configuration and source code, both in numbered listings and inline with standard text. In both cases, the source code is formatted in a `fixed-width font like this` to separate it from ordinary text.

The book shows only the relevant sections of a configuration file in most cases. The configurations are annotated to illustrate the configurations. In some cases, even this is not enough, and listings include line-continuation markers (➡).

You can get executable snippets of code from the liveBook (online) version of this book at https://livebook.manning.com/book/logs-and-telemetry. Source code for the examples in this book is available for download from the publisher's website at https://www.manning.com/books/logs-and-telemetry or the GitHub repository at https://github.com/mp3monster/Logs-and-Telemetry--Using-Fluent-Bit.

liveBook discussion forum

Purchase of *Logs and Telemetry* includes free access to liveBook, Manning's online reading platform. Using liveBook's exclusive discussion features, you can attach comments to the book globally or to specific sections or paragraphs. It's a snap to make notes for yourself, ask and answer technical questions, and receive help from the author and other users. To access the forum, go to https://livebook.manning.com/book/logs-and-telemetry/discussion. You can also learn more about Manning's forums and the rules of conduct at https://livebook.manning.com/discussion.

Manning's commitment to our readers is to provide a venue where meaningful dialogue between individual readers and between readers and the author can take place. It is not a commitment to any specific amount of participation on the part of the author, whose contribution to the forum remains voluntary (and unpaid). We suggest that you try asking the author some challenging questions lest his interest stray! The forum and the archives of previous discussions will be accessible on the publisher's website as long as the book is in print.

about the author

PHIL WILKINS has spent more than 30 years in the software industry, with broad experience in businesses and environments from multinationals to software startups and consumer organizations to consultancy. He has worked with household names and has been part of award-winning teams. He started as a developer on real-time, mission-critical solutions and worked his way up through technical and development leadership roles, primarily in Java-based environments. Along the way, Phil became TOGAF-certified. Phil now works for Oracle as a cloud architect and evangelist specializing in cloud-native development, APIs, and integration technologies and is involved with the development of a new generation of SaaS products.

Phil was a peer reviewer of books for several publishers before coauthoring several titles on API and integration, as well as *Logging in Action*, which is the partner to this book. Outside his daily commitments, Phil is an active blogger and contributor to websites such as Software Daily, DZone, and InfoQ. He has made presentations physically and virtually at conferences in the United Kingdom and around the world.

about the cover illustration

The figure on the cover of *Logs and Telemetry* is "Cephalonien," or "Man from Cephalonia," taken from a collection by Jacques Grasset de Saint-Sauveur, published in 1788. This illustration is finely drawn and colored by hand.

In those days, it was easy to identify where people lived and their trade or station in life by their dress alone. Manning celebrates the inventiveness and initiative of the computer business with book covers based on the rich diversity of regional culture centuries ago, brought back to life by pictures from collections such as this one.

Part 1

From concepts to running Fluent Bit

Any good thriller starts by introducing its protagonists, along with their motivations, backgrounds, and strengths and weaknesses. The environment(s) in which the key players operate is shown in the first 20 minutes.

This is what the first part of the book is about. The first chapter introduces our hero, Fluent Bit; it sets the scene by presenting the context, the use cases, and so on. If we are in the process of discovering Fluent Bit or thinking about the things that will help us make a case to colleagues for adopting it, this chapter gives us plenty of fuel for thought.

If chapter 1 is about our principal player, chapter 2 is about the environments in which Fluent Bit can operate. We will start by taking our first practical steps with Fluent Bit and follow the time-honored tradition established by Brian Kernighan, in which the first solution is "Hello, World."

Introduction to Fluent Bit

This chapter covers

- Examining the drivers behind the rapid growth of Fluent Bit
- Identifying the essential parts of Fluent Bit
- Reviewing the technologies used with Fluent Bit
- Understanding the relationship and differences between Fluentd and Fluent Bit

Lewis Carroll wrote in *Alice in Wonderland* that you should "begin at the beginning," so that's what we'll do in this chapter. Before we get down to the details, let's take a moment to understand what Fluent Bit is and answer some important questions about it, such as why it is so important and worthy of a book and how it fits into the IT ecosystem. We'll also address the elephant in the room: the relationship between Fluentd and Fluent Bit.

1.1 Why is Fluent Bit so important?

Fluent Bit is, at its heart, a specialized event capture and distribution tool. Let's break that statement down a bit. Why is it specialized? Fluent Bit focuses on log events, metrics, and traces (sometimes called *signals*):

- *Log*—Can be seen as each output message or line in a log file or, put another way, a string of text that provides some information about what has happened. The message can range from completely unstructured to a fully structured and self-describing message.
- *Metrics*—Measurements, usually numeric values with a descriptive label, generated by our IT hardware and software. Examples are the use of each CPU core on a computer or the number of transactions processed in an application per minute.
- *Traces*—A trace is a linked set of values recorded at important waypoints in the execution of our software, often aligning with transactions. Traces have a lot in common with log events. The key difference is that trace events have a relationship with each other, and sometimes, a trace is not shared until a transaction ends or an error occurs. It's important to note that trace identifiers are carried through the different parts of the application. Traces have become more significant with Kubernetes and the adoption of microservice strategies because, when used properly, they can make following what is happening across distributed solutions far easier.

We'll explore types of event data in greater depth as we progress through the book. The ability to handle various events within a single tool isn't unique, but it does distinguish Fluent Bit from technologies it's sometimes compared with, such as Logstash (https://www.elastic.co/logstash).

Because Fluent Bit reacts to and processes events, typically in near real time as they're received or tracked from sources such as a file, it's described as *event-driven*. Why do we need Fluent Bit to be event-driven? After all, we look at the data when something isn't right. Although we may adopt the traditional approach of looking at logs when someone has declared there to be an issue, people still like to see stats and metrics closer to real time. We should also remember that we can derive meaningful time-sensitive metrics from log events. In our code, we are interested in the events when our software has done something that may be of interest to confirm that all is well, understand which decision branch was taken, or find the answer to a calculation applied to data. Even when a scheduler triggers the monitored solution, we want the logs, events, and traces to be provided when they are still meaningful.

Clever words, then, for something mundane? It would be easy to think that. Unfortunately, this thinking can lead us to miss a wealth of possibilities and opportunities that Fluent Bit offers to make our lives a lot easier. If we consider a log event as just a block of text from our code, for example, we may overlook that we can derive meaning from it and determine whether something else needs to occur there and then. If the event is a health check indicating everything is fine, we could send the data to the operations dashboards and do no more. But if the event reports the receipt of a large, malformed payload, it could indicate a more serious problem that needs immediate intervention before users start calling to complain.

1.1.1 *The value of event distribution*

Tackling the pain of identifying (and possibly needing to resolve) an issue with a system benefits us all individually, whether we're part of a team working within an environment practicing some variation of DevOps, part of a tiered support system on the operational front line, or the developer last in an escalation chain for a testing issue.

When an issue reaches us, we need to know what happened or, better, be able to engage with it as it is happening. The issue might be a serious system failure or a question about how something or someone was or is interacting with our system(s). To address the issue, we must have this information available and a tool that fits our needs.

The information we need could be as simple as the complete log message. Often, we need to understand what happened before, during, and after the event of concern to establish cause and effect. (For example, a database may be producing errors because we've run out of storage. Did we run out of storage because the housekeeping process failed, or did we overlook the need to monitor our storage capacity?) We need to capture and aggregate data from many different sources. Logs, metrics, and traces are the building blocks of observability, and monitoring data (logs, events, and traces) is generally transient. Using Fluent Bit and tools like it enables us to gather data from all sources and put it somewhere secure. It's been my experience that when things go seriously wrong, people aren't worrying about preserving state information, logs, and the like. Their concern is returning to an operational status, which can mean that logs and stored metrics in the production environment may easily be trashed.

Aggregating log events doesn't just mitigate the risk of data loss but also helps us see the complete picture. COBOL solutions, for example, usually were made up of multiple programs run in sequence. Processes were sequential, but distribution processes were already possible. As technology advanced, we adopted two- or three-tier solutions running concurrently (application and database servers, usually with separate UIs). Even if we're operating monolithic application servers, work can be spread across multiple virtualized load-balanced servers, and microservices have led to a further explosion of distribution. To make sense of what is happening, we need to bring together all the events spread across all these distribution points to get an accurate picture of what is happening.

Aside from being able to preserve information that can help us diagnose an issue, we can easily overlook one challenge: the more time we take to get from issue to diagnosis, the more damage can occur, and therefore, the more painful the recovery process becomes. Whether we're fixing failed transactions or working out the scale of a security breach, by processing the metrics and logs as they occur, we can automate the evaluation of whether they indicate an issue occurring now or, better, an imminent problem. Thus, we can reduce the amount of pain because we've avoided or kept the effect of the issue as small as possible.

The ability to distribute data easily also allows us to adopt different tools for different tasks. If the data is difficult to distribute, we end up with the lowest common denominator or with tools that support the most vocal team using the data rather than ones that address different needs. PagerDuty (https://www.pagerduty.com), for example, is ideal for notifying the right person depending on the identified system and the time and day of the week.

1.1.2   *Fluent's place in CNCF*

The Fluent tools, Fluentd and Fluent Bit, are key players in the Cloud Native Computing Foundation (CNCF; https://www.cncf.io) ecosystem, helping us gather, secure, and, ideally, analyze logs and metrics. These solutions allow us to get the observability data (logs, traces, and metrics) in a form that another tool can render in an easily digestible format. Fluent Bit is having a greater effect than Fluentd in terms of adoption and support for the latest observability standards and tools, as we'll see.

Within the CNCF, projects are classified to reflect their process, quality, maturity, support, and adoption. Graduated projects such as Fluentd and Fluent Bit need contributors from multiple organizations with processes that demonstrate good project governance and development processes. Most important, these projects need several public adopters so the wider community can be confident that it will not likely adopt something that could be abandoned overnight.

1.2   Core Fluent Bit concepts

We've looked at why Fluent Bit is important. Now, let's address some core concepts that influence almost every aspect of Fluent Bit. The most critical thing that we've encountered is the event. We should also consider what Fluent Bit does and doesn't do to make events useful.

The other key concept in Fluent Bit is plugins. As we progress through the book, we'll dig deeper into plugins, but at this stage, I'll describe them as the building blocks of Fluent Bit's functional capabilities.

1.2.1   *Payload structure*

To interact with Fluent Bit's events (whether they represent log events, traces, or metrics), we need to understand how each event is represented within Fluent Bit, which is the same way Fluentd does, with three mandatory elements. As figure 1.1 illustrates, Fluent Bit has three core elements with some additional elements that are opaque to us right now:

- *Metadata*—*Metadata* is a list of key-value pairs with a mandatory key called `Tag` and related value. The `Tag` is a logical name associated with the events. We use the `Tag` to route events to the correct operation(s). As we progress through the book, we'll introduce strategies that allow us to manipulate a `Tag` and use intelligent naming conventions to help us. In Fluent Bit v1 and Fluentd, the metadata was only the `Tag`. To increase flexibility and allow Fluent Bit to carry other types of events (and traces), Fluent Bit v1.9 changed the metadata to hold additional key-value pairs about the nature of the record content, such as the type of event. As we'll see later in the book, we can access the `Tag` value without referring to the fact that it's part of the metadata, as Fluent Bit v1 and Fluentd have.

■ *Timestamp*—Events without a timestamp are of limited value. Without the timestamp, we can't determine whether an issue is current or new because we have no sense of when the event occurred. We can't determine whether the event is a cause or an effect because we don't know the order in which things occurred. As a result, many input plugins offer a means to locate where in the event the correct timestamp to use or apply the moment when the input is received as the timestamp.

■ *Record*—A record contains the event data (log, metric, or trace). The ability to access and manipulate the record within various plugins depends on the plugin type and the metadata describing the record. When the record contains a log, Fluent Bit (depending on the input and parsing) treats the record's value as a list of key-value pairs or a single block of text. We can extract content and convert the payload to JSON, among other things. When we're not processing an event, the record is held efficiently by serializing the record using the MessagePack (https://msgpack.org) library. (Appendix B has additional details on MessagePack.)

The metadata can also denote that the record represents metrics or traces. In this case, the record takes on the following characteristics:

– *Metrics*—When we send and receive metrics, the data is in line with the Prometheus format (a non-JSON structure). But Fluent Bit gives us the means to retrieve and manipulate metrics data. Internally, metrics are handled by a library called CMetric, which other projects are starting to use.

– *Traces*—Traces are also handled as a special record payload and can be made into a record and interacted with.

We'll explore these aspects in greater detail as we explore these data sources. Although the movement of the content between the visible record and the opaque structure is not completely free today, it is this author's opinion that handling this movement will become easier over time.

Figure 1.1 shows the data structure of Fluent Bit v1.9 and later, alongside the equivalent Fluent Bit v1 and Fluentd structure. Although the difference is subtle, it is noticeable when handling non-log events. It is worth noting that in the exceptional situation of caching log events in a file with a pre-1.9 version of Fluent Bit, trying to get a post-1.9 version of Fluent Bit to read those cached files will result in errors.

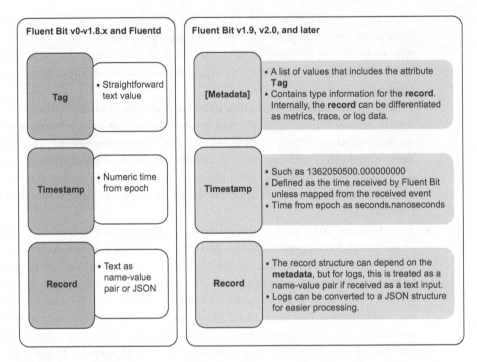

Figure 1.1   Log event structure for Fluent Bit v1.x and Fluentd (left) and Fluent Bit from v1.9 (right)

1.2.2   *Logical architecture*

Figure 1.2 shows Fluent Bit's architecture. We'll use this diagram throughout the book to help orient us to the capabilities we're exploring within Fluent Bit. The figure shows these logical components:

- *Input plugin (listener), input plugin (pulled)*—Many representations of Fluent Bit don't differentiate the types of input plugins. Although the contract between the plugin and the core of Fluent Bit (the pipeline processing) is unaltered, there are differences in how the plugin is implemented that affect configuration and tuning considerations. Network-centric inputs can be described as listeners; we connect to the network, and when data is received, we must process it. Large, sudden spikes here can cause backpressure; the source system invoking Fluent Bit can't continue until we consume the event.

  The pulled events, such as those that capture log events from a file as they're written, require us to poll the file periodically to determine whether any new content has been added. The implementation of the input plugin can dictate the system's throughput.

- *Custom input plugin*—This capability can be characterized as a pulled or listener plugin. As we have support for network sources with HTTP, unless we have specialist encoding that is best handled by an input plugin rather than a decoder (a specialist feature available to parsers), this feature is likely to adopt a pulled model. A custom plugin differentiates itself from other plugins because it is not part of the standard Fluent Bit release—any plugin built directly into the binary by a third party or through the extension options, which we'll discuss in section 1.3.3.

- *Parser*—This provides the means to transform the received content into meaningful data, such as extracting the important values from the record or transforming it to JSON. A range of prebuilt parsers is available; many of these parsers are specializations of regular expressions. Parsers are typically used in conjunction with filters, but some input plugins can also use them.

- *Buffer*—Depending on the plugin, buffering can be used in several places. Logically, it fits well here, as the primary objective of buffering is to allow us to flex to input and output performance differences that might occur, such as spikes in outputs from our sources or a slowdown in the consumption of our outputs. The buffer, therefore, prevents Fluent Bit from being a potential throughput constraint or point of data loss. If you're sensitive about the risk of data loss, you can switch the buffer to use file storage, which can be read when the Fluent Bit process restarts. This approach does have a performance cost. The buffer has a storage interface layer that manages the data going into and out of the buffer and its physical implementation (file or memory); it also interacts with any relevant stream processors.

- *Filter, custom filter*—Filters are the pipeline's heavy lifters, providing the means to interact and manipulate events that have been received. Filters fetch and return the events that they process to the buffer. Normal filters are completely configuration-driven, but custom filters can be implemented in two ways:
  - The typical approach is to invoke Lua scripts.
  - We can implement more demanding or complex filters with C, Go, and WebAssembly, following the approach used by custom input and output plugins.

- *Stream processing*—Stream processing represents how we configure the new, advanced analytics capabilities. We can loop data from this analytical process back as an input so we can use the analytical values to enrich processing, such as creating time series data based on received events.

- *Output plugin, custom output plugin*—As with the inputs, we've separated these types of plugins to draw attention to extensibility. The output plugin's role is to retrieve events from a buffer and then store them or pass them to a third-party solution for onward processing (this may be data storage, but we may output to other Fluentd or Fluent Bit instances to delegate or aggregate work), depending on the plugin's implementation.

We have defined the logical components more granularly than the official documentation does to help you understand their behavioral characteristics. The official documentation focuses principally on input, filter, and output—three of the four horizontal groups in figure 1.2.

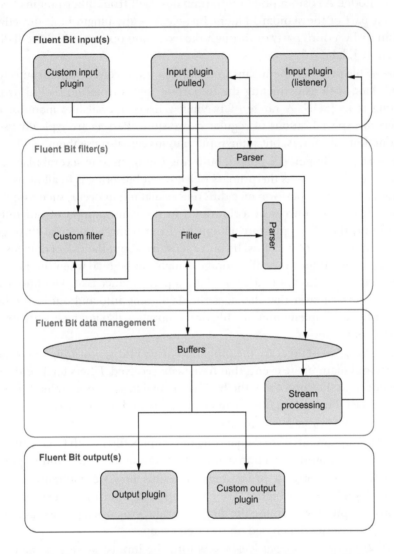

Figure 1.2   Logical Fluent Bit architecture, with the blocks representing logical features and the lines representing the possible flow of events. The standard Fluent Bit groupings are overlaid, but I've separated and illustrated the buffers slightly differently, as their positions are more logical than how they fit into the code base.

1.3   Drivers of Fluent Bit adoption

The drivers that make Fluent Bit a significant player come down to a few key factors:

- The way Fluent Bit is implemented perfectly addresses the cloud and cloud-native industry drive for small size, efficiency, and quick startup, making it easier to exploit the elasticity of containerized environments.
- Fluent Bit is equipped to meet the rapid acceleration and adoption of OpenTelemetry (often referred to as OTel), bringing together log processing, metrics, and tracing to harmonize the different aspects of observing our applications. As a result, tasks such as tracking individual transactions across multiple services and servers can be standardized.
- Fluent Bit provides out-of-the-box support for other dominant cloud-native technologies, particularly those used to support monitoring and observability, such as Prometheus and Grafana's Loki.

There are a couple of additional factors that we think are in play, but the trends are harder to isolate:

- Support for ideas and approaches to streaming and stream analytics have been seen with technologies such as Apache Kafka, Spark, and Beam. Fluent Bit's capability to support stream-processing ideas may not be influencing adoption currently, but it is likely to make a difference in the future. Streaming is more notable in the cloud and cloud-native domains, but depending on how it is addressed, it can deliver dividends for monitoring and observability across all industries and technology domains, new and old. Fluent Bit's streaming capabilities allow it to become more dynamic and adapt to what happens—an idea we'll explore further when we look at stream processing in chapter 8.
- One of the most dominant players in the monitoring space is Fluent Bit's older sibling, Fluentd. We could attribute its dominance to several things, such as being early in the market and part of CNCF or the ease with which new sources and targets can be plugged into their custom integrations. Fluent Bit has all these benefits. In addition, Fluent Bit can communicate transparently with Fluentd deployments, removing or minimizing disruption in transitions between Fluentd and Fluent Bit and blending deployments of both across an organization as needed.

1.3.1   Small footprint, efficiency, and speed

Fluent Bit may have started by supporting Internet of Things (IoT) use cases, but the characteristics that IoT requires fit nicely with cloud-native, particularly containers and Kubernetes. First, maximizing the dynamic scaling of containers through orchestration engines such as Kubernetes makes the ability to go from a standstill to running quickly exceptionally easy to do when an application is designed to run with a small footprint (typically needed on IoT devices). Further, with the overhead of the container itself, anything we can do to reduce the amount of CPU and memory consumed is desirable. One way is to employ precompiled native binaries (sometimes called ahead-of-time [AoT] compilation). This approach eliminates the overhead of running an interpreter layer (such as the time to start the interpreter before any application logic is loaded and the additional memory needs of the interpreter). Using a just-in-time (JIT) compiler helps with performance but still has a compilation overhead that we see with language virtual machines such as the JVM. As Fluent Bit has been written with C, it has always compiled into a binary and, therefore, has no overhead. The value of scaling exceptionally quickly and being resource efficient and high perform-ing means that Fluent Bit has been adopted by cloud providers such as Amazon Web Services (AWS), Azure, Google, and Oracle, as well as cloud service providers such as LinkedIn and Lyft because these characteristics translate into tens of thousands of dollars in savings.

Although Fluent Bit is very compact, it can scale to handle workloads with con-trols that allow inputs and outputs to run in separate threads. Separating input and output operations reduces the chance that backpressure will affect multiple inputs. Threading control options in Fluent Bit also have the potential to increase through-put. Still, when we're working within a containerized environment, we need to use threading with care; we no longer have an assured allocation of CPU cores, and more threads could make the real CPU perform more context switching than is optimal.

1.3.2   *Effect of OpenTelemetry and how Fluent Bit relates to It*

Before OpenTelemetry (OTel), the primary specifications that informed the observ-ability of metrics, traces, and logs came from several standardization efforts within CNCF in the form of OpenTracing (https://opentracing.io), OpenCensus (https://opencensus.io), and implicitly, given its dominance, Fluentd and, by association, Flu-ent Bit for the structure of logging. Different standards often required different tool-ing to capture such data. Fluent Bit has always caught some metrics data; the IoT ecosystem needs to keep software footprints small, so one service capturing both logs and metrics is preferable. As a result, it made sense for Fluent Bit to capture not only logs but also local metrics such as CPU, memory, and storage use. Bringing all these data sources together has driven the simplification of operational monitoring, result-ing in rapid uptake and shown to be disruptive.

Fluent Bit's support of the OpenTelemetry standards and its ability to work within the OTel ecosystem hasn't required any radical changes, although it has driven some upgrades of parts of its implementation. In some respects, the upgrades have formal-ized what Fluent Bit was already doing. With this alignment, Fluent Bit is well-equipped to support the adoption of OpenTelemetry standards without imposing them, allowing its adoption to be more incremental.

When we start digging into the input and output capabilities of Fluent Bit, we'll look further into the relationship with OpenTelemetry and leading products in the observability space, such as Prometheus (https://prometheus.io), which has helped propel OTel further forward, and Grafana (https://grafana.com/grafana). We'll also look at commercial vendors that have worked to support OTel's standards, creating a rapidly growing ecosystem of connectable monitoring tools.

> **NOTE** If you need a quick reference on the acronyms and terminology, you can find a handy glossary at https://opentelemetry.io/docs/concepts/glossary. Also, appendix B lists several excellent resources.

The heart of OTel is the OpenTelemetry Protocol (OTLP), which details the data structures, encoding, and transmission of the telemetry data. Currently, OTLP supports transmission using gRPC (Remote Procedure Call) with HTTP/2 using Protocol Buffer (Protobuf) and JSON with HTTP synchronously. OTLP promotes the use of gRPC as the first-choice approach to communication and JSON as a step-down or fallback.

OTel, as a project, goes far beyond defining OTLP. It also provides implementations of the functionality described in the standard (sometimes described as a reference implementation), along with tools and libraries. The tools and libraries are implemented in multiple languages; we can use them to help inject logic into applications and quickly get data applications producing traces. OTel also has functionality such as log appenders that allow logging frameworks to send the logs using the OTLP specification.

To understand how Fluent Bit could fit into an open telemetry solution, let's look at what Fluent Bit can do using OTel terminology (https://opentelemetry.io/docs/concepts/components). Given its ability to gather monitoring and observability data from different sources and transform it into the OTLP structure, Fluent Bit can fill the role of an *OpenTelemetry Collector.* Because Fluent Bit was built to work in a distributed environment and can pass data in OTLP format to any other OpenTelemetry compliant collector (which could be a Fluent Bit node or another product), we can describe Fluent Bit as being able to perform as an *OTLP Exporter.*

Figure 1.3 shows how Fluent Bit can fit into an OpenTelemetry environment with its ability to handle logs (L), metrics (M), and traces (T) generated by an application with or without the help of OTel libraries or tools, along with its ability to interact with an OpenTelemetry Collector.

Because OTel provides implementations of collector and exporter capabilities, calling Fluent Bit an OpenTelemetry Collector or OpenTelemetry Exporter can be a source of confusion. The standard itself is called OTLP, so referring to Fluent Bit as being OTLP-compliant is clearer, even if less obvious about the task we might deploy Fluent Bit to perform. In addition, there is some sensitivity within the OpenTelemetry community about the difference between the project's own implementation of a collector (called OpenTelemetry Collector) and other implementations of that capability. We are erring on the side of describing Fluent Bit as an OTLP Collector (after all, protocol compliance is key to the collector's function) and reducing ambiguity among CNCF projects.

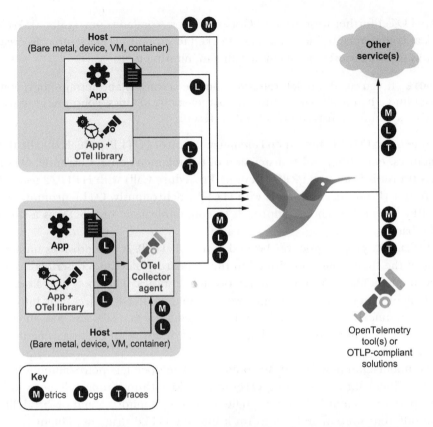

Figure 1.3   Fluent Bit's relationship with OpenTelemetry with apps generating OTel logs, metrics, and traces and Fluent Bit facilitating their transmission to an OTel-compliant point of aggregation or processing. Applications can send OTLP data directly or via an OTel component, and we can route data to other OTel services or analysis tools.

Protocol Buffers (Protobuf)

Protocol Buffers are a key technology for gRPC, which OTel uses. Protocol Buffers have a concisely defined schema, which is used with the Protobuf tooling to generate the code for sending and receiving payloads. A well-defined schema allows the tooling to create the code that creates a compressed binary payload representation. This schema is both a strength and a potential constraint. The strength comes from the efficient payload transmission. The downside is that a schema change affects both the provider and consumer and makes realizing the tolerant reader integration pattern more challenging. Also, given that the Protobuf-generated payload is a compressed binary format, it is a lot harder to inject into any communication middleware that can accommodate transformation. Links to OTel, Protobuf, and related technologies are in appendix B.

As we progress through the book, we'll examine more closely how Fluent Bit and OpenTelemetry perform different functions. Note that OpenTelemetry protocol support before Fluent Bit v3 was restricted to HTTP and JSON. Version 3 brought enhancements that support HTTP/2, enabling Fluent Bit to use gRPC. This, in turn, means that Fluent Bit can provide a fully compliant OTLP implementation without needing to take advantage of the step down to HTTP and JSON.

1.3.3 *Extending Fluent Bit with C, Go, WebAssembly, and Lua*

The ability to extend Fluent Bit's core capability is important. The number of third-party plugins built for Fluentd clearly demonstrates this need. In addition to source and targets, small pieces of custom logic for actions such as filtering are also needed. For inputs, outputs, and filters, we can connect precompiled solutions using C, Go (also referred to as Golang), and WebAssembly (WASM), which we can use to further increase our choice of languages for implementation and elevate decoupling.

As Filters often need a quicker, easier way to define small pieces of logic, using Lua as a scripting language makes sense. We'll explore these technologies and the pros and cons of the different approaches in chapter 9.

1.3.4 *Fluent Bit and stream processing*

The goal of implementing processing logic as events flow through a pipeline is not new. As software frameworks developed to support that goal, we saw what we now know as stream processing or stream analytics as *Complex Event Processing* (CEP). You could argue that we've had basic stream processing in the form of service bus (https://www.devx.com/terms/enterprise-service-bus) products for a long time; stream processing is less about the technology and more about how the technology is applied. If you accept the argument about service buses, it is reasonable to assert that Fluentd and Fluent Bit also provide basic streaming capabilities. What has evolved is how we look at stream processing and stream analytics. Today, we can identify a couple of distinctive characteristics of stream processing and analytics:

- The large volume of data we're trying to push through the pipeline is a key characteristic of stream processing. Fluent Bit is no stranger to these data volumes, but the volumes we want to process demand an enormous scale for service buses to meet such demands. Also, service buses need to address a level of complexity, such as data integrity across multiple systems—something that is typically not an issue for stream processing.
- As we focus on data, using SQL is the nearly universal way to work with data. If we can express the examination of the log events by using SQL, we make the data a lot more accessible.

1.3.5 *OTel vs. Fluent Bit and Fluentd*

We should emphasize that when considering whether to use Fluentd or Fluent Bit and even Fluent Bit or OTel, the answer need not be one or the other. From the outset,

Fluent Bit and Fluentd have been built to communicate easily and seamlessly. Because of the way that the Fluent Bit and Fluentd solutions structure their payloads internally, we can take an OTel payload, wrap it inside the Fluent model, and unpack it again. The key to answering the question about Fluentd lies with the adoption of OTel for more than microservice use cases and the speed at which additional adaptors are developed.

In my opinion, new developments will become Fluent Bit–based over the next couple of years because developers who may have considered Logstash will look to Elastic APM agents (https://mng.bz/x6n6). However, solutions in production will see a slower rate of change with Fluent Bit replacing Fluentd. The most likely driver of change in existing software will be the adoption of OpenTelemetry. Highly scaled OTel solutions with even small footprint savings will create measurable cost savings or a solution that reaches the point of replacement or significant overhaul.

With the data captured within Fluent Bit, we can parse semistructured content to extract more meaning from the event, allowing more informed actions to be performed downstream. This process can be as simple as extracting a value from some text, such as whether the log entry contains an error or extracting a numeric value for Prometheus to use or to influence the routing of the event. The process can also be as complex as converting a custom format to a JSON representation.

The natural next step is filtering events, perhaps to discard them when they are insignificant or to route them to one or more outputs. We could send the data to a central log repository and pass the event's numeric elements to Prometheus as a metric.

Transferring data in groups of events is more efficient than transferring one event at a time. The start and end of each conversation have some small overhead, such as opening and closing network connections or opening and locating the end of a file and then closing the file handle. Buffering or grouping events helps us make tradeoffs in these activities, which is one of the roles of buffers regardless of where they are. Because a buffer may not be a simple in-memory structure, it's better to perform buffering after filtering, so if the buffer involves more than managing the data we already have in memory, we're minimizing the effort.

The final step is putting the events somewhere. That might well be another Fluent Bit (acting as an OpenTelemetry node or a simple log event processor) or Fluentd (taking advantage of its larger collection of plugin options or existing deployed monitoring infrastructure), or it could be one of the supported data stores or custom outputs that have been plugged in.

In figure 1.4, we have taken our architecture view and add some example sources, destinations, and technologies that allow us to enhance Fluent Bit. This figure underlines the flexibility and compatibility of Fluentd and OpenTelemetry-compliant tools in addition to a diverse range of other applications and technologies.

You'll probably have noticed that Fluent Bit doesn't do anything about data presentation or visualization. This comes down to the philosophy that an application has a single responsibility: do one thing and do it well. For Fluent Bit, that one thing is

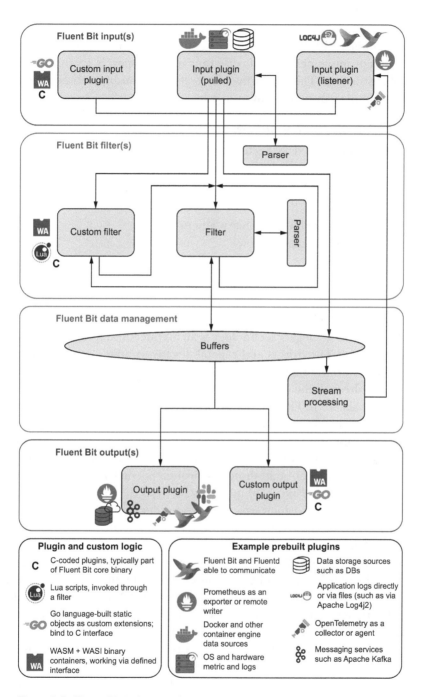

Figure 1.4   Fluent Bit logical architecture with some of the available plugins

getting observability data from what needs to be observed to the tools that allow us to visualize and analyze the data.

If you're familiar with the architecture of Fluentd, you'll recognize that the architecture, although implemented with different technologies, is reasonably similar at this level of abstraction. This similarity reflects the relationship between the two solutions and is a simple truism of event processing.

1.4   Is Fluent Bit a child or a successor of Fluentd?

Although Fluent Bit started as a sibling of Fluentd (https://www.fluentd.org), with support for OTel and other features arriving in the late 1.x versions and as part of v2.0, it is fair to say that it has grown up to be Fluentd's equal. This fact spawns a couple of questions:

- Do I need to learn Fluentd to learn Fluent Bit?
- Is Fluentd a legacy solution now?

To come to grips with Fluent Bit, you don't need to know anything about Fluentd. But if you understand Fluentd at a high level, you'll find that getting to grips with Fluent Bit is easy. There is no dependency between the products. In many respects, although the two products have a lot of overlap, they are complementary.

Whether Fluentd is a legacy technology is an architectural question. The answer is always, "It depends." The drivers and capabilities incorporated into Fluent Bit mean that it fits neatly into the modern Kubernetes-centered, cloud-native ecosystem, with the means to address all the demands of that ecosystem, although some features currently are not available in Fluentd. As previously discussed, Fluent Bit has a smaller, lighter footprint, making it suitable for containerized use cases. Another factor is OpenTelemetry support. At the time of this writing, we have not seen a road map to equip Fluentd with support for OTel, which makes Fluent Bit by far the better choice for deploying into container-orchestrated environments such as Kubernetes and working with services such as Istio. Nothing stops us from deploying Fluent Bit in non-cloud-native environments, which typically have a wider portfolio of technologies with which to work. This scenario lends itself more to Fluentd for the foreseeable future, given the number of adapters it has available. The skills required to create custom plugins are also more readily available; you simply need to grasp Ruby or another object-oriented language with built-in memory management, as listed in the TIOBE Index (https://www.tiobe.com/tiobe-index). Although WASM can enable extensions to Fluent Bit in languages such as Java and Ruby, it demands additional skills for a technology that is still proving itself to the mainstream.

As to whether Fluentd is history, the answer is no. Major vendors have invested in and used Fluentd for a long time, and that sort of investment is not one to walk away from. Furthermore, Fluentd and Fluent Bit have different technologies, and although they have some common ideas, they execute those ideas differently. Many of the key contributors to the development of Fluentd are also working on Fluent Bit. Both solutions are being propelled forward to meet the demands and innovation needed by the CNCF ecosystem. Cloud-native ideas and CNCF influence the world of software; not all cloud software deployments are as tightly bound to Kubernetes as others. Put simply, Fluent Bit can do a lot and be applied to many use cases, but today, Fluentd fits some use cases better than Fluent Bit, and vice versa.

> **NOTE** The way that Fluent Bit's name is written has fluctuated, at times being *Fluentbit*. The two ways of writing the name are interchangeable. The spellings *fluent-bit* and *Fluentbit* have also been used for code and executable artifacts. But the official, correct spelling is *Fluent Bit*.

1.5 *How we're going to discover Fluent Bit*

This book sequences chapters to get you started quickly, focusing on sources and destinations. Then it adds advanced capabilities, such as filtering and creating plugins. We want this book to be both a tour guide for those who are new to Fluent Bit and a resource for reference for both new and experienced users. Like a good tour guide, we will reflect on Fluent Bit's history and how it affects today as we travel through Fluent Bit's capabilities. We'll look at the most common configuration scenarios with real-world applications. The scenarios don't simply involve clicking this and typing that and seeing something happen; we'll explain what is going on and why. After all, the better you understand how things work, the easier it is to derive new configurations and other use cases.

Every scenario has a working solution in a GitHub repository (https://mng .bz/vJKa) and in Manning's book-download pack (https://www.manning.com/downloads/2686), and we'll describe how to run those scenarios in the book. As the examples get more advanced, we may not include every bit of the configuration in the book—only the bits that are relevant to the subject at hand. The complete configuration is available in the files referenced in the GitHub repository.

Just as a tour guide doesn't explain every detail of every exhibit as they guide you along, we're not going to look at every edge case of Fluent Bit. Like a guide, we will give you the means to go back and explore different aspects more deeply on your own time. We've included several appendices for that purpose. The appendices include setup instructions for the tools used in the book and references to further supportive reading, tools, lookup information, and examples that will help.

The scenarios in each chapter sometimes develop logically from the preceding ones as we build sophistication and illustrate different possibilities. But don't worry—if you need to jump back to a chapter, you won't need to return to the beginning. Each scenario configuration is independent of the others. We'll also give you some additional challenges; the solutions are in the downloadable content. These challenges allow you to try different ways of configuring Fluent Bit without having the answer in front of you.

The biggest possible challenge is creating realistic log behavior. We'll solve that issue by using a LogGenerator/LogSimulator that can create different log events. To learn more about this utility, see appendix A.

1.5.1 How much Kubernetes will this book involve?

The way the industry references Kubernetes can confuse those who are new to the technology. To be precise, Kubernetes is the orchestrator for a set of technologies that are compliant with its APIs. We often talk about Docker when referring to containers, but we actually mean Open Container Initiative (OCI)–compliant containers and the associated container engines. Product names like Kubernetes are shorthand for the broader ecosystem rather than detailed specifics of container orchestration. Within this book, we have worked to use Kubernetes in the broader use, and when we're talking about specific parts of Kubernetes, we've tried to use the specific component names.

The objective for many people is to understand Fluent Bit in the context of building and operating containerized applications. Using Fluent Bit to monitor containerized applications requires only a basic understanding of how containers can be orchestrated. Likewise, 10 years ago, only a basic understanding of VMs was needed to monitor applications that ran in environments managed by VMWare. Few people need to know how VMWare moves VMs or Kubernetes moves containers within a server cluster, for example. Applications shouldn't be aware of the world outside their container or VM unless you're producing a Kubernetes controller.

For a detailed look at the Kubernetes log and observability, we would recommend checking out a Kubernetes-specific book to understand its administration (several resources are mentioned in appendix B). Most of us will start with a prepared Kubernetes cluster, and these Kubernetes environments are opinionated; compare OpenShift, Tanzu, K3s, Minikube, and the cloud-provider setups, and you'll see. Many prepared Kubernetes deployments tell you how they have configured things, so it's worthwhile to look at their documentation; sometimes, there are preconfigured Fluent Bit settings to monitor Kubernetes at the lowest level, so the question is how to build on this feature. When you've considered this question, come back to this book to see how you can use the events generated by Kubernetes and apply Fluent Bit.

We use containers in this book, but to keep things simple and to emphasize that Fluent Bit is not just a tool for Kubernetes, we will focus on running Fluent Bit locally. This approach means we don't have to worry about container configuration when trying to master Fluent Bit configuration. It also helps us see that Fluent Bit can work with more traditional application deployments.

1.5.2 Logging in Action

The final question in this chapter is how this book relates to *Logging in Action* (https://www.manning.com/books/logging-in-action). That book touches on Fluent Bit but just enough to provide context. Like the two technologies, that book and this one can be used together, but neither is beholden to the other. Don't dismiss *Logging in Action*, however. That book has content relevant to Fluent Bit, particularly a deeper look at the theory of observability and monitoring, such as deployment strategies and ways to mix the two technologies.

Summary

- We have taken a whirlwind tour of what has made Fluent Bit so popular and how it is particularly good in a microservices context, such as its small footprint and operability with other technologies, particularly Fluentd.
- We looked at the high-level ideas, architecture, and components of Fluent Bit, so we are in a better position to understand the application of Fluent Bit, which we'll explore in the coming chapters.
- We also examined the relationship between Fluent Bit and OpenTelemetry and saw that they can coexist and complement each other.
- We reviewed the high-level ideas and elements of Fluent Bit, enabling you to be able to start asking questions about Fluent Bit and getting a sense of the elements we'll explore in the coming chapters, starting by looking at the different ways we can run Fluent Bit and implement a "Hello, World" configuration.

From zero to "Hello, World"

This chapter covers

- Learning ways to configure Fluent Bit
- Examining the Fluent Bit command-line interface (CLI)
- Creating a Fluent Bit version of "Hello, World"
- Looking at classic and YAML Fluent Bit configurations
- Working with dynamic configuration features

When it comes to getting Fluent Bit up and running with a scenario, we'll be quicker than Nic Cage in *Gone in 60 Seconds*. Although the chapter will take you a little longer to read than others, we'll certainly have the Fluent Bit equivalent to the developer's "Hello, World" going with minimal effort. Understanding different configuration approaches and the ways they can be dynamic means you can decide which approach best fits your deployment needs.

For this chapter, all we need are Fluent Bit and a tool of our choice to edit configuration files, such as Visual Studio Code. If the tool can understand YAML (YAML Ain't Markup Language), that's a bonus. All the instructions for installing Fluent Bit are provided in appendix A.

The content relating only to v3 has been explicitly called out. The core capabilities described will work all the way back to Fluent Bit v1, but the console output differs slightly.

NOTE The book focuses on Fluent Bit v2 and v3. Despite the major version change, the configuration files are backward compatible.

2.1 Multiple ways to configure Fluent Bit

Fluent Bit allows us to provide configurations in multiple ways—through the command line or several different file formats. Before examining how to configure Fluent Bit, we need to take a moment to understand the various options and how we will address them in the book.

2.1.1 Configuration formats

Using the command-line interface (CLI) can be a powerful way to configure Fluent Bit. This approach also has limitations and becomes difficult to work with when implementing anything more than basic use cases, such as retrieving log events or standard environment metrics and outputting them to a file.

The command-line capability is one way to simplify a container configuration. A configuration tweak affects only a single layer in the container and does not require a container to be rebuilt from scratch as a result of needing to copy configuration files into the image. We could also bypass this with smarter container management that mounts volumes to retrieve a configuration file(s), or have the container startup perform a configuration pull from somewhere like a Git repository every time a container is started. If the Fluent Bit container is being used with Kubernetes, it is common practice to insert configuration files into a container by using a `ConfigMap`—the approach we'll use with Kubernetes in chapter 4.

To understand the possibilities, we'll walk through the process of using the CLI to define a simple Fluent Bit configuration. The rest of the book focuses on using a configuration file.

2.1.2 CLI controls

The Fluent Bit command line can be used to provide parameters that tell Fluent Bit how to execute, as well as set several status and control behaviors. As with most applications, the CLI uses a hyphen and a single letter or double hyphen with a full name for each parameter value. The short parameters are case sensitive. Fluent Bit supports the near-universal shortcut `-h` (`--help`) to display command-line help. Let's start with the parameters we're likely to use regularly, particularly during the development of Fluent Bit configurations (table 2.1).

Table 2.1 Fluent Bit execution CLI controls

Short parameter	Long parameter	Description
-h	--help	This parameter displays detailed CLI help on the console.
-b	--storage_path	When buffering uses the filesystem, the files are stored in this location.
-c	--config	As with Fluentd, this parameter directs Fluent Bit to work with a specific configuration file identified by the path to the file provided.
-d	--daemon	This parameter tells Fluent Bit to run as a daemon process, so it will be executed as an OS process.
-D	--dry-run	The --dry-run option directs Fluent Bit to evaluate the configuration to ensure that it is correct without running the pipelines and generating output.
-q	--quiet	The --quiet parameter reduces output to warnings and errors, and -qq makes things very quiet, with only errors being output.
-S	--sosreport	This parameter builds a detailed summary of the Fluent Bit deployment, including flags used to build the binary, which helps anyone better understand any operational issues.
-v	--verbose	The --verbose and --quiet controls work in the same manner. -v enables Fluent Bit to log to the debug level, and -vv goes to the trace level.
-V	--version	This parameter gets Fluent Bit to provide information on the version number and related details.

Using parameters, we can validate the version of Fluent Bit we have deployed. When we run the command fluent-bit -v, we should see a message confirming that our Fluent Bit deployment is v2 or later. If not, revisit appendix A's deployment guidance, as we will be doing things in the book that can't be run. Try generating an SOS report with the -s parameter. We'll use other options, such as --dry-run and --config (-c), later in the book.

Let's look at more advanced configuration options that allow us to control Fluent Bit behavior in a more operational context, such as directing where Fluent Bit writes its log files, and where it can write temporary files, such as when file buffers are used (table 2.2).

Table 2.2 Log operation CLI controls

Short parameter	Long parameter	Description
-C	--custom	Enables the use of custom sources (inputs) or sinks (outputs).

Table 2.2   Log operation CLI controls *(continued)*

Short parameter	Long parameter	Description
-e	--plugin	Identifies where an external plugin should be loaded from.
-f	--flush	Allows us to change the flush frequency by providing an integer representing a number of seconds. (No value means that flush defaults to every second.) The flush represents the frequency at which the log events are processed downstream, regardless of how full the buffering capacity is.
-l	--log_file	Allows us to direct the log events to a log file rather than the console. The console still gets a brief startup configuration summary.
-w	--workdir	Defines where Fluent Bit puts any temporary files.
-H	--http	Enables the HTTP server, which can be used to address HTTP GET REST calls that can be used to retrieve information about the Fluent Bit node, such as health, metrics, and build details. Except for the response to the root URL, the other endpoints start with /api/v1/.
-P	--port	Allows a different port from the default 2020 to be defined for the HTTP server.
-s	--coro_stack_size	Sets the stack size for coroutines (defaults to 24 KB).

Using the parameters in table 2.2, run Fluent Bit so that it logs to a file called fb.log, run the command, and terminate the process after about 10 seconds. The command you should arrive at is fluent-bit -l fb.log. When you've stopped Fluent Bit, you should see a local file called fb.log. The file will contain text showing Fluent Bit log information reflecting the startup, like this:

```
[2024/04/14 16:57:29] [ info] [fluent bit] version=2.2.2,
➥ commit=eeea396e88, pid=30060
[2024/04/14 16:57:29] [ info] [storage] ver=1.5.1, type=memory,
➥ sync=normal, checksum=off, max_chunks_up=128
[2024/04/14 16:57:29] [ info] [cmetrics] version=0.6.6
[2024/04/14 16:57:29] [ info] [ctraces ] version=0.4.0
[2024/04/14 16:57:29] [ info] [sp] stream processor started
[2024/04/14 16:57:34] [ warn] [engine] service will shutdown
➥ in max 5 seconds
[2024/04/14 16:57:35] [ info] [engine] service has stopped
➥ (0 pending tasks)
```

Table 2.3 shows the key controls for defining a pipeline from the command line. We'll put these controls to use soon. We previously saw the architecture of Fluent Bit, so it shouldn't surprise you that it heavily informs how the CLI and the configuration files are structured.

Table 2.3   Log event–processing CLI controls

Short parameter	Long parameter	Description
`-i`	`--input`	Identifies the input plugin and must be followed by the plugin name.
`-o`	`--output`	Identifies the settings for the output. `-o` needs to be followed by the name of the output, such as `stdout`.
`-F`	`--filter`	Starts the definition of a filter.
`-m`	`--match`	Controls the events that an output can process.
`-p`	`--prop`	Identifies the following value provided to define the name and value for a configuration property for the plugin, filter, etc. The property is provided as a name-value pair, such as `name=value`.
`-R`	`--parser`	Allows us to define the data in the log event's record that can be manipulated.
`-t`	`--tag`	Allows us to define the tag to be applied to the input event.
`-T`	`--sp-task`	Allows us to define a stream processor.

We can also retrieve a help summary for specific inputs, outputs, and filters by specifying the input, output, or filter followed by `-h` or `--help`. For example, we can retrieve details about the `dummy` input plugin using the command `fluent-bit -i dummy -h`. Try formulating a command line to get the configuration details for the `stdout` output plugin.

What does plugin mean?

We've encountered references to plugins. The term is key to Fluent Bit but can be a source of misunderstanding because *plugin* can be used to describe features compiled directly into the core of Fluent Bit. This term comes from Fluent Bit's older sibling, Fluentd, which is built with Ruby and takes advantage of Ruby's modularity and dynamic class loading. Different parts of Fluentd are exposed by defined interfaces that could be easily built on with Ruby's language features. These interfaces are provided to help ensure that the code is implemented with good software engineering practices, regardless of whether the code is part of the core product or used by others to implement their own inputs, outputs, and filters. There are other interfaces, but they are far less frequently used. As functionality that uses these interfaces typically comes in separately deployable files and could be visualized as being plugged into the core, they've become known as *plugins*.

Fluent Bit defines *interfaces* to manage coupling and extensibility as sound software engineering practices. As a result, the term has continued in Fluent Bit even though many of the plugins are compiled into the executable for the Fluent Bit file. In this book, we will continue using the language of plugins, whether they are compiled into the core of Fluent Bit or custom developed using WebAssembly or Go.

2.1.3 Defining a monitoring pipeline using the CLI

As we've seen from the command-line options, we can use the CLI to define a monitoring pipeline. This capability makes it possible to configure containerized Fluent Bit and embody the behavior in a Kubernetes Pod declaration, including the command declaration. Let's put it to the test by creating a simple Fluent Bit command that works with a `dummy` input and pushing it to the console.

INPUT

Within the command line, we can define one or more inputs by repeating the input delimiter, followed by the input plugin name. For our "Hello, World" example, we'll use the simplest possible option: a plugin called `dummy`. `dummy` doesn't source any log events; it creates them internally with a JSON payload, which we can define or allow to have defaulted values. With each input, we need to define the tag associated with that source. Let's use the value `dummy1`, which means that after the input, we need to provide the `-t` parameter with the value `dummy1`.

We want to output the JSON `{"hello": "my world"}`, so we need to supply the configuration for the attribute or property used by the plugin to change the payload. Now things get a little tricky, as JSON expects quotes, but the logic that consumes the property wants only the whole value quoted. As a result, the quotes within the JSON need to be escaped with a leading forward slash, for example: `"{\" hello\" :\"my world\"}"`. Bringing these CLI parameters together gives us the definition of the input. Note that the order is important.

OUTPUT

Next, we define the output, which we'll keep simple, directing the log events to the `stdout`. We use the `-o` option followed by the output name—in this case, `stdout`. We need to define the tag-based filter (or event *match*, to use the correct Fluent Bit term). We do this with the `-m` parameter applied to the output identified immediately before the declaration. Because we want to log all events, we can use a wildcard (`*`). (We'll address the role of matching in chapter 5 when we start to explore the ideas of routing.)

As we're running the command from a script, wrapping the asterisk in single quotes has become necessary. Single quotes are unnecessary if we run the command directly from the console.

The last addition to our command, `-q`, makes the logging quiet, so we don't get any unnecessary noise from the logging. We recommend incorporating the behavioral settings into the CLI statement before expressing any log event–handling elements. The built-up CLI command should look like the following listing; see `chapter2\fluentbit\hello-world.cli.[sh|bat]`.

Listing 2.1 Command-line-configured Fluent Bit

```
fluent-bit -q -i dummy -p dummy="{\"hello\":\"my world\"}" -t dummy1
⇨  -o stdout -m '*'
```

The download/GitHub bundle (identified in appendix A) provides the command wrapped up as a shell script to make it easy to run. When we run the command `./hello-world.cli.sh`, we should see a result like figure 2.1.

```
chapter2>./hello-world.cli.sh
Fluent Bit v2.1.7
* Copyright (C) 2015-2022 The Fluent Bit Authors
* Fluent Bit is a CNCF sub-project under the umbrella of Fluentc
* https://fluentbit.io

[0] dummy1: [[1697918353.085813857, {}], {"hello"=>"my world"}]
[0] dummy1: [[1697918354.085851108, {}], {"hello"=>"my world"}]
[0] dummy1: [[1697918355.086278162, {}], {"hello"=>"my world"}]
[0] dummy1: [[1697918356.086084709, {}], {"hello"=>"my world"}]
[0] dummy1: [[1697918357.085891951, {}], {"hello"=>"my world"}]
```

Figure 2.1   Output generated from running the CLI version of the "Hello, World" configuration

INTERPRETING CONSOLE OUTPUT

Figure 2.1 shows our output, and we can clearly see the strings used in our JSON set by the `dummy` property and a timestamp showing when the log entry was created. But the payload isn't the expected format for JSON because the output plugin can present information in a few ways, and the default isn't JSON; it's a representation of how Fluent Bit stores each event internally. The internal representation uses a serialization library, MessagePack (https://msgpack.org/index.html), that converts the string to a binary format, reducing the number of bytes needed to hold the message. This library is also used when communicating between Fluent Bit and Fluentd instances. MessagePack is an open source data format designed to be compact and fast in serializing and deserializing. We address this topic further in chapter 3, but first, we'll explain what the data elements in figure 2.1 represent:

- The first value in square brackets is a counter for that event in the current chunk of events. The process of outputting the event is dictated by how much of the buffer is full and by the flush frequency, which by default is 1 second. The `dummy` plugin generates events once per second, so we can expect this value to be only 0. To illustrate this behavior, alter the script and add `-f 15`, which flushes the buffer every 15 seconds. As a result, we'll see the counter increment to 14 (or 13, if any nanosecond drift occurs in the timing).
- The next value is the tag associated with the log event. If no tag is defined, the tag is derived from the input type, such as `dummy`. If no tag is set, we see the plugin name and a numeric counter for each instance of the plugin used, e.g., `dummy.0`).
- The third numeric value is the timestamp in seconds from the epoch, with fractions of a second as the decimal place number.

- Later versions of Fluent Bit (v2 and later) follow the timestamp with any metadata associated with the event as we described in chapter 1.
- Finally, we have the record body, which contains a representation of the JSON formatted text from our `dummy` attribute: `{"hello"=>"my world"}`.

EXTENDING THE CLI TO DEFINE MULTIPLE INPUTS

A single input, such as a CPU or an application log alone, doesn't tell a comprehensive story. Ideally, we might want to collect multiple log event data sources. We can see how multiple inputs work by creating an additional `dummy` input on the command line with different values.

When we use multiple inputs or outputs, the sequence of the properties provided in the CLI declaration is important. The tag (`-t`) and properties (`-p`) are always associated with the preceding defined input, output, or filter. Given this information, we should be able to enhance the existing `dummy` input with a tag value of `dummy1`. We should be able to define an additional `dummy` input. This second `dummy` input uses the tag `dummy2` and generates the JSON `{"more": "stuff"}`. We should be able to configure this second `dummy` input by copying the first `dummy` input and then editing the properties.s

All the exercises so far have provided solutions. The answer should look like the following listing; see `chapter2\fluentbit\hello-world-2.cli.[sh|bat]`.

Listing 2.2 Parameterized CLI run

```
fluent-bit -q -i dummy -t dummy1 -p dummy="{\"hello\":\"my world\"}"
➥ -i dummy -t dummy2 -p dummy="{\"more\":\"stuff\"}" -o stdout -m '*'
```

In developing the enhanced version of the command, we'll have picked out the following points:

- Ordering the input and associated properties
- Using escape characters for the `dummy` input on the input plugin

As a result, we expect to see a result that looks like figure 2.2.

```
chapter2>./hello-world-2.cli.sh
[0] dummy1: [[1697918565.085824475, {}], {"hello"=>"my world"}]
[0] dummy2: [[1697918565.085916821, {}], {"more"=>"stuff"}]
[0] dummy1: [[1697918566.085856320, {}], {"hello"=>"my world"}]
[0] dummy2: [[1697918566.085887660, {}], {"more"=>"stuff"}]
[0] dummy1: [[1697918567.085860424, {}], {"hello"=>"my world"}]
[0] dummy2: [[1697918567.085898636, {}], {"more"=>"stuff"}]
[0] dummy1: [[1697918568.085833550, {}], {"hello"=>"my world"}]
[0] dummy2: [[1697918568.085873446, {}], {"more"=>"stuff"}]
[0] dummy1: [[1697918569.085850756, {}], {"hello"=>"my world"}]
[0] dummy2: [[1697918569.085879471, {}], {"more"=>"stuff"}]
[0] dummy1: [[1697918570.085833329, {}], {"hello"=>"my world"}]
```

Figure 2.2 Output from Fluent Bit when running with two `dummy` sources configured with different `dummy` attribute values

MULTIPLE OUTPUTS

Let's extend our example so that we have multiple outputs and can differentiate the outputs. We'll continue to use stdout, but for one of the outputs, we'll configure the output plugin to format the entire message as JSON for its output, and we'll configure the date and timestamp to use ISO 8601 format. To do so, we'll add properties to the output definition, specifically setting format to a value of json. The default is msgpack, which results in an unpacked representation of the data held in Fluent Bit. Other options are json_lines and json_stream, both of which force the output to be syntactically correct JSON, but json_lines forces each record onto its own line, and the json_streams option does not. The property json_date_format should be set to iso8601. As a result, the date is included in the log event output formatted in line with the ISO standard. The resulting command should look like this listing (chapter2\fluentbit\hello-world-3.cli.[sh|bat]).

Listing 2.3   CLI with multiple inputs

```
fluent-bit -f 5 -q -i dummy -t dummy1
  -p dummy="{\"hello\":\"my world\"}"  -i dummy -t dummy2
  -p dummy="{\"more\":\" stuff\", \"1\":\"2\"}" -o stdout -m "*"
  -o stdout -m "*" -p Format=json_lines -p json_date_format=iso8601
```

The result should resemble figure 2.3, where outputs occur twice (once for each output definition). One of the outputs is displayed in proper JSON format and uses the ISO 8601 date representation.

```
[0] dummy1: [[1698069182.432607543, {}], {"hello"=>"my world"}]
[1] dummy1: [[1698069183.432610340, {}], {"hello"=>"my world"}]
[2] dummy1: [[1698069184.432603807, {}], {"hello"=>"my world"}]
[3] dummy1: [[1698069185.432610894, {}], {"hello"=>"my world"}]
{"date":"2023-10-23T13:53:02.432607Z","hello":"my world"}
{"date":"2023-10-23T13:53:03.432610Z","hello":"my world"}
{"date":"2023-10-23T13:53:04.432603Z","hello":"my world"}
{"date":"2023-10-23T13:53:05.432610Z","hello":"my world"}
[0] dummy2: [[1698069182.433265925, {}], {"more"=>"stuff", "1"=>"2"}]
[1] dummy2: [[1698069183.432634876, {}], {"more"=>"stuff", "1"=>"2"}]
[2] dummy2: [[1698069184.432627693, {}], {"more"=>"stuff", "1"=>"2"}]
[3] dummy2: [[1698069185.432648796, {}], {"more"=>"stuff", "1"=>"2"}]
{"date":"2023-10-23T13:53:02.433265Z","more":"stuff","1":"2"}
{"date":"2023-10-23T13:53:03.432634Z","more":"stuff","1":"2"}
{"date":"2023-10-23T13:53:04.432627Z","more":"stuff","1":"2"}
{"date":"2023-10-23T13:53:05.432648Z","more":"stuff","1":"2"}
```

Figure 2.3   Output from Fluent Bit when running with multiple inputs and outputs

Defining the inputs, outputs, and filters in the order in which we expect them to be used is generally good practice because it helps with ease of reading. Sometimes, however, definition order can have an effect, particularly when we're introducing filters. In this case, there aren't any factors that will make Fluent Bit have to consider order. We can confirm this fact by changing the declaration order of the inputs and outputs.

2.1.4 *Fluent Bit prebuilt Docker container*

When the Fluent Bit project performs a release, a basic Docker container is published (https://hub.docker.com/r/fluent/fluent-bit). We can run the Docker image version by editing our `hello-world-2.cli.sh` file, and replacing the `fluent-bit` binary reference with the command `docker run` and the path to the latest Fluent Bit, such as `cr.fluentbit.io/fluent/fluent-bit:latest`. We should see the same outcome as Docker allows its `stdout` to reach our console. We've provided an implementation of the answer with the script file `hello-world-2.cli.answer.[sh|bat]`.

2.2 *Fluent Bit configuration in two forms*

Fluent Bit has two configuration file styles. The original, or classic, format looks like a Fluentd configuration file and a new YAML format. The YAML format was introduced with Fluent Bit v1.9 and is considered a production fit from Fluent Bit v2.0. Adopting a YAML format for Fluent Bit helps align with a common notation used across the cloud-native ecosystem of the Cloud Native Computing Foundation (CNCF) and Kubernetes. It also allows us to exploit any tooling that supports YAML or can template YAML configuration files, such as Carvel (https://carvel.dev/ytt). Eventually, YAML will become the default configuration approach. As new features arrive for Fluent Bit, we'll see the approach to configuration support through YAML first and possibly not in the classic format (such as the recent addition of the processor feature, which we'll discuss in chapter 9). As Fluent Bit is mature and has an established install base, we need to maintain backward compatibility so we don't expect breaking changes when it comes to the classic configuration notation.

As many existing users are working with the classic format, we'll use that configuration format for most of the book (but equivalent YAML files are provided). This chapter looks at both formats and addresses the differences.

2.2.1 *Fluent Bit vs. Fluentd configuration comparison*

Chapter 1 introduced the relationship between Fluent Bit and Fluentd. If you're already using Fluentd and considering migrating to Fluent Bit, then we need to understand the similarities and differences of the configuration file formats. Unfortunately, while there are a lot of similarities in the configuration formats, they aren't a perfect match. Table 2.4 shows how a classic Fluent Bit configuration file compares with a standard Fluentd configuration using `dummy` and `stdout` plugins.

Table 2.4   Classic Fluent Bit vs. Fluentd configuration comparison

Classic Fluent Bit	Fluentd
```[SERVICE] flush 1 daemon Off log_level info```	``` log_level info ```
```# define the Dummy source [INPUT] name Dummy dummy {"hello": "my world"}```	```# define the Dummy source <source> @type Dummy dummy {"hello": "my world"} </source> # after a directive```
```# Accept all log events regardless of tag and write # them to the console [OUTPUT] name stdout match *```	```# Accept all log events regardless of tag and write them to the console <match *> @type stdout </match>```

The key difference is that the XML style tags have been replaced by square brackets with no termination, which is now implicit. Our core types of directives have had some name changes. The configuration for the node, for example, is called SERVICE in Fluent Bit and system in Fluentd.

TIP If you elected to migrate from Fluentd to Fluent Bit, it's worth adopting a coexistence strategy and migrating directly to the YAML format.

2.2.2   Comparing Classic and YAML configuration

We've seen how classic and YAML Fluent Bit configurations differ. Now let's look at the same configuration side by side (table 2.5). The comparison uses dummy and stdout plugins to implement the "Hello, World" configuration.

Table 2.5 Classic Fluent Bit vs. Fluent Bit YAML configuration

Classic Fluent Bit	Fluent Bit YAML (without Kubernetes idiomatic formatting)
``# Hello World config will
take events received on
port 18080 using TCP as a protocol

[SERVICE]
    flush   1
    daemon   Off
    log_level info

define the TCP source that will
provide log events
[INPUT]
    name   Dummy
    dummy {"hello":"my world"}

Accept all log events regardless
of tag and write them to the
console
[OUTPUT]
    name   stdout
    match *``` | ```# Hello World config will
take events received on
port 18080 using TCP as a protocol

service:
  flush_interval: 1
  log_level: info

pipeline:
  inputs:
    - name: dummy
      dummy: '{ "hello": "my world" }'
      tag: test
  outputs:
    - name: stdout
      match: *``` |

As we can see from the side-by-side representation of the classic and YAML formats, the difference is more than minor changes to align the attributes and core blocks. The change isn't just moving [input] to input, for example; we have the additional structure in the form of a pipeline element, and input is called inputs. Likewise, output is now the plural rather than the singular representation and resides within the pipeline definition. There is also a variation in the YAML format, sometimes referred to as Kubernetes Idiomatic YAML.

TIP If you're new to YAML, appendix B includes links to resources that can help, including the YAML specification, IDE plugins, and online formatters.

Configuration files

This book supports both classic and YAML configuration formats. When illustrating configurations, we will use the classic format, which is arguably a little easier to read, and present YAML when we need to show how configurations may appear differently or features without a classic configuration option. These files are in the download package from Manning and available in the GitHub repository (https://mng.bz/vJKa).

CONFIGURATION FILE STRUCTURE FOR A CLASSIC FILE

We've seen similarities and differences in the formatting. Now let's look at the formatting rules for the classic file.

Indentation within classic-format configuration files is significant, as it is in YAML (see appendix B if you're unfamiliar with YAML). The main directive blocks (sometimes described as *sections*), such as [SERVICE], [INPUT], [OUTPUT], and [FILTER], must be left-aligned with no spaces. The case is not important in the declarations; [SERVICE] and [service] are equally valid.

Each block's attributes (also referred to as *properties*) need to be indented, usually with four spaces (but we've opted to use only two spaces to help with layout in this book). The indentation must be consistent within the configuration file.

A property (sometimes referred to as an *attribute* or *key*) and value can't be split across lines. The spacing between the attribute and its value needs to be at least one space. Some people like to space the attributes and values so that the configuration appears in a more tabular form with the values lining up, as shown in table 2.4. Others prefer single-space separation, the approach adopted within the provided configuration files. The following listing highlights a few key rules; see `chapter2\fluentbit\` `hello-world.conf`.

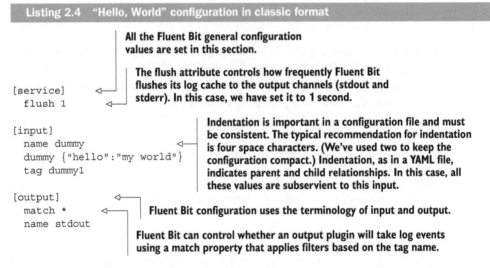

Listing 2.4 "Hello, World" configuration in classic format

All the Fluent Bit general configuration values are set in this section.

The flush attribute controls how frequently Fluent Bit flushes its log cache to the output channels (stdout and stderr). In this case, we have set it to 1 second.

```
[service]
  flush 1

[input]
  name dummy
  dummy {"hello":"my world"}
  tag dummy1

[output]
  match *
  name stdout
```

Indentation is important in a configuration file and must be consistent. The typical recommendation for indentation is four space characters. (We've used two to keep the configuration compact.) Indentation, as in a YAML file, indicates parent and child relationships. In this case, all these values are subservient to this input.

Fluent Bit configuration uses the terminology of input and output.

Fluent Bit can control whether an output plugin will take log events using a match property that applies filters based on the tag name.

To execute these configuration files, rather than use a lengthy set of parameters, we can use the command `fluent-bit -c` followed by the name of our configuration file. We assume you have the folder with the `fluent-bit` executable in the $PATH (%PATH% for Windows) environment variable, as advised during installation. Otherwise, you'll have to use the full path. For this book, we have assumed that you have the executable in the PATH, so a command such as this will work:

```
fluent-bit -c hello-world.conf
```

For a YAML configuration, the only thing we need to do is change the file extension to

```
fluent-bit -c hello-world.yaml
```

CONFIGURATION FILE STRUCTURE FOR A YAML FILE

We've seen that while there are some similarities, there are also some important differences. So, we should take a closer look at the configuration file and the rules that apply.

Fluent Bit has traditionally named its attributes using snake-case convention (separating words with underscores `like_this`). Kubernetes, however, adopted an approach that has cascaded to many other CNCF projects: camel case. (The first character of each word except for the first word is capitalized, so no underscore is necessary, `likeThis`.) You can find the specifics at https://mng.bz/ZVA9. The style differences can be jarring when reading Fluent Bit configuration inside a Kubernetes Pod configuration. To address this, Fluent Bit adopted the ability to translate attribute names between the two representations. `log_level` and `logLevel`, for example, are recognized as the same attribute. In this book, we will use snake case and reserve camel case only for Kubernetes YAML configurations to help you appreciate both formats. The following listing highlights a few key rules of the YAML formatting; see `chapter2\fluentbit\hello-world.yaml`.

Listing 2.5 "Hello, World" config using YAML

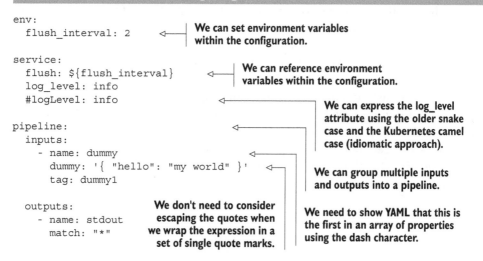

Let's incorporate the additional sources and outputs described when we extended the CLI with an additional `dummy` input and the `stdout`. We created a version of the classic configuration and YAML files. We can see from the resulting files that the classic configuration file has a near-perfect correlation to how we define the command line, as shown in the following configuration. The only notable difference is that we don't need to escape the quotation marks, as we can assume everything after the property name belongs to the payload to use; see `chapter2\fluentbit\hello-world-2.conf`.

Listing 2.6   Multi-input configuration file

```
[service]
  flush 3

[input]
  name dummy
  dummy {"hello":"my world"}
  tag dummy1

[input]
  name dummy
  dummy {"more":"stuff"}
  tag dummy2

[output]
  match *
  name stdout

[output]
  match *
  name stdout
  format json
  json_date_format iso8601
```

We repeat the input block for each input we define.

We create an additional output block for each event output type, including associated properties.

Defines the additional formatting using JSON

Sets the date formatting to use ISO 8601 format

The YAML format, by contrast, doesn't map perfectly. First, we use the `pipeline`, which offers an interesting opportunity to create a behavior a bit like a `Label` in Fluentd. In effect, we can group `inputs` and `outputs`. The next difference is that each input within a pipeline no longer needs to reuse the `inputs` declaration if the inputs are defined consecutively, which makes sense of that previously discussed change in plurality; instead, we start a fresh list of properties. The `inputs` element may be worth using to support readability, of course. We can visualize this pipeline using Calyptia's Visualizer tool (part of which we can see in figure 2.4), which allows us to design pipelines and generate visualizations from an existing configuration (another option for validating that the configuration will perform as expected). Listing 2.7 shows the configuration; see `chapter2\fluentbit\hello-world-2.yaml`.

Figure 2.4   Two dummy (Mock Data) plugins, which will be consumed by two standard-output (`stdout`) plugins

Listing 2.7 Multi-input config using YAML

```yaml
env:
  flush_interval: 1

service:
  flush: ${flush_interval}
  log_level: info

pipeline:                         ◁──┐  We have the additional
  inputs:                              pipeline declaration.
    - name: dummy
      dummy: '{ "hello": "my world" }'   ◁──    We don't need to escape the quotes,
      tag: dummy1                               but the string still needs to be
                                                wrapped with a single quote.
    #inputs:                      ◁──┐
    - name: dummy                     │
      dummy: '{ "more": "stuff" }'    │  The second input and output
      tag: dummy2                     │  declarations don't require the
                                      │  parent element to be used.
  outputs:                            │  We've commented them out
    - name: stdout                    │  here so you can try the
      match: "*"                      │  configuration with and
                                      │  without the declarations.
    #outputs:                     ◁──┘
    - name: stdout
      match: "*"
      format: json
        json_date_format: iso8601
```

Classic and YAML differences

As of this writing, the classic configuration formats have a few features that are not yet in YAML format. I expect that the gaps will be addressed over time so that adopting YAML format will become a superset of capabilities. Check the GitHub issues (https://github.com/fluent/fluent-bit/issues) and discussions (https://github.com/fluent/fluent-bit/discussions) sections if a feature doesn't appear to exist.

At the same time, the latest features for Fluent Bit are getting YAML configurations first and may not be backported to the classic notation. A key example is the processor feature, which we'll look at in chapter 9.

2.3 Checking configuration with a dry run

Having progressed to running the `hello-world` example via the CLI and a configuration file, we have an ideal opportunity to address the command-line option `--dry-run`. A dry run allows us to start up Fluent Bit so that it validates the configuration without running it. If any problems occur with the configuration, Fluent Bit provides log output information to tell us. To see a valid execution of the dry run, try it with a valid configuration by using this command:

```
fluent-bit --dry-run -c hello-world.conf
```

The result ends with a simple message that says

```
configuration test is successful.
```

To prove its behavior, either edit the `hello-world.conf` file and make a change (such as changing the plugin's name from `dummy` to `dumm`) or run the provided faulty file `hello-world.error.conf`. When you run the erroneous file, you should see an error such as `[error] [config] section 'dumm' tried to instance a plugin name that doesn't exist`.

The validation checks performed by Fluent Bit are not exhaustive. The error reports in the Fluent Bit GitHub repository show some limitations.

Because the validation checks are applied to the configuration when they're loaded, the `--dry-run` option can be used on the YAML configuration just as easily. Try performing a dry run with the YAML version of the erroneous configuration file `hello-world.error.yaml`. The loading of the YAML file is also aware of how the file should be constructed.

2.3.1   *Exercise: Using --dry-run to help fix a conf file*

We have provided an additional configuration file with errors (`hello-world.error2 .conf`); use the `--dry-run` option to identify the problem(s) and get the configuration running. We've provided a version of the configuration file with the errors commented out and the corrections applied; the file is called `hello-world.error.conf.answer`.

> **TIP**   Incorporating the `--dry-run` command within a software build pipeline can help you identify and eliminate configuration errors during the build process; you don't have to wait until the software is deployed and is producing errors during startup.

2.4   *Configuring file inclusions*

When Fluent Bit configuration files start getting larger and more complex, we can break them down and create the configuration through a series of files, which are pulled together with `@include` declarations. This approach makes each part of the configuration easier to manage. Handling inclusions is a process of performing a text substitution, so you need to be aware of considerations such as these:

- *Sensitivities such as indentation*—The substitution is applied only at the root level rather than the attribute level.
- *Any declaration sequencing issues*—These issues include referencing variables, which need to be defined before they're used.

We can see this at work by using `hello-world-includes.conf`, which includes two files that make up our `hello-world` example; see `chapter2\fluentbit\hello-world-includes.conf`.

Listing 2.8   **Using file inclusions**

```
@include hello-world-input.conf
@include hello-world-output.conf
```

◁─── ⌐ **Example of the inclusion of a configuration file**

◁──────────────────────┐

**When a relative path is provided, the path is
relative to the configuration file with the inclusions.**

Figure 2.5 shows how this process works.

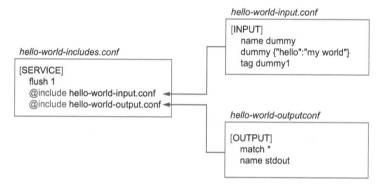

Figure 2.5   Visualizing how configuration is inserted when using the
`@include` **feature**

We can run this example with the command - `fluent-bit -c hello-world-includes`
`.conf`. This will yield the same result as running `hello-world.conf`.

2.4.1 Creating dynamic configuration by using inclusions

Simplifying our configuration files is the beginning of using the `@include` feature. We
can also use it to be more sophisticated in varying monitoring configurations based on
deployment needs. If we're deploying Fluent Bit with our application (which could be
Kubernetes itself), we may want to track the logs and information about the host, such
as CPU logs. The input plugin for CPU logs is a Linux-only source. If we keep two versions of only the CPU bit of our configuration—one for use in Linux and the other
for non-Linux deployments—we can swap the appropriate file version depending on
the environment. The core configuration never changes.

Figure 2.6 illustrates this approach. We apply `Linux-cpu.conf` or `noLinux-cpu`
`.conf` by symbolically linking, copying, or using other strategies to make a file called
`cpu.conf` with the appropriate content for the two options.

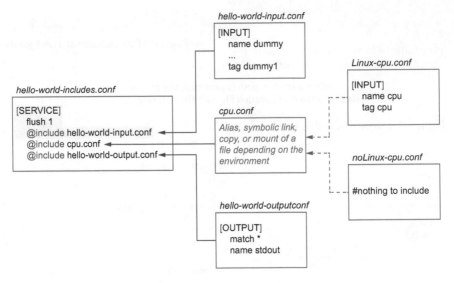

Figure 2.6 Injecting the appropriate file into a configuration depending on the deployment context

2.4.2 *Proving stub inclusions*

For this exercise, we can illustrate this dynamic behavior without the `hello-world` configuration. We can create the new version by copying the `hello-world-includes .conf` (let's call the new file `hello-world-includes2.conf`) and adding an includes declaration, including a file we'll call `dynamic.conf` (e.g., `@include dynamic.conf`). The `stub.conf` file is empty, as would be the case for our Windows environment. We need to establish the relationship between `dynamic.conf` and `stub.conf`. In Linux, we can copy (`cp stub.conf dynamic.conf`) the file or establish a symbolic link (`ln -s stub.conf dynamic.conf`). The best approach in Windows is to copy the file (`copy stub.conf dynamic.conf`, comparable to `noLinux-cpu.conf` in figure 2.6). Run our copied scenario (`fluent-bit -c hello-world-includes2.conf`). We should see the same results as before.

Now let's simulate the Linux environment; the inclusion should bring in the additional configuration. We don't have to change our main file. We need to copy or change the symbolic link, so if we look at `dynamic.conf`, we'll see the same contents as `stub-content.conf`, including an additional dummy input plugin. We can rerun our copied scenario (`fluent-bit -c hello-world-includes2.conf`). This time, the output includes an additional output message saying `hello stubby` with the tag `stubby`. We can change the output by swapping the mapping of `dynamic.conf` without changing any configuration.

> **TIP** Avoid using wildcard inclusions. It's possible to define inclusions with wildcards in the names. If we had the files `FBInclusionOne.conf` and `FBInclusionTwo.conf`, we could include them both with `@include`

`FBInclusion*.conf`. The problem is that this approach can result in the inclusions being applied in arbitrary order. In the case of interdependency or implications of ordering, there are no guarantees. Therefore, this approach is best avoided.

2.5 Environment variables in the configuration

Another way to make our configurations more dynamic in behavior is to use environment variables. Fluent Bit configuration can reference environment variables. Then, during startup, we can retrieve and use the values within the configuration file. This technique can be particularly helpful if, for example, we want to have the same monitoring configuration for our preproduction environment and our production environment, with all logged content going to an instance of OpenSearch or Elasticsearch for each environment. We could define an environment variable with the URL and a location to retrieve credentials (such as a vault) for the different connections and then reference those variables in the configuration. Alternatively, we could operate a single instance of a logging service and differentiate the environments by changing tags or adding an attribute to the logged event.

2.5.1 Applying environment variables

In this section, we're going to use an environment variable to change the "Hello, World" message—something that is about as invasive as we can get. For this change to work, we need to introduce an environment variable called `myTag` and give it a value, for example, `my-dummy-tag`. In Linux, we can use the command `export myTag=my-dummy-tag`. In Windows, we would use the shell command `set` instead of `export`. Appendix A includes additional details on exporting environment variables as part of the Fluent Bit setup.

Next, we need to copy `hello-world.conf` to `hello-world-variable.conf` to introduce the variable into the expression, or we can use the provided version. We reference environment variables by placing the variable name inside curly braces with a leading dollar symbol, as shown in the following configuration fragment (`chapter2\fluentbit\hello-world-variable.conf`).

> **Listing 2.9 Using environment variables**

```
[input]
  name dummy
  dummy {"hello":"my world"}
  tag ${myTag}
```

> References the environment variable to set as the tag

With the changes made, we need to set the environment variable. When the environment variable is in place, we can run the example:

```
fluent-bit -c hello-world-variable.conf
```

We can see the output change when we run this, replacing the tag's value of `dummy1` with the value of the environment variable. If the environment variable isn't set, Fluent

Bit produces an error complaining about an unknown property because the value substitution failed.

> **NOTE** The use of environment variables has some constraints. Some configuration attributes, such as `dummy`, expect to be given a literal string. In situations like this, we can use the `Modify` or `Record` filters, which we'll see in chapter 7. These filters allow us to add or change the event payload.

2.5.2 *Setting environment variables*

In addition to referencing environment variables, we can set them from within a configuration by using the `@set` declaration. For example, if we wanted to set an environment variable within our configuration called `myTag` with the value of `TestingTesting`, we'd need to include it in the configuration `@set myTag=TestingTesting`.

The applications of this feature aren't as broad as the `@include`, but the most useful use case is for sharing configuration values between included configuration files. Also, any needed environment variables can be captured within a Fluent Bit configuration file in a platform-agnostic manner. `@set`, for example, takes care of whether the environment is Linux, Windows, or a different OS with different syntaxes for setting up the values of these shared variables. If the `@set` declaration uses the same name as an OS-level environment variable, the environment variable's value will be overridden.

Let's try setting and overriding an existing environment variable by copying listing 2.9 (`hello-world-variable.conf`) to `hello-world-variable2.conf` (we've provided the configuration so you can run the example), adding `@set myTag=NotTesting` as the first line, and rerunning the configuration. The result will be that the tag displayed in the output will now be `NotTesting` rather than the original environment variable value `my-dummy-tag`.

If the configuration fails to start up with an error message like `unknown configuration property 'tag'`, it indicates that Fluent Bit isn't able to resolve the environment variable or the environment variable is an empty or null string.

2.6 *Monitoring Fluent Bit's health*

When teams start investing in observability and monitoring more generally, effort goes into checking that our applications are running smoothly. Often, the absence of an alert is interpreted as a sign that all is well. But what if the monitor has stopped? In this case, the absence of events is a problem. For this reason, microservices in a Kubernetes environment should implement a health endpoint, traditionally set as `/health`. This leads to the question, does Fluent Bit have anything to which we can connect the container health check?

Background on health checks

To enable containers or Kubernetes Pods to be effectively managed, we must be able to interrogate their condition. To this end, Dockerfiles include the ability to define health check actions. For more information on defining health checks in Dockerfiles, see https://mng.bz/RN4a. For Pods, we can describe several different checks (also called *probes*), including liveness. For more information, see https://mng.bz/2gnw. If the Pod doesn't respond quickly enough to the health check from Kubernetes, we can assume that the Pod is unhealthy and needs to be replaced by a new instance. A healthy response for Kubernetes is a response typically containing an HTTP response code of `200` (which may be accompanied by a body containing `ok`). Any HTTP response code outside the `200–299` range is deemed unhealthy. It's common practice for a containerized app to include some sort of endpoint implementation that can respond to invocations on `localhost:8080/v1/health`, which provides details on the application's health.

To enable Fluent Bit to communicate and listen to web-delivered events, we need to include a web server, which gives us the means to communicate with and interrogate Fluent Bit. The first step is configuring Fluent Bit to start the web server, which we do with an attribute in the `[SERVICE]` block called `http_server`. We can also configure the IP and ports the server should use (`http_listen` and `http_port`, respectively).

With the server active, we can also configure how Fluent Bit responds to health checks. We need to switch on the feature with the `health_check` attribute with a value of `on`; otherwise, the default web server response is provided. With the health response enabled, we can control what Fluent Bit considers healthy. Health is characterized by a count of errors from all the output plugins measured against a threshold defined by `hc_error_count` and the number of failed retries for output plugins (`hc_retry_failure_count`). We don't want the error count and retry-error count to be a cumulative score from the start of Fluent Bit, so we need to define a period expressed in seconds (`hc_period`) over which the count is applied. If we had an output trying to write to a file that kept failing because the filesystem was full, we should expect the error count or retry failure count to exceed a threshold quickly. As a result, the response to the health check URL will be bad.

When we use the health check feature, we should take into account what Fluent Bit considers to be an error and its implications. Any failing output will result in an unhealthy response even if we can live with the loss of those outputs. To put it another way, there is no way to define a tolerance to losing some outputs temporarily; the approach is an all-or-nothing approach. The other challenge is that the health check doesn't test inputs to see whether they're working successfully. If the `tail` (file tracking) input can't read the input file, an unhealthy state won't be successfully produced because the plugin is considered OK as the plugin exists and the parameter values are at least defined. The following listing shows the config for the health check feature; see `chapter2\fluentbit\hello-world-server.conf`.

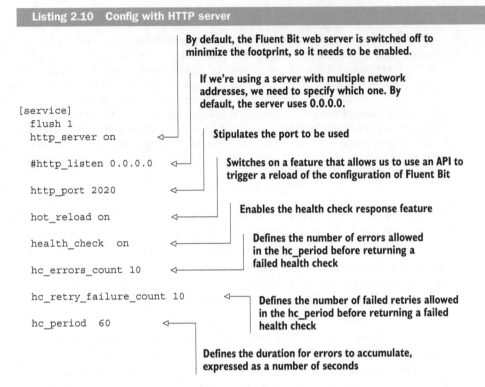

Listing 2.10   Config with HTTP server

With this included in our `hello-world` configuration, we can run Fluent Bit (`fluent-bit -c hello-world-server.conf`) and then use a tool such as curl or Postman (or even a browser) to access the information about Fluent Bit. The URL to use is `0.0.0.0:2020`, giving us a JSON payload and details about the Fluent Bit instance. If we use this approach, we can use `jq` to make things more readable:

```
curl 0.0.0.0:2020 | jq
```

In addition to the curl commands, we have created Postman configurations that can be used to exercise the different API endpoints, including the hot reload. Details on setting up Postman are in appendix A.

> **NOTE** Because Fluent Bit treats all its data as JSON, it can be useful to have a tool such as `jq` that can format the output to be more readable (sometimes referred to as *pretty print*). To get `jq` or understand how it works, go to https://jqlang.github.io/jq. Additional information is included in appendix B.

Fluent Bit provides APIs that go beyond simply retrieving a summary view. Some of the APIs have two versions available: v1 is accessed via the URL path `/api/v1/`, and v2 is accessed via the path `/api/v2/`. The version changes represent feature improvements; the older URL version is retained for backward compatibility. An example is the

`/metrics` endpoint; v1 provides a JSON payload, and v2 responds with Prometheus-formatted data and more data than `/v1/metrics`.

For a Kubernetes health check, a simple response returning `ok` indicates that the container instance is running smoothly. To get this response, we need to access one of the more meaningful operational endpoints in the path `/api/v1/`, such as `/api/v1/health`. If we invoke the health check URL with a `curl` command, we can expect to get a response of `ok`:

```
curl 0.0.0.0:2020/api/v1/health
```

In subsequent chapters, particularly chapters 3 and 5, we'll revisit the available APIs.

Summary

- We can configure and run Fluent Bit by using the following approaches: CLI, classic file format, and YAML file format.
- Fluent Bit and Fluentd are different even at the configuration level.
- We can create a simple "Hello, World" configuration and then extend it to explore some of the different means by which we can validate and structure its configuration.
- We can validate the configuration by using the `dry-run` option.
- Fluent Bit's configuration can be made dynamic by using inclusions and environment variables.
- We can monitor and obtain health and metrics data in different formats from Fluent Bit, making it easy to ensure that our monitoring operations are working properly.

Part 2

Digging deeper

Part 1 set us up for our deep dive into Fluent Bit. The next five chapters cover different types of input and how to output, filter, and route. By the end of chapter 7, we'll be able to solve many of our routine problems in monitoring and measuring our systems.

Chapter 3 is about ingesting data from common sources, from files to network communications. Chapter 4 dives deeper, focusing on Kubernetes. Most of our interactions are about input from Kubernetes, and the chapter touches on other concepts, such as filters, because we may not be inputting but enriching our observability data with details from Kubernetes.

Chapter 5 is about getting the captured events to the right places. As we saw in chapter 1, Fluent Bit looks to other tools to provide visualization and exploration of observed data. As in chapter 3, we'll look at different types of destinations. We may not see every type of plugin we can output with, but we'll have the foundation to use any plugin we encounter. Now we have "stuff coming out, stuff going in," as Peter Gabriel sang.

But we need to make sense of what we have, which means filtering the wheat from the chaff and making sense of what is being said. Chapter 6 covers parsers, which allow us to break up and change the noise to signals. Then we can apply meaning with filters in chapter 7. Filters are for removing noise, but they give us the opportunity to enrich and transform our events.

Capturing inputs

This chapter covers

- Reading log events from files
- Capturing console logging
- Ingesting OpenTelemetry data
- Integrating with logging frameworks

This chapter is all about capturing metrics, traces, and (most important) logs using Fluent Bit and a variety of plugins that support the latest techniques in the form of OpenTelemetry, as well as the established practices of using stdout and log files. We'll focus on logs, as Fluent Bit originated from log handling. Logs also offer the most flexible signals and can be easily used to provide data that embodies metrics and traces; we'll touch on techniques that allow us to change a signal's type. We'll come back to this subject in other chapters, including chapter 9.

3.1 Fluent Bit plugins

Fluent Bit has a respectable portfolio of plugins. To understand the relationships between the parts of Fluent Bit, let's see how the inputs fit into the overall logical architecture, shown in figure 3.1.

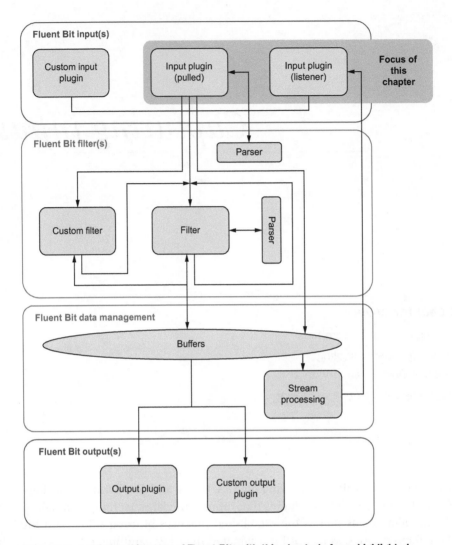

Figure 3.1   Logical architecture of Fluent Bit, with this chapter's focus highlighted

If we tried to illustrate every available plugin, we could easily fill this book and never get around to looking at what to do with the captured events. To address this challenge, we can group some of the inputs with similar characteristics and then look at representative plugins in each group. As Fluent Bit has a high level of consistency, an example in each group provides a sound basis for extrapolating what can be expected of similar source plugins that the book doesn't discuss. The inputs can be characterized this way:

- OS-level events from `systemd`, Windows event logs, and serial interfaces
- System metrics such as CPU, disk I/O, and memory metrics

- Application-level sources such as log files with prebuilt or custom log formats
- Event-driven sources such as MQTT, OpenTelemetry, and other Fluent nodes
- Network-/web-based pulled data such as Prometheus scraping and Kubernetes-style health checking

One important thing to remember is that Fluent Bit and Fluentd can work together. Consequently, we can take advantage of Fluentd having more plugins than Fluent Bit but still do the bulk of the work with Fluent Bit, which, as we have seen, is more efficient. We can do this because the `forward` plugin has a defined standard that both Fluent Bit and Fluentd use. As a bonus, some external products have also adopted this protocol so they can be connected directly to Fluent Bit. (Docker, for example, has a logging driver supporting the `forward` protocol.) In addition to the `forward` plugin, there are several other general-purpose standard protocol-based plugins available, such as `http` and `TCP`, available in Fluent Bit and Fluentd.

The `forward` and `http` plugins aren't the only ones we can use to send and receive data from third-party products without having a specific input plugin implementation. Fluent Bit supports the OpenTelemetry (OTLP) protocol, so applications configured to generate compliant logs, traces, and metrics can also be connected with Fluent Bit.

Traditionally, application-logging frameworks are associated with creating log files. Some logging frameworks can work with the `forward` protocol or `http`, and the OpenTelemetry (OTel) project has provided telemetry frameworks that can be used, as well as adapters or appenders for the most common logging frameworks.

What does this mean for us? Well, for new or modernized solutions, we can consider alternatives to traditional monitoring strategies, such as log files, without resorting to custom plugins to obtain metrics and trace data (although custom plugins can be a highly efficient way of implementing data transformation).

When capturing events, we should consider the options and the pros and cons rather than accept the default and traditional approaches to capturing observability data. We'll explore the `opentelemetry`, `forward`, and `http` plugins later in the chapter. First, we should consider the common monitoring needs and proven strategies.

3.2 OS and device sources

Input plugins for OS-based resources work in a similar manner; they use a time-based sampling approach that yields a JSON payload, which becomes a log event in Fluent Bit. Because these plugins behave in the same way, we can combine them into a single scenario. When monitoring infrastructure, we should consider memory, CPU, disk storage, and network utilization.

3.2.1 Monitoring infrastructure with native executables

Although prebuilt binary solutions produce faster executables than interpreted solutions such as Python or just-in-time (JIT) compiled solutions such as Java and Ruby, the downside is that there is no language abstraction layer providing platform-specific

OS and hardware interfaces. As a result, different platform binaries have certain features disabled; typically, the interpreter or JIT has been implemented to address any platform difference or capability gaps. Because there is no virtual machine (VM), we depend on libraries that talk directly to the OS or hardware. We have a problem if those libraries don't work for a particular environment. This challenge has been addressed through feature switches, so some features are unavailable for some builds. The most common occurrence is when features are switched off for Apple silicon chipsets (such as M2) and macOS.

The benefit of open source is that we can address these problems ourselves either because no binary executable was built for our CPU and OS combination or because we need a feature and are willing to invest the effort in developing the solution. The latter option is a serious undertaking.

An alternative to this problem (which may come up if you're using macOS) is adopting a VM or chipset emulator such as QEMU or using a cloud vendor's free tier. To help you understand what is available, appendix B includes a table of plugins, listing which plugins work for various platforms.

These resource measures, even in a container context, are useful even at a low refresh rate to ensure that our services have the capacity they need to run efficiently. (We don't want our services to use swap space, for example, as that wastes allocated CPU capacity.) Have we correctly configured the amount of CPU resources for Kubernetes to allocate to a container? If we're operating on real hardware, the answer is more critical. In such circumstances, we can't intervene quickly by dialing up the allocated resources or scaling out with another container or Pod.

Treating these measures as log events within Fluent Bit rather than metrics may seem perverse. But we do it for a couple of reasons:

- The ability to handle metrics differently came in v2 of Fluent Bit, and the plugins haven't been changed to protect backward compatibility.
- The ability to handle logs is more flexible and more efficient for data manipulation than the metrics structure. But if this data needs to be transformed to metrics, we can do that. Other plugins, such as `node_exporter`, can be used to generate metrics with this data from the outset, as we'll see in chapter 5.

To capture these metrics, we need to define four `input` blocks. Each input block identifies the source plugin by using the `name` attribute, such as `disk`, `cpu`, `mem` (memory), and `netif` (network interface). All these plugins use the attributes `interval_sec` or `interval_nsec`, which allow us to define the frequency at which we pull the measures as integers (expressed as seconds or nanoseconds, respectively). We can define tags for them or let Fluent Bit set a default tag. We recommend setting the tags explicitly, as it can help if you want to use them as values for filtering data. In our example, the tag `book_vm_<plugin name>` uses a full name rather than just the plugin name, such as `memory` instead of `mem` and `network` instead of `netif`.

NOTE Some naming conventions that have been adopted are worthy of note. Most source and target plugins have a degree of consistency in attribute naming conventions (such as `interval_sec` or `interval_nsec`) when polling physical or virtualized resources. When data is being pulled from another web service, the attributes typically refer to scraping, so the frequency becomes `scrape_interval`. Timing typically defaults to being expressed in seconds.

For now, let's continue the chapter 2 practice of pushing the events to the console. We need the output declaration with the `name` attribute having the value `stdout` and the `match` attribute having the value of * (asterisk). This configuration allows us to start monitoring if we want to, as we see in `os-monitoring-basic.conf`. See the following listing and `chapter3/fluentbit/os-monitoring-basic.conf`.

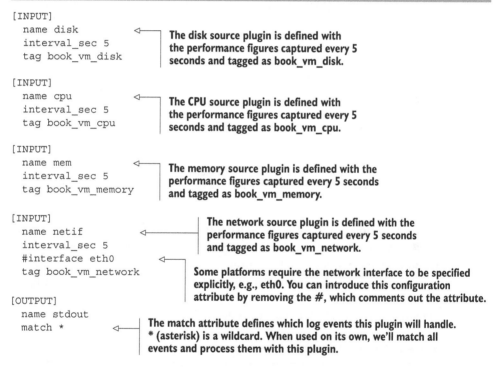

Listing 3.1 Performing basic OS monitoring

```
[INPUT]
  name disk              ◁────    The disk source plugin is defined with
  interval_sec 5                  the performance figures captured every 5
  tag book_vm_disk                seconds and tagged as book_vm_disk.

[INPUT]
  name cpu               ◁────    The CPU source plugin is defined with
  interval_sec 5                  the performance figures captured every 5
  tag book_vm_cpu                 seconds and tagged as book_vm_cpu.

[INPUT]
  name mem               ◁────    The memory source plugin is defined with the
  interval_sec 5                  performance figures captured every 5 seconds
  tag book_vm_memory              and tagged as book_vm_memory.

[INPUT]                           The network source plugin is defined with the
  name netif             ◁────    performance figures captured every 5 seconds
  interval_sec 5                  and tagged as book_vm_network.
  #interface eth0        ◁────
  tag book_vm_network             Some platforms require the network interface to be specified
                                  explicitly, e.g., eth0. You can introduce this configuration
[OUTPUT]                          attribute by removing the #, which comments out the attribute.
  name stdout
  match *                ◁────    The match attribute defines which log events this plugin will handle.
                                  * (asterisk) is a wildcard. When used on its own, we'll match all
                                  events and process them with this plugin.
```

WARNING Not all OSes support all plugins. The input plugins for storage (`disk`), memory (`mem`), CPU, and network (`netif`) are not available in the current standard builds of Fluent Bit for macOS. We have detailed which plugins are different OSes in appendix B.

Let's run this configuration with the command

```
fluent-bit -c chapter3/fluentbit/os-monitoring-basic.conf
```

Figure 3.2 shows the outcome of this command.

```
* Fluent Bit is a CNCF sub-project under the umbrella of Fluentd
* https://fluentbit.io

[0] book_vm_cpu: [[1690827214.930491800, {}], {"cpu_p"=>0.025000, "user_p
"=>0.025000, "system_p"=>0.000000, "cpu0.p_cpu"=>0.000000, "cpu0.p_user"=
>0.000000, "cpu0.p_system"=>0.000000, "cpu1.p_cpu"=>0.000000, "cpu1.p_use
r"=>0.000000, "cpu1.p_system"=>0.000000, "cpu2.p_cpu"=>0.200000, "cpu2.p_
user"=>0.200000, "cpu2.p_system"=>0.000000, "cpu3.p_cpu"=>0.000000, "cpu3
.p_user"=>0.000000, "cpu3.p_system"=>0.000000, "cpu4.p_cpu"=>0.000000, "c
pu4.p_user"=>0.000000, "cpu4.p_system"=>0.000000, "cpu5.p_cpu"=>0.000000,
 "cpu5.p_user"=>0.000000, "cpu5.p_system"=>0.000000, "cpu6.p_cpu"=>0.2000
00, "cpu6.p_user"=>0.200000, "cpu6.p_system"=>0.000000, "cpu7.p_cpu"=>0.0
00000, "cpu7.p_user"=>0.000000, "cpu7.p_system"=>0.000000, "cpu8.p_cpu"=>
0.000000, "cpu8.p_user"=>0.000000, "cpu8.p_system"=>0.000000, "cpu9.p_cpu
"=>0.000000, "cpu9.p_user"=>0.000000, "cpu9.p_system"=>0.000000, "cpu10.p
_cpu"=>0.000000, "cpu10.p_user"=>0.000000, "cpu10.p_system"=>0.000000, "c
pu11.p_cpu"=>0.000000, "cpu11.p_user"=>0.000000, "cpu11.p_system"=>0.0000
00, "cpu12.p_cpu"=>0.000000, "cpu12.p_user"=>0.000000, "cpu12.p_system"=>
0.000000, "cpu13.p_cpu"=>0.000000, "cpu13.p_user"=>0.000000, "cpu13.p_sys
tem"=>0.000000, "cpu14.p_cpu"=>0.000000, "cpu14.p_user"=>0.000000, "cpu14
.p_system"=>0.000000, "cpu15.p_cpu"=>0.000000, "cpu15.p_user"=>0.000000,
"cpu15.p_system"=>0.000000}]
[0] book_vm_memory: [[1690827214.930545161, {}], {"Mem.total"=>16052504,
"Mem.used"=>1372648, "Mem.free"=>14679856, "Swap.total"=>4194304, "Swap.u
sed"=>0, "Swap.free"=>4194304}]
[0] book_vm_disk: [[1690827219.930214835, {}], {"read_size"=>0, "write_si
ze"=>0}]
```

Figure 3.2   Output fragment from running the OS-monitoring configuration that collects CPU, memory, and disk. You could run the command and pipe the content to `jq` to help with formatting.

Let's take a moment to understand what the console output of the captured host metrics shows. The output records are prefixed with the timestamp, metadata, and so on, introduced in chapter 2. The output should contain the entries tagged from the sources defined in the input definitions and sent to the console using our output plugin. With the data from the `cpu` plugin, which has the tag `book_vm_cpu`, we can see CPU measurements in JSON form (table 3.1).

Table 3.1   The `cpu` plugin output values and their meanings

Attribute name	Description
p_cpu	Provides the overall measure of total CPU utilization
p_user	Shows how much CPU use is from user processes, such as running developer tools, as a percentage of the total
p_system	Shows how much of the CPU use is from system processes, such as the OS, as a percentage of the total

These metrics are reported against each CPU core, with each CPU ID used as a prefix, such as `cpu0`. In this example, the measurement reflects the capabilities of eight dual-core CPUs. We can capture this information in a more nuanced way by providing Fluent Bit with the specific process we want to measure (PID). We'll come back to this topic.

The output also includes records with the tag `book_vm_memory`, which includes the actual memory available to the environment, the swap space, and the amount of memory being utilized expressed in kilobytes (KB). To compare the numbers with an alternative view, use the command `cat /proc/meminfo` in Linux or the Task Manager tool in Windows (`taskmgr` on the command line).

The output from running this configuration includes a record tagged `book_vm_network` and shows the volume of network traffic passing through the network. (The network interface to be monitored can be identified with the `interface` attribute, but we have omitted this attribute, so the measurement is for all available networks.) The figures are split into `rx` (received) and `tx` (transmitted) for each interface being measured. Then the transmitted and received are split to show the volume of bytes, how many packets they represent, and how many network errors are detected.

The last record in our output is `book_vm_disk`, which lists the data for the amount of read (`read_size`) and write (`write_size`) activity measured. Because we haven't been generating activity (unless we have another process going while running this scenario), we will report zero values.

3.2.2   *Tuning monitoring sources*

Our first exercise is to adapt and tune the configuration we've just used in listing 3.1 to gather OS-based metrics. We need to change the CPU, network, and memory monitoring inputs from 5 to 1.5 seconds. As the interval values are expressed as integers, we can't simply modify the `interval_sec` value attribute to a decimal value of 1.5, as it accepts only whole (integer) values. However, Fluent Bit provides an alternative attribute called `interval_nsec`. This attribute allows us to stipulate a number of nanoseconds, so we can express 1.5 seconds with an integer. Therefore, we could replace the configuration attribute `interval_sec 5` with the attribute `interval_nsec 1500000000`. With that change applied, we rerun the Fluent Bit configuration. This change can be run using the prepared answer configuration `fluent-bit -c chapter3/fluentbit/bos-monitoring-answer.conf`. As a result, many more log events will be pushed to the console.

3.2.3   *Device sources*

In addition to typical, basic, host-environment measurements, Fluent Bit can capture other infrastructure values depending on the hardware and the OS. For example, in Linux environments, we can also collect temperature metrics with the `thermal` input plugin. In Windows environments, we can pull data via the Windows Exporter Metrics source (`windows_exporter_metrics`), based on the Prometheus plugin that targets specific drives, CPU, and thermal sensor data.

In addition, Fluent Bit allows us to pick up OS kernel log events from Windows and Linux using platform-specific plugins. To make these plugins work, you need to understand and have the relevant user permissions associated with the user or process that runs Fluent Bit and is allowed to access the relevant data.

Exporter metrics plugins such as Windows Exporter Metrics generate proper Fluent Bit metric structures rather than log structures. These plugins are based on the Prometheus Node Exporter functionality (https://prometheus.io/docs/guides/node -exporter). These plugins produce a metrics event rather than the previously described structured content within a log event. The metrics produced are comprehensive but need to be converted to log events to perform meaningful calculations, as we have a lot more tooling capability with logs. It's reasonable to assume that this capability will improve over time, so eventually, we won't need to convert.

3.3   *Using stdout*

If you've been actively involved with software development in the past 5 to 10 years, there's a fair chance you'll have come across the twelve-factor app (https://12factor .net), which lays out some high-level principles for software development. The 11th factor addresses the use of logs (https://12factor.net/logs). Specifically, it recommends:

- Logs are the stream of aggregated, time-ordered events collected from the output streams of all running processes and backing services. Logs in their raw form are typically in text format with one event per line (though backtraces from exceptions may span multiple lines). Logs have no fixed beginning or end but flow continuously as long as the app is operating.

- A twelve-factor app never concerns itself with routing or storage of its output stream. It should not attempt to write to or manage log files. Instead, each running process writes its event stream, unbuffered, to stdout. During local development, the developer will view this stream in the foreground of their terminal to observe the app's behavior.

- In staging or production deployment, each process's stream will be captured by the execution environment, collated with all other streams from the app, and routed to one or more final destinations for viewing and long-term archival. These archival destinations are not visible to or configurable by the app and instead are completely managed by the execution environment. Open source log routers (such as Logplex and Fluentd) are available for this purpose.

- The event stream for an app can be routed to a file or watched via real-time `tail` in a terminal. Most significantly, the stream can be sent to a log indexing and analysis system such as Splunk or a general-purpose data warehousing system such as Hadoop/Hive.

3.3.1 *The twelve-factor app and Fluent Bit*

Let's explore what the twelve-factor app statement means when working with Fluent Bit. The first statement reflects a point we made in chapter 1, and Fluent Bit has features that align with this idea. We agree that the application shouldn't need to know where the logging goes beyond passing it to an output. However, whether you should state that you are sending all logging to stdout is more debatable. We would argue that where the events go should be configuration driven so the application logic doesn't address routing or storage. Although Fluent Bit can handle catching stdout, applying this approach presents several challenges, particularly if the guidance is taken literally (such as the use of `printf`, `println`, and other language-equivalent statements):

- If this guidance is taken literally, we're unlikely to be using a logging framework, which means we can't change the logging detail (such as logging debug messages or only errors).

  Operationally, we rarely want to generate debug-level logs, although if a problem can't be re-created in nonproduction environments, it may be necessary. If we only push logs to stdout, there isn't any logic to filter out this overhead, and we end up with overly chatty production solutions or code that can be hard to diagnose due to information scarcity. If we start wrapping the output calls with conditions and our own flags, we're reinventing the wheel; a logging framework can do this work for us with more consistency and flexibility.

- Although not using a logging framework doesn't automatically mean that log output will be structured inconsistently, experience shows that output inconsistency is far more likely, and it is much harder to ensure that code logs consistently without using even a simple logging framework.

- If any part of the solution generates sensitive log data and we use a logging framework, we have the chance to suppress logging in a targeted manner quickly (such as setting logging thresholds so that a particular class never creates log events), even temporarily, by tuning the logging configuration.

- If the log structure has no consistency, to make logs actionable, we have to incorporate logic into the monitoring that has more understanding of the source application (which messages are errors and which aren't, which messages are formatted as JSON and which are free text). If we incorporate logic conflicts with the idea of cohesion and low coupling, as our monitoring must understand the innards of another piece of software, and change the application, which affects logging or metrics, we must also modify the log management tooling because the changes are far more likely to have knock-on effects.

Regardless of what the twelve-factor app says, we believe the right thing to do is to use a logging framework that knows how to push the log events to Fluent Bit. Because Fluent Bit can communicate in the same way as Fluentd, a wide range of possible logging frameworks is available. If a logging framework isn't possible, we can identify an intermediary that can be efficiently consumed.

TIP   *Logging in Action* (https://www.manning.com/books/logging-in-action) includes a chapter on logging frameworks and compatibility with Fluentd. As we'll see later in this chapter and in chapter 5, Fluent Bit can be interchanged with Fluentd because both support several common protocols. You can find details on compatible frameworks at https://mng.bz/lrVd.

The goal is to not need the core application logic to know where the logs are going, which all comes down to the separate configuration of the logging framework. We get the benefits of tuning logging and structural standardization, reducing labor, and having no file management performance problems or storage overhead to worry about. At the same time, we don't need the infrastructure during unit testing to capture failed test outputs. If you agree with this approach, you'll find some helpful material in the *Logging in Action* book, which looks at a range of frameworks in multiple languages. Not everyone agrees, however, so let's look briefly at the stdout capture approach.

To generate stdout traffic, we'll use the LogSimulator with a simple configuration. Appendix A describes how to set it up. Using it is even easier than writing a little script that creates a steady flow of stdout messages. To capture the stdout stream, we need to set up Fluent Bit with the `stdout` input plugin, which is simple because it has no attributes other than the tag to attribute the stdout content, as shown in the following listing; see `/chapter3/fluentbit/stdout-monitoring.conf`.

Listing 3.2   Capturing stdout

```
[SERVICE]
    flush 1

[INPUT]
    name stdin          ◁——   Identifies the plugin to be
    tag book_stdout     ◁——   configured using the name
                               attribute

[OUTPUT]                      Imposes a specific tag for the captured
    match *                   events. We will see in chapter 5 how it can
    name file                 help direct log events through the correct
    path .                    processes in Fluent Bit.
    file captured.txt
```

3.3.2   *Running the containerized Log Simulator*

To simplify the command, we've wrapped the Docker container call inside a simple shell script called `stdout-formatted-run.sh` (we've used a naming convention of postfixing the properties file with `-run.sh` or `-run.bat` instead of `.properties`). The script looks like this:

```
docker run -v .:/vol/log \
    -v $flbBookRootDir/chapter3/SimulatorConfig/:/vol/conf \
    -v $flbBookRootDir/TestData/:/vol/test-data \
    --env run_props=stdout-formatted.properties \
    --env data=medium-source.txt \
    logsimcontainer-logger
```

We're mounting directories for the test data files, the location of the configuration files for the log simulator, and the output location (the current directory). Then, via environment variables, we're telling the log simulator which configuration file and test data file to use. For the rest of the book, we'll show the provided script for simplicity. If you prefer, this script can be substituted with the following command. Using this configuration, we can run the process with the command (from the chapter 3 folder):

```
./SimulatorConfig/stdout-formatted-run.sh | fluent-bit
⟼ -c ./fluentbit/stdout-monitoring.conf
```

> **NOTE** As we're using Docker to simplify the use of the Log Simulator, you may see additional Docker output in the `SimulatorConfig` folder during the execution of the scripts, such as warnings about Java incubator modules. This output is a byproduct of the container dependencies and isn't a problem.

When we review the `captured.txt` file, we see that it contains lines like this:

```
[1683312768.616811852, {"message":"The first computer dates back to
⟼ Adam and Eve. It was an Apple with limited memory, just one byte.
⟼ And then everything crashed."}]
```

Note that the body of the log is a simple JSON structure because we configured the LogSimulator to print messages in a JSON structure. We can see this structure if we remove the piping of the simulator into Fluent Bit (`./SimulatorConfig/stdout-formatted-run.sh`). That's fine, but few applications write to stdout with nice, simple JSON structures, although adopting a framework often gives use that option. By default, this structure is what Fluent Bit expects because we want to consume the stdin in an unstructured manner. We have an alternative configuration to generate it: `stdout-formatted2.properties`. The best way is to copy and edit `stdout-formatted-run.sh` or use the one I've provided, called `std-formatted-run2.s`, and change the `run_props` reference to the new file. Try running this configuration against the same Fluent Bit configuration to see what happens. (It may be helpful to delete `captured.txt` before repeating.) Our command becomes

```
./SimulatorConfig/stdout-formatted-run2.sh | fluent-bit
⟼ -c ./fluentbit/stdout-monitoring.conf
```

The file won't be created, but we won't see any indication of a problem from Fluent Bit. From chapter 2, we know how to use the command line to move the log level to debug: by setting the log level in the configuration file, using the attribute `log_level` in the `service` block or `--verbose` on the command line. If we rerun the command with the changed log level, we'll see messages like this one:

```
[input:stdin:stdin.0] invalid JSON message, skipping
```

To overcome this problem, we need to introduce a parser. (We'll explore the use of parsers in detail in chapter 6.) At this time, we need to worry only about adding an

attribute called `parser`, which identifies a named parser to be pulled from the identified file referenced by the `parser_file` attribute, which is part of the `services`
definition. See the following listing and stdout: `/chapter3/fluentbit/stdout-`
`monitoring2.conf`.

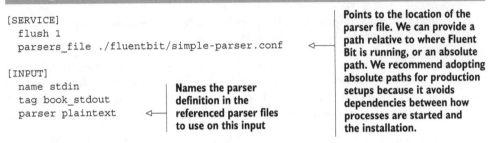

Listing 3.3   Capturing stdout (fragment): `stdout-monitoring2.conf`

```
[SERVICE]
  flush 1
  parsers_file ./fluentbit/simple-parser.conf     ◁─┐

[INPUT]
  name stdin
  tag book_stdout
  parser plaintext     ◁─┐
```

Points to the location of the parser file. We can provide a path relative to where Fluent Bit is running, or an absolute path. We recommend adopting absolute paths for production setups because it avoids dependencies between how processes are started and the installation.

Names the parser definition in the referenced parser files to use on this input

To run this configuration, we need to feed the Log Simulator's output to the stdin of
Fluent Bit, but we don't want the output from Fluent Bit to mingle with it accidentally.
Therefore, the safest thing is to direct our output to a file. We've added the necessary
output declaration to the configuration file, so we'll see the log entries being put in
the `captured.txt` file, with the log event formatted as a simple JSON structure. Here
is the command to execute this configuration:

```
./SimulatorConfig/stdout-formatted-run.sh | fluent-bit
➥ -c ./fluentbit/stdout-monitoring2.conf -v
```

Risks of using the stdin plugin

Piping the output from one application to another is generally not recommended, irre-
spective of the twelve-factor app. If the application generating the stdout traffic is producing faster than Fluent Bit can consume it, we'll have a lot of issues. Precisely how
these problems will manifest depends largely on the Linux configuration, but situations such as backpressure blocking the source from working are a likely outcome.
In addition, some Linux flavors have control of the use over stdin for `systemd`-con-
trolled processes.

As a result, if this approach is necessary, keep the parser simple, use buffering, and
push the heavy lifting to a separate node downstream. Alternatively, consider piping
the output to a log file using the `tail` plugin. If the log file becomes unwieldy in size,
you may need to consider introducing the Linux logrotate utility (https://linuxconfig
.org/logrotate). For Windows, you may need to consider something like https://github
.com/plecos/logrotatewin.

3.4   *File-based log events*

Writing logs to files has, for the longest time, been the default way of sharing logs,
metrics, and traces from an application. During development and testing, it is often

the easiest way (after using stdout) to inspect what is going on in an application. If we take the DevOps principle "You build it; you run it" to its logical conclusion, we're most likely to carry forward the approaches that served us well during development: handling logs through files. We'll probably dial down the amount of logging going on.

The downside is that when it comes to containerization—particularly when the container is being managed with Kubernetes—when the container is deleted, the container's local storage is also deleted. Only mounted external persistent volumes remain. So if our application using Kubernetes health checking indicates a problem, Kubernetes will recycle our container, taking the logs with it. But this point is when we want the logs most. Why did our application in the container start reporting problems? We have two options: reconfiguring our logging for production or finding a way to secure that file content. We think that over time, we'll see new developments, and the code that is given time to be refactored to adopt aspects of OpenTelemetry will help, along with changing approaches to logging during development and testing. Although newer developments may take a more optimal approach, lift and shift developments are more likely to repackage existing modules for containerized environments. But we still need to solve the current problem, which we can do in several ways:

- *Make the containers more complex by ensuring that logs are written to storage that isn't transient.* This option involves using persistent volume claims, making our Kubernetes configuration and deployment more complex.
- *Use logging frameworks with a different adapter that can send the logs somewhere over the network.* We can use the sidecar pattern to deploy tools like Fluent Bit as part of the same Pod and capture logs (we'll see more of this in chapter 4).
- *Deploy a process that knows where the logs are being written, collect the log content as it is generated, and send it elsewhere.* This option is effectively the least invasive for existing code. It works where a logging framework can't support alternative plugins and where logging is done by capturing stdout and sending it to a file. Whichever way we slice it, logging in to files isn't going to go away, and we need to get that content somewhere more secure. Given Fluent Bit's small footprint and its capability to be incorporated into a machine startup (virtual or physical), it's an ideal candidate for this task.

Therefore, let's continue our journey with Fluent Bit by looking at how we can capture log events from a file so that the log events are captured as soon as possible after they're written. For this task, we need to use our LogSimulator to mimic our application generating log files. We'll provide the configuration and commands necessary to run the log-generation process for each example or exercise.

> **Using the LogSimulator in the real world**
>
> Although we'll use the LogSimulator to help us master the configuration of Fluent Bit, the utility can also play real-world logs as though they're happening in real time. This feature allows us to develop and test our monitoring configurations without needing to run large, complex applications and, harder still, set them up to induce unhappy scenarios—the kind that are most important to capture.

3.5   *Capturing log files*

Fluent Bit's input plugin for handling files is called `tail`. The plugin is so named because it comes from the Linux command `tail`, which allows us to see the end of a file. With the right parameters, the Linux `tail` (`tail -f`) can read from the start of the file and then track how a file is appended to. This behavior is also available to our plugin. If the end of a file is the tail, it's easy to appreciate why the start of a file is often referred to as the head.

The plugin expects us to provide attributes that help Fluent Bit identify files and where they exist in the filesystem. We can tell the plugin to record how far it has progressed through reading a file so Fluent Bit can pick up where it left off if it restarts. The attributes that control this behavior can be identified with the name `DB.<something>`. In the following sections, we'll look at various configuration options for the `tail` plugin and address common use cases.

3.5.1   *Simple file consumption*

The first approach to parsing a file is ingesting the lines. Don't try to turn the content into something meaningful; that task can come later. We'll use the configuration that is most beneficial for injecting existing log files into our monitoring tools. We want the logs to be consumed from the top of the file rather than track changes to the bottom of the file from the moment we start Fluent Bit. For now, we want the content to go to the console, as we did with the "Hello, World" example in chapter 2. We need to use the `tail` input plugin to perform this task and set several attributes.

First, we need to identify the file to ingest. We can do that with combinations of setting the `path`, `path_key` and excluding content from the path (`exclude_path`) so that we don't accidentally try to process files that could be in the same file location, such as compressed log files in `.zip` or `.tar` format. As we saw in chapter 1, we also need to associate a tag with the log event. We can either define the tag explicitly or tell the plugin which part of the payload to pull the tag from. Because we are treating the log events as an unstructured string, we need to impose the tag. To ensure that we read from the start of the file, we set the `read_from_head`. We can also tell Fluent Bit to terminate when it reaches the end of the file by setting the `exit_on_eof` attribute. Taking these considerations into account, the simplest configuration is shown in the following listing; see `/chapter3/fluentbit/basic-file-read.conf`.

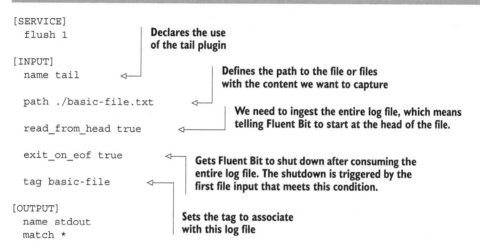

Listing 3.4 Illustrating a file tail: `basic-file-read.conf`

```
[SERVICE]
  flush 1                    Declares the use
                             of the tail plugin
[INPUT]
  name tail                  Defines the path to the file or files
                             with the content we want to capture

  path ./basic-file.txt
                             We need to ingest the entire log file, which means
  read_from_head true        telling Fluent Bit to start at the head of the file.

  exit_on_eof true           Gets Fluent Bit to shut down after consuming the
                             entire log file. The shutdown is triggered by the
  tag basic-file             first file input that meets this condition.

[OUTPUT]
  name stdout                Sets the tag to associate
  match *                    with this log file
```

> **WARNING** Appendix A describes how to build or retrieve the required Docker image. We recommend building the image locally to ensure that any security patches will be picked up from the dependency tree. If you pull the Docker Hub image, make sure to follow the actions identified in appendix A. If you don't complete this step, Docker may complain that it can't find or access the container image.

Let's run our basic file-read setup. To do that, we need to start the LogSimulator with its configuration and test data using the command

```
./SimulatorConfig/basic-log-file-run.sh
```

To avoid the need for absolute paths and minimize the need to configure environment variables to resolve where we put the downloaded content, we used relative paths, which rely on the download's directory structure. So we need to run the command from the correct location. With the LogSimulator generating log content, we can start Fluent Bit properly with the command

```
fluent-bit -c ./fluentbit/basic-file-read.conf
```

The output from the internal logging of Fluent Bit is the log file entries, as shown in figure 3.3.

```
[2023/07/20 19:10:57] [ info] [fluent bit] version=2.1.7, commit=, pid=13313
[2023/07/20 19:10:57] [ info] [storage] ver=1.4.0, type=memory, sync=normal, checksum=off, max_chunks_up=128
[2023/07/20 19:10:57] [ info] [cmetrics] version=0.6.3
[2023/07/20 19:10:57] [ info] [ctraces ] version=0.3.1
[2023/07/20 19:10:57] [ info] [input:tail:tail.0] initializing
[2023/07/20 19:10:57] [ info] [input:tail:tail.0] storage_strategy='memory' (memory only)
[2023/07/20 19:10:57] [ info] [sp] stream processor started
[2023/07/20 19:10:57] [ info] [output:stdout:stdout.0] worker #0 started
[2023/07/20 19:10:57] [ info] [input:tail:tail.0] inode=562949953750272 file=./chapter3/basic-file.txt ended, st
op
[2023/07/20 19:10:57] [ info] [input:tail:tail.0] inotify_fs_add(): inode=562949953750272 watch_fd=1 name=./chap
ter3/basic-file.txt
[2023/07/20 19:10:57] [ warn] [engine] service will shutdown in max 5 seconds
[2023/07/20 19:10:57] [ info] [input] pausing tail.0
[0] basic-file: [[1689876657.703341849, {}], {"log"=>"hello"}]
[1] basic-file: [[1689876657.703377617, {}], {"log"=>"hear about the new O Reilly book called —Essential Changin
g stuff and seeing what happens"}]
[2] basic-file: [[1689876657.703378939, {}], {"log"=>"Job requirement - must understand core programming concept
s - able to code without cut and paste from StackOverflow"}]
[3] basic-file: [[1689876657.703379801, {}], {"log"=>"dictionary definition of a programmer - A machine that tur
ns coffee into code"}]
[4] basic-file: [[1689876657.703380522, {}], {"log"=>"Programmer - A person who fixed a problem you don't know y
ou have, in a way you don't understand"}]
[5] basic-file: [[1689876657.703381164, {}], {"log"=>"algorithm - word used by programmers when they dont want t
o explain what they did"}]
[6] basic-file: [[1689876657.703381745, {}], {"log"=>"hardware - the part of the computer that you can KICK"}]
```

Figure 3.3   The output of reading the LogSimulator-generated log file, as consumed by our Fluent Bit input

Looking at the configuration, we've set the `read_from_head` attribute to `true`. Every time we start Fluent Bit, that attribute will log every record from the start of the log file(s). If Fluent Bit is deployed as part of a container that is regularly destroyed and re-created, this situation doesn't present a problem. But if we're capturing logs from a long-running process, we don't want the log-capture process to return to the start every time, as this would result in the downstream solution receiving duplicated log entries.

The second problem with the current configuration is that we set the attribute `exit_on_eof` to be `true`. This attribute means that as soon as the reading process reaches the end of any files being input, Fluent Bit shuts down (it's possible to exit before all files are fully read). This approach may sound strange, but it's ideal when we want to use Fluent Bit to bulk process existing log files, such as ingesting historical logs into an analytics platform. But typically, we want Fluent Bit to wait until new records are detected. So let's eliminate that attribute and try again (we've provided this as `./fluentbit/basic-file-read2.conf`). We'll see the console update as the LogSimulator generates logs. Note that the log simulation is configured to loop through the test data set and then stop.

3.5.2   *Supporting long-running processes*

For typical long-running application log capture, we're going to collect logs that will accumulate over time, as we would expect for application servers or web servers running on bare metal, VMs, or even in containers. We're more likely to handle large log files (covering a long time) and rotate because we can't allow log files to become too large and unwieldy. If environments are snapshotted or backed up, having a monolithic log file can burden the process unnecessarily.

In noncontainerized deployments, there is a chance that the server will generate the logs, Fluent Bit will start and stop at different times, and existing log files may be extended as servers start and stop. Hence, we need to avoid missing logs but not reingest logs that have already been consumed. Consequently, we need to track our progress through the capturing of log events and understand how to handle log rotation. We also need to parse the log file to derive attributes such as the event time recorded by the application rather than impose a timestamp stating when the log event was read.

In a Kubernetes ecosystem, we have another challenge: Kubernetes may decide to evict Pods, particularly if we're manipulating taints. If we're not running Fluent Bit as a sidecar, the starting and stopping will differ.

TRACKING PROGRESS

Tracking our progress through log files means we can stop and start Fluent Bit and, if we're unfortunate, address process-recovery scenarios without reingesting logs. To do so, we need to maintain a separate record of how far through a log file we've progressed and which log files have been partially or fully ingested by using some sort of database (in the most generic sense). Fluent Bit uses SQLite, a database implemented in C with a small footprint. Fluent Bit is written in C, which keeps things nice and simple. Although SQLite may seem heavy-handed for the task, there are good reasons to use it. Many mobile devices use SQLite to hold data for state and locally stored data to accommodate the possible lack of network connectivity. Furthermore, as SQLite handles the storage files at a low level, its I/O is optimized and can be faster than handling the tracking data with text files.

SQLite is built into the Fluent Bit binary, so we need to provide the appropriate configuration values only for the DB attribute, which defines the file that will be used to store the data. DB.locking allows us to tell SQLite whether multiple processes can update the database file. Ideally, each database is updated by a single Fluent Bit process at any time. Giving each source of logs its own database files provides good isolation. We may hold a few more file handles if we use workers (a Fluent Bit feature that enables parallelization, explored in chapter 5) to optimize performance, which minimizes the chance of limiting the benefits of workers by needing to manage the database reading and writing. Note that we can still query the database from other processes.

The remaining configuration options made available by Fluent Bit focus on more traditional database applications, covering the journaling of DB changes (DB.journal_mode) and how the low-level file I/O disk synchronization works (DB.sync) to ensure that the database updates are fully secured on the filesystem. To track the progress of reading log files, we should be able to tolerate the risk of file corruption in the unlikely event of a problem, such as a power failure during the low-level I/O process. We would be more concerned about the possible corruption of the actual log file. This attribute is geared to more transactionally sensitive use cases with SQLite. Given this fact, we should be able to leave the value DB.sync unset so that it defaults or lowers the setting to gain a little more performance. Because the journal_mode is incompatible with shared network filesystems, we should leave DB.journal_mode unset. We're likely to be working with network filesystems except for Internet of Things (IoT) use cases. Do we want or need the overhead for database journaling? Our configuration will look like the following listing; see `/chapter3/fluentbit/basic-file-read.conf`.

Listing 3.5   An enhanced file tail: `basic-file-read.conf`

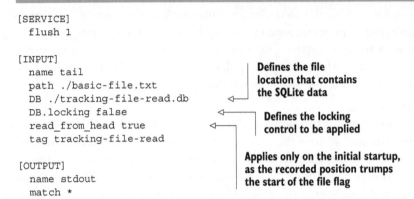

```
[SERVICE]
  flush 1

[INPUT]
  name tail
  path ./basic-file.txt
  DB ./tracking-file-read.db
  DB.locking false
  read_from_head true
  tag tracking-file-read

[OUTPUT]
  name stdout
  match *
```

Defines the file
location that contains
the SQLite data

Defines the locking
control to be applied

Applies only on the initial startup,
as the recorded position trumps
the start of the file flag

TIP The downside of using SQLite is that we need to deploy additional tools to inspect the contents of the database file. Fortunately, the SQLite website offers prebuilt downloads for this purpose (https://SQLite.org/download .html). In addition to tooling, the SQLite website has lots of useful information.

To run our log file–tracking configuration with the progress-tracking scenario, we'll use the LogSimulator with a version of the data file that has each line numbered sequentially. This version allows us to understand what is happening with log consumption. When we've got Fluent Bit logging the file contents to the console, we'll stop the process (press Ctrl-C) in the shell running Fluent Bit to bring the process to a graceful end. Then, to make it easy to see where the logging output picks back up, we'll use a command along the lines of

```
echo ------------------
```

which displays a visible separator on the console. Then we can restart the Fluent Bit process and review the content pushed to the console. We can start Fluent Bit with the command

```
fluent-bit -c ./fluentbit/tracking-file-read.conf
```

and run the Log Simulator with the command

```
./SimulatorConfig/basic-log-file-run-2.sh
```

We should have observed the logs displayed in the console output from the start of the file. After we stop and restart Fluent Bit, the output should continue from where it left off.

NOTE   Using a database to track progress through a file isn't unique to consuming application log files. Other types of log event sources are realized with files, such as `systemd`. As a result, we need to provide a plugin with the attributes necessary to allow the plugin to record its progress, so processing can resume where it left off as expected.

LOG ROTATION

Log rotation prevents log files from becoming too large due to endless appending to the file. Without rotation, a log file eventually becomes difficult to use, and it's harder to ensure we don't exhaust storage resources. Log rotation is typically managed in one of two ways. In a Linux environment, we have the OS utility logrotate (https://mng.bz/1aoR). Many logging frameworks offer rotation options as well. Typically, log file rotation works by writing to a log file. When the file reaches a certain threshold based on size or time (for Linux's logrotate, only on time, as a `cron` job triggers it), it gets renamed, and we start with a new file with the same name. We must also ensure we've fully exhausted reading log events from a file. We can see this log rotation process in figure 3.4.

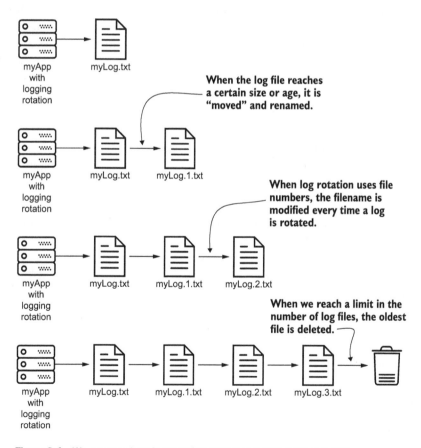

Figure 3.4   We can see how log rotation moves and then deletes log files.

Using any log-capture framework, including Fluent Bit, raises several questions. Apart from managing potential file growth, do we want log rotation? If we're capturing the logs as they get written to the file, the old files are redundant. Challenges also come from monitoring applications with Fluent Bit. Fluent Bit may not be in place in environments such as dev and test, where log files are an essential part of development and testing, and we don't want to change configurations unnecessarily.

If we use log rotation, we need to tune our logging settings to minimize the possibility that a file will be rotated before we've read all the content. If we're using the database, how do we know that we'll start from the beginning again? Also, how do we prevent reading the rotated log files again, as we have already read them before they rotated?

Fluent Bit addresses these questions by tracking the underlying file identifiers. When a file is rotated, the new file may have the same name, but the identifier for the file is new. Fluent Bit provides an attribute that allows us to change our read interval so we can be sure that we've picked up the last of the log entries. This attribute, called `rotate_wait`, takes a value in seconds (e.g., `rotate_wait 1` means we wait 1 second to accommodate any final flush). We can also control which files get picked up by using the `ignore_older` attribute, which takes a numeric value and a character that indicates the type of duration (such as hours, minutes, or seconds; appendix B defines a full list of duration types). If we set the attribute as `ignore_older 5m`, files over 5 minutes old are not processed. This setting allows us to track our progress. We also need to amend file properties to support rotating logs, so we need to understand how log files are rotated. The easiest way to create the effect of log rotation is to use a modified Log Simulator configuration that drives log rotation via the logging configuration file. We can run the earlier scenario, a modified configuration file, `./chapter3/SimulatorConfig/jul-log-file.properties`. The command to run the script that uses this new configuration file is

```
./SimulatorConfig/jul-log-file-run.sh
```

Let's also extend our previous configuration by adding to the properties mentioned. See `/chapter3/fluentbit/rotating-file-read.conf`.

Listing 3.6   Illustrating log rotation: `rotating-file-read.conf`

```
[SERVICE]
  flush 1

[INPUT]
  name tail
  path ./basic-file.txt
  DB ./tracking-file-read.db
  DB.locking false
  read_from_head true
  tag tracking-file-read
  rotate_wait 1              <—— Adds the new attribute
  ignore_older 1m
```

```
[OUTPUT]
  name stdout
  match *
```

Running the log-rotation scenario, we see the same output on the console, but we also see log files accumulate in the folder. Try setting up a logrotate configuration file and triggering logrotate manually to see its effect.

3.5.3 *Capturing logs from short-lived applications*

Capturing logs from short-lived applications is often overlooked. But we can build solutions using Amazon Web Services (AWS) Lambda, OpenFaaS (https://www .openfaas.com), and other serverless function-based solutions. We can also have scheduled jobs with Kubernetes. Or, in more traditional environments, we may log/audit trail batch processes such as housekeeping managed by `cron` jobs. If the underlying infrastructure and storage are transient, as in AWS Lambda, OCI Functions, and similar serverless cloud options, trying to trail logs can be an issue.

Given our understanding of this behavior, we should be able to adapt the configuration to accommodate deployments, which are more likely to occur when we use code deployed as a Function as a Service (FaaS) such as AWS Lambda, Oracle Functions, or local deployments using the open source framework provided by OpenFaaS. The task is to adapt our existing configuration to such a use case.

We can address this constraint in several ways. The approach depends on the preferred design style and software development frameworks being used. We could configure the application and Fluent Bit so that the application's stdout goes to Fluent Bit's stdin, and Fluent Bit uses its `stdin` source plugin to capture the log events. We can take a more advanced approach to long-running solutions by using an application-logging framework. Many logging frameworks have a configurable element typically described as an appender that can communicate directly with Fluent Bit or Fluentd. As the native Fluentd and Fluent Bit implementations work the same way, logging frameworks can connect to Fluentd or Fluent Bit interchangeably.

NOTE Chapter 11 of *Logging in Action* (https://mng.bz/XVxE) is devoted to looking at the frameworks, so we won't invest any more effort into how to do this. But if you have the book, it is worth experimenting with swapping Fluentd with Fluent Bit.

3.6 *Network events and communication between Fluent Bit and Fluentd*

The source of log events (or, as we'll see, all three types of OpenTelemetry signals) can be sent and received over the network by Fluent Bit. In many respects, this situation is desirable; we escape the possible latency of storage devices, and we have a great deal of freedom in the way we deploy Fluent Bit. Not only can we receive data from applications this way, but we can also have Fluent Bit and Fluentd nodes work together using several approaches, such as the `forward` protocol, simple `http`, and Fluent Bit. Fluent Bit also has the option of using OpenTelemetry. As a result, we can create sophisticated scaling and deployment patterns described in chapter 7 of the *Logging in Action* book (https://mng.bz/XVxE).

Given the importance and value of network-based communications, we're going to look at the `http`, `forward`, and OpenTelemetry plugins. Because we don't need to worry about event volume at this stage, we're going to use Postman as the tool to send the events to Fluent Bit. Appendix A provides details on installing Postman and explains how to set up the payloads or import the provided configuration file. If you want to try invoking the use cases by other means, such as curl (https://curl.se), feel free to do so.

3.6.1 *Network input sources*

The input plugins for the core Fluent Bit that uses network connectivity have several common attributes, including `forward`, `http`, and Splunk. These common characteristics help manage Fluent Bit's performance and resource needs. Fluent Bit has control of incoming data from most non-network sources, even if that control is how many bytes are read from a file at a time. This task is harder on a network because network data is transient, so we have to consume it as it appears. The attributes we need to be aware of are

- `buffer_max_size`—Sets the amount of memory available in the buffer (in other words, the maximum amount of pre-allocated space). If a single log event exceeds this amount, we can expect operational errors. The default is 4 MB, which should be more than sufficient in most scenarios. If we need more capacity, we're likely to be facing challenges such as these:
  - Someone is trying to push events containing the entire works of Shakespeare or their holiday photos through your monitoring as a single event. Neither activity is recommended.
  - We're trying to buffer up too much content as a result of factors such as waiting too long to allow data to be flushed. Holding data in memory for long periods creates a higher risk of losing events in the event that Fluent Bit stops ungracefully (if Kubernetes kills a container, for example).
  - This sort of data volume for a message suggests a possible denial-of-service (DoS) attack on the monitoring infrastructure.

  We can change this value by providing an integer and, optionally, an explicit data size (e.g., 64 MB or 32 KB). If the value is unset, the number is treated as bytes. Appendix B lists the data volume names that can be used.

  If the source is batching events before sending them to Fluent Bit, and the space of all the events in a single call to Fluent Bit exceeds the buffer size, errors can result. In this situation, however, we might consider reducing the number of events batched up in the source.

- `buffer_chunk_size`—Defines how big an individual chunk is. Fluent Bit starts processing a buffer chunk as soon as it is full (or sooner if the flush interval occurs before the buffer chunk is full). The default is 512 KB. Each chunk holds one or more events.

There are only two realistic situations in which we might want to change these defaults:

- *When we're operating a Fluent Bit instance as a point of aggregation for many upstream sources*—In this case, we may want to increase the capacity.
- *When we need to optimize memory use and reduce the allocation*—This situation might occur when we're running Fluent Bit on a small IoT device.

3.6.2   HTTP source

The HTTP source supports the HTTP verb POST with a JSON body, which is treated as the log event. The timestamp attributed to each log event is based on the time when the event was received according to the system clock.

To receive HTTP traffic, we need to define the network(s) that we want to listen to and which port on the network to listen to. Typically, we define the network address to listen to as `0.0.0.0`. This setting allows us to accept traffic from all networks to which our environment is connected. When we're deployed to a server running at a network boundary, the server will likely have multiple network connections. As a result, we need to be mindful of which network is being used so we don't accidentally create a network security vulnerability. The identified port needs to be the one to which the sender expects to send their HTTP traffic.

When the HTTP payload is received, if it is valid JSON, we can influence the response provided by setting the HTTP response code by using the `successful_response_code` attribute. (For details on HTTP codes, see https://mng.bz/PNn5.) The successful response code, if unconfigured, defaults to `201`. Still, we may want to return the generic OK (`200` to indicate that we received the payload), in which case we need to explicitly declare the attribute and the value in the configuration. For this example, we'll return the generic `200` response code. We can also add name-value pairs to the HTTP header response by using the `success_header` attribute. This attribute gives us an easy way to return information to the sender. For example, we may want to use a custom header to indicate the recipient type or the instance identifier of a Fluent Bit node. We can add as many custom headers as we need by repeating the attribute followed by the name and value. In this example, we're using it to distinguish between a Fluent Bit and a Fluentd consumer. As with all inputs, we can also stipulate the tag. See the following listing and `/chapter3/fluentbit/http.conf`.

Listing 3.7   Using custom headers: `http.conf`

```
[SERVICE]
  flush 1
  log_level debug

[INPUT]
  name http              ◁┘  Declares the input source plugin name
  listen 0.0.0.0         ◁
  port 9881
  successful_response_code 200    ◁
  success_header x-fluent-bit received
  tag http               ◁

[OUTPUT]
  name stdout
  match *
```

Declares the input source plugin name

Defines the network to listen to. In this case, we're listening to all network sources. We've also set the port.

Defines the HTTP response code to be returned when the invocation is successful, restricted to 200, 201

The tag we set is important in this case, as it influences which output will be used.

To run our HTTP source configuration, we need to start Fluent Bit with the command

```
fluent-bit -c ./fluentbit/http.conf
```

Next, we start Postman and load the configuration provided (`chapter3/Postman/FluentBit-Chapter3.postman_collection.json`). With the HTTP Call option selected, we can see the configuration (or set it up with the `log.json` file, following the configuration guidance in appendix A). When we click the Send button, the response should be nearly instant. Looking at the bottom half of Postman, which contains the response, we see that the Body section is empty, but the Headers tab contains values. When we select the Headers tab, we can see our custom response header includes `x-fluent-bit` and a received value, as shown in figure 3.5.

In addition to verifying the outcome in Postman, as we've directed the output to stdout, we'll see the log message payload in the Fluent Bit console. With the basic configuration working, try modifying the configuration to return multiple headers and different payload bodies. We've provided `chapter2/fluentbit/http-answers.conf` to give you something to compare or try.

What if we want to receive different event feeds over the HTTP input? We can configure inputs on different ports or continue with a single input. After the base part of the URL (in the preceding example, `localhost:9881`), the remaining path can be used as the tag value. So, if we made an HTTP post to the URL `localhost:9881/myURLTag`, we'd see that the tag has a value of `myURLTag`. Let's amend the scenario to omit the `tag` attribute and add a path name to the URL we want to see as the tag, such as `/myURLTag`. As a result, only the console output will display the extracted path as the tag value.

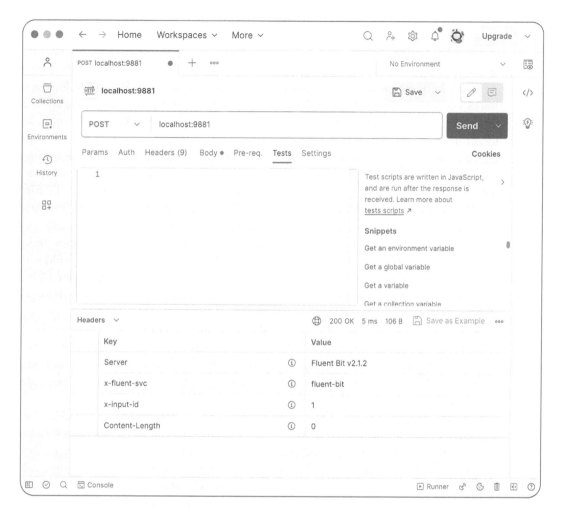

Figure 3.5   When we use Postman to perform the send, we can expect a result with an empty body and several header values received, such as the Server value shown in the bottom half of the screenshot. This element changes depending on the version of Fluent Bit and may be omitted.

3.6.3   *Securing communication with SSL/TLS*

So far, we've used HTTP without any form of security. Historically, this approach has been acceptable within a closed environment. Now, however, we work in a world that is increasingly security conscious, recognizing that security should no longer be at the perimeter of our networks but be on every layer so that if one level of security is bypassed, the next should protect us. This approach is often referred to as *zero trust*. We recognize the fact that bad actors may be in our organization, performing malicious acts as a result of either social engineering or other staff unaware of the consequences of how they're working. Today, computer performance and capacity are such that security is no longer a large overhead. In addition, our systems are becoming connected but decoupled and highly distributed. Solutions originally assumed to be run in private data centers are now potentially spread across multiple cloud vendors in different cloud regions and in what is left of our data center.

It would be easy to assume that observability data in the form of metrics, logs, and traces doesn't need security, but this assumption would be a mistake. During application development, it isn't unusual to log complete message payloads. Although we might tidy up our logging as our development reaches maturity, it is easy to overlook a log statement or log attributes that we think aren't sensitive. Still, if someone misuses the application, such as recording customer credit details in a notes field, if we don't have some security, we're logging and transmitting sensitive data. For credit card details, we'd have problems with the Payment Card Industry Data Security Standard (PCI DSS), which can have serious consequences.

To help address this problem, any network-based plugin in Fluent Bit can utilize Secure Sockets Layer/Transport Layer Security (SSL/TLS) certificates. If you build your own plugin and repackage Fluent Bit accordingly, it's best to ensure that your plugin builds on the foundations provided, which include SSL/TLS. As all the network source plugins have a common foundation, we can apply the same attributes to all those plugins.

Let's make this example more practical by looking at how we can secure the HTTP source from the preceding example. We need a certificate (see appendix A for generating a certificate) to use SSL/TLS. The first attribute we need to set is the `tls` flag, which defaults to `off`. For this reason, we don't see TLS attributes in most configuration examples. In real applications, consider setting this attribute even if the value is `off` because it acts as a prompt to think about security. When we use a certificate, we can accept the certificate at face value or use the information in the certificate to ask the certificate authority (CA) to perform an authenticity check. We can control whether this check happens by using the `tls.verify` attribute. When we're using self-signed certificates, no recognized CA is associated with the certificate, so no CA can perform a verification process; as a result, this attribute needs to be switched off. In production use cases, we recommend using a proper CA-provided certificate. CAs also maintain records of certificates that have been revoked.

Certificate authorities and certificate management

Certificates have lifespans, and the shorter a certificate's lifespan is, the better the security is because any certificate compromise can last only as long as the certificate's life. The problem is that deploying and refreshing certificates can be a messy, time-consuming process, and any error will break a system that uses HTTPS. The Linux Foundation addressed this challenge by developing Let's Encrypt (https://letsencrypt.org). Let's Encrypt provides a short-period certificate (six months). The foundation also led the development of the Automatic Certificate Management Environment (ACME), which is now an Internet Engineering Task Force (IETF) RFC (Request for Comments; https://datatracker.ietf.org/doc/html/rfc8555). The implementation of

> ACME requires you to deploy an additional piece of software but manages the autore-newal of certificates for you.
>
> There are now several implementations of the ACME standard, some of which can be embedded in other programs or frameworks. A solution such as the CNCF project's certification manager (https://cert-manager.io) can automate the distribution of cer-tificates in a Kubernetes environment and work with Let's Encrypt. Appendix B lists some additional resources on creating and managing certificates.

To use a certificate, whether it is self-signed or issued by a recognized CA, we need to tell Fluent Bit where to find the certificate by stipulating the certificate to use. The file location is defined by the attribute `tls.ca_file` for a specific certificate. Or we can point to a location that contains certificates with `tls.ca_path`.

When we create a certificate, it has two components: a public key file and a private key file. The private key file is part of the server verification process, so we must pro-vide the private key location by using the `tls.key_file` attribute, which points to the location of the private key. The last aspect of a certificate is providing a password, which is optional. If a password has been set, we must provide it by using the `tls.key_passwd` attribute.

Regarding the CA, we can either configure the OS or container so that it knows about the CA or provide the root certificate. Given this information, we can adapt the preceding example so that it looks like the following listing; see `/chapter3/fluentbit/https.conf`.

Listing 3.8   HTTP input example: `https.conf`

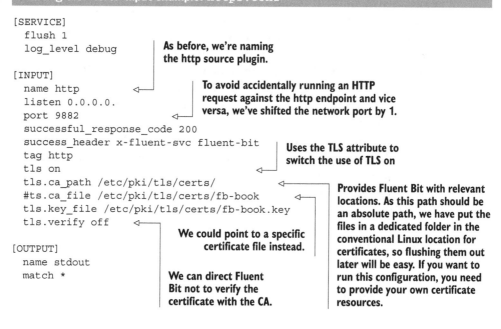

```
[SERVICE]
  flush 1
  log_level debug

[INPUT]
  name http
  listen 0.0.0.
  port 9882
  successful_response_code 200
  success_header x-fluent-svc fluent-bit
  tag http
  tls on
  tls.ca_path /etc/pki/tls/certs/
  #ts.ca_file /etc/pki/tls/certs/fb-book
  tls.key_file /etc/pki/tls/certs/fb-book.key
  tls.verify off

[OUTPUT]
  name stdout
  match *
```

As before, we're naming the http source plugin.

To avoid accidentally running an HTTP request against the http endpoint and vice versa, we've shifted the network port by 1.

Uses the TLS attribute to switch the use of TLS on

We could point to a specific certificate file instead.

We can direct Fluent Bit not to verify the certificate with the CA.

Provides Fluent Bit with relevant locations. As this path should be an absolute path, we have put the files in a dedicated folder in the conventional Linux location for certificates, so flushing them out later will be easy. If you want to run this configuration, you need to provide your own certificate resources.

We've shifted the port number to ensure we know we're running the HTTPS configuration, so we need to modify the port number in the Postman URL. When the configuration is executed, we'll see the same process of invocation and response.

3.6.4   *forward source*

As we touched on in previous chapters, Fluent Bit and Fluentd can interoperate seamlessly. Both products can use a plugin implemented for input and output called `forward`. Because the implementations are in different languages and some other products have adopted the protocol, interoperability can't be achieved simply through a common code base. Therefore, the protocol and payload have been formally defined; you can find the definitions at https://mng.bz/w5og. To take advantage of protocol compliance, we can use Fluent Bit and Fluentd to receive log events from a Docker Fluentd logging driver.

Because `forward` and `http` have many features in common—both can use networking to send and receive events, for example—let's take a moment to highlight key differences between them. The payload structure is prescribed for `forward`, for example. Perhaps more significant is using a binary serialization library called MessagePack (https://msgpack.org; shortened to `msgpack` in code), which encodes the payload and improves transmission performance. Unlike gRPC, which can be used with Open-Telemetry, MessagePack doesn't need a schema to generate code before being used for a payload. The upside is flexibility, but `msgpack` can't compress the payload as efficiently as gRPC. Also, the tag and timestamp are preserved with the core message payload, unlike the `http` plugin.

Because Fluent Bit can use the `forward` protocol/plugin as both input and output, we can use Fluent Bit to connect to itself. This approach saves us from deploying additional tools and shows how we can create networks of Fluent Bit that can be connected to route data to a common location. We'll use a `forward` output, which we'll examine in more depth with the other types of output plugins. The `forward` output sends a payload it has received to a second Fluent Bit instance with its own configuration, which receives the `forward` input and sends the received message to its console. As a result, our setup will use two separate configuration files. Our configuration will look like figure 3.6.

As we explore the `forward` output plugin with the other output plugins, we won't consider the `http-forward` configuration file (illustrated in figure 3.6). Instead, we'll concentrate on the `forward-out` configuration file using the `forward` input plugin.

The configuration attributes of the `forward` input plugin work the same way as those of the `http` input plugin. Now the `name` attribute is `forward`, and we need to identify the network and the port to listen to. In this case, we've set the `port` attribute to `9980`. As with `http`, we can control the buffer behavior with `buffer_max_size` and `buffer_chunk_size`, but we'll accept the default values.

Differences between `http` and `forward` configuration start with how the events are tagged. We can impose a tag with the standard `tag` attribute that overrides the log

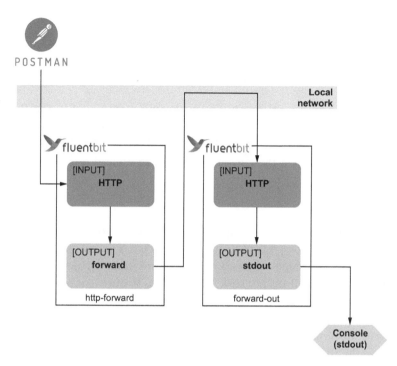

Figure 3.6 When we use Postman to perform the send, we can expect a result with an empty body and several header values.

event's existing tag in the `forward` payload, or we can prefix it using the attribute `tag_prefix`. Prefixing the tag name makes it easy to route a received event based on whether the event originated in this Fluent Bit instance or another instance. In this scenario, we want to carry the tag from the original source as it helps to show the continuity between the Fluent Bit instances. See the following listing and `/chapter3/fluentbit/forward-out.conf`.

Listing 3.9 `forward` plugin example: `forward-out.conf`

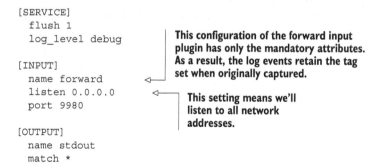

```
[SERVICE]
  flush 1
  log_level debug

[INPUT]
  name forward          ◁── This configuration of the forward input
  listen 0.0.0.0             plugin has only the mandatory attributes.
  port 9980                  As a result, the log events retain the tag
                             set when originally captured.

                       ◁── This setting means we'll
                           listen to all network
                           addresses.

[OUTPUT]
  name stdout
  match *
```

We need two shell sessions to run this `forward`-based configuration, one to each of the following commands:

```
fluent-bit -c ./fluentbit/http-forward.conf
fluent-bit -c ./fluentbit/forward-out.conf
```

With the processes running, we need to reuse Postman as we did in the first HTTP exercise. In doing so, we should see the first shell's console receive the message and report sending it by using `forward`. In the second shell, we should see the message being received and printed to the console, with the tag set and the timestamp reflecting the initial receipt.

3.6.5   *Beyond network ports*

Fluent Bit's forwarding mechanism goes beyond the standard network model to enable us to exploit Linux sockets (or domain sockets). This mechanism allows processes that reside on the same server to communicate more efficiently, for example, eliminating the need to address network routing. This feature can be useful when Fluent Bit is deployed as part of a Kubernetes control plane, deployed on the host alongside services such as CRI-O (https://cri-o.io) and containerd (https://containerd.io), which we need to monitor to understand any problems with a Kubernetes worker node. Because the socket approach depends on being co-resident, we don't recommend it unless the deployment model is certain. We need to set the Linux/UNIX path for the socket by using the attribute `unix_path`. The existence of this attribute results in the `listen` and `port` attributes being ignored regardless of their settings. We also need to define the permissions of the Linux socket file done with the `unix_perm` attribute. Example values are `unix_path /tmp/fluent-bit-in.sock` and `unix_perm 440`.

3.6.6   *Internode communication*

In Kubernetes-based environments, one of the key reasons for sending data between Fluent Bit instances is to simplify Pod configurations and handle Pod scaling by embedding the Fluent Bit with the primary application in a container or, more likely, using a sidecar pattern. By including Fluent Bit within a Kubernetes Pod, we eliminate the complexities of managing persistent volumes; different Pods won't clash when writing to storage, and we can handle the consequences of dynamic scaling of Pods and worker nodes. We can also manage the dynamics that come in as Kubernetes retires unhealthy nodes as well as the transitioning of nodes and Pods with changes driven by canary or blue/green deployment patterns. With the sidecar pattern, we capture the logs from the service within the Pod. If we do so via tailing files, then we simply use the Pod's transient storage, or (better) the service's logging framework sends to the Fluent Bit sidecar via the localhost network. The sidecar can route the data to a centralized node to consolidate it and direct it to the appropriate backend services, such as a security information and event management (SIEM) solution for security, a time series data store for metrics dashboarding, and so on. Pod-related deployment of Fluent Bit may also capture details on the Pod, clearly showing us when a Pod becomes unhealthy. We can see some of these internode communication configurations in figure 3.7.

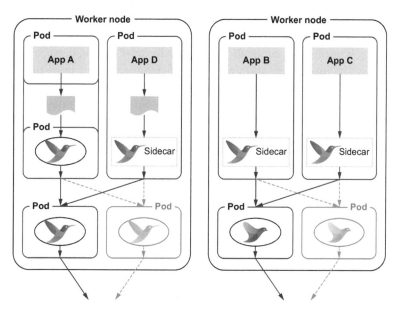

Figure 3.7   Deployment options for using Fluent Bit and Fluentd. The arrows reflect the flow of forwarded log events. The dashed arrows reflect the ability to forward to secondary connections if a connection fails to respond, giving us a resilient configuration if needed. These options work because the `forward` plugin works for both services. The right worker uses Fluentd as the concentrator node. App A uses common storage. App D works via a flat file visible within the Pod.

Two things to keep in mind when using multiple Fluent Bit nodes are the startup sequence and what could happen if an upstream node starts before the downstream node. In this situation, the upstream nodes are consuming events, but when they try to forward them, the destination node is unavailable. We can configure retries to mitigate this problem, but we will see errors. If we can arrange it, starting Fluent Bit instances with other Fluent Bit instances connected to them first and working outward can overcome the problem. This approach minimizes reported errors about failed connections as nodes start and connect because the send action always initiates the connection and reports an error. In figure 3.7, we would start with the nodes at the bottom and work our way up. As a result, we don't start processing events until the network is up and everyone is connected. In production, this kind of control may not be possible, but in nonproduction environments, controlling the startup sequence means we don't receive errors that can be distracting.

3.6.7   *OpenTelemetry*

OpenTelemetry (often shortened to OTel) radically affected the landscape for monitoring solutions, bringing together the key elements (sometimes called *signals*) of logs, metrics, and traces. Although this book isn't about OpenTelemetry, OTel continues to influence the growth and adoption of Fluent Bit. In all likelihood, through working with Fluent Bit, you'll encounter some of the challenges that OTel presents. We can't underestimate the effect of OTel. In our opinion, OTel's effect on observability is similar to Log4j's effect on application logging. Because of Log4j, we've seen multiple derivatives of its implementation across many languages and even programming languages that incorporate logging as a native feature. OTel is not trivial; it's much more advanced than traditional logging frameworks. So we should take time to understand it before we examine how Fluent Bit works with it.

OTel refers to types of observability data as signals. The types of signals are

- *Logs*—Cover traditional application logging.
- *Traces*—Have some features in common with logs but in a specific context, such as a parent trace or typically a specific transaction. A trace can have *baggage* that includes additional metadata for the transaction, such as the business transaction identifier and associated accounts. A trace treat spans like baggage that represent the start and end of significant activities, such as the execution of a transaction. Applications can be composed of smaller pieces, such as services or nested transactions, so we need spans to represent composition as well. Spans within a trace can be nested; as a result, we can have a hierarchy of spans.
- *Metrics*—Represent the usual measurement data we associate with monitoring. This data can be associated with resource monitoring, such as CPU use, but can measure business-centric values, such as the number of transactions handled per minute.

Traditionally, we would have focused on logs and metrics using different tools. The adoption of cloud-native technologies and microservices made handling traces even more critical. The execution of an end-to-end process can occur across different services on different servers, which may change from moment to moment, so correlating activities for a single transaction is far more complex. The OTel project has propelled the handling of observability forward in several ways:

- Harmonization and formalization of the definition and transmission of different types of signals
- Reference implementations for certain capabilities, protocols, and connectors to other cloud-native projects
- Tooling to support the creation of different types of metrics, including injecting into existing code-trace generation

One nice thing about the standardization of logs events is that the format drew a lot of its structure from de facto standards provided by Fluentd and Fluent Bit. Although the OTel log format is more complex than Fluentd's and more prescriptive than Fluent Bit's, you can still see some connections. As discussed in chapter 1, Fluent Bit will become an important technology in the observability space because it can handle different types of signals discretely but also act as an OTLP collector (bringing the different signal types together) and an exporter sending the signals to another OTel service (which could include another Fluent Bit instance) or to specialist services such as Prometheus and Grafana for additional analysis and visualization. Figure 3.8 represents the stages that the signals pass through from the viewpoint of OTel. You can see how Fluent Bit fits in.

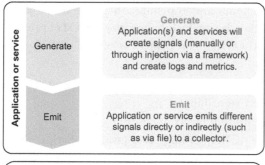
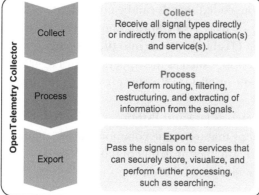

Figure 3.8 The phases and separation of steps involved in Open Telemetry traffic

We need to be aware of some challenges. OTel is still evolving, and the signal data structures have only recently been identified as stable. To accommodate the needs of different stakeholders, we can transmit the different signals in a couple of ways, and not everyone has implemented all the different mechanisms defined by the standard. As a result, there is a chance of mismatches in capability. The standards allow us to send the signals as follows:

- gRPC requires HTTP/2. gRPC uses Protobuf3 to encode the payload in a compact binary form. When using gRPC, if the communication recipient can't handle HTTP/2, the sender is meant to step down to the widely supported HTTP/1.1. But this may not always be the case.

- The use of the compressed Protobuf3 payloads over HTTP/1.1 is allowed.
- The signals may also be transmitted via JSON-formatted messages over HTTP/1.1.

Fluent Bit v3 adopted HTTP/2; before, it handled the signals by using HTTP/1.1 as JSON or in Protobuf3-formatted messages. To invoke these endpoints, we'll use JSON payloads over HTTP/1.1. This approach is the most basic one, but we can use Fluent Bit endpoints with v2. HTTP/1.1, and JSON handling is almost universal, so even if our existing tools do not understand the payload, they can at least handle it. We can easily see the complexity and details of the payloads for different types of signals.

Although this discussion isn't representative of the potential sources, the key is compliance with the payload schema and transmission protocol. However, seeing the diversity of origins of OTel data is worthwhile because the OTel project isn't just about the Collector or standard OTLP. The project provides tooling and libraries to support

- Logging frameworks with an OTel-compliant interface. The OTel project has built tooling to enable this extensibility.
- Code instrumentation at different layers, including
  - Language libraries (C++, .Net, Erlang, Go, Java, JavaScript, PHP, Python, Ruby, Rust, and Swift). This instrumentation includes access to libraries and agent logic so that custom-coded signals can be created with SDKs.
  - Language frameworks, such as Java's SpringBoot and Python's Flask, can have modules that inject OTel invocations into the app engine.
  - Plugins to logging frameworks, such as the Appender for Log4j2 or Go's Zap, so the log events are sent to an OTLP collector due to the logging framework's configuration.
  - Language annotations such as Java and Python.
  - Kubernetes configurations that use some commonly used languages, such as Node, Python, .Net, and Java, have instrumentation injected.
- Monitoring agents that can generate OTel data.

Protobuf background

Google developed Protobuf (short for Protocol Buffers) and made it freely available. Protobuf takes a predefined schema and generates code with objects and logic to (de)serialize it. The schema provides details such as data type and the order of fields, allowing the code to compress the message payload and limit the amount of metadata in the payload. For example, if you know the order of the elements and their types, when types are a fixed size, you no longer need to encode the start and end of the attributes in a record or state for which attribute the following bytes are. Protobuf supports the generation of code for all the major programming languages. Protobuf has been through a couple of evolutions, with v3 being the latest; v2 and v3 are not fully backward compatible. You can find the full specification at https://protobuf.dev.

As we progress through this book, we'll see features that allow us to transform non-compliant events into OTel-compliant payloads, use Fluent Bit's ability to act as an exporter in OTel terminology, and send payloads onward in a compliant format. As a result, Fluent Bit can act as an observability agent or proxy for noncompliant sources.

MessagePack vs. Protobuf3

Fluent Bit's preferred way to send messages is through MessagePack. Although MessagePack and Protobuf3 have the goal of helping data communication, MessagePack does not need to know the message schema ahead of time, whereas Protobuf3 requires ahead-of-time code generated against a message schema. This gives Protobuf3 a performance edge over MessagePack at the price of having to work with predefined schemas.

To handle the different signals, we can have separate Fluent Bit endpoints or a single endpoint for all signals. Because some attributes apply to certain signals, we've separated them out for clarity. As before, we're going to direct the received events to stdout. The first thing to note about the configuration in listing 3.10 is that we create a separate `[INPUT]` declaration for each signal type. This declaration is not unique to OTel; it's how we can handle as many inputs as our Fluent Bit configuration. Regardless of the signal type, the plugin `name` is `opentelemetry`.

Because an OTLP collector expects data over the network, we also need to set the `listen` attribute for the network and the `port`. We chose to separate the signals into different inputs, so we need to set each input to listen to its own port. Each signal uses a different port. The OTel source plugin allows us to define the payload element to use for the tag rather than impose a value. For now, let's see how Fluent Bit will set the value; when we derive the tag, we can use the `tag_key` attribute.

Because traces and logs have many common characteristics, Fluent Bit provides an attribute called `raw_traces` that allows Fluent Bit to treat traces as though they are log bodies when set to `true`. Our input for traces has this attribute set. As a result, we end up with the configuration as shown in listing 3.10. As you can see in the configuration, we haven't specified the URL path for receiving the different metrics because Fluent Bit imposes the URL endpoints standardized by the OTel specification:

- `<server address e.g., localhost:4618>/v1/logs`
- `<server address e.g., localhost:4618>/v1/traces`
- `<server address e.g., localhost:4618>/v1/metrics`

Keep in mind that the event sizes for the OTel signals, particularly traces, have the potential to be large. They're not going to be in the megabytes range, but kilobytes are a possibility when using JSON format. A trace is made up of records called *spans*, which record the start and end of an operation, against which we need to record information that makes it unique. But a span can contain more spans within it. For example, a parent span may represent the trace of a business transaction from start to end. Within that business transaction, we may record inner spans. Each child span may cover each SQL or API call to aggregate content from other services. If we have multiple SQL or API calls, the parent span can end up with multiple child spans, and this relationship can be recursive. Also, if an automated injection of traces is adopted, the number of data points and associated data values (known as *baggage*) captured in the trace has the potential to be significant. You can see an example of OTel automated instrumentation with the Python Flask framework at https://mng.bz/9oV0. See the following listing and `chapter3/fluentbit/otel-consumer.conf`.

> **Listing 3.10 OTel input example:** `otel-consumer.conf`

```
[SERVICE]
  flush 1
  log_level debug

[INPUT]
  #use this for Logs
  name opentelemetry
  listen 127.0.0.1
  port 4318

[INPUT]
  # use this for Traces
  name opentelemetry
  listen 127.0.0.1
  raw_traces true
  port 4317

[INPUT]
# use this for metrics
  name opentelemetry
  listen 127.0.0.1
  port 4316

[OUTPUT]
  match *
  name stdout
```

With this input, we want to ingest the log events, so we've got the port and network to listen to.

A second input for traces, which differs because we need to have a port separate from logs

Here, we set the raw_traces attribute to true; as a result, the traces will be consumed as logs (treating the event in its raw form rather than as a special kind of event.

This input is for our metrics. Although we have the same attributes as logs, we may wish to configure the tag differently to separate metrics routing from logs or traces.

Because we're using JSON over HTTP for OTel communications, we can use Postman to execute the configuration. Within Postman, we have provided three configurations to post, one for each signal type: OpenTelemetry V1 Log, OpenTelemetry V1 Trace, and OpenTelemetry V1 Metric. Take a look at the JSON body in each configuration. The content is much more substantial than our pure HTTP example because although the log structure is derived from Fluentd (and, by implication, Fluent Bit), it has much more additional metadata. It can link the log back to spans within traces, for example. (See `resourceLogs.scopeLogs.logRecords[0].traceId` and `resourceLogs.scopeLogs.logRecords[0].spanId`.) Our JSON contains two records within `resourceLogs.scopeLogs.logRecords`.

Let's start Fluent Bit with

```
fluent-bit -c chapter3/fluentbit/otel-consumer.conf
```

and test the Logs signal first by selecting the OpenTelemetry V1 Log configuration and then clicking the Send button in Postman. What we see on the console may surprise you. Figure 3.9 shows an example.

```
[2023/07/31 19:49:30] [ info] [output:stdout:stdout.0] worker #0 started
[2023/07/31 19:50:13] [debug] [input chunk] update output instances with
new chunk size diff=209, records=2, input=opentelemetry.0
[2023/07/31 19:50:13] [debug] [task] created task=0x7fb79c053150 id=0 OK
[2023/07/31 19:50:13] [debug] [output:stdout:stdout.0] task_id=0 assigned
 to thread #0
[0] v1_logs: [[1581452773.2910168880, {"app"=>"FluentBit OTel demo", "Key
"=>"Value", "instance_id"=>{"myValue"=>"1", "myServer"=>"server1"}}], {"l
og"=>"This is a log message"}]
[1] v1_logs: [[1581452773.2910168880, {"customer"=>"acme", "env"=>"dev"}]
, {"log"=>"something happened"}]
[2023/07/31 19:50:13] [debug] [out flush] cb_destroy coro_id=0
[2023/07/31 19:50:13] [debug] [task] destroy task=0x7fb79c053150 (task_id
=0)
```

Figure 3.9   The console output for handling logs in with Open Telemetry

We don't see the entire JSON payload provided in Postman when looking at the console output, only the `resourceLogs.scopeLogs.logRecords` (as we can see in the JSON body of Postman). The content has been restructured for us, so we no longer see additional values such as `resourceLogs.resource.attributes` or the associated values needed to provide the data type information. As the OTel payload described two log events, we correspondingly see two complete entries on the console. When it comes to the tag value, we see the type and the URL path that received the event.

> **NOTE** There are some additional considerations for processing Open-Telemetry data. As the payload shows, the core schemas allow part of the data to be self-describing: for example, `resourceLogs.scopeLogs.logRecords` `.attributes[]`. The attributes included will vary depending on the source of the OpenTelemetry signal and may change based on ingestion. Examples are illustrated in the OTel documentation (https://mng.bz/EO0D). It is easy to expect OTel to enforce a single schema, but internal adoption for services may have to make compromises, such as imposing some structure on the log body, which isn't ideal and could impede adoption. Without OTel, we would see a divergence in the low-level protocol layers and even basic payload structures. So, while this may appear overly complex, we are better off. The way to handle such considerations is to apply good practices from the integration world, as we are addressing a specialist integration challenge. You can read more about some of these ideas in the *Logging in Action* book.

UNDERSTANDING TRACES WHEN THE RAW_TRACES ATTRIBUTE IS NOT SET

In the configuration `otel-consumer.conf`, we included the attribute `raw_traces` and set it to `true` so the trace data would be consumed as log events rather than as the OTel Trace. We need to remove the `raw_traces` value from our configuration or change it from `true` to `false` and then rerun Fluent Bit with this configuration. We also use Postman to send the Trace event to our Fluent Bit instance. What would you expect to see on the console? At present, we don't see anything; there isn't any data within the log event itself.

How do we know that Fluent Bit has received the event to process it? The answer is that we have to review the HTTP response returned, which we can see in the same way as with the `http` source plugin. You should see an `HTTP 201` response in Postman. Fluent Bit is only acknowledging its receipt, and there are no guarantees about the processing of the payload, so a corrupt JSON body will get the same response. How do we know the event has been processed correctly? The simple answer is that if Fluent Bit experiences an error when trying to process an event, it will generate error events itself. Should we force the source to wait until an event is processed, and if so, what could the source do? If we force the source to wait until an event is processed, we are likely to create backpressure problems and slow throughput. But even if the source waited for the event to be processed, if we pushed back an error message instead of trying to send the same event again, the chances of having some intelligence to address the problem are minimal.

SENDING METRICS

Having run the logs and traces of OTel cases, let's run the metrics case. With Fluent Bit still running, we only need to switch to the OpenTelemetry V1 Metric configuration in Postman and click Send again. Just as the traces were not treated as raw events, we don't see anything on the console.

SIMPLIFYING CONFIGURATION

As you may have ascertained from the explanation of the URL, we could consolidate the traces into a single endpoint if we are not concerned about using tags to separate the sources. Therefore, take the provided configuration, change the tag to OTel, simplify so that we have a single input for all metrics, and rerun the configuration. To rerun Postman, we need to correct the URLs to be consistent. As before, we have provided the answer configuration in the form of `chapter3/fluentbit/otel-consumer-answer.conf`.

> ### Learning more about OpenTelemetry
> OTel is a significant answer to the need for observability, and we've only scratched the surface of the subject here. But our focus is on Fluent Bit, not the OTel standards and tools. The OTel docs (https://opentelemetry.io/docs) are substantial and useful resources but not necessarily the easiest guides if you don't have at least a basic

understanding of the cloud-native ecosystem (Kubernetes, Prometheus, and so on). This is understandable, given that OTel is part of the CNCF ecosystem, but also unfortunate, as OTel is just as valid and useful in non-Kubernetes environments. Appendix B lists titles that can help.

3.7 Fluent Bit buffers and chunks

We've started to talk about attributes, such as `chunk_size`, that relate to how buffering is managed. Now we should provide a bit more detail on buffers and chunking. We'll address them in more depth later in the book, but here, we'll take a high-level look.

To be efficient, Fluent Bit captures and holds log events in buffers, which are made up of chunks. Each input has its own discrete buffer. The buffers and chunks are defined based on capacity. Normally, we can expect a chunk to hold multiple events from a source. To make processing efficient, input plugins hand off chunks of the buffer for processing when they reach capacity; in doing so, they make handling events more efficient. A chunk doesn't have to be full before it is passed on for processing, as we also have the `flush` attribute to control behavior by triggering data movement on a time basis. The number of chunks available is determined as a function of the total buffer storage allowed and the size of a chunk (buffer size/chunk size). If or when it becomes necessary to tailor the buffering, you need to consider several factors:

- You want multiple chunks so that as one is being handed off for processing, the next is being filled.
- The size is always greater than the largest single event to be handled, as chunks hold only complete events. To put that into context, this chapter is a bit over 1 MB as a PDF with all its images and formatting.
- Which is more important: event processing throughput speed or efficiency? If efficiency is more important, make each chunk larger. If throughput is more important, keep chunks smaller.
- The more events held in the buffer, the greater the effect of data loss in the event of a failure, such as when the Fluent Bit process terminates ungracefully.

Buffering is typically performed as an in-memory mechanism, but some plugins also support using the filesystem for buffering. This can be defined in the plugin by the attribute `storage.type`, which takes the value of the `filesystem` or `memory`. But using the filesystem does come with the price of the fact that file I/O is much slower, having additional effects on performance. To use the filesystem with a plugin's buffer, we need to stipulate with the other service attributes the location of the storage to be used (`storage.path`) and whether chunks that can't be recovered from the filesystem should be deleted (`storage.delete_irrecoverable_chunks`). We can also switch on checksumming on storage by setting the attribute `storage.checksum` to `on`. Depending on the type of storage being used, we can control synchronization by using the `storage.sync` option, which can be set to `full`, ensuring that data is synchronized to the filesystem if Fluent Bit crashes. To better understand this concept, look at the Linux-mapped memory file capability when set to MAP_SYNC (https://man7.org/linux/man-pages/man2/mmap.2.html). Using the full `storage.sync` can have performance implications.

3.8   *Other sources*

There are more source plugins than we can address in a single chapter, and available plugins will continue to evolve. As you'll have read, input plugins have common themes. The points we have focused on will provide a solid grounding for understanding other sources. It's worthwhile to touch on some sources and approaches for getting data into Fluent Bit.

3.8.1   *Container-related plugins*

As Fluent Bit's characteristics lend themselves to container and container orchestration use cases, it is not surprising to see its adoption within the Kubernetes ecosystem and its plugins to support the specific needs of the Kubernetes environments. In chapter 4, we'll explore the input possibilities for containers and Kubernetes.

3.8.2   *Getting data from other processes*

We can invoke external processes by using the `exec` plugin or the `exec-wasi` plugin. The `exec` plugin is similar to its Fluentd namesake, but there are some constraints when using it in a containerized world. For exec to work, it needs certain OS features, which (depending on your container) may not be present. This is true of distroless containers. (For more information on distroless containers, visit https://mng.bz/mRO0.)

Still, a simple trick that can help capture some data, albeit less efficiently than a proper plugin, is to execute a shell script or command. With a script, we can tailor the response to make it consumable.

Unlike `exec`, the `exec-wasi` plugin uses the WebAssembly System Interface (WASI), which provides the means to invoke a WASM solution. As we're using WASI rather than a shell like Bash to execute, this approach is unaffected by distroless container constraints like `exec`. We'll explore WASM and WASI in chapter 9.

The final approach, which differs slightly from using `exec` or `exec-wasi`, is to produce a freestanding script or application that can act like a probe that captures the desired data, such as pinging third-party services to confirm availability and then sending the result to the `http` endpoint as a JSON payload, using a curl command. Such probes could be as simple as a little bit of Bash scripting. We can monitor our external (to the Fluent Bit process) probes by using the `proc` plugin. Running such a process as a `cron` job would mean we can be confident that the process is executed. Such an approach can be more challenging to make operationally resilient, but if the probe is simple, the chances of needing intervention are low. We may want to monitor the state of print queues on a print server. We could build a custom plugin for this task or produce a short script that uses the Linux tool `lpstat` (https://mng.bz/5OQq), which wraps and sends the result to Fluent Bit via a curl command.

3.8.3 *Observing the observers*

We want to ensure that our observers are behaving themselves and monitoring the environment. Fluent Bit has a plugin that can generate its own health data. Ideally, that is sufficient, but if we're operating observability tools with their own built-in self-monitoring, we may want to capture that data as well. After all, if our ability to observe is failing, we want to know before we go blind. We should also keep in mind some of these tools are destinations for our outputs. As a result, it is possible to pull data from them. Prometheus, for example, exposes a metrics API that can be used to source data. (Read more about Prometheus' self-monitoring at https://mng.bz/DpDg.)

Summary

- We can receive log events from several different sources and push the events out to stdout, including files, HTTP, and forwarding.
- OpenTelemetry (OTel) significantly affects how observability and monitoring happen and how Fluent Bit supports these changes.
- Fluent Bit can handle metrics and traces as well as logs.
- The twelve-factor app advocates logging via stdout, which we can address with Fluent Bit's `stdin` plugin. However, this approach can present additional challenges.
- When capturing logs from long-running processes, we can mitigate processes starting and stopping by using SQLite to record how far through a log file we are.
- There are some options for executing processes to capture metrics and logs using plugins such as `exec`.
- Fluent Bit and Fluentd can send logs to each other without knowing or caring which Fluent implementation the other is. This is achieved using the `forward` plugin.
- Applications through log appenders can talk directly to Fluent Bit, which offers several benefits, particularly for short-lived processes.
- We can secure network-centric traffic with SSL/TLS and control how the certificate is validated.

Getting inputs
from containers
and Kubernetes

This chapter covers

- Finding ways to capture events from containerized apps
- Investigating how we can observe containers and Kubernetes itself
- Discussing deployment patterns and tools to power our monitoring
- Applying techniques for adding container or Kubernetes context to events

Chapter 3 looked at a variety of input plugins that can be used in cloud-native and traditional deployments. These input plugins provide insights into applications and environments in which they are deployed: bare metal, virtual machine (VM), or container. Although these technologies provide the means to execute applications, they don't address how we can orchestrate and manage these sources. This chapter examines how we can observe containers and container orchestration, particularly with Kubernetes, and the approaches available to manage our Fluent Bit configuration effectively. Understanding the complexities of how containers and container orchestration can work is important. It can influence how we approach observing our applications and the way we understand what container runtimes and container orchestration are doing and how they affect our solutions.

4.1 Architectural context

Figure 4.1 shows our architecture diagram again, highlighting the parts of Fluent Bit relevant to this chapter. We're still on the top layer of our diagram, which reflects the importance of ingesting events. Without that capability, Fluent Bit's value becomes rather limited.

In this chapter, we're going to start with containers. Containers and their engines are used not only as part of Kubernetes but also as a more contemporary, lighter-weight

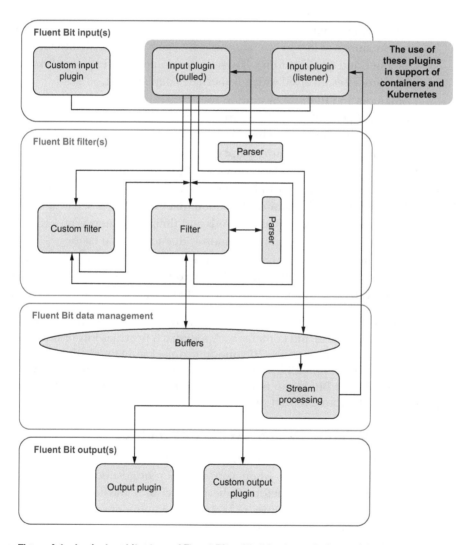

Figure 4.1 Logical architecture of Fluent Bit, with this chapter's focus highlighted

way to achieve virtualization without the complexity, such as running individual containers or a simple composition such as Docker Compose. Although Kubernetes is the dominant container orchestration technology, other options of varying sophistication are available, from Docker Compose and Docker Swarm to Podman and Hashicorp's Nomad (https://mng.bz/5OwD). After we've looked at containerization, we'll look at Kubernetes (or, more accurately, the Kubernetes ecosystem of components). For containerized environments and container orchestration, we need to consider several perspectives:

- How the container engine(s) are performing, as they are discrete processes hosting the application logic. After all, our application may be reporting problems because the engine running it is having its own problems.
- Whether the container orchestration is reporting issues that, in turn, can affect the container's ability to operate correctly (such as being able to locate another container and connect to it). These issues could stem from etcd, kubelet, and other processes involved with a Kubernetes deployment.
- Containers and their orchestration present a different approach to deployment to help propel scaling and resource efficiencies; as a result, they offer us additional deployment approaches. What are the approaches and patterns?
- Containers are more transient and no longer have unique configurations in the way that VMs usually do. How do we handle those consequences?
- We want to know whether Kubernetes and containers are operating properly; ideally, we also should look for confirmation that everything is behaving as we expect. A Kubernetes cluster with all the Pods and their containers is an extremely complex animal that can morph continuously due to external factors.
- If we're hosting services that can incur costs (licenses, support agreements, service fees, and so on) in a dynamic environment, we need to understand our commercial obligations and possible cost exposures.

NOTE This chapter is about the features Fluent Bit provides and supports to work with Kubernetes and containers. Appendix B provides lots of references for more detailed information. If you want to package Fluent Bit with Helm, for example, the appendix provides details on packaging and deployment options for Fluent Bit, but to find out how to use Helm, it would be better to read a book dedicated to that subject.

4.2 *Fluent Bit capturing Docker events and metrics*

Today (and in the foreseeable future) Docker is the most dominant container runtime and toolkit, particularly when you consider non-Kubernetes container and development environments. Before Kubernetes v1.5, it was integrated directly into Kubernetes (kubelet), although we're seeing more containerd and CRI-O for cloud-provided Kubernetes environments. Therefore, it makes sense that Fluent Bit has the means to tap into Docker's event records. Currently, these plugins are available only for Linux because the Docker Events plugin uses UNIX sockets to communicate with Docker, so we need the deployments to be coresident.

4.2.1   *Docker Events*

The Docker Events plugin allows us to observe the events that the container engine handles. It helps us understand the container life cycle and related events that can affect container operations.

> **NOTE** Docker use (particularly Docker Desktop) can be constrained or prevented in some organizations because of licensing implications, which may result in having to pay for commercial licenses.

If our Docker installation is standard, we can use the plugin without any configuration attributes. Otherwise, we need to define the location of the Docker socket for Fluent Bit with the attribute `unix_path`. We can tune the buffer size (the amount of storage being allowed to hold events) with the `buffer_size` attribute, which takes the number of bytes. Docker's event outputs may be formatted as JSON or structured text output. To mitigate against possible connection loss, we can stipulate the maximum number of reconnection attempts with `reconnect.retry_limits` and how many seconds to wait between retries using `reconnect.retry_interval` as a number of seconds.

When the events are received as structured text, we can tell Fluent Bit the name of the JSON key (the attribute is called `key`), the value of which will contain the event output we want to use. By default, this output has the value of the `message`, as shown in the following output. As with many other text-based inputs, we can identify a parser to use with the attribute called `parser`. Start Fluent Bit to use the `docker_events` plugin and output to the console using this command (to start, accept all the default attribute settings for the plugin):

```
fluent-bit -i docker_events -o stdout
```

Then we need to get something happening with Docker, so let's run the "Hello, World" container with this command in the terminal:

```
docker run hello-world
```

If you haven't already run this container, Docker first attempts to retrieve it from Docker Hub (https://hub.docker.com/_/hello-world). When the container has been retrieved and started, logs, like the following example, will be sent to the console. Note that each output starts with `{"message"=>"{`, reflecting the default setting of the key attribute for the configuration of the plugin. We've also simplified the long hex value of the ID to help with the readability of the output, but it offers an ideal value to correlate messages when logs are combined:

```
[2] docker_events.0: [[1699637206.996666301, {}],
    {"message"=>"{"status":"create","id":"hex-id-string",
    "from":"helloworld","Type":"container","Action":"create",
```

```
➥ "Actor":{"ID":"hex-id-string","Attributes":
➥ {"desktop.docker.io/wsl-distro":"Ubuntu-22.04",
➥ "image":"hello-world","name":"vigorous_wescoff"}},
➥ ""scope":"local","time":1699637206,"timeNano":1699637206996174521}"}]
[3] docker_events.0: [[1699637207.011748547, {}],
➥ "{"message"=>"{"status":"attach","id":"hex-id-string",
➥ "from":"hello-world","Type":"container","Action":"attach",
➥ "Actor":{"ID":"hex-id-string","Attributes":
➥ {"desktop.docker.io/wsl-distro":"Ubuntu-22.04",
➥ "image":"hello-world","name":"vigorous_wescoff"}},
    "scope":"local","time":1699637207,"timeNano":1699637207010889920}"}]
```

It is interesting to see the attributes included with each captured event. We can observe how the container is being run (note the values in the output for the JSON elements, like `Action` update) and the amount of detail provided. Let's change from the command line and use the default settings to use a configuration file with the `key` set to the value of `DockerDoes`. We should also set the retry values. We've provided a solution configuration called `docker-events-in.conf.answer` if you want to see the solution. We can rerun the scenario with the command

```
fluent-bit -c fluentbit/docker-events-in.conf
```

Then we start Docker as before, using the command

```
docker run hello-world
```

In the console output, the only difference is that the element name for the log event content itself is not `{"message"=>"{"` but `{"DockerDoes"=>"{"`. This time, rather than terminate things gracefully, let's stop Docker but leave Fluent Bit running. If you're running Docker Desktop, use the UI to terminate the process; if you've only installed Docker, use the command `sudo service docker stop`. Then we'll see Fluent Bit reporting errors like this:

```
[2023/11/10 20:33:40] [error]
➥ [/tmp/fluent-bit/plugins/in_docker_events/docker_events.c:57
➥ errno=111] Connection refused
[2023/11/10 20:33:40] [error]
➥ [input:docker_events:docker_events.0] failed to re-initialize socket
[2023/11/10 20:33:40] [debug]
➥ [input:docker_events:docker_events.0] close socket fd=40
[2023/11/10 20:33:40] [ info]
➥ [input:docker_events:docker_events.0] Failed. Waiting for next retry..
[2023/11/10 20:33:45] [ info]
➥ [input:docker_events:docker_events.0] Retry(2/2)
```

Note how many retries Fluent Bit attempts to execute. Finally, the events that can be received from Docker are substantial, covering all of the container's life cycle events and user commands, such as attaching to the container and checking its health. You can see the list at https://mng.bz/o02j. Figure 4.2 illustrates the Docker events that

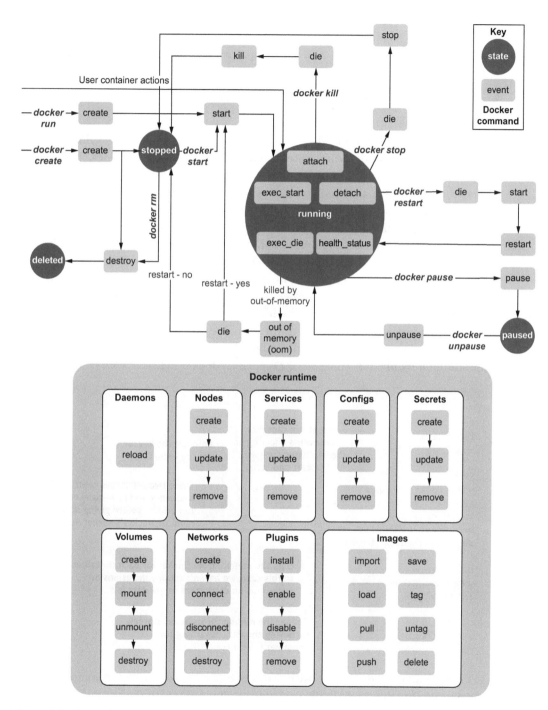

Figure 4.2 Illustration of the events that Docker emits and where in the container life cycle or platform they originate

are emitted as commands and how Docker-received commands or the container moves through its life cycle. Understanding these details means we know what should be happening and looking for in the events received and how any commands issued should affect them. As a result, we can apply filters (covered in chapter 7) to examine particular aspects of the container's behavior.

4.2.2   Docker Metrics

The Docker Metrics plugin (identified with the `name` attribute with a value of `docker`) gives us the means to determine the resources the container consumes. This information can be beneficial for ensuring that a container is getting sufficient resources (an oversubscribed node may see containers being rationed) and that we're not asking the container orchestration to allocate unnecessary resources to a container.

This plugin allows us to define in seconds the frequency of collecting the data (`interval_sec`). We can also define containers to include or exclude by using attributes called `include` or `exclude` with space-separated values for each container. If neither `include` nor `exclude` has values specified, data for all containers is gathered.

Let's copy and extend our `docker-event.conf` to capture the Docker metrics. We don't need to include or exclude anything, as we're using the `hello-world` container. Let's set the interval to 5 seconds, as the container runs briefly. We've saved a copy of the enhanced configuration as a file called `docker-all-in.conf`. Our configuration file should look like this (`chapter4/fluentbit/docker-all-in.conf`).

Listing 4.1   Performing Docker monitoring: `docker-all-in.conf`

```
[SERVICE]
    flush 1
    log_level debug

[INPUT]
    name docker_events
    tag myDockerEvents
    key DockerDoes
    reconnect.retry_limits 2
    reconnect.retry_interval 5

[INPUT]
    name docker
    interval_sec 5

[OUTPUT]
    name stdout
    match *
```

This plugin captures the events affecting the container, such as start and stop.

Enforces the key for the log events

These two attributes control the retry frequency and how many retry attempts to perform before giving up trying to monitor Docker's socket outputs.

Gets the metrics from Docker for each container. In this case, we haven't set any inclusions or exclusions on containers to get data for.

Defines the number of seconds between retrieving the data regarding the container's resource consumption

---

Let's run our revised scenario with the `busybox` container, which remains alive until we exit the container's shell. We can run this Fluent Bit with the command

```
fluent-bit -c fluentbit/docker-all-in.conf
```

NOTE Depending on your environment, running Fluent Bit as an admin or root may be necessary.

Then start the Docker container using the command

```
docker run -it --rm busybox
```

As a result of the command, we should see outputs like this:

```
[0] docker.1: [[1699904074.688616190, {}], {"id"=>"cc5d19f82359",
"name"=>"distracted_keldysh", "cpu_used"=>39952, "mem_used"=>524288,
"=>18446744073709551615}]
```

Even if we don't do anything further with the container, we see additional log entries being recorded with the container metrics. After a minute, we'll have seen sufficient logs flow through Fluent Bit and can now stop the container, which we can do by using the `exit` command in the container's shell. Note that, in the output, we see the `name` reflecting the container name Docker provided and the container's `id` in addition to the memory and CPU measurements.

NOTE Depending on your environment, Docker commands may be rejected, typically due to a permissions problem. To overcome this problem, use the `sudo` command; an example is `sudo docker run -it --rm busybox`.

TIP You can find more about `busybox` at https://hub.docker.com/_/busybox. Like `hello-world`, it's an official Docker image. BusyBox is convenient for trying scripting within a container's shell.

To handle Docker metrics in a Prometheus format, we can use cAdvisor (container advisor), which has been implemented to export metrics from Docker via an API. We can find this utility at https://github.com/google/cadvisor.

4.3 Using Podman as a Docker alternative

An alternative to Docker is Podman (https://podman.io). Podman has the benefit of working with Kubernetes Pod definitions rather than directly with a container, although there are pros and cons to using Podman instead of Docker. Exploring arguments such as licensing and support models, particularly for the support tooling, is best addressed elsewhere. Technically, the decision whether to use Docker or Podman is more about the decision to use Pods or container configurations and runtimes, which always override how we want to use monitoring, as well as what observability is implemented and how. Here, we need to examine how to interact with Podman because it differs from Docker.

If we use Podman, we can access metric events when we understand the configuration file and several container-related filesystems. We can read these files using the Podman plugin on a polling cycle. The input plugin has more in common with a node exporter in configuration, which extends to having attributes like a polling frequency expressed as several seconds (`scrape_interval`) and a Boolean value for whether the plugin should scrape on startup (with `scrape_on_start` taking a `true` or `false` value). Then we can define the paths to configuration for Podman (`path.config`) and the locations for sysfs (`path.sysfs`) and procfs (`path.procfs`), which relate to Linux kernel virtual filesystems. The output from the plugin is formatted like node exporter content, adopting the Prometheus metrics format.

The following listing provides an illustrative configuration (`chapter4/fluentbit/Podman-basic.conf`). If you use it, you may want to adjust the configuration for your Podman deployment.

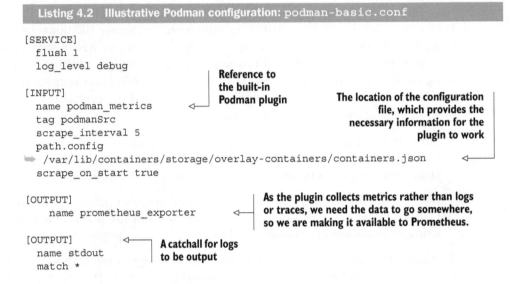

Listing 4.2   Illustrative Podman configuration: `podman-basic.conf`

```
[SERVICE]
  flush 1
  log_level debug

[INPUT]
  name podman_metrics          Reference to the built-in Podman plugin
  tag podmanSrc
  scrape_interval 5            The location of the configuration file, which provides the necessary information for the plugin to work
  path.config
  /var/lib/containers/storage/overlay-containers/containers.json
  scrape_on_start true

[OUTPUT]
    name prometheus_exporter   As the plugin collects metrics rather than logs or traces, we need the data to go somewhere, so we are making it available to Prometheus.

[OUTPUT]                       A catchall for logs to be output
  name stdout
  match *
```

TIP You can find background on sysfs (short for *system filesystem*) at https://linuxhint.com/linux-sysfs-file-system and https://mng.bz/n0N8. Find background on procfs (short for *process filesystem*) at https://mng.bz/q042 and https://mng.bz/75Ky.

4.4   *Other containers*

We have looked at Docker and Podman, both of which have dedicated Fluent Bit plugins and are well known. They also illustrate differing approaches to exposing data to tools such as Fluent Bit. When it comes to enterprise-class deployments of Kubernetes, containerd and CRI-O are more dominant. Both container runtimes focus on delivering against the Kubernetes interface specifications. As a result, their approach to events and logging is influenced by Container Runtime Interface (CRI; https://mng.bz/vJ6q), which provides the specification for communication between kubelet and the container. In addition, we have the Open Container Initiative (OCI), which provides the interface for the container implementation.

Neither CRI nor OCI prescribe specific ways for container implementations to handle stdout and stderr. As a result, containers could use journald and systemd for outputting details. CRI requires that logs be communicated using CRI logging format. Fortunately, Fluent Bit has a predefined parser to support handling such formatted outputs. The Kubernetes standards also define a means to pull back metrics needed to help ensure that scheduling is observed.

Tracing is not prescribed, but containerd, for example, can be configured directly to work with OpenTelemetry. Working with the plugin that supports this feature requires an appreciation of the workings of containerd, which is true of all the container runtimes. As figure 4.3 illustrates, several layers exist between how we typically interact with Kubernetes and the container execution layer.

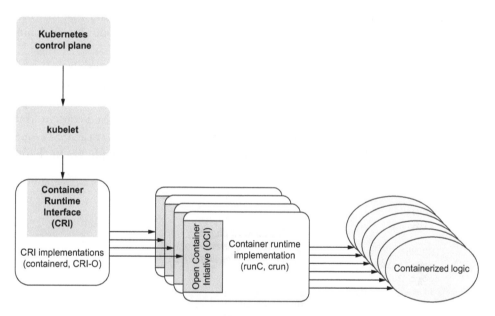

Figure 4.3 The relationship between Kubernetes and containers for logging, traces, and metrics. The shaded segments highlight the elements guaranteed to be consistent across Kubernetes deployments. As you can see, a lot of variability and flexibility makes Kubernetes powerful and adaptable, and it is harder to apply a universal observability approach.

As we can see, it is a complex challenge to interact directly with container logging for containers designed specifically to work with Kubernetes. Although Docker can work with Kubernetes, its heritage is not exclusive. But simply using stdout and stderr with the container isn't the only way to communicate our events.

We've covered several popular container engines and the newer engines built with Kubernetes specifically in mind. It's worth keeping in mind that these processes run on the host OS, and although they perform specialized tasks (including helping manage container logs,) ultimately, they are like other applications and generate logs. Therefore, the secret is understanding how the software generates and shares its signals (logs, traces, and metrics). Some specifics are available at https://mng.bz/M1D8. We'll discuss Kubernetes from an application perspective in section 4.7 (Kubernetes and observability).

4.5   Container logging drivers

Different container engines support logging differently, but it is common practice to offer a feature called *log driving*—the process in which the container's stdout and stderr I/O streams are captured and sent to an output location based on the driver that has been configured. Podman defaults to using a journald logging driver (which we can tap by using the `systemd` plugin provided by Fluent Bit) along with several other file formats. Log-driven content can be but is not guaranteed to be enriched with information about the container, such as the container ID, name, and output source (stdout or stderr).

Docker has a broad range of drivers, including a Fluent driver that uses the `forward` format we saw in chapter 3. Docker's documentation talks about Fluentd, but as we've already seen, Fluent Bit can handle the `forward` protocol.

Let's repeat the `"Hello World"` container exercise but, this time, tell Docker about a Fluent Bit instance that is ready to receive the log events from Docker. To do this, we need a simple configuration that uses the `forward` input plugin, listens to port `24224` on all networks (`0.0.0.0`) or `localhost`, and directs the received content to the stdout for convenience. The following configuration (`chapter4/fluentbit/docker-log` `-driver-out.conf`) is likely to be familiar, as we've used these plugins in chapter 3.

> ### Listing 4.3   Receiving Docker log events: `docker-log-driver-out.conf`

```
[SERVICE]
  flush 1
                              The forward plugin
                              receives log events from
[INPUT]                       the Docker logging driver.
  name forward         ◁───┘
  port 24224
  listen 0.0.0.0
                            The stdout output directs
[OUTPUT]              ◁───   the received events from
  name stdout               Docker to the console.
  match *
```

Before we run the scenario, we need to start Fluent Bit and make it ready to receive the events with the command

```
fluent-bit -c ./fluentbit/docker-log-driver-out.conf
```

We can start the container now, but we need to give Docker additional parameters that tell it to use the Fluentd logging driver and where to direct the logging traffic (by passing `--log-opt` parameters). As a result, our command becomes

```
docker run --log-driver=fluentd --log-opt
➥ fluentd-address=localhost:24224 hello-world
```

As a result of this command, Fluent Bit sends to the console log events like these samples (with a `container_id` string substituted for readability):

```
[0] d2525377a000: [[1701015147.000000000, {}],
⮕ {"container_id"=>"hex-id-string", "container_name"=>"/jolly_mestorf",
⮕ "source"=>"stdout", "log"=>""}]
[1] d2525377a000: [[1701015147.000000000, {}],
⮕ {"source"=>"stdout", "log"=>"Hello from Docker!",
⮕ "container_id"=>"hex-id-string", "container_name"=>"/jolly_mestorf"}]
[2] d2525377a000: [[1701015147.000000000, {}],
⮕ {"log"=>"This message shows that your installation appears
⮕ to be working correctly.", "container_id"=>"hex-id-string",
⮕ "container_name"=>"/jolly_mestorf", "source"=>"stdout"}]
[4] d2525377a000: [[1701015147.000000000, {}],
⮕ {"log"=>"To generate this message, Docker took the following steps:",
⮕ "container_id"=>"hex-id-string",
⮕ "container_name"=>"/jolly_mestorf", "source"=>"stdout"}]
```

If the chosen container runtime doesn't have a logging driver that supports Fluentd/ Fluent Bit protocols (as may be the case with a service provider), we can resort to driving the logs to a known, accessible file location where a Fluent Bit instance can track the file. If you adopt this approach, I recommend considering the following points:

- Security on access to the log file should support data sensitivity/classification of the most sensitive container that could be run.
- The storage I/O performance is sufficient to match the log event generation rate. You don't want the container engines to experience buffer problems.
- Make sure that the storage location has capacity, assuming that applications are chatty. This can be important if the logging mechanism records voluminous trace data.
- Make sure that the context covering the container instance is recorded in the log.

4.6 Application direct to Fluent Bit

Chapter 3 described arguments for using or not using stdout for logs, such as the additional work required, particularly for correctly recombining multiline log events that occur when logging stack traces. We've also seen how containers can capture stdout and stderr streams. But if our application uses a logging framework, our application could optionally talk directly to a Fluent Bit instance, which can make handling logs in our containerized environment easier and maintainable in the following ways:

- Our monitoring configuration will be agnostic about the monitoring stack and how the containerization handles logs as well as traces and metrics.
- Minimize potential latency in getting logs from the transient containerized environment to a secured persistent location. If Kubernetes chooses to kill a container or node because it has become unhealthy, you want to know what was happening just before and when the container was terminated so you can perform root-cause analysis or determine whether a transaction was disrupted.

- Configuring and tuning the application's logging levels and which parts of the code base produce logs are part of application configuration. If someone incorporates sensitive data into a log, we can selectively tune it out, reducing data sensitivity and security implications as we aggregate data.
- Using a framework makes it easier to control and direct the generation of signals so that the core application meets your logging strategy. If logging to stdout is the mandated strategy, so be it.
- We can use the logging framework to eliminate newline characters before output, eliminating a lot of issues or the need to recombine such information. Log4j2, for example, allows us to define layouts and exclude particular characters. Log4j provides documentation on this topic at https://mng.bz/aVvX. Although a lot of development may not be Java-based, Log4j is a good place to look, as it has a history of leading the way with language logging frameworks, and the various Apache language derivatives provide language-specific implementations such as log4net (https://mng.bz/w5gQ).

A potential downside is that the logging framework and Fluent Bit may not know that they are being run within a container. How do we differentiate our logs between container instances? We could approach this problem in several ways:

- *Look to our logging framework.* Log4j2, for example, provides capabilities to help with this task (https://mng.bz/QVve). Many logging frameworks are extensible, so we can always build our own mechanism to interrogate the container environment.
- *Inject into the container environment variables that can identify the instance.* These variables can be incorporated into the logs by the framework or Fluent Bit.
- *Set OS attributes such as the hostname explicitly and uniquely.* Some containers set the hostname to be container unique, but OCI doesn't mandate this, so it can't be taken as a guarantee unless you know which container engine will be used.
- *Configure logging to target a specific Fluent Bit endpoint or file.* Fluent Bit can derive the necessary contextual information from that endpoint or file and inject it into the log events.

The approach you adopt to solve this problem depends on how you prefer to work and how you're generating the application logs, metrics, and traces. My preference is to inject the values into the container as environment variables and have the Fluent Bit sidecar inject what is necessary. This approach keeps the application code deployment agnostic, like Fluent Bit.

NOTE The sidecar pattern is a well-documented approach and is covered in Kubernetes' documentation (https://mng.bz/gAaG) and the excellent *Microservice Patterns* book by Chris Richardson (https://www.manning.com/books/microservices-patterns).

TIP You can find information about application logging frameworks at https://mng.bz/pxKw and https://mng.bz/OmBa. Remember that if you're investigating frameworks and framework plugins that could extend a framework's capabilities, Fluentd is often mentioned when you could use Fluent Bit and Fluentd.

4.6.1 OpenTelemetry's approach to containerized applications

Although we have been focusing on logging frameworks, we shouldn't forget that OpenTelemetry allows us to log from the application directly to an OpenTelemetry Protocol (OTLP)–compliant collector, which can be a Fluent Bit instance. Figure 4.4 shows that the application logs are sent directly to the collector rather than indirectly via a file or the container management tier.

Routing more directly makes it easier to associate and correlate the logs with metrics data and traces. To this end, the OpenTelemetry project has produced SDKs (https://opentelemetry.io/docs/specs/otel/logs/sdk) to send logs directly, using

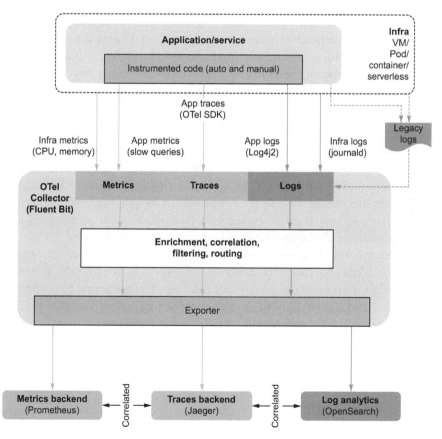

Figure 4.4 Application direct to a Collector (based on https://opentelemetry.io/docs/specs/otel/logs)

APIs within the application code. Alternatively, the OpenTelemetry project provides the Logs Bridge API, which enables existing frameworks to build new appenders that allow the logging framework to send logs to the OTLP-compliant collector (in our case, Fluent Bit). You can find the Bridge API at https://mng.bz/YVDa.

You're welcome to try this API. The repository includes details on deploying into minikube (https://minikube.sigs.k8s.io/docs), and the configurations need tweaking to authenticate with your Elasticsearch deployment. We aren't going to put this API into action, as it is all about the application-development side of things, and Fluent Bit would see the results purely as OpenTelemetry calls.

4.6.2 *Deploying for application direct logging*

The sidecar pattern is the most common way to deploy a supporting service. This pattern makes it easy to define monitoring in a manner suited to an application and deal with application-specific considerations by deploying only the relevant inputs, filters, and formatters related to the application. This drives lower coupling, as each Fluent Bit deployment is aligned to the application in one container. This capability has a price:

- There is overhead in running an instance of Fluent Bit per application Pod deployed. But given the size of Fluent Bit's footprint, it is arguably a fair price for lower coupling and empowering the DevOps ethos (you build it, you run it).
- Additional effort is required to ensure that all the Pods are using the correct patched version of the sidecar container.

Compare this approach with the DaemonSet approach, in which output from each application is pushed to stdout or stderr and collected by Kubernetes. Then we have Fluent Bit deployed per worker/master node as a DaemonSet, and all containers running on that node have their logs picked up by that node's Fluent Bit instance(s). Any application-specific filtering in the configuration is now held within the same Fluent Bit instance, so any logging configuration change (such as routing, filtering, or enriching) affects all the applications in containers on that node.

In addition, the sidecar model reduces the overhead of parsing the container's stdout, which is necessary with the DaemonSet approach. Because the sidecar approach has an implicit context, the match and filtering configurations have the potential to be simpler, and the configuration does not need to understand how the Kubernetes environment is configured, making the development effort simpler.

The sidecar doesn't have to work with network connectivity to the application generating logs, but doing so keeps the network connection within the local host scope. However, the sidecar can access the transient storage provided to the Pod, so logs can also be handled.

The following Kubernetes configuration file (`chapter4/kubernetes/sidecar-config-map.yaml`) defines a Pod configuration with two containerized sources. The first uses `busybox` to generate log files, which we can collect by using a second container in which Fluent Bit is operating. To keep the Fluent Bit configuration separated, we define it in a `ConfigMap`, which needs to be passed to Kubernetes before providing the Pod declaration (`sidecar-config-map.yaml`).

Listing 4.4   Kubernetes sidecar: `sidecar-config-map.yaml`

```
apiVersion: v1
kind: ConfigMap
metadata:
  name: fluentbit-config
data:
  fluent-bit.conf: |
    [SERVICE]
      flush 1

    [INPUT]
      name tail
      tag source1
      path /var/log/1.log

    [INPUT]
      name tail
      tag source2
      path /var/log/2.log

    [OUTPUT]
      name file
      match *
      file /var/combined-output.txt
      format plain

    [OUTPUT]
      name stdout
      match *
```

Defines the name of this configuration so it can be referenced by the Pod configuration. A separate configuration means we can deploy an update to the config and need only refresh the existing containers.

Sets the tag for the first input file so we can easily differentiate the entries in the combined file

Sets the path to the file based on a common view of shared folders

Sets the location for the common output file (assuming that the container configuration allows you to write to the filesystem)

We also send the output to the container's terminal, so if we attach it to the container to see its console, we can observe the outcome.

Deploying this configuration requires a Kubernetes environment and the Kubernetes command-line tool (kubectl). With Kubernetes running, we can run the command

```
kubectl apply -f ./kubernetes/sidecar-config-map.yaml
```

This configuration is simple, taking the two file inputs and writing them to a different output file (`chapter4/kubernetes/sidecar-example.yaml`).

Listing 4.5   Config with sidecar: `sidecar-example.yaml`

```
apiVersion: v1
kind: Pod
metadata:
  name: side-car-demo
spec:
  containers:
    - name: log-generation
      image: busybox
      command: ["/bin/sh", "-c"]
```

The name of the container in the Pod that will generate the logs that Fluent Bit is going to be tailing

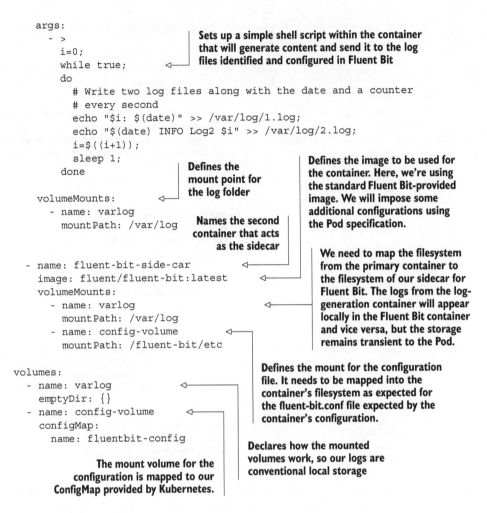

We need to deploy the Pod configuration with the command

```
kubectl apply -f ./kubernetes/sidecar-example.yaml
```

With the Pod deployed, we should see it start. When the containers are running, to see the results, we need to connect to the container `fluent-bit-side-car`. We can do this in several ways:

- Use the Kubernetes command-line interface with the command `kubectl exec`.
- Access the Pod using the Kubernetes dashboard and the UI navigation options, which is particularly easy with minikube.

When we've connected to the container, we can execute the Linux command using our preferred Kubernetes:

```
tail -f /var/log/combined-output.txt
```

As a result, we'll see Fluent Bit generating a single log file from the `1.log` and `2.log` file sources. It isn't wise to keep logs within the containers because if a container or Pod is removed, its local storage is deleted because the local filesystem, as previously mentioned, is transient. If the local filesystem isn't mapped to external storage, we can expect to see the content lost. Given this fact, it would be better for our Fluent Bit deployment to send the logs to an external destination, such as an OpenSearch instance. Writing directly to an external service like OpenSearch can eliminate transient storage but create various other challenges. A better option is to bypass local storage, map a logging framework to HTTP, and address the sidecar container using the localhost network address.

4.6.3 *Enriching log events with Pod context by injection*

Using the sidecar deployment model means that we're operating within the context of a container, and of course, the application shouldn't need to be explicitly aware of this fact. Therefore, how can we differentiate logs from different instances of the same Pod? After all, in a production environment, we may create multiple instances of a Pod, even if only for simple cutover to new Pod instances. Then, if we scale up, we may get more instances of the same Pod. Fluent Bit doesn't address that situation as part of the input but uses a plugin called `Kubernetes`, which enriches the logs with the relevant information. This plugin is intended to be used with Fluent Bit operating as part of a DaemonSet processing stdout or anywhere that has a tag set following the format `<pod name>_<namespace>+<container name>-dockerId`. We will explore the use of filter plugins in chapter 7, although we'll discuss aspects of the Kubernetes filter in the next section.

If this approach is not an option, we can take advantage of Kubernetes configuration options that can direct the convention for the hostname to reflect the Pod's fully qualified domain name (FQDN). Then a container script can be used to define environment variables for the necessary values based on the FQDN. Alternatively, the environment variables are set by the container configuration, taking advantage of the downward API, which is well illustrated in the Kubernetes documentation (https:// mng.bz/dZWw). Although these approaches also require filters to enrich the events, you could look to the log source to use this mechanism, so when Fluent Bit receives the log events, we already have the information in the event.

4.6.4 *Enriching log events with Pod context by filter*

An alternative approach to enriching the events received through Kubernetes logging involves using a Kubernetes filter. The Kubernetes filter works by exploiting how input plugins such as `tail` and `systemd` customize the event's tag (sometimes referred to as *tag expansion*). Tag expansion incorporates the tags, including several attribute details, such as the Pod name and container ID, into the filename. These name elements are extracted from the full path and enable the plugin to look up additional metadata using the Kubernetes APIs.

TAG EXPANSION

We tell the plugin that the tag needs to be expanded to include the full file path by adding the asterisk at the end of the tag name. The easiest way to see tag expansion in action
is to apply it to the file-reading configuration in chapter 3. Let's copy the `basic-file`
`-read2.conf`. (We've called our copy `basic-file-read-tag-expansion.conf`.) Then
we change the tag attribute from `tag-basic-file` to `tag basic-file.*` in the following
listing and `chapter4/fluentbit/basic-file-read-tag-expansion.conf`.

Listing 4.6   Tag expansion fragment: `basic-file-read-tag-expansion.conf`

```
[INPUT]
  name tail                              We have modified the tag to use a dot as
  path ./chapter3/basic-file.txt         a separator and then expand. For the tail
  read_from_head true                    plugin, expansion is supported by appending
  tag basic-file.*        ◁              the absolute pathname of the file being read.
```

We can run the configuration using the following command (which must be run from
the parent folder of the chapter resources):

```
fluent-bit -c ./fluentbit/basic-file-read-tag-expansion.conf
```

When this command is executed, we see log entries that look something like this:

```
[0] basic-file.d.dev.Fluent-Bit-with-Kubernetes.chapter3.basic-file.txt:
➥ [[1712088985.065352000, {}], {"log"=>"hello"}]
```

Note that in the example log entry, the tag now includes after `basic-file` the full
path of the filename. The tag value uses dots where we would usually see a slash in
the pathname.

KUBERNETES FILTER

The Kubernetes filter is closely aligned with handling an input related to Kubernetes.
Because we're looking closely at containers and Kubernetes, it makes sense to introduce the filter now. But don't worry if the topic isn't entirely clear yet. We'll take a
good look at parsers in chapter 6 and filters in chapter 7.

   When operating as a DaemonSet, Fluent Bit is deployed as an instance per node,
and with the right mount configuration for the DaemonSet, Fluent Bit can see the
logs that are being generated by Kubernetes' routing of stdout and stderr. With the
appropriate information in the file path and filename, we can exploit the tag expansion and parse the tag to obtain the attributes necessary to query Kubernetes for additional metadata. The parser is looking for the following:

- Pod name
- Kubernetes namespace
- Container name
- Container ID

Then we can obtain the following details by calling the Kubernetes API server or kubelet:

- Pod ID
- Labels
- Annotations
- Namespace labels
- Namespace annotations

Tapping into a container's logs this way requires either Kubernetes configurations for output to remain standard or an understanding of how the path is constructed so that we can create an alternative parser configuration to extract the necessary values. Otherwise, we can't derive all the essential information, and the tail configuration keeps up to date as the container deletes the associated log files when it is evicted. The filter configuration offers a lot of options, but these options can be reduced to several core themes:

- Securely connecting to the Kubernetes API (`kube_URL`, `kube_CA_file`, `kube_CA_path`, `kube_token_file`, `kube_token_TTL`, `tls.debug`, `tls.verify`) or kubelet (`use_kubelet`, `kubelet_port`, `kubelet_host`, `kube_token_command`)
- How the additional metadata is incorporated into the log event (`merge_log`, `merge_log_key`, `merge_log_trim`, `merge_parser`, `keep_log`, `dummy_meta`)
- Controlling the caching and metadata applied (`annotations`, `kube_meta_preload_cache_dir`, `kube_meta_cache_TTL`)

As you can see from the groups of configurations, we can either configure Fluent Bit to talk to the Kubernetes API server or a kubelet. Although communicating with the server is preferable in large clusters where this server is already going to be working hard, it may be preferable to communicate with the kubelet, which will be a more local endpoint with fewer components talking to it. But for our example configuration, we're going to talk with the server using the default DNS address. Because we need to communicate securely, we need to know where the certificates are and ideally expose them to the DaemonSet via a mount. Because this connection is using Transport Layer Security (TLS) and the filter builds on the TLS framework within Fluent Bit, we inherit the network controls to enable or disable details such as TLS certificate verification.

In addition to securing the connection to the Kubernetes API server using TLS, Kubernetes expects a token to participate in the exchange, so we need to supply a bearer token. This token is sourced from a file identified by the `kube_token_file`. (For more information on authentication with Kubernetes, check https://mng.bz/ GNeJ.) We don't want to reread the token file every time we call the API. So the filter caches the value, but as the token is rotated, it needs to be refreshed. To address this situation, we set a time to live (TTL) before Fluent Bit rereads the file. The TTL value is set with the attribute `kube_token_TTL`.

Although connecting to Kubernetes securely and efficiently is important, ideally, we want to cache data so that we're not recalling the API for another log event from the same container. The filter includes attributes we can use to control how and when caching is applied, including the aging of the cache. The cache's primary age control is set via the `kube_meta_cache_TTL` attribute. This attribute follows the common Fluent Bit syntax for defining seconds, milliseconds, and other time intervals with a character code. (See appendix B for the options.) If the Docker ID is included in the path and the Docker ID changes, we can use it to trigger a refresh by setting `cache_use_docker_id` attribute. Obviously, the tradeoff is a small chance that something such as the labels will change before the cached value is refreshed. As a result, old labels are attached to log events. Because the logs are typically written as semistructured text or journal formats, the filter has the logic to handle both formats; by default, it assumes semistructured text, but we can switch it to journald by setting the `use_journal` attribute to on.

Finally, we can control the data added by setting the attributes `annotations` and `labels` to on or off. We can also control how the additional attributes are added if the `merge_log` attribute is set. The filter determines whether the log event is in JSON format; if so, the new values are added to the log event as additional JSON elements. When we merge, we have the option to consolidate all the log attributes under a single element defined by using the `merge_log_key` attribute.

If the payload isn't JSON, we can still parse it by naming the parser to use with the `merge_parser` attribute. This attribute identifies the parser from a parser file, as we'll see in more depth in the coming chapters.

Perhaps one of the most valuable options for the filter is the `merge_log_trim` attribute. When switched on, this attribute tells the filter to strip any line-feed and carriage-return characters from the log event. The attribute makes downstream processing simpler if the log has to be written to file because we remove the complexity of processing multiline use cases. See the following listing and `chapter4/fluentbit/kubernetes-filter.conf`.

Listing 4.7 Kubernetes filter fragment: `kubernetes-filter.conf`

> Because the source will have used the tag expansion technique to get the full source name, which we need to process to obtain metadata, we need a wildcard in the match.

> Declares the address of the Kubernetes server; this is the default DNS name.

> The configuration to secure and validate our call to the Kubernetes API server

> Declares the metadata we want to include in the enriched log event

> Controls the caching of results from Kubernetes. Here, we're setting the cached values to be held for a minute before refreshing.

```
[FILTER]
   name kubernetes
   match kube.*
   kube_URL https://kubernetes.default.svc:443
   kube_CA_file
/var/run/secrets/kubernetes.io/serviceaccount/ca.crt
   kube_token_file
/var/run/secrets/kubernetes.io/serviceaccount/token
   kube_meta_cache_TTL 60s
   cache_use_docker_id on
   labels on
   annotations on
   use_journal off
```

```
kube_tag_prefix kube.var.log.containers.
merge_log on
merge_log_key log_processed
merge_log_trim on
```

Because the complete file path is included in the tag, we may want to strip the base part of the path and prefix from the tag.

Asks the filter to strip carriage-return and line-feed characters from the payload so that we limit the problem of multiline log reading downstream if the contents need to be written to file at any time

Given the number of attributes involved in configuring the connection to Kubernetes and identifying essential values to get the information needed to query Kubernetes, using the filter can be a concern, and it can be challenging to get the configuration correct. If you haven't been involved in the detailed configuration of Kubernetes, finding all the correct values won't be easy. This challenge can be compounded when you use a managed Kubernetes service, as all the necessary information may not be available or even accessible. Focusing on the application layers rather than the low-level Kubernetes configuration, we prefer to adopt two approaches to this scenario:

- Keep the Fluent Bit configuration as vanilla as possible and trust your Kubernetes subject matter expert or service provider to supply all the details for the source and filter. Connect this configuration using Fluent Bit (see chapter 2), which allows you to bring your configuration in. As a result, details such as where to direct the events, additional filters, and so on can be managed separately from the Kubernetes configuration details managed by your Kubernetes expert.
- Aim to capture your logs and events by directing the data through logging frameworks and OpenTelemetry SDKs. Although this approach is at odds with the twelve-factor app guidance (chapter 3), it isn't at odds with OpenTelemetry, and it reduces computational workload and deployment complexity.

4.7   Kubernetes and observability

Kubernetes looks at logs and logging from multiple perspectives: logging, measuring, and tracking what a container does, what the wider Kubernetes cluster does (although the container and cluster can be considered the same), and what the application within the container does. As a result, we need to think about how to capture these forms of events.

4.7.1   Understanding Kubernetes' position on logging

As far as Kubernetes is concerned, logging from applications run by containers is the responsibility of the container runtime. The norm is for the container to handle standard out and standard error. In addition to using stdout and stderr, most container runtimes have adopted the idea of a logging driver, which allows for different ways to handle captured application logs. Other than typically implementing the stdout and stderr using the logging-driver model, implementations have little consistency.

Just handling what the container is doing doesn't address logging at a cluster level, such as recording what is happening across the cluster, eviction of Pods, and the starting and stopping of nodes. Again, Kubernetes does not prescribe a specific solution but promotes the idea of using logging agents in a sidecar configuration or having a logging agent operate on every node (as part of a DaemonSet). Kubernetes has its own logging library, known as klog (https://github.com/kubernetes/klog), and more recently has moved toward adopting logr (https://github.com/go-logr/logr). Logr has a stronger decoupling between the logging interface and log-content output, so logr can be used to create klog and other outputs.

4.7.2   Kubernetes auditing

In addition to understanding what is happening with the applications within a Kubernetes ecosystem, we should be auditing Kubernetes. We may want to find out, for example, who or what instructed Kubernetes to evict a container. Kubernetes addresses this situation with auditing capability, which we can configure to talk to a logging backend by using a webhook or writing the events in a log file in JSON Lines format (https://jsonlines.org). We shouldn't confuse this auditing with the event capability that Fluent Bit supports as a plugin source, as we'll see. With the correct audit configuration, we can collect such data by using Fluent Bit. For more information on configuring Kubernetes auditing, see https://mng.bz/znZA.

4.7.3   Kubernetes events input

Kubernetes exposes its activities and events to anyone requesting them via its API server. Through the Kubernetes events plugin (called `kubernetes_events`), we can grab those events and put them in the log events pipeline. You'll recognize many attributes that have the same or similar names and purposes as the `tail` plugin and a network-based plugin.

The plugin uses an SQLite database as we can with `tail` (identified by the `db` attribute) so that events aren't accidentally duplicated into the pipeline; we are given the same events each time we call the API server. Because the process is based on polling, we have attributes to define the number of seconds or nanoseconds (`interval_sec` or `interval_nsec` attribute).

We need to be mindful that we can have only one active Fluent Bit instance running this plugin because of the constraints on the way SQLite works. This restriction isn't catastrophic; we can lean on Kubernetes to monitor the health of the container. A large cluster, however, will have a lot of events, so a single Fluent Bit instance needs sufficient resources to keep up with Kubernetes. If more than one Fluent Bit instance starts retrieving the event data, we'll see a duplication of events.

When it comes to connecting with the Kubernetes API to collect event data, this plugin has a common set of attributes with the Kubernetes filter plugin for defining the URL for the server, certificate location, TLS checking, token, and token time to live (TTL) (`Kube_URL`, `Kube_CA_File`, `Kube_CA_Path`, `tls.debug`, `tls.verify`, `Kube_Token_File`, `Kube_Token_TTL`). See the following listing and `chapter4/fluentbit/kubernetes-out.conf`.

Listing 4.8   K8s events plugin illustration: `kubernetes-out.conf`

```
[SERVICE]
  flush 1
  log_level debug

[INPUT]
  name kubernetes_events
  tag kubernetes_events
  kube_url https://kubernetes.default.svc
  tls.verify off
  interval_sec 5
  kube_token_file
    /var/run/secrets/kubernetes.io/serviceaccount/token
  kube_request_limit 100
  kube_retention_time 15m
  #kube_namespace

[OUTPUT]
  name stdout
  match *
```

Reference to the Kubernetes events plugin

Address of the Kubernetes API server. Standard DNS addresses will work.

This value needs to be configured based on the deployment instance.

We haven't restricted the namespace, so this receives all events.

Assumes that Fluent Bit is running within the Kubernetes environment, so we have to attach it to the container to see the log events being generated

This plugin's configuration raises challenges, specifically, safely exposing the Kubernetes token and the certificates to Fluent Bit. Assuming that this Fluent Bit deployment occurs within a Kubernetes Pod, a good way to overcome this challenge is to store the files as Kubernetes secrets and then, in the Pod specs, define a mount point that maps to the secrets. Data is kept securely, but we can map the value to whichever containers need the value. Within the Pod, the file is seen as normal. It's best not to provide the credentials via environment variables, as they're fixed for the lifetime of the container. As a result, the configuration will fail if the credentials are rotated.

We should be careful how we interpret the Kubernetes event data. As the documentation says, "Events should be treated as informative, best-effort, supplemental data" (https://mng.bz/0MQv).

> **NOTE** With the Kubernetes filter, `kubernetes_events` plugins, or any other way of interacting directly with Kubernetes APIs, role-based access control (RBAC) must be configured so that the service accounts used to run these containers have the necessary privileges to request data from the API server. We can find an illustration of the configuration at https://mng.bz/KDGO. Books such as *Core Kubernetes*, by Jay Vyas and Chris Love (https://www.manning .com/books/core-kubernetes), are good guides to how RBAC works.

4.7.4   *The many parts of the Kubernetes ecosystem*

When we talk about Kubernetes, we're also talking about multiple other processes, such as etcd (https://etcd.io), container managers such as Docker and CRI-O (https:// cri-o.io), container runtimes such as `runc` and `crun`, and container networking with

Calico (https://www.tigera.io/project-calico) and flannel (https://github.com/flannel
-io/flannel). Different components behave differently even if they comply with the
Kubernetes interfacing specifications such as Container Network Interface (CNI)
and OCI.

Then we can overlay the challenges of the Kubernetes deployment with opinionated deployments in the form of OpenShift (https://mng.bz/9oYr) and Tanzu (https://
tanzu.vmware.com/tanzu), for example. Cloud-vendor-hosted packaging of Kubernetes
such as Google Kubernetes Engine (GKE), Azure Kubernetes Service (AKS), Amazon
Elastic Kubernetes Service (EKS), and Oracle Container Engine for Kubernetes (OKE)
can provide additional dimensions to monitoring because the infrastructure and even
parts of Kubernetes management can be abstracted from you. OKE, for example, doesn't
allow you to monitor the management nodes because this part of the service is managed.
You can elect to have the worker nodes managed, eliminating the tasks of adding nodes
to and removing nodes from a cluster and deploying the Kubernetes component.

> **NOTE** To learn more about the Cloud Native Computing Foundation (CNCF)
> software ecosystem, including projects such as flannel, Calico, and CRI-O, as
> well as interfaces such as CNI (https://www.cni.dev) and related explicit or
> implicit standards, the easiest place to start is from the CNCF landscape web-
> site (https://landscape.cncf.io).

4.7.5 Container Images

As part of Fluent Bit's release cycle, different image builds are created for Fluent Bit
(available at https://packages.fluentbit.io), as well as OCI container images using a
distroless base image, benefiting from the smallest footprint possible and, therefore,
the smallest number of vulnerabilities. An image can be configured via the command
line, as illustrated in the Docker Hub documentation.

But if we want to use a configuration file, we need to override the provided configuration. We can address this problem in different ways. To manipulate the container
directly, a quick and easy approach is to do it locally with the `docker run` command,
which overwrites the container's configuration file with a local one:

```
docker run -v $PWD/fluent-bit.conf:
➥ /fluent-bit/etc/fluent-bit.conf:ro fluent/fluent-bit
```

An alternative option is to use the `docker cp` command to copy our own configuration
file(s) to the container's file: `/fluent-bit/etc/conf/fluent-bit.conf`. For a long-
term solution, however, we need to build our own container extension using the `from`
declaration. Today, the container expects a classic file format, but overriding the `CMD`
declaration allows us to change which file and configuration format are executed.

Other providers of container images with Fluent Bit exist. By default, the Fluent
Operator, for example, uses an enhanced container image provided by KubeSphere
(`kubesphere/fluent-bit`). We need to be mindful of which image we use and the lay-
ers on which it is built.

The last option, probably the most common one, is to use Kubernetes configuration files, define a `ConfigMap` containing the Fluent Bit configuration, and then map it to the container filesystem, which is how our example sidecar configuration works (listing 4.5). Although we used this approach on the sidecar, we can apply it to other scenarios, such as configuring the DaemonSet.

4.7.6 Helm charts

Helm is the default package manager for deploying into Kubernetes. The project includes Helm charts, which include Fluent Bit. The chart (`chapter4/helm-charts/chart/fluent-bit/values.yaml`) provides a configuration that can be used as a foundation for a DaemonSet that configures Fluent Bit. It shows how we can incorporate the configuration rather than the container into the chart. Much of this configuration will be explored in later chapters and is here only for illustrative purposes.

Listing 4.9   Extract from Helm chart: `values.yaml`

We'll see in chapter 7 how we can use Lua. As we're looking at a Helm chart, it's worth showing how a separate Lua script can be declared and referenced. Here, we declare the Lua code, which will be referenced later in the configuration.

The start of the Fluent Bit core configuration. The following declarations of the inputs, outputs, and filters are children of this YAML element.

These declarations should be familiar, as the values set are the same as when we used a conventional Fluent Bit configuration file.

As the configuration is still a YAML file, we need to declare the different plugin types using YAML and use | notation to include all the subsequent lines as part of the declaration.

When Fluent Bit is installed, it includes predefined filters. Here, we're referencing them based on the standard deployment location. Note that we can define multiple parser files by repeating the Fluent Bit attribute.

Here, we're telling the input to use the multiline parser, which can expect to parser Docker-formatted lines or those provided by CRI-O managed containers, reflecting the fact that configuring monitoring for Kubernetes can be challenging.

```
luaScripts:
  filter_example.lua: |
    function filter_name(tag, timestamp, record)
      -- put your lua code here.
    end

config:
  service: |
    [SERVICE]
        Daemon Off
        Flush {{ .Values.flush }}
        Log_Level {{ .Values.logLevel }}
        Parsers_File /fluent-bit/etc/parsers.conf
        Parsers_File /fluent-bit/etc/conf/custom_parsers.conf
        HTTP_Server On
        HTTP_Listen 0.0.0.0
        HTTP_Port {{ .Values.metricsPort }}
        Health_Check On

  inputs: |
    [INPUT]
        Name tail
        Path /var/log/containers/*.log
        multiline.parser docker, cri
```

```
        Tag kube.*
        Mem_Buf_Limit 5MB          ◁────  Because the container can be constrained explicitly
        Skip_Long_Lines On               within the configuration of the Pod, we need to ensure
                                         that Fluent Bit works within those constraints.
    [INPUT]
        Name systemd
        Tag host.*
        Systemd_Filter _SYSTEMD_UNIT=kubelet.service
        Read_From_Tail On

  filters: |
    [FILTER]
        Name kubernetes
        Match kube.*
        Merge_Log On                           References the Lua
        Keep_Log Off                           script mentioned
        K8S-Logging.Parser On                  previously. Note that
        K8S-Logging.Exclude On                 the reference is a
                                               predetermined path
    [FILTER]                                   but uses the name
        Name     lua                           provided in the
        Match    <your-tag>                    luaScripts YAML
        script   /fluent-bit/scripts/filter_example.lua  ◁─┘ element.
        call     filter_name

  outputs: |
    [OUTPUT]
        Name es              ◁────   Identifies an Elasticsearch output
        Match kube.*                 plugin. The host address needs to
        Host elasticsearch-master    be resolvable, as seen by the
        Logstash_Format On           container within Kubernetes.
        Retry_Limit False
```

For this solution to work, the Helm chart adds a mount point called `config` to the Helm chart's `values.yaml`, into which the configuration is injected. To take advantage of the Helm charts provided, assuming that you have Helm installed, run the following commands:

```
helm repo add -force fluent https://fluent.github.io/helm-charts
helm upgrade --install fluent-bit fluent/fluent-bit
helm show values fluent/fluent-bit
```

When applying the `tail` input configuration to these log files, we also have to work with the assumption that they may span multiple lines. We see in listing 4.9 the use of the attribute `multiline.parser`, which tells the `tail` input plugin that it needs to use the more advanced multiline parser.

But the problem doesn't end there. The Kubernetes logs could be generated using Container Runtime Interface (CRI) format or possibly Docker format. We can overcome this problem by telling the parser about both formats by separating them with commas, as the listing shows (`docker, cri`). The parser will attempt to apply the first parsing format. If that format yields errors, it attempts to use the next parser format. If you're confident about the format your Kubernetes environment will support, it is worth setting the configuration to reflect this format.

Keep in mind that multiline parsing requires greater computational effort. The parser has to determine which line is the last line of the event before it can do anything, compared with the normal single-line approach. If we can do anything upstream to avoid or minimize multiline outputs, it's worth doing, such as following development practices that discourage multiline outputs (checks with static code analysis) or using logging frameworks to strip newline characters.

> **TIP** Calyptia (part of Chronosphere) has great troubleshooting blogs that are worth examining if you encounter additional problems, particularly when working with the DaemonSet approach to log capture. You can find these blogs at https://calyptia.com/blog and https://mng.bz/j0pe.

4.8 Kubernetes operator

Although Kubectl and Helm are typical ways to deploy and manage resources in Kubernetes, we can also manage Fluent Bit in a Kubernetes environment through the Fluent Operator. The Fluent Operator (https://github.com/fluent/fluent-operator) defines the following custom resource definitions (CRDs):

- `FluentBit`—Defines node monitoring via a DaemonSet (https://mng.bz/WV2W). It identifies the image to use to run and the configuration to use.
- `ClusterFluentBitConfig`—Defines cluster-wide plugin configurations for inputs, outputs, and filters as secrets, so embedding credentials in the configuration, although not optimal, is secure. We also have the option to target specific namespaces with the cluster configuration.
- `FluentBitConfig`—Selects namespace-level configurations for inputs, outputs, and filters. These configurations follow the same conventions as their cluster namesakes for `Input`, `Output`, `Filter`, and `Parser` resources.

Because `ClusterFluentBitConfig` and `FluentBitConfig` work the same way, let's examine part of the standard `ClusterFluentBitConfig` configuration files. The following configuration files come directly from Fluent Operator's configuration samples (https://mng.bz/86OD).

The easiest way to visualize the configuration process is to consider https://mng.bz/EOwR, a configuration file with the different selectors defined as enhanced, including declarations that we would see in a conventional Fluent Bit configuration file. The critical difference is that what it includes is more dynamic here.

Listing 4.10 Helm chart config: `fluentbit_v1alpha2_fluentbitconfig.yaml`

```
apiVersion: fluentbit.fluent.io/v1alpha2
kind: FluentBitConfig
metadata:
  name: fluentbitconfig-sample
```

```
spec:
  service:              ←——┐ Having seen the service block in our configurations,
    flush: 1              │ we recognize the contents of this block.
    daemon: false
    logLevel: info
    parsersFile: parsers.conf     ┐ The configuration kind drives which configurations to use.
  inputSelector:          ←————————┘ (An inputSelector looks for objects of kind input and so on.)
    matchExpressions:
    - key: fluentbit.fluent.io/enabled     ←—— The match selector looks in the labels section
      operator: In                            of the configuration for a corresponding key.
      values: ["true"]
  filterSelector:         ←——————┐   ┌ The label needs to have a value that
    matchExpressions:              │   │ produces a Boolean result when evaluated
    - key: fluentbit.fluent.io/enabled │ against this list of value(s) using the
      operator: In                     │ operator.
      values: ["true"]
  outputSelector:                     ┌ The same configuration as the inputSelector is
    matchExpressions:                   followed for a filter. We can add or remove
    - key: fluentbit.fluent.io/enabled  inputs, outputs, and so on to the configuration
      operator: In                      by varying the label(s) in each config file,
      values: ["true"]                  affecting the outcome of the match rule.
```

As the preceding configuration shows, the Helm chart defines the selectors for the parts that make up a complete Fluent Bit configuration (https://mng.bz/NBwd). The next two examples show input and output configurations.

Listing 4.11 Input config: `fluentbit_v1alpha2_fluentbitconfig.yaml`

```
apiVersion: fluentbit.fluent.io/v1alpha2
kind: Input
metadata:
  name: input-sample
  labels:
    fluentbit.fluent.io/enabled: "true"     ←
spec:
  tail:              ←——┐ Identifies the plugin
    tag: kube.*          │ to use by its name
    path: /var/log/containers/*.log     ←
    parser: docker
    refreshIntervalSeconds: 10
    memBufLimit: 5MB
    skipLongLines: true
    db: /tail/pos.db
    dbSync: Normal
```

Here, we define a label that the match rule will evaluate. As we can see by comparing it with the code in listing 4.10, our label key is identified, and the operator value produces a positive result, meaning that it will be included in the final Fluent Bit configuration. As a result, we could easily remove it by changing true to false.

Now we have the same configuration attributes using the camel-case notation of the attributes.

Note that the input configuration has also put performance constraints on the configuration with the `memBufLimit` and `skipLongLines`. As a result, we can be more confident the output will not be a source of backpressure because we're not going to consume lots of resources; any log entries that are large and could demand too much effort are skipped. We're controlling how much compute effort is needed compared with the main application logic. See the following listing and `https://github.com/fluent/fluent-operator/blob/master/config/samples/fluentbit_v1alpha2_output.yaml`.

Listing 4.12 Output config: `fluentbit_v1alpha2_output.yaml`

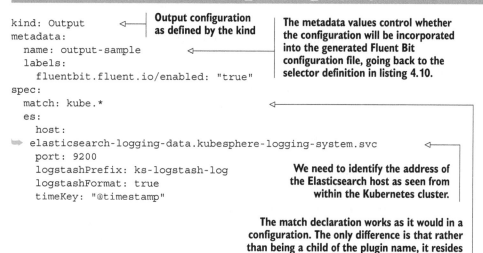

```
kind: Output
metadata:
  name: output-sample
  labels:
    fluentbit.fluent.io/enabled: "true"
spec:
  match: kube.*
  es:
    host:
      elasticsearch-logging-data.kubesphere-logging-system.svc
    port: 9200
    logstashPrefix: ks-logstash-log
    logstashFormat: true
    timeKey: "@timestamp"
```

Output configuration as defined by the kind

The metadata values control whether the configuration will be incorporated into the generated Fluent Bit configuration file, going back to the selector definition in listing 4.10.

We need to identify the address of the Elasticsearch host as seen from within the Kubernetes cluster.

The match declaration works as it would in a configuration. The only difference is that rather than being a child of the plugin name, it resides outside the plugin's attributes.

Fluent Operator contains a configuration that watches these resources for changes. When it detects a change, it pushes the revised configuration changes out to the secrets repository, which is synced with the DaemonSet. The result is that the Fluent Bit configuration changes are picked up and applied. This sequence of events is illustrated in figure 4.5.

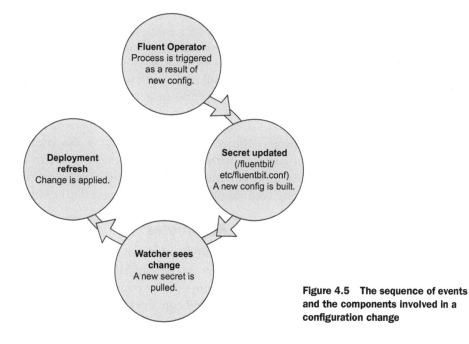

Figure 4.5 The sequence of events and the components involved in a configuration change

TIP Using alpha versions involves an elevated risk of errors. The gain is a more flexible solution. By the time you read this chapter, a more up-to-date version may be available, possibly even a general-availability release. But I don't expect the configuration and intended behavior to change.

If you're sending log events to a service such as Elasticsearch, which also runs within the same Kubernetes cluster when the cluster starts, the DaemonSet will start before the other Pods. As a result, it becomes possible for a Fluent Bit instance in a Daemon-Set to complain that it can't send logs to Elasticsearch during the startup phase. We might be able to control the startup by using an init container (https://mng.bz/DpwV), but this approach has the potential to create unexpected side effects. If a container fails during startup before our Fluent Bit DaemonSet is started, for example, we'll lose visibility into what happened because logs will be removed before Fluent Bit has had the chance to capture them. Another possibility is using the scheduler to retry sending the events, as we'll see in chapter 5. The question is whether we can live with the possibility of losing the log events while Elasticsearch is starting or whether the retry configuration is a workable option.

Today, Fluent Operator assumes that the Fluent Bit instances deployed on each node (due to the DaemonSet) will consolidate all the logs to a Fluentd instance based on the premise that Fluentd can connect to more end systems. Although this may be true, the situation is changing because of OpenTelemetry.

NOTE Using Fluent Operator with new or custom plugins requires updating the operator configuration with one CRD YAML file for each type of plugin. You can find the provided CRDs at https://mng.bz/lrZo. The YAML file contains the descriptors for the data types and attribute names. Because these files are maintained manually, we must ensure that attribute names are synchronized to prevent confusion. The build process for the CRD plugins uses Kustomize (https://kustomize.io), which could be tailored to add your own plugins, minimizing problems of forked code and the ability to accept future updates.

The Fluent Operator project isn't the only source of a logging operator for Kubernetes. The Logging Operator project (https://kube-logging.dev) is also available. This implementation has a lot in common with the Fluent Operator project. The most notable difference is that this implementation allows the option of using Fluentd or syslog-ng (https://www.syslog-ng.com) as the consolidation point for the cluster.

4.9   *Observations on Fluent Bit with Kubernetes*

Having looked more closely at Fluent Bit and its relationship with Kubernetes, we've seen that the relationship is more about how the plugins allow us to examine what is going on with a particular type of application (for the main part addressed by some specific input plugins) than how Kubernetes and container management wraps around and uses Fluent Bit.

What we've referred to as *application direct* logging or observability (achieved by injecting or using a framework that communicates directly with observability tooling) is the approach OpenTelemetry leans toward. OpenTelemetry also offers an elegant solution to some of the challenges that arise from using stdout and stderr and accepting whatever a Kubernetes environment offers. These challenges include

- Any events with content that have a newline character get separated into multiple events to be recombined. In a direct approach, the multiline content is passed to Fluent Bit as a single event.
- Additional management (and budgeting) of the additional processing workload of parsing text back to a structured payload.
- Although we want to monitor Kubernetes when using an opinionated configuration or deployment, we're better off thinking of it as being more of an OS. We don't ignore it; we trust it to surface problems for us.

4.10 *The next frontier of observability with Fluent Bit: eBPF*

The next potential consideration for observability, primarily in the Kubernetes space, is the growing interest in the Extended Berkeley Packet Filter (eBPF; https://ebpf.io). This has come about because of CNI implementations such as Cilium (https://cilium.io) and Falco (https://falco.org), which have taken advantage of eBPF support in the Linux kernel and provided a means to help ensure network traffic security. Any anomalies are captured and reported, which makes Fluent Bit a natural fit for facilitation.

eBPF is a safe, controlled way to inject logic into the Linux kernel, allowing us to customize kernel behavior, among many other things. We can observe how data flows through the network layers and how applications are performing at even the lowest levels, such as memory management. Although the tooling for eBPF started by supporting activities such as OS and kernel observation and diagnostics, this approach made it easy to tap in and observe what is happening with virtual networks implemented through CNI, such as Cilium and flannel.

Due to the effect eBPF is making, Microsoft is developing an eBPF implementation for Windows (https://github.com/microsoft/ebpf-for-windows) so that eBPF tools can be used within a Windows environment. An example of this space is Aqua-Security's Tracee (https://github.com/aquasecurity/tracee), working with Fluent Bit using the `forward` plugin (https://mng.bz/Bgz2). An interesting configuration requirement arises. Because Fluent Bit is likely to generate network traffic sending eBPF-related log events to the event capture and log analytics tools, we need to ensure that Fluent Bit's network activities don't, in turn, create eBPF events that must be logged.

Summary

- Fluent Bit can capture events from Docker and Podman, although they have different technical approaches—with Docker pushing events and Podman pulling via an API.
- We can use logging drivers to capture log data. The benefits of this approach include reduced effort to extract meaning, routing, and potential for greater contextual information (inferred or explicitly sent).
- Applications can communicate more directly to Fluent Bit while remaining agnostic to how the events (logs, traces, and metrics) are captured by using a sidecar and/or adopting OpenTelemetry.
- Kubernetes logging is a complex landscape due to different container runtimes and the ability to swap the implementation of some components with different observability approaches. Other challenges exist when operating in cloud-provided Kubernetes services, such as whether we can interact with the compute node for managed Kubernetes services.
- Configuring container images can be addressed in several ways. The basic container approach embeds configuration, so we need to extend the container or override the configuration. When using a container in Kubernetes, we can adopt an injection approach using `ConfigMaps` or by overriding parts of a container configuration, such as the CMD or mount points.
- Helm charts allow us to apply the configuration to the Fluent Bit container. By defining the Fluent Bit configuration as a `ConfigMap`, we can control the effect of change as part of Kubernetes package management.
- Kubernetes operators enable us to apply monitoring, although we have a more complex approach to the configuration. Through operator definitions, we can ensure that valid configuration values are supplied to Kubernetes. The selector mechanism allows us to choose which configurations to apply.
- The application of eBPF and Fluent Bit is a potentially powerful use case, particularly with further security insights from low-level network activity.

Outputting events 5

This chapter covers

- Examining the common characteristics of output plugins
- Generating logs for the console, files, and other local outputs
- Storing logs and metrics with Prometheus and PostgreSQL
- Forwarding signals to an OpenTelemetry or Fluent Bit node
- Exploring other monitoring tools using HTTP and hyperscaler endpoints

We've explored capturing events (logs, traces, and metrics) from various sources, such as files, OS data, and network-based events, using OpenTelemetry and different plugins. Having captured these events, we need to put them somewhere so that the data can be visualized, analyzed, and communicated to those who need it, from SecOps to developers running regression tests. We should start this activity by understanding the components of Fluent Bit that are involved.

5.1   *Architectural context*

Figure 5.1 shows the part of the architecture we'll be looking at in this chapter. Although it may look like we're jumping a lot of steps, as with mastering any programming language, we start with I/O before mastering the clever constructs. But we will touch on some basic details, such as filters.

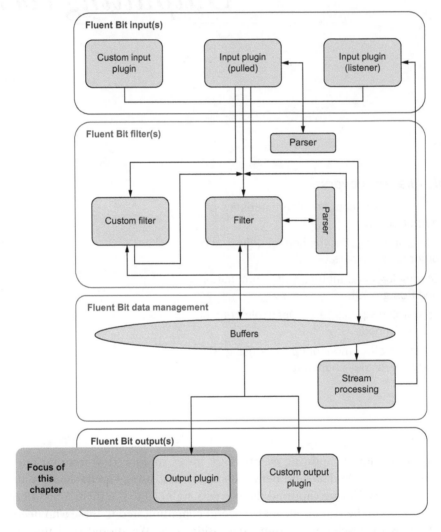

Figure 5.1   Fluent Bit architecture and which areas will be covered by this chapter

Output covers a wide range of possible destinations for our logs, traces, and metrics, from simply storing the captured events in a file to forwarding the events to a product. With the advent of OpenTelemetry, it has become possible to send data to more systems without needing custom adapters. In addition to the growing adoption of OpenTelemetry, some de facto standards have developed, such as the data format adopted by Prometheus and even Fluent Bit's own `forward` specification (https://mng.bz/6YD6). As with the input plugins, we can characterize the output plugins. With a few exceptions, such as `file`, `flowcounter`, and `Null`, the outputs have a network component. Some have authentication attributes and attributes to help map the event to product characteristics, such as which elements of the message need to be labeled or identify the service we're sending events for. This makes the groupings much harder. However, we can best group them based on the ability to customize/configure the destination's behaviors, which leads us to

- Technology or standards-defined protocol solutions, such as OpenTelemetry, WebSockets, and HTTP.
- Data store and query services that can be deployed locally and can be self-managed or offered as a managed solution, such as Loki (https://grafana.com/oss/loki) and PostgreSQL.
- Data store and query cloud services, such as Datadog (https://www.datadoghq.com) and Google Cloud BigQuery (https://cloud.google.com/bigquery). Some services offer generic query capabilities, while others have enhanced and domain-specific features.

To get a handle on Fluent Bit's output capabilities, we will focus on `null`, `:stdout` (console), and file outputs, as `stdout` and `null` are helpful for developing or solving configuration issues, and file outputs are almost universal. Next, we will focus on the first two characterizations in terms of pure technology and then the self-hostable solutions, which are representative of distributed and Kubernetes environments. We don't need to be so concerned about having multiple examples from data stores. Mastering a service like PostgreSQL provides plenty of insight for the last category because most data store–related plugins have similar characteristics to achieve connectivity. In addition, many operational considerations are addressed as part of the data store operations or by a service provider and aren't a problem for the environment running Fluent Bit itself.

5.2 *Common characteristics of Fluent Bit output plugins*

Fluent Bit's framework supports several reusable capabilities, although not all output plugins support all these features, such as workers and network timeouts. Therefore, a table in appendix B shows which plugins support these behaviors.

5.2.1 *Output resilience through retries*

As previously mentioned, many of our output plugins involve networks, and even when we're using localized outputs like files, there is a chance that networking will be hidden from us. This is very much the case for Kubernetes and enterprise environments where storage is network-attached.

We like to think networks are highly resilient and never fail, but this is not the case. The internet is robust; if a linkage fails, traffic usually gets rerouted around such problems. However, private networks don't always have such levels of redundancy. We tend to forget that between our source and destination can be a plethora of physical or software devices that can decide that our network traffic might not be allowed to progress because of the type or size of the payload or a raft of other possible rules that may be in place. Or maybe demand has overwhelmed the device, as happens in a successful denial-of-service (DoS) attack, including network proxies, caches, firewalls, and load balancers between source and destination. Then, networks are increasingly software-defined within our Kubernetes environment, and they will certainly be a component of operations. We can change and affect networks so much more easily. The bottom line is that we have to assume networks aren't resilient and are fallible.

To help address this problem, all Fluent Bit output plugins return a result from their actions, which can indicate success (`OK`), error, or a request that a retry be scheduled. We don't see this within the configuration, but this is important when building our own plugins, as we'll see later in the book. As this is a plugin-wide behavior, we can configure Fluent Bit to pause and retry outputs before giving up. This behavior can be controlled by service-wide attributes specified in the service block. The two key controlling attributes are

- `scheduler.cap`—Defines the maximum number of seconds a delay can have before a retry
- `scheduler.base`—Sets the minimum number of seconds a delay can have before a retry can be attempted

The actual delay before retrying is calculated as a random number between the base and a maximum value that is never greater than the `scheduler.cap`. The max number for the range in which we get a random delay is adjusted exponentially. This means that the first retry should happen at a time on or soon after the `scheduler.base`. But the more times we retry, the greater we want to potentially delay, as the chances of other processes also retrying increases. Therefore, we need to increase the spread of the retries over time. If we count the number of retries, the upper limit becomes `min(scheduler.base * 2n, scheduler.cap)`. Figure 5.2 illustrates the retry periods and shows when multiple tries will be attempted.

This is an elegant way to distribute the retry load, particularly as the number of processes trying to connect to a service increases. But we can't let retries continue forever, as this could result in backpressure issues. So, we need the option to stipulate a retry limit. The retry limit relates to the possibilities of backpressure and how critical data is from a particular cause. We can stipulate within the output configuration for a specific plugin a configuration called `retry_limit`. This configuration has several options. We can provide a numeric maximum number of retries. `retry_limit 3`, for example, gives us three retries after the first attempt. We may never want a retry, so we can set the attribute value as `no_retries` (such as `retry_limit no_retries`), or we might want the retries to go forever, in which case we set the attribute with a value of `false` or `no_limits`.

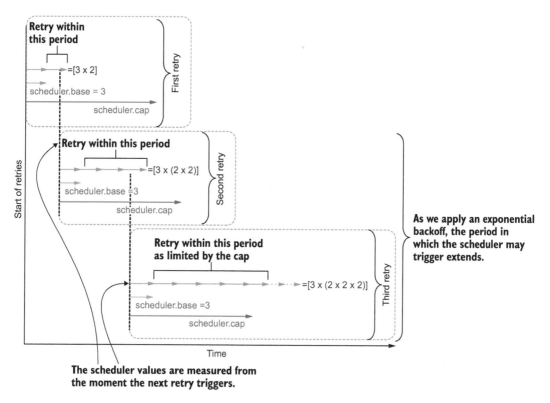

Figure 5.2 Fluent Bit's scheduler retry timing is represented with a timeline.

To see this in action, let's reuse chapter 3's configuration, illustrating the use of receiving an HTTP event and then routing it to the forward plugin. But rather than run the second instance of Fluent Bit in which we had the input forward plugin configured, we won't start that process. Thus, we're going to configure our retry controls into the scenario. To keep things fairly quick, we'll

- Specify the schedule base as 2 seconds and the cap as 15 seconds.
- Set the output option on the forward output configuration.
- Set the limit to five retries.

We should have a configuration like the following listing (chapter5/fluentbit/http-forward-retries.conf).

Listing 5.1 Controlling retries: `http-forward-retries.conf`

```
[SERVICE]
  flush 1
  log_level warn
  scheduler.base 2
  scheduler.cap 15
```

Here, we're defining the minimum backoff duration in seconds.

Defines the maximum period for which we can delay the retry. This maximum isn't used immediately because of the backoff algorithm.

```
[INPUT]
  name http
  listen 0.0.0.0
  port 9881
  successful_response_code 201
  success_header x-fluent-bit received
  tag http

[OUTPUT]
  name forward
  match *
  host 0.0.0.0
  port 9980
  retry_limit 6
```

Sets an explicit limit on how many attempts we'll try to forward to the events before giving up

With this scenario running, the first thing to note is that we're likely to see errors (depending on how a plugin is implemented; it certainly is the case for HTTP plugins) when the output plugin tries to send the events. The next step is to start Postman and, using the HTTP Single Call configuration in the chapter 5 collection, use the Send button to send the request, which will report a 201 HTTP success response. Things will appear on the console where we're running Fluent Bit. The invocation will immediately fail, and we'll see a series of messages reporting failures to send and how long before the output plugin attempts to send again, as illustrated in the console output in figure 5.3.

```
[2023/08/06 15:53:33] [error] [output:forward:forward.0] no upstream connections available
[2023/08/06 15:53:33] [ warn] [engine] failed to flush chunk '420-1691333612.907425771.flb', retry in 3 seconds: task_id
=0, input=http.0 > output=forward.0 (out_id=0)
[2023/08/06 15:53:36] [error] [output:forward:forward.0] no upstream connections available
[2023/08/06 15:53:36] [ warn] [engine] failed to flush chunk '420-1691333612.907425771.flb', retry in 4 seconds: task_id
=0, input=http.0 > output=forward.0 (out_id=0)
[2023/08/06 15:53:40] [error] [output:forward:forward.0] no upstream connections available
[2023/08/06 15:53:40] [ warn] [engine] failed to flush chunk '420-1691333612.907425771.flb', retry in 8 seconds: task_id
=0, input=http.0 > output=forward.0 (out_id=0)
[2023/08/06 15:53:48] [error] [output:forward:forward.0] no upstream connections available
[2023/08/06 15:53:48] [ warn] [engine] failed to flush chunk '420-1691333612.907425771.flb', retry in 8 seconds: task_id
=0, input=http.0 > output=forward.0 (out_id=0)
[2023/08/06 15:53:56] [error] [output:forward:forward.0] no upstream connections available
[2023/08/06 15:53:56] [ warn] [engine] failed to flush chunk '420-1691333612.907425771.flb', retry in 10 seconds: task_i
d=0, input=http.0 > output=forward.0 (out_id=0)
[2023/08/06 15:54:06] [error] [output:forward:forward.0] no upstream connections available
[2023/08/06 15:54:06] [ warn] [engine] failed to flush chunk '420-1691333612.907425771.flb', retry in 7 seconds: task_id
=0, input=http.0 > output=forward.0 (out_id=0)
[2023/08/06 15:54:13] [error] [output:forward:forward.0] no upstream connections available
[2023/08/06 15:54:13] [error] [engine] chunk '420-1691333612.907425771.flb' cannot be retried: task_id=0, input=http.0 >
 output=forward.0
```

Figure 5.3   The console reports the retry attempts and fails because the destination Fluent Bit instance isn't running and can't be connected to it.

When we review the figure, we see that the retry interval typically increases, as reflected by the growing range from which a randomized number is being taken. We also see six retry messages plus the final report of being unable to retry after the last attempt. Remember that six retries will mean seven calls—the first attempt and then the retries, but the retry is reported off the back of the first attempt.

The configuration we've used with the scheduler applies to all the output plugins because we've applied the configuration attributes within the service block. However, is it also possible to apply these configurations at the individual output plugin level? If the scheduler is set globally, any attributes defined for a specific output will override the service-level settings. We can disable retry attempts or set things to retry infinitely by setting the `retry_limit` attribute to `no_retries` or `no_limits`, respectively.

5.2.2 *Network controls*

We've looked at resilience through retries for outputs. But when the network aspect of the output is visible to us (as when we are explicitly addressing servers and ports), we also need to have a chance to dictate how quickly we decide a connection is not responding. In other words, we manage the timeout, and when we can maintain or keep a connection such as WebSockets alive, we minimize the overhead of reestablishing the connection.

5.2.3 *Worker threads*

Worker threads allow us to increase the performance of Fluent Bit by establishing multiple threads to handle the workload for output plugins. In doing so, we minimize the chance of creating backpressure, where our ability to output events affects the ability to consume events because of buffer constraints, which can then create issues for the log source, such as slowing down the consumption confirmation if the source is synchronously connected to Fluent Bit. Not all plugins support workers today, but the stdout and file output plugins do. We configure the number of workers wanted for an output with the attribute `workers` and provide the number of workers (threads) wanted.

The following configuration illustrates the use of workers with the `stdout` plugin (`chapter5/fluentbit/std-output-workers.conf`). The input almost doesn't matter, as we're only interested in seeing what Fluent Bit does, so we've switched the logging to debug, which helps show what is happening.

Listing 5.2 Allocating workers for output: `std-output-workers.conf`

```
[SERVICE]
    flush 1                        A dummy input is used for
    log_level debug                simplicity, as the input doesn't
                                   matter unless we want to see Fluent
[INPUT]                ◁────────   Bit's behavior under extreme load.
    name dummy
    tag dummy
    dummy {"name" : "blah", "message" : "a dummy message"}

[OUTPUT]
    match *                        We allocated four workers
    name stdout                    (threads) for this output plugin.
    workers 4          ◁────────   By default, this value is 1.
```

When we run this scenario, we should see a couple of things displayed on the console in addition to the dummy message. We can expect to see log messages indicating the creation of the output threads (numbered from 0, so four threads would be numbered 0–3). As the buffer is flushed through the output, we'll see an indication of the threads in use. To run the scenario, we need to use the command

```
fluent-bit -c fluentbit/std-output-workers.conf
```

The result is messages like this:

```
[2024/04/07 17:04:06] [debug] [stdout:stdout.0]
➥ created event channels: read=23 write=24
[2024/04/07 17:04:06] [ info] [output:stdout:stdout.0] worker #0 started
[2024/04/07 17:04:06] [ info] [sp] stream processor started
[2024/04/07 17:04:06] [ info] [output:stdout:stdout.0] worker #2 started
[2024/04/07 17:04:06] [ info] [output:stdout:stdout.0] worker #1 started
[2024/04/07 17:04:06] [ info] [output:stdout:stdout.0] worker #3 started
```

As the `stdout` plugin is triggered, we'll see messages like this:

```
[2024/04/07 17:04:07] [debug] [output:stdout:stdout.0]
➥ task_id=0 assigned to thread #0
```

Note how the thread is identified at the end of the event. Scrolling through the outputs, we notice that the thread number increments until all the threads have been triggered and then returns to 0. So, we can see, all things being equal, that each thread is used in turn. Finally, when we're shutting Fluent Bit down, we see messages like this for each worker (thread.) Again, notice near the end of the log event the number for each worker:

```
[2024/04/07 17:04:14] [ info] [output:stdout:stdout.0]
➥ thread worker #0 stopping...
[2024/04/07 17:04:14] [ info] [output:stdout:stdout.0]
➥ thread worker #0 stopped
```

5.2.4 *Considerations for using threads*

We have to consider whether using workers is beneficial, however. Events may arrive in the target system out of order because of how the CPU allocated time to different threads. Log events being slightly out of order in a database or a security information and event management (SIEM) tool is unlikely to be an issue as the query process can resolve the sequence. But logging events in a file for engineers to read will make life harder if correct ordering is lost. Another possibility with worker threads is that we allocated more worker threads than the end system can handle. As a result, we risk the connection timing out or increasing the workload on the destination service as it has to switch between servicing different connections.

As a rule of thumb, unless you know about the destination you're outputting to and have certainty about the actual capacity for concurrency within the environment in which Fluent Bit is running, mitigating possible bottleneck effects on the sources is best achieved using buffering. After all, if we're in a virtual environment without guaranteed CPU capacity, we could create more threads that the OS needs to context-switch between within a virtual machine (VM), which itself is context-switched because more VMs are running than real CPU threads are available.

> **TIP** The natural thing to do when you want to help Fluent Bit performance in a Kubernetes environment is to increase the amount of memory or CPU allocated to the Fluent Bit container. But this additional resource doesn't deliver any gains and goes unused. Fluent Bit can be I/O intensive. Potential causes are that processes wait for I/O resources or access is blocked because another process has locked the resource. One way to overcome this is by using threads and workers. This may seem counterintuitive, but it allows the process to switch to another thread that may not be blocked by I/O and can be executed using the currently available capacity. As we've mentioned, threads come with a cost, so they are best used wisely.

In addition to worker threads for output, input plugins can be moved into dedicated threads with the additional attribute `threaded` set with a value of `on`. This feature was introduced in Fluent Bit v2.0.2, but little has been said about it since then, so we recommend being cautious when adopting its use.

5.3 Null output

When dealing with data pipelines, it is worthwhile to ensure that all the data has an output. In doing so, we can see how much is being received and data being discarded as long as we're using Fluent Bit's routing, so we don't direct data to both the bin and a genuine endpoint. The easiest way to bin data is to use the `null` output plugin. In Fluent Bit, this is the equivalent of directing output to /dev/null as the output is going to consume the data and do nothing with it. The plugin needs two attributes. The `name` attribute identifies the plugin (in this case, `null`), and the `match` attribute identifies the data it is to output.

In addition to measuring the amount of event data not being put to use, the `null` output plugin can be helpful for examining performance problems. Routing the captured events to the `null` output plugin makes it possible to determine whether a throughput problem is caused by the ability to ingest data or at the backend output phase.

5.3.1 Monitoring with Fluent Bit

Before we try to see how the `null` output plugin affects the Fluent Bit operation, we need to understand what is happening with resources. Fortunately, Fluent Bit has an API that we can enable to observe what is happening. To use the API, we need to switch the web server on by providing some additional attributes in the service block:

- `http_server` set to `on` (the alternative is `off`)
- `http_listen` and `http_port` set to the network(s) and port to listen to

Let's listen to all network sources (0.0.0.0) on port 2020 for our configuration. We also need to tell the server to enable the collecting of metrics from the plugins by adding the attribute `storage.metrics` with a value of `on` to the `service` declaration. With the server configured, we need to understand the URLs available to us, shown in table 5.1.

Table 5.1   Standard URLs for Fluent Bit metrics and health data

URI (http://host:port)	Description
/	Returns the build flags that have been set. The build process allows us to enable or disable the inclusion of features and plugins using build flags. So, if we need to compact the Fluent Bit binary footprint, we can exclude particular plugins, such as FLB_HAVE_AWS, if we don't want to interact with the Amazon Web Services (AWS) plugins, such as Kinesis.
	In addition, we have the version of Fluent Bit and the edition returned, which represents whether we've got the open source (community) version or an enhanced version from an organization such as Calyptia.
/api/v1/health	Same as the root response.
/api/v1/metrics	Provides the throughput of the plugin as the number of records and data volume in bytes. Other measures may be provided, depending on the plugin. Output, for example, will include errors and retries. These figures are cumulative.
/api/v1/metrics/ prometheus	Presents the same metrics data but in a manner that Prometheus can collect and process, allowing us to combine it with tools like Grafana to visualize what Fluent Bit is doing.
/api/v1/storage	Provides meaningful information about how the buffers are being used with the number of chunks, the amount of physical storage involved, and the amount of memory being consumed.
/api/v2/metrics/ prometheus	Exposes any metrics provided by loaded plugins (such as those used in the loaded configuration, in addition to the core measurements that the v1 API produces. The response is formatted as a Prometheus metrics payload.
/api/v2/metrics	Uses a new CMetrics (https://github.com/fluent/cmetrics) library, which has taken its inspiration from a Go Prometheus package format (https://mng .bz/o01v).
	The key difference between this metrics output and the Prometheus v2 path is that the Prometheus #HELP and #TYPE entries are not included in the output. The actual metric value is still in Prometheus format but prefixed with a timestamp.
/api/v2/reload	Triggers the Fluent Bit node to execute a hot reload of its configuration without requiring the Fluent Bit instance to restart. It requires Fluent Bit to have the hot reload option switched on using the command-line parameter --enable-hot-reload, http_listen, and http_port.
	This endpoint responds to both GET and POST HTTP verbs. The GET returns a simple JSON structure showing the number of reloads that have occurred. To trigger the hot reload, we need to use the POST verb, as in curl -X POST -d '{}' localhost:2020/api/v2/reload.

These endpoints mean we can understand where the data is coming from and going to. Based on the configuration described, we have some API calls configured in the Postman chapter 5 collection that we can use to grab the data easily. We also captured the outputs in `chapter5/api-output-examples` if you want to review and compare the outputs.

We'll also look at the Prometheus exporter plugin later in the chapter. This plugin can be used to expose Fluent Bit metrics, which doesn't need the main HTTP server capabilities, allowing us to separate security controls.

5.3.2   *Configuring null output*

To generate a reasonable volume of events quickly so we can clearly see the null output statistics changing, we could use the LogSimulator, or we could use a source plugin such as `mem` and `cpu`, which we saw in chapter 3 for capturing CPU and memory use at the OS level. We'll use these plugins and take advantage of the nanosecond timing we can configure, giving us a steady, consistent volume of data. We'll add the output definition in the Fluent Bit configuration but with the output commented out. As a result, we should have the following configuration (`chapter5/fluentbit/null-output.conf`).

Listing 5.3   Using the `null output` plugin: `null-output.conf`

```
[SERVICE]
  Flush 1
  log_level debug
  HTTP_server   On          ◁─┐  We've enabled the HTTP server so
  HTTP_listen   0.0.0.0        │  we can access the internal metrics
  HTTP_port     2020           │  and data to confirm events are
  storage.metrics On           │  being generated.

[INPUT]
  name cpu
  interval_nsec 10
  tag book_vm_cpu

[INPUT]
  name netif
  interface eth0
  interval_nsec 10
  tag book_vm_network

[INPUT]
  name mem
  interval_nsec 10
  tag book_vm_memory      ─┐  Declares and
                           │  matches all outputs
[OUTPUT]                   │  to the null plugin
  name null          ◁────┘
  match *
```

Given this information, we can create or run the configuration provided (`chapter5/fluentbit/null-output.conf`). Then, we can run the configuration with the command

```
fluent-bit -c fluentbit/null-output.conf
```

With Fluent Bit generating and ingesting the events, we can select the `Get FB Metrics` configuration in Postman and then click Send. The result will be returned data from Fluent Bit, as illustrated in figure 5.4. We should expect to see the outputs listed with the number of records and bytes generated by the input plugins. The output plugin should be listed with similar metrics. As we're directing everything to the same output plugin, the total record processed by the inputs should correspond to the output. There will always be a potential small margin of error depending on when the metrics are retrieved from the plugins compared with which record(s) have been processed in the pipeline. To explore further, use the other Postman API calls to retrieve health and storage data.

Figure 5.4   A screenshot of Postman with JSON metrics response shows the different plugins' throughput.

5.4 Sending log events to the console

We directed output to the console (stdout) in chapter 4. However, this topic is worth exploring further, as it makes for an easy way to see how other common features can affect output behavior and touch on use cases that can be beneficial.

When applying the stdout plugin, the use cases may not stand out beyond helping the development of Fluent Bit configuration, particularly if our configuration is modifying or filtering log events. As we did in previous chapters, we can easily see the outcomes of our configuration changes. We remove the output when we're happy with filtering and record manipulation.

The value may be less obvious when using the plugin beyond the development of our Fluent Bit configuration. stdout may help in the following production use cases:

- In a Kubernetes environment, the stdout can be captured by Kubernetes. Some complexities and challenges arise from trusting this approach, which is described in the *Logging in Action* book, so we would advocate it only as a fail-safe method.
- Almost the opposite approach is to direct only the most critical of errors to stdout. That way, if the console displays any output, it stands out, and we'll know the problem is considered serious.
- Considering the value, let's examine what is needed to direct output to the console. Each output definition is preceded by the [OUTPUT] directive. Then we need to define the match attribute, which declares which tag(s) will be handled by this output. We can provide an asterisk (*) as a wildcard for all outputs. Alternatively, we can provide names or combine them with the wildcard. We can have only a single wildcard within the match. We'll see more in chapter 7 when we dig into filtering.

NOTE The general convention for tag naming is to adopt dot-based notation to represent any logical hierarchy needed (much like JSONPath). If we have sources defined for a computer's CPU, memory, and disk, we might tag them as server.cpu, server.memory, and server.disk. If we captured multiple log sources for App1 and App2, we might call those sources something like app1.container_log, app1.db_log, and app2.console. Now, if we want a single output for just the host machine metrics, we could set the match to server.*. Although there aren't any formally defined legal or illegal characters for tags, we know that the asterisk has a special meaning. We recommend keeping tag names constrained to alphanumeric values, dash, underscore, and dot characters, which will make it much easier if we need to wildcard or process the tag's value somehow, within the same constraints as legal characters for JSON attributes, to avoid problems.

As with any plugin, we need to name the plugin to use; for the console, as we've seen, this is stdout. We can also direct Fluent Bit on how to format the output. For now, we've set this to json_lines. We'll explore the options a bit more shortly. We can add to the JSON structured log event the timestamp that the log event was received and how to format it. We provide the JSON element name via the configuration attribute `json_date_key` and the supported format for the value with the attribute `json_date_format`, which will accept the value `double` as the numeric data type, with the whole number denoting seconds from the epoch (midnight, January 1, 1970) and the fractional part being milliseconds: `1690230582.488276600`. We can change that to milliseconds from epoch, with the value `epoch` or its synonym `epoch_ms` or `epoch_millis` or by using the ISO 8601 convention `YYYY-MM-DDTHH:MM:SS.nnnnnnZ` with the value `iso8601`. The last option is `java_sql_timestamp`, a simplified version of ISO 8601, as it omits the use of the characters `T` and `Z`.

All our output configurations have used the `match` attribute, which is set with an asterisk as its value. The `match` attribute defines which events can be handled by the output definition (and, as we'll see in the coming chapters, used for most types of operations). The match compares the value it has with the tag value set. As you've probably realized, the asterisk is effectively a wildcard match.

Using this, we can construct a configuration that sends the log events to the console in JSON format, with each log event having its own line, and includes the timestamp for when we received the events in ISO format, as shown in the following listing and `chapter5/fluentbit/std-output.conf`.

Listing 5.4   Formatting output: `std-output.conf`

```
[SERVICE]
    flush 1
    log_level error

[INPUT]
    name http
    listen 0.0.0.0
    port 9881
    tag http-in

[OUTPUT]
    match *
    name stdout
    format json_lines
    json_date_key received-date
    json_date_format iso8601
```

Controls Fluent Bit's own log output. We don't want the console to receive anything except Fluent Bit errors or content directed to the console by an output plugin, so we can easily see the difference between Fluent Bit logging and the output plugin.

Matches against all tags (so all inputs will be output)

As with all plugins, we name the plugin to use.

Defines the format for the output. In this case, each log event is displayed as JSON on a single line.

Definition of the element in the JSON structure to place the recorded date and time of when the event was received by Fluent Bit

The formatting to use for representation of the date and time to be used with the field named by json_date_key

To run this scenario, within the provided Postman configuration, we have a collection for the chapter that has a `POST` invocation named `HTTP Call`. We can send the log event by clicking the Send button. But first, we'd recommend looking at the HTTP body provided. Although simple, it is a little more complex than in chapter 4, as we have nested JSON content with multiple records within the body declaration. Next, we need to start Fluent Bit with our configuration file using the following command:

```
fluent-bit -c fluentbit/std-output.conf
```

With Fluent Bit running, let's send the log event. We should see that each log event in the REST payload gets its own log line on the console, as shown in figure 5.5.

```
* Fluent Bit is a CNCF sub-project under the umbrella of Fluentd
* https://fluentbit.io

{"received-date":"2023-07-27T16:06:51.442464Z","helloGrp":[{"hello":"Fluent","val":"1"},{"hello":"Fluent","val":"2"},{"h
ello":"Fluent","val":"3"},{"hello":"Fluent","val":"4"},{"hello":"Fluent","val":"5"}],"my-date":169023185000}
{"received-date":"2023-07-27T16:06:51.442464Z","hello":"Fluent","val":10,"my-date":169023145000}
{"received-date":"2023-07-27T16:06:51.442464Z","hello":"Fluent","val":20,"my-date":169023182000}
```

Figure 5.5   Console output with one line per log event, with long text wrapping

If we compare the console output to the body of the message in Postman, we see that we have a new leading element in the JSON, which reflects our use of the `json_date_key` and `json_date_format` attributes. We can experiment with the output to try the format options described in the next section.

5.4.1   Formatting outputs

Not all outputs support the use of formatting, and the formats that the outputs support can differ between output plugins. Table 5.2 describes the incorporated formatters. Appendix B includes a table that shows which outputs allow which formats.

Table 5.2   The different output formatting options and what they produce

Format type	Description
`msgpack`	MessagePack (`msgpack`) doesn't behave entirely as you might expect. Rather than writing to stdout, the binary representation (of the `msg`), we see a string representation of the payload carried within Fluent Bit. We don't see the binary representation, as this can have some unexpected consequences for the terminal. The mildest effects can be that the character sequences affect how the console session renders content; the worst is that character sequences trigger the console to start messing with memory buffers, printer configurations, and so on. Check out https://www.xfree86.org/current/ctlseqs.html for details.
`json`	`json` ensures that the event's record is represented in a JSON structure. This doesn't include the tag and timestamp associated with the log event's record.
`json_lines`	`json_lines` ensures that each record is represented by its own line.
`json_stream`	Here, we continue to see the log events in JSON format. But rather than give each log entry its own line, now we have everything on the same continuous line or stream.

Now that we understand the different options, let's try a couple to see the differences. We can edit and rerun the previous configuration. We'd recommend trying `json_stream` and `msgpack` (also used if no format is specified).

5.4.2   *Seeing matching at work*

We can use this configuration to see how the match attribute can affect behavior. Table 5.3 defines different values to try with the match attribute and the expected outcomes. You can try these by editing the configuration file and rerunning Fluent Bit configuration, taking an HTTP input and output to stdout, and resending the log event using Postman.

Table 5.3   **Different match values and how they affect the outcomes**

match value	Outcome
http-in	We have set the match value to be the same as the tag value. We will continue to see the received log events on the console as before.
HTTP-IN	Here, we're seeing how the match behaves with case sensitivity. We don't see any output this time as the match is case sensitive.
http*	We've included the asterisk as a wildcard. We will continue to see the log events pass through to the console because of the wildcard behavior.
http	As the match is literal, without a wildcard, the match is not exact, and the log events won't make it to the console.
nothing	We have a different tag, so our events won't reach the console.

5.5   *Writing to files*

Storing log events for easy consumption later is done using a shared filesystem. When the files are written to by multiple processes at the same time, with or without a logging framework, there's a risk of corrupting the log entries, which are intermingled on the same line. By consolidating log events through Fluent Bit, we avoid file write collisions while still being able to bring log events together. As we'll see later in the book, the other benefit of using Fluent Bit rather than application log appenders is the ability to enrich stored data. Also, we can enhance security so that only Fluent Bit needs to have write permissions to the filesystem being used. Finally, if the application process communicates with Fluent Bit via networking, we may be able to improve application performance by offloading the overhead for slow I/O throughput of disk storage.

As with console output, we have the option to format outputs in different ways. This time, we will configure multiple file outputs using different formats so that we can compare the outputs. This does mean we need to duplicate some of the attributes. First, we need to define the filename for the output file using the file attribute. If this is left undefined, the filename defaults to the tag value, which we don't want, given that we're outputting the same source with the same tag to multiple files. To avoid this issue, we will set the file attribute for each output as output1 but use different extensions to reflect the formatting. We have the option to define the path to the output folders. If the path attribute is unset, the folder from which we have executed Fluent

Bit will be used as the path. In production, we'd recommend setting this value, but to make it easier to exercise the configuration without the path being defined (everyone will have different environment setups), we've omitted it. We have provided a `clean-c5.sh` script to delete the files generated, which assumes the same thing as Fluent Bit regarding location. Let's look at the formatting options and the ones we will use:

- `plain`—The `plain` format takes the log events and pushes them out to the file in an unmodified format.
- `csv`—The `csv` (comma-separated values) format allows you to choose a separator using the `delimiter` attribute, which allows values `comma`, `space`, and `tab` (or `/t`). It is also true to its name, as the output process treats the record's root elements as name values, so just the values are output. If the record contains nested JSON, the nested JSON is treated as a single value.
- `ltsv`—The `ltsv` (label tab-separated values) format is similar to the `csv` format, except we can include the labels and choose among the same options to delimit the labels but use the attribute name `label_delimiter`.
- `msgpack`—The `msgpack` format takes advantage of the `msgpack` serialization mechanism. This results in the payload generated appearing more like binary.
- `template`—The `template` format is much more interesting, as we can now incorporate whatever content and then reference values using curly braces around the keys to the payload, including the log record's time value, using the key of `time`. The ability to reference the log event record content includes traversing nested JSON elements using a subset of the `JSONPath` notation—dot notation to traverse hierarchy, such as `<parent element name>.<child element name>`.

At this stage, we need to know that all output plugins will receive all log events as long as the `match` clause allows. With this, we can configure the log events to be output to multiple files, allowing us to see the different formatting side by side. See the following listing and `chapter5/fluentbit/simple-file.conf`.

Listing 5.5 Different file formats: `simple-file.conf`

```
[SERVICE]
  flush 1
  log_level error

[INPUT]
  name http
  listen 0.0.0.0
  port 9881
  tag http-in

[OUTPUT]
  match *
  name stdout
  json_date_key received-date
  json_date_format iso8601
  format json_lines
```

We've retained the console output so we can see when the event has been received.

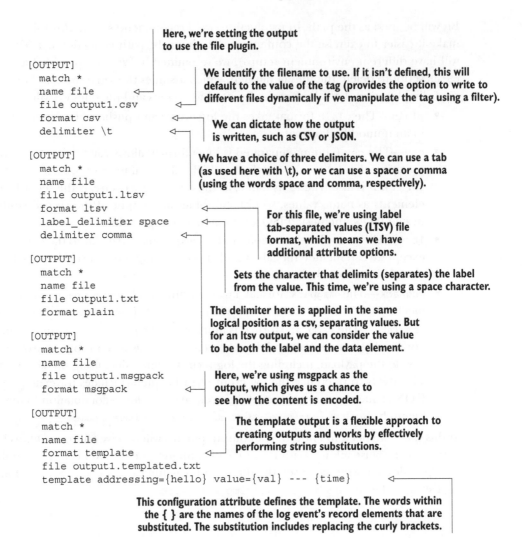

Here, we're setting the output
to use the file plugin.

```
[OUTPUT]
  match *
  name file
  file output1.csv
  format csv
  delimiter \t
```

We identify the filename to use. If it isn't defined, this will
default to the value of the tag (provides the option to write to
different files dynamically if we manipulate the tag using a filter).

We can dictate how the output
is written, such as CSV or JSON.

We have a choice of three delimiters. We can use a tab
(as used here with \t), or we can use a space or comma
(using the words space and comma, respectively).

```
[OUTPUT]
  match *
  name file
  file output1.ltsv
  format ltsv
  label_delimiter space
  delimiter comma
```

For this file, we're using label
tab-separated values (LTSV) file
format, which means we have
additional attribute options.

Sets the character that delimits (separates) the label
from the value. This time, we're using a space character.

```
[OUTPUT]
  match *
  name file
  file output1.txt
  format plain
```

The delimiter here is applied in the same
logical position as a csv, separating values. But
for an ltsv output, we can consider the value
to be both the label and the data element.

```
[OUTPUT]
  match *
  name file
  file output1.msgpack
  format msgpack
```

Here, we're using msgpack as the
output, which gives us a chance to
see how the content is encoded.

```
[OUTPUT]
  match *
  name file
  format template
  file output1.templated.txt
  template addressing={hello} value={val} --- {time}
```

The template output is a flexible approach to
creating outputs and works by effectively
performing string substitutions.

This configuration attribute defines the template. The words within
the { } are the names of the log event's record elements that are
substituted. The substitution includes replacing the curly brackets.

To run this configuration, we will continue using Postman as our log event source. We also want to start Fluent Bit, as we haven't stipulated a configuration value for the `path` attribute; the output files will be written in the folder in which Fluent Bit is being executed. So, it's best to ensure that we have read and write privileges in the folder in which we're about to execute Fluent Bit.

Unlike when reading, we don't need to worry about tracking progress, as we'll keep adding to the end of the current file. In chapter 3, we talked about log rotation and the fact that some logging frameworks include the ability to rotate logs. Fluent Bit doesn't have this feature and will continue to add new log entries to the end of the file each time they need to be written. This means we need to use an external service to perform log rotation. Within Fluent Bit, we can apply some control on the output using techniques such as these:

- Omit the file attribute so that it defaults to using the tag, but before the output plugin processes the log events, manipulate the tag name. We will see how we can manipulate log events in the coming chapters.

- Another strategy is to use a variable as part of the path attribute. We can periodically manipulate the variable and force a hot configuration refresh (not available on all platforms), which will induce the variable to be picked up. This can, of course, be used only if the log event sources can tolerate Fluent Bit restarting periodically. Sources where Fluent Bit is reading the source won't be a problem, but network-centric source plugins need to have the ability to retry or fail to a standby instance of Fluent Bit.

In later chapters, we will see how to manipulate values such as the tag.

5.6 *Prometheus outputs*

When it comes to more sophisticated times series data storage for metrics (numeric) and visualization, Prometheus and Grafana are often the default tools for Kubernetes-based use cases. When it comes to Prometheus, there are two ways we can enable data to be passed from Fluent Bit to Prometheus:

- We can allow Prometheus to scrape data from Fluent Bit on a scheduled interval, which is the traditional way for Prometheus to work. This allows Fluent Bit to serve dual purposes. For Prometheus to capture environmental data, it traditionally uses a local agent to gather the data (an exporter). As we're deploying Fluent Bit with access to the same information, we can use Fluent Bit as the agent. As a result, the input plugin for this way of working is known as the `prometheus_exporter`. As we potentially also want Prometheus to capture the metrics relating to our Fluent Bit deployments, another input plugin called `fluentbit_metrics` exists. These plugins generate the metrics data in a format that is readily consumable by Prometheus.

- More recently, Prometheus introduced an API to push data to Prometheus. We'll look at why this approach is necessary shortly. The ability to remotely write means we use the `prometheus_remote_write` plugin instead.

In this part of the chapter, we'll evolve the configuration to support different ways we can work with Prometheus. The first thing we need to do is deploy Prometheus with the appropriate configuration. We will be running Prometheus using Docker Compose, as this allows us to configure Prometheus easily in a manner that looks like Kubernetes without needing to run a Kubernetes environment. Appendix A details the steps to set up all the prerequisites. We aren't deploying Grafana, as Prometheus provides a basic interface and query expression syntax called PromQL that is sufficient to meet our requirements.

> **Understanding Prometheus and Grafana**
>
> Prometheus is a feature-rich and powerful tool, as is Grafana. Plenty of resources can help you dig deeper into these tools. Aside from the product documentation websites https://prometheus.io/docs/introduction/overview and https://grafana.com/docs, we recommend looking at *Cloud Observability in Action*, by Michael Hausenblas (https://www.manning.com/books/cloud-observability-in-action), for more context on Prometheus. See *Learn Kubernetes in a Month of Lunches*, by Elton Stoneman (https://www.manning.com/books/learn-kubernetes-in-a-month-of-lunches), to put these tools in action.

5.6.1 *Prometheus Node Exporter*

To capture the data that the Node Exporter would generate, we need to add a new input plugin called `node_exporter_metrics`. At the simplest level, we need to identify only the frequency at which it retrieves the data from the compute node using the `scrape_interval` attribute, which takes a numeric number of seconds per poll. As with all plugins, we can define the tag to use, as well as the `tag` property. It is worth noting that this is a Linux-only plugin today, although there is a Windows-comparable plugin called `windows_exporter_metrics`. Although it is not ideal that this is a Linux-only plugin, we must accept that there are more Linux production environments, particularly when considering Kubernetes-based environments.

With the input of node data defined, we can focus on the output plugin. The `prometheus_exporter` plugin takes data provided in the record part of the internal data structure, which needs to be formatted as a Prometheus record, and shares the data with Prometheus when it makes an HTTP call to the Fluent Bit instance using the URL `<host address>:<port>/metrics`, which is the standard URL that Prometheus uses. We can specify the `port` number, which can be different for different Prometheus outputs. For example, an infrastructure team wants to monitor servers to understand overall enterprise health. It is not interested in differentiating between production and nonproduction environments. Or an application development team wants to have a Prometheus instance of their own as they're using the metrics to ascertain factors that might influence the performance of their application during testing or in production. We're not suggesting that this is a good way of working. But the way organizations work has a material effect that Fluent Bit can address. The attribute `host` identifies the networks that should be listened to; in our case, we're saying all networks. Finally, to help distinguish this exporter from others, we can provide additional name-value pairs that function as labels in Prometheus. This can be done using the `add_label` property with a space character to separate the name and the value. Note that Prometheus has strict rules on naming conventions for the labels that need to be kept to upper- and lowercase alphanumeric characters and no special characters. We can combine this and get a configuration.

Labels allow us to dimension the data (group data values) from different perspectives. We might want a view per Fluent Bit deployment, so we'd add a label to reflect that. (Container instance or server ID are possibilities depending on the deployment.) We may also want to group the metrics based on a functional characteristic, such as all Fluent Bit instances deployed to monitor a group of servers running a particular service (sometimes described as a *server group* or *fleet*). As using predefined data values such as server name, type, and ID has minimal overhead, these labels are worth adding to metrics even if there isn't an identified immediate requirement, as it creates options for later custom querying when trying to perform fault diagnosis or event correlation.

TIP A key consideration when using Prometheus is the size of the cardinality (the number of dimensions) of the data being handled. High levels of cardinality have a real effect on Prometheus. This challenge is explored in depth by Jaime Riedesel in chapter 14 of *Software Telemetry* (https://www.manning .com/books/software-telemetry).

The following listing illustrates configuring Fluent Bit as a node exporter for Prometheus (`chapter5/fluentbit/prometheus-exporter-output.conf`).

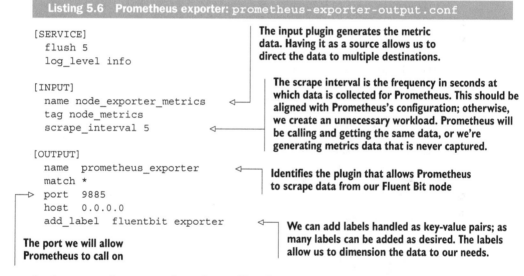

Listing 5.6 Prometheus exporter: `prometheus-exporter-output.conf`

```
[SERVICE]
  flush 5
  log_level info

[INPUT]
  name node_exporter_metrics
  tag node_metrics
  scrape_interval 5

[OUTPUT]
  name  prometheus_exporter
  match *
  port  9885
  host  0.0.0.0
  add_label  fluentbit exporter
```

The input plugin generates the metric data. Having it as a source allows us to direct the data to multiple destinations.

The scrape interval is the frequency in seconds at which data is collected for Prometheus. This should be aligned with Prometheus's configuration; otherwise, we create an unnecessary workload. Prometheus will be calling and getting the same data, or we're generating metrics data that is never captured.

Identifies the plugin that allows Prometheus to scrape data from our Fluent Bit node

We can add labels handled as key-value pairs; as many labels can be added as desired. The labels allow us to dimension the data to our needs.

The port we will allow Prometheus to call on

As the output is communicated over HTTP, we can see the result of our configuration without starting Prometheus. Let's start Fluent Bit with this command:

```
fluent-bit -c fluentbit/prometheus-exporter-output.conf
```

We can see what data is generated for Prometheus to scrape by using a browser or Postman to execute a GET on the URL `http://localhost:9885/metrics`. We provided the configuration in Postman, called Prometheus Scraper. When the data is retrieved, we'll see a considerable amount of detail provided in the output. This includes comments describing groups of output values (provided by the exporter) followed by each measurement in the format `measurement-name {label="value",` label="value"} measurement-"value". Note that the label(s) added appear in every record, and other label values help differentiate each of the readings, such as which processor the value relates to in a multicore CPU. (We saw this in chapter 3 when looking at the cpu input plugin.) We've extracted illustrative fragments from the output, as well as leaving a blank line to show where each fragment starts and ends:

```
# HELP node_cpu_seconds_total Seconds the CPUs spent in each mode.
# TYPE node_cpu_seconds_total counter
node_cpu_seconds_total{fluentbit="exporter",cpu="0",mode="idle"}
➥ 84200.880000000005
node_cpu_seconds_total{fluentbit="exporter",cpu="0",mode="iowait"}
➥ 811.76999999999998
node_cpu_seconds_total{fluentbit="exporter",cpu="0",mode="irq"} 0
node_cpu_seconds_total{fluentbit="exporter",cpu="0",mode="nice"} 0
node_cpu_seconds_total{fluentbit="exporter",cpu="0",mode="softirq"}
➥ 111.56999999999999
node_cpu_seconds_total{fluentbit="exporter",cpu="0",mode="steal"} 0
node_cpu_seconds_total{fluentbit="exporter",cpu="0",mode="system"}
➥ 70.010000000000005
node_cpu_seconds_total{fluentbit="exporter",cpu="0",mode="user"} 101.28
```

Note that the label presents itself within the Prometheus-formatted output. The JSON-like labels can be used to dimension the data sets, such as viewing data for CPU 0 or the idle time across all CPUs:

```
# HELP node_cpu_guest_seconds_total Seconds the CPUs spent in
➥ guests (VMs) for each mode.
# TYPE node_cpu_guest_seconds_total counter
node_cpu_guest_seconds_total{fluentbit="exporter",cpu="0",mode="user"} 0
node_cpu_guest_seconds_total{fluentbit="exporter",cpu="0",mode="nice"} 0

# HELP node_disk_reads_completed_total The total number of reads completed
     successfully.
# TYPE node_disk_reads_completed_total counter
node_disk_reads_completed_total{fluentbit="exporter",device="sda"} 1141
node_disk_reads_completed_total{fluentbit="exporter",device="sdb"} 111

# HELP node_disk_flush_requests_time_seconds_total This is the
➥ total number of seconds spent by all flush requests.
# TYPE node_disk_flush_requests_time_seconds_total counter
node_disk_flush_requests_time_seconds_total{fluentbit="exporter",
➥ device="sda"} 0
node_disk_flush_requests_time_seconds_total{fluentbit="exporter",
➥ device="sdb"} 0.0060000000000000001

# HELP node_vmstat_pgpgin /proc/vmstat information field pgpgin.
# TYPE node_vmstat_pgpgin counter
node_vmstat_pgpgin{fluentbit="exporter"} 2624237

# HELP node_network_transmit_fifo_total Network device statistic fifo.
# TYPE node_network_transmit_fifo_total counter
node_network_transmit_fifo_total{fluentbit="exporter",device="lo"} 0
node_network_transmit_fifo_total{fluentbit="exporter",device="eth0"} 0
```

```
# HELP node_systemd_units Summary of systemd unit states
# TYPE node_systemd_units gauge
node_systemd_units{fluentbit="exporter",state="activating"} 0
node_systemd_units{fluentbit="exporter",state="deactivating"} 0
node_systemd_units{fluentbit="exporter",state="inactive"} 94
node_systemd_units{fluentbit="exporter",state="active"} 240
node_systemd_units{fluentbit="exporter",state="failed"} 2
# HELP node_systemd_version Detected systemd version
# TYPE node_systemd_version gauge
node_systemd_version{fluentbit="exporter",
⮕ version="249.11-0ubuntu3.9"} 249.11000000000001
```

The default configuration for the `node_exporter` plugin yields a great deal of data, so the plugin provides additional attributes that allow us to tailor and tune the data collected, such as controlling characteristics like these:

- Linux paths to the data on processes and filesystem metrics for collection
- Ability to specify which metrics are collected
- The option to override the `scrape_interval` attribute for specific data regarding CPU, memory, disk, and filesystem load
- Regular expressions for allowing parts of the filesystem to be ignored when it comes to collection metrics
- Regular expressions for collecting and excluding systemd data

To show all the attributes and their options, we created a configuration file called `prometheus-exporter-output-all.conf` that you can review and experiment with.

5.6.2 Running our Prometheus configuration

We can try capturing this data quickly with our Prometheus configuration. To do this, we need to start Fluent Bit with our configuration (if we haven't shut it down). Then, in a separate terminal, navigate to the `chapter5/prometheus` folder and run the command

```
docker compose up
```

We need to run the command from a specific folder as we pass some basic configuration information into Prometheus. Prometheus needs configuration to know from where to scrape its metrics data and how frequently. We don't want to do a deep dive into the Prometheus configuration. To understand all the configuration attributes, we recommend reviewing https://mng.bz/n0W4. But we will call the critical elements that affect our exercise. First, in the global declaration section, we can define the frequency at which we scrape data unless there is an overriding configuration for a specific source. In our case, we want to run quickly at 10-second intervals, so we set the `scrape_interval` to `10s`. Next, we need to define all the scrape sources. In our case, we've left in the configuration where Prometheus is scraping its own metrics. We've added a block of values in the `scrape_configs` section. Each scrape process is described as a job with a `job_name`. The job name is important as it is a way to distinguish the data source when we perform queries using the Prometheus UI. Then we need to point Prometheus to an address, ideally, DNS rather than IP, which makes things a little more robust if IPs are reallocated. With the address, we also need to provide the ports being used. Looking back at our configuration, we see that we have already set the port number to 9885.

As we're running Fluent Bit locally, and Prometheus is in a container, we need to consider how we connect the container networking to our host network. We can do this by telling Docker through the compose configuration to use the host's network (network_mode: host), in which case Prometheus and Fluent Bit will appear to be running on the same network address. Therefore, we can use a network address of 127.0.0.1 (aka localhost) in our Prometheus configuration.

The alternative is to allow Docker to use bridge mode (my preference, as it avoids conflicting network ports). In this case, we need to edit chapter5/prometheus/ prometheus.yaml to replace occurrences of 127.0.0.1 with our host machine's IP address; for me, 192.168.0.205.

We can use the command docker compose up again to start Prometheus so that we can see it generating logs, and we'll see it executing and scraping the data. As we've not put the container into the background, we can terminate things simply with con- trol d, and Docker should report the deployment shutdown.

5.6.3   *Prometheus Fluent Bit Exporter*

More appropriate for us is a similar input called fluentbit_metrics. This works using the same principle as the node_exporter_metrics plugin but instead provides metrics about Fluent Bit itself. Unlike node_exporter_metrics, the configuration is much simpler. We need to provide the scrape_interval in seconds as before, the tag, and an optional scrape_on_start, which, if unset, defaults to false, so let's set it to true. Getting the data to Prometheus doesn't require changes to the output plugin. Unlike the node_exporter_metrics plugin, this source is not platform sensitive. As a result, we have a configuration that looks like the following listing (chapter5/fluentbit/ prometheus-fb-exporter-output.conf).

> **Listing 5.7   Fluent Bit metrics: prometheus-fb-exporter-output.conf**

```
[SERVICE]
  flush 5
  log_level info

[INPUT]
    name fluentbit_metrics
    tag fluentbit_metrics
    scrape_interval 5        ◁──   Tells Fluent Bit how frequently to
    scrape_on_start true     ◁──   gather its own metrics, expressing the
                                    frequency as a number of seconds

[OUTPUT]                            We can force the scrape to happen as soon as Fluent
    name  prometheus_exporter       Bit starts up or when it starts processing events. By
    match *                         capturing metrics at startup, we are likely to see a
    port  9885                      start-state measurement for Fluent Bit (assuming
    host  0.0.0.0                   that the Fluent Bit process doesn't immediately hit
    add_label  fluentbit exporter   with pushed inputs such as HTTP).
```

Let's start this version of the configuration and repeat the process of using Postman to retrieve the log metrics. The command line to start Fluent Bit is

```
fluent-bit -c fluentbit/prometheus-fb-exporter-output.conf
```

With Fluent Bit running, we can use the same Postman configuration as before (Prometheus Scraper). As with the previous output, we'll see Prometheus-style metrics, but this time, they relate to Fluent Bit. Let's see how Prometheus sees this data by starting up Prometheus again.

Prometheus provides a simple presentation layer that allows us to formulate and run queries against the data it stores. This can be accessed using the `<host>:<port>/graph` URL, such as `localhost:9090/graph`. We can then use the UI to help build the graph. For example, we could query the metric `fluentbit_input_metrics_scrapes_total`, and then we need to tell Prometheus the time period and interval for the data points on the Graph tab. For our demo, we want to set the interval to a short value (5 minutes in the following example), and as we don't have much data, we can go for the latest (obtained by clicking the cross icon in the time field). When we're happy with the query parameters, we click the Execute button to direct the browser to a URL with the parameters defined and render the graph. The result should look figure 5.6.

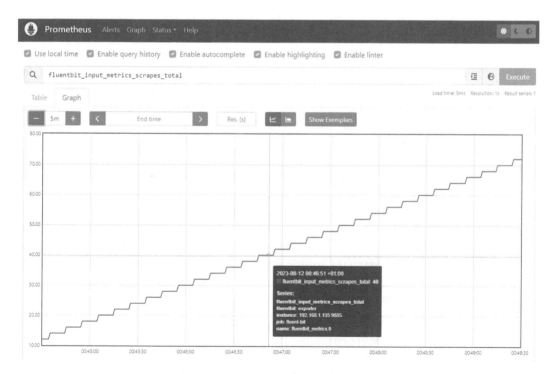

Figure 5.6   A simple example output metric from Prometheus showing how many times Prometheus scraped data from Fluent Bit

We could jump directly to the graph using the URL `http://localhost:9090/graph?g0` `.expr=fluentbit_input_metrics_scrapes_total&g0.tab=0&g0.stacked=0&g0&g0` `.range_input=1m` (assuming that localhost is where Prometheus is being run).

5.6.4 *Prometheus remote writer*

We have seen how we can let Prometheus scrape data from Fluent Bit. But the scraping (or polling) approach to collecting data has some limitations. It may be easy to have Prometheus calling nodes to retrieve the metrics data from a central control perspective, as we can control operations from one place and present a server being swamped with data. But it also means we risk missing or losing important data:

- Short-lived or transient processes generating metrics data may no longer be alive by the time Prometheus knows and tries to connect with the metrics exporter on the node. For example, it generates metrics from within a Pod, which Kubernetes may shut down as it controls the number of instances based on demand. Other short-lived scenarios that would be affected are metrics from serverless solutions such as Fn Project and AWS Lambda.

- Connecting to node exporters across networks can present some real problems for network security. This is most visible when Prometheus is running in one cloud and needs to scrape data from node exporters in another cloud or private data center. Allowing an external service to connect with a node exporter within a private subnet within a data center is the sort of thing that will give an IT security officer a heart attack. Suppose the idea was even considered. In that case, we'd likely need to put into place a complex array of network security processes, such as proxies or API gateways, to introduce additional authentication checks.

- Reaching out to node exporters is, in effect, a process of polling, which can be inefficient as we may end up going through the overhead of connecting to a node exporter to find there is no new data. We must trade off the latency of important metrics, such as a metric showing something has reached a critical threshold, against the efficiency of calls. Ideally, we should make calls only when we have a high probability of retrieving the data. Call too quickly, and we won't get any new data in each call; call too slowly, and we'll hit critical thresholds before we know and can do anything about them. As a result, communicating using a push model or streaming approach is attractive. With a push model, when there is data, the source sends it to the central service, or the central service creates an open connection where the data source can send back data when it occurs over the connection initiated by the server.

To address these challenges with Prometheus, the team behind Prometheus developed a remote write specification (https://mng.bz/vJPr). Prometheus provides an endpoint to support this specification but isn't the only software to implement it; it can be used to send metrics to solutions that can handle time series data, such as Thanos. As the interaction is standardized, we can communicate with Prometheus or data stores but also use this output plugin to send data to cloud services that support that standard, such as New Relic, Logz.io, and Grafana Cloud.

Let's set up our configuration so that we can remotely write to our locally hosted Prometheus instance. To illustrate configuration differences, we're also going to define an output to send data to a cloud-hosted solution. We opted to use Grafana Cloud, as it has a free tier and a period of unrestricted use. The way the service is built also allows us to differentiate among Grafana, Prometheus, and other components. Appendix A describes how to set up Grafana Cloud. If you don't want to use one or the other, delete the output declaration or comment it out using the hash character.

We'll continue to use the Fluent Bit metrics as the source (making the deployment platform neutral). We need to define an output that uses the `prometheus_remote_write` plugin (identified with the `name` attribute). We need to specify the host address. For our local configuration, this can be the IP of the machine running our Prometheus container. For the cloud deployment, we'd expect this to be a DNS address, which will vary depending on which cloud provider and cloud region the managed service is operating. As we're based in the United Kingdom, it makes sense for us to use a region in the United Kingdom. (During setup, you may choose a different deployment location, but you should note the URL you're provided.)

Next, we need to identify the URI—the path to the endpoint, which will differ depending on the service. Prometheus, out of the box, expects this to be `/api/v1/write`. For the Grafana Cloud, the changes to `/api/prom/push` reflect how they've structured their endpoints across multiple service components. We can derive these details from the remote write endpoint provided by the Prometheus setup (https://grafana.com/orgs/<subdomainname>/hosted-metrics/<userId>). We need to indicate which port to use to call Prometheus, which can be affected by whether we're using Transport Layer Security (TLS). Locally, we're using the default port of `9090`, and we're not using TLS or credentials. For a cloud deployment, we'd expect to use TLS and the standard TLS port to be used, which means we need to set the `port` attribute to the standard `443` TLS port for our cloud service but to `9090` locally. Also, we need to enable the TLS option for our cloud service using the attribute `tls` and set the value to `on`, but for a simple local configuration, we set the attribute to `off`. We would expect any cloud service to authenticate requests to provide data to prevent a third party from poisoning our data or disrupting the service by sending it masses of junk data. Authentication can be done through basic authentication, so we need to define the username with the attribute `http_user` and the associated password with `http_passwd`. Locally, to avoid the additional complexities of setting up an authentication solution and adding more complexity to the Prometheus setup, we will forgo authentication so we don't need to supply such credentials. Our example references environment variables to minimize the exposure of such credentials. We can provide the additional labels using the `add_label` attribute.

As we're initiating the data transmission, we have the option to record what the consumer says about the data. We can control whether Fluent Bit will log this (and we'll be able to see it on the console) using the attribute `log_response_payload`, which we'll enable with the value of `on`. Our configuration looks like the following listing (`chapter5/fluentbit/prometheus-remote-output.conf`).

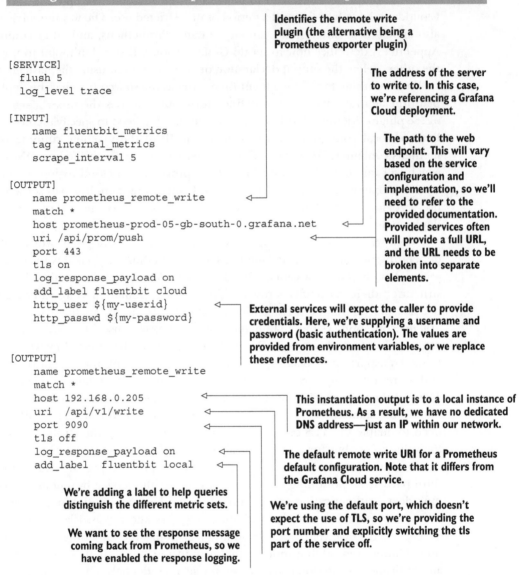

Listing 5.8 Prometheus writer: `prometheus-remote-output.conf`

Identifies the remote write plugin (the alternative being a Prometheus exporter plugin)

```
[SERVICE]
  flush 5
  log_level trace

[INPUT]
    name fluentbit_metrics
    tag internal_metrics
    scrape_interval 5

[OUTPUT]
    name prometheus_remote_write
    match *
    host prometheus-prod-05-gb-south-0.grafana.net
    uri /api/prom/push
    port 443
    tls on
    log_response_payload on
    add_label fluentbit cloud
    http_user ${my-userid}
    http_passwd ${my-password}

[OUTPUT]
    name prometheus_remote_write
    match *
    host 192.168.0.205
    uri  /api/v1/write
    port 9090
    tls off
    log_response_payload on
    add_label  fluentbit local
```

The address of the server to write to. In this case, we're referencing a Grafana Cloud deployment.

The path to the web endpoint. This will vary based on the service configuration and implementation, so we'll need to refer to the provided documentation. Provided services often will provide a full URL, and the URL needs to be broken into separate elements.

External services will expect the caller to provide credentials. Here, we're supplying a username and password (basic authentication). The values are provided from environment variables, or we replace these references.

This instantiation output is to a local instance of Prometheus. As a result, we have no dedicated DNS address—just an IP within our network.

The default remote write URI for a Prometheus default configuration. Note that it differs from the Grafana Cloud service.

We're adding a label to help queries distinguish the different metric sets.

We're using the default port, which doesn't expect the use of TLS, so we're providing the port number and explicitly switching the tls part of the service off.

We want to see the response message coming back from Prometheus, so we have enabled the response logging.

With the cloud environment configured and our Docker version of Prometheus running using the previously described `docker compose up` command, we can run the scenario using the command

```
fluent-bit -c fluentbit/prometheus-remote-output.conf
```

We should see Fluent Bit's console report sending the metrics to Grafana Cloud. We can then navigate to the dashboard using the URL `https://<subdomain name>.grafana .net/dashboards>` we've set up to see the effect of the incoming data, as described in appendix A.

5.7 PostgreSQL output

If we want a general-purpose tool that allows us to query our log events (as well a metrics and tracers), the ideal is a database with native support for JSON, which means the database can easily accommodate varying log structures and we avoid Fluent Bit's having to do a lot of heavy lifting restructuring the different payloads. Also, Fluent Bit handles log events using a JSON data structure. Out of the box, Fluent Bit supports databases such as Elasticsearch and the OpenSearch variant, as well as Postgres. We could also include Kafka and Prometheus in this list, as they can operate as time series databases. As Postgres is not difficult to work with and is a converged database (works with relational and nonrelational data models), it makes a good illustration.

Appendix A provides setup information for PostgreSQL, which we'll need to run this scenario. In addition, within the chapter's download folder are convenience scripts `start-postgres.[sh|bat]` to help make things easier with the Docker command and all the relevant parameters.

The PostgreSQL plugin (`pgsql`) is subject to build flags; as a result, it may not be in your Fluent Bit deployment. By default, it is in the official binary download for Linux but not for Windows or macOS and won't be on if you have compiled Fluent Bit yourself (unless the plugin has been explicitly enabled). The easiest way to confirm the plugin's availability is to use the `fluent-bit --help` command line, which includes a list of the available plugins in the output.

Let's start with the simplest scenario and configuration. We will continue consuming events from Postman as an HTTP input, and output the received events to a table in Postgres. To do this, we need to provide the details of how to authenticate the database connection using the attributes `user` and `password`. Including credentials in the core configuration is not ideal, and we'll return to this consideration shortly. Then we need to provide the network connection address for the database server using the attributes `host` and `port`, which are configured just like any other network-based connection. Although our example is going to work with localhost for simplicity, when we get into real-world deployments, particularly in containerized use cases like Kubernetes environments, localhost is unlikely to be an option (the one case where localhost will be fine is sidecar deployments), and we're best using DNS addresses. We won't collocate Fluent Bit within a single container with Postgres. We need to ensure that we can still access the Postgres service.

As the database server can support multiple database instances, we need to name the database instance using the `database` attribute. The plugin allows us to name the table with the attribute called `table`. This means we can direct different types of logs or log sources to different tables if we want Fluent Bit to filter and route events (chapter 7), but we've already seen how we can use the match attribute. Finally, we need to incorporate the log event's timestamp into the JSON payload to make it easier to perform JSON queries when examining time ranges or ordering data. We could do this by manipulating the payload upstream of the output, but the plugin has made this simple for us. For our scenario, we will use the provided Postgres database and the users' setup (again, an action to avoid extra setup effort and good for production use cases). See the following listing and chapter5/fluentbit/db-output.conf.

Listing 5.9 PostgreSQL output example: db-output.conf

```
[SERVICE]
  flush 1
  log_level info
```
Provides the name of the plugin being used. This is the name for PostgreSQL.

```
[INPUT]
  name http
  listen 0.0.0.0
  port 9881
  tag input1
```
As the database has been deployed on the same host as Fluent Bit, we can reference localhost. But in a Kubernetes use case, we'll want to use an IP or DNS address.

The port to be used for communicating with Postgres

```
[OUTPUT]
  name  pgsql
  match *
  host  localhost
  port  5455
  user  postgresUser
  password  postgresPW
  database  postgres
  table  fluentbit
  timestamp_key ts
```
As a Postgres server can handle multiple schemas, we need to identify which schema. We can use the default schema rather than set up an additional schema. But in production, we should have a separate schema for monitoring use cases.

We need to declare the attribute's name in the JSON payload, to which we'll add the timestamp for the record.

To execute this HTTP-to-Postgres scenario, we need to start our container with Postgres, as described in appendix A. Then we need to run either a Postgres command-line interface (CLI) client or an installed UI tool such as pgAdmin, which we're going to use (appendix A). Finally, we're going to use Postman again. When our prerequisite tools are running, we can start Fluent Bit with the command

```
fluent-bit -c fluentbit/db-output.conf
```

When Fluent Bit is running, we can select the HTTP call configuration in the collections within Postman and click Send. We should see log messages on the Fluent Bit console indicating activity. With that, we can explore what happened in Postgres. Using the navigation tree, we can open the database and expand the tables, which should include a table called fluentbit that the plugin generated for us. Then, using the context menu on the table, we can use pgAdmin to View/Edit Data > All Rows. This will populate the Query panel, execute the SQL, and show the results in the lower panel, as shown in figure 5.7.

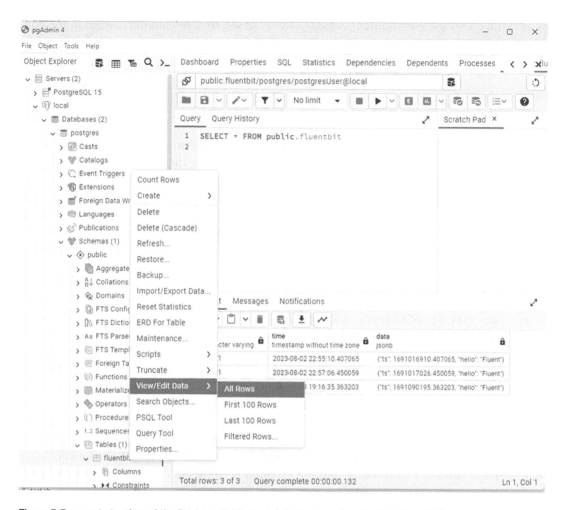

Figure 5.7 pgAdmin **view of the Postgres table containing log events output by Fluent Bit**

As the figure shows, the table contains a record for each log event received, with columns for the tag, timestamp, and data in JSON format. Depending on the environment and time zone, the timestamp will reflect Coordinated Universal Time (UTC). This prevents the records from getting out of sequence when moving in and out of daylight-saving clock shifts.

We previously identified that having credentials in clear text is not recommended. The easiest way to address this is to reference an environment variable for this value. When operating within a Kubernetes environment, we can retrieve the credentials from a Vault and inject them into the container via the Pod configuration. This ensures the credentials are stored securely and not in the configuration, which ideally would be held in a version control tool such as Git. The downside of this approach is that after the environment variable values are set, they remain unchanged in the container for as long as it is running.

> **TIP** For more information on how to configure Secrets management within Kubernetes, we recommend looking at *Kubernetes Secrets Management* by Alex Soto Bueno and Andrew Block (https://www.manning.com/books/kubernetes-secrets-management).

Let's modify our configuration to illustrate that the password comes from an environment variable. The first step is defining and populating the environment variable. We can do that with the command `export PostgreSQLPassword=postgresPW`. Then we modify the attribute so that, rather than `password postgresPW`, we have the attribute set as `password ${PostgreSQLPassword}`. With that change, repeat the previous steps of starting Fluent Bit, sending the event from Postman, navigating to the `fluentbit` table, and retrieving the records with pgAdmin. The result of the query on the table will show the additional record.

In addition to security, we need to consider the performance of the database to ensure that we can send the logs to the database quickly enough. Like many databases, PostgreSQL supports connection pools and allows many concurrent connections. To exploit this, we have configuration attributes that allow us to configure how many connections we may want to use concurrently. Each connection, in effect, can process a chunk of log events. There is always an outside chance that one connection may get serviced before another, resulting in log events being stored slightly out of sequence. But as we mentioned, we can protect against this by using `order-by` clauses in our SQL. To enable this behavior, we need to switch on the asynchronous behavior using the attribute `async` and providing a value of `true`. Then we can define how many connections it maintains as a minimum (avoiding the initial overhead of starting additional connections) and the maximum number of connections using the attributes `min_pool_size` and `max_pool_size`, respectively.

To increase the workload, we need to use the LogSimulator. Trying to induce the workload to guarantee the use of the additional connections is difficult as it is dependent on the environment being used in terms of CPU, memory, and so on. The LogSimulator command and configuration to generate a large load is provided in `chapter5/SimulatorConfig/volume.properties`, along with the convenience scripts previously illustrated. (Appendix A describes setting up and running the LogSimulator.) You may need to experiment with configurations of LogSimulator and Docker to see the connection pooling being used. We've included a configuration called `scaling-test.conf` in `chapter5/fluentbit`, which includes the pool size attributes.

The `pgsql` plugin has also been enabled to work with CockroachDB (https://www.cockroachlabs.com), available as an open source or managed cloud service, which is fully compliant with PostgreSQL syntax and can work with PostgreSQL drivers. To exploit this, an additional attribute called `cockroachdb` needs to have a value of `true` set.

Cockroach DB offers some interesting capabilities suited to deployment in cloud/containerized environments as it is resilient through the use of multiple nodes, able to scale and balance workload across its nodes, and retains integrity and ACID (atomicity, consistency, isolation, durability) properties expected of a relational database.

5.8   HTTP output

Today, the use of HTTP and JSON (described as RESTful if it's used according to several good principles) is so pervasive that when there isn't a plugin available, it is likely that we can direct Fluent Bit using the HTTP output or extending it to overcome any special needs, such as specific payload encryption or authentication. The `http` output plugin is restricted to using the POST verb; this reflects the idea that we're unlikely to be updating or replacing a log record, typically done with the PATCH or PUT verb.

To illustrate the HTTP output, we're going to use a tool called WireMock (appendix A), which allows us to create a local HTTP server that can be configured to respond to different requests and validate header details, such as basic auth credentials and return payloads. We've prepared configuration files for WireMock and supplied a shell script (`start-wiremock.sh`) to start the container.

To create an HTTP output, we need to start with the `match` and `name` attributes. As we're passing on what we receive from an HTTP input, we can set the output to match all traffic, and the output plugin is called `http`. As with all network-based outputs (where we invoke the endpoint rather than accept a call from another party, such as Prometheus), we must provide the `port` and `host` properties. As this output is a general-purpose plugin, we can't assume the URI/path of the destination. So, this needs to be provided using the `uri` property. We'll use a simple path with `/simple`. Combining these properties should produce a qualified URL, and depending on the HTTP verb (POST, PUT, GET, PUSH, and so on), we can use curl or a web browser, `http://localhost:8080/simple`. We can get the output plugin to format the payload, which means using a format property to define what format we'd like. For readability, let's use JSON. As we've seen previously, we can also stipulate the formatting of the date-time provided using the property `json_date_format`. We can add HTTP header values using the `header` attribute followed by name and value for the header with a space separating the key and value. In our example (`chapter5/fluentbit/http-output.conf`), we provide a key of `Fluentbit` and a value of `http`.

Listing 5.10   HTTP output example: `http-output.conf`

```
[SERVICE]
  flush 1
  log_level error

[INPUT]
  name http
  listen 0.0.0.0
  port 9881
  tag http-in
```

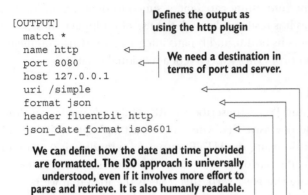

```
[OUTPUT]
  match *
  name http
  port 8080
  host 127.0.0.1
  uri /simple
  format json
  header fluentbit http
  json_date_format iso8601
```

**Defines the output as
using the http plugin**

**We need a destination in
terms of port and server.**

**In addition to a network address, we
need to supply the URI that defines
where in a specific server to
communicate. In our example, we're
addressing 192.168.0.135:8080/simple
as the complete address. The full path is
separated out to make it easier to
adjust the addressing dynamically.**

**We can define how the date and time provided
are formatted. The ISO approach is universally
understood, even if it involves more effort to
parse and retrieve. It is also humanly readable.**

**By providing additional header attributes, we can provide
additional values dynamically; these could be additional
tokens for authentication through useful metadata about
which instance of Fluent Bit we're sending the event from.**

**We can define the formatting of
the output. In most cases, we'd
expect this to be JSON.**

To run our scenario, we need to start WireMock using the script

```
start-wiremock.sh
```

If you choose to run WireMock differently, such as deploying to a Kubernetes environment, ensure that you can see the console output. Then start up Fluent Bit with the command

```
fluent-bit -c http-output.conf
```

The last step is to start Postman. Using the chapter 5 collection, select the HTTP single Call configuration and click the Send button. We expect to see this result on the console displaying the HTTP input. Postman should receive an HTTP 201 response code. Then, examining the WireMock console output, we should see it write out the header and body details to the console.

This is a good start, but if we're sending a great deal of JSON data, ideally, we want to take advantage of the fact that HTTP allows payloads to be compressed. This can be enabled by defining the compress property and providing the type of compression to be used. Today, the only option for applying compression is gzip, which reflects the broad availability of gzip as both ends of the connection must support the compression algorithm. When Fluent Bit is supported by distributed solutions, particularly when crossing data centers, there is a good chance that a proxy will be involved. In this case, we can identify the proxy server using the proxy attribute and supply the proxy's address.s

More important, when using the network, we should ideally use security, and many HTTP endpoints will expect at least basic authentication to secure the destination data store from being tainted with random or poisonous data. The http output plugin supports basic authentication and has also been extended to support AWS authentication. HTTP Basic authentication requires a user and password, provided by the `http_user` and `http_passwd` attributes. We previously discussed different approaches to avoiding hardwiring credentials into the configuration. For simplicity, we have set these to have the value test in our configuration `http-auth-output` `.conf` file.

Let's restart WireMock and Postman. This time, we'll run Fluent Bit with the command

```
fluent-bit -c fluentbit/http-auth-output.conf
```

We should see the header and body again written to the console. Note the additional header line for authorization, which indicates we are using basic authentication and a random-looking string. The string represents the Base64 encoding of our username and password, separated with a colon. We can verify the string using the website https://www.base64encode.org. As we haven't set up WireMock to support HTTPS, we are passing credentials in the clear, which isn't recommended. The benefit of Wire-Mock is that it can be set up with certificates to enable HTTPS traffic. Figure 5.8 shows the expected output.

```
2023-08-20 16:40:52.273 Verbose logging enabled
2023-08-20 16:40:52.819 Verbose logging enabled
 /$$        /$$ /$$                    /$$        /$$                     /$$
| $$       /$ | $$|__/                   | $$$      /$$$                    | $$
| $$      /$$$| $$ /$$   /$$$$$$   /$$$$$$| $$$$    /$$$$   /$$$$$$   /$$$$$$$| $$   /$$
| $$/$$ $$ $$| $$| $$  /$$__  $$ /$$__  $$| $$ $$  $$ $$  /$$__  $$ /$$_____/| $$  /$$/
| $$$$_  $$$$| $$| $$ | $$  \__/|  $$$$$$ | $$  $$$$| $$ | $$  \ $$| $$      | $$$$$$/
| $$$/ \  $$$| $$| $$ |  $$      |  $$____/| $$\  $ | $$ | $$  | $$| $$      | $$_  $$
| $$/   \  $$| $$| $$ |  $$$$$$$| $$ \/  | $$ \/  | $$ |  $$$$$$/| $$$$$$$| $$ \  $$
|__/     \__/|__/|__/  _____/|__/      |__/ _____/  _____/|__/  \__/

port:                      8080
enable-browser-proxying:   false
disable-banner:            false
no-request-journal:        false
verbose:                   true

2023-08-20 16:41:03.419 Request received:
172.17.0.1 - POST /simple

Host: [192.168.1.135:8080]
Content-Length: [360]
Content-Type: [application/json]
Authorization: [Basic dGVzdDp0ZXN0]
User-Agent: [Fluent-Bit]
fluentbit: [http]
[{"hello":"to all my Fluent bit friends - Patrick Stephens, Eduardo Silva, Anarug, Takahiro Yamashita, Leonardo Albertov
ich, Hiroshi Hatake, Wesley Pettit, Phillip Whelan, David Korczynski, Fujimoto Seiji, Jorge Niedbalski, Yann Soubeyrand,
 Masoud Koleini, Don Bowman, Zero King, Jeff Luo, Matthew Fala, Thiago Padilha","more":"","val":20,"date":169023182000}]

Matched response definition:
{
  "status" : 200
}

Response:
HTTP/1.1 200
Matched-Stub-Id: [f4cdfaa4-730d-4cb0-82b2-a52c16f8fca7]
```

Figure 5.8 WireMock console output for the configuration using basic authentication

5.9   *Forwarding to other Fluent nodes*

Chapter 4 introduced the `forward` plugin to illustrate how we can configure Fluent Bit to receive log events. Let's take a close look at the `http-forward.conf` file we used, as shown in listing 5.11 (`chapter5/fluentbit/http-forward.conf`). As we described earlier, the network-centric plugins have the same core attributes, such as `host` and `port`. We can also secure connectivity using TLS with the attribute and value `tls on`. The same TLS configuration values need to be provided as described with the HTTP plugin use. When TLS is enabled, Fluent Bit, when communicating with Fluentd, can use several additional security properties, such as basic authentication (`username` and `password` attributes) or a shared token (defined using `shared_key` or disabled with `empty_shared_key` attributes).

Listing 5.11   Using the `forward` plugin: `http-forward.conf`

```
[SERVICE]
  flush 1
  log_level debug

[INPUT]
  Name http
  listen 0.0.0.0
  port 9881
  successful_response_code 202
  success_header x-fluent-bit received
  Tag http

[OUTPUT]
  name forward
  match *
  host 0.0.0.0
  port 9980
```

> The forward output plugin uses the same core attributes as HTTP and other network plugins.

We can repeat chapter 3's `forward` plugin configuration, as shown in figure 5.9, where we use a Postman configuration (or curl) to trigger the pipeline. (The Postman chapter 3 collection configuration was called HTTP `call`, and in chapter 3, the JSON file is called `log.json`.) A more adventurous configuration exercise would be to set up Fluentd as described in chapter 7 of the *Logging in Action* book but using the `http-forward.conf` configuration from chapter 3 to direct the Postman traffic to Fluentd, which, in turn, will reach our Fluent Bit deployment.

To rerun the scenario to see the configuration perform, in our shell, we need to go back to the `chapter3` folder and execute the command

```
fluent-bit -c ./fluentbit/http.conf
```

Although the results will be the same as in chapter 3, we can understand the `forward` plugin from both an input and output case.

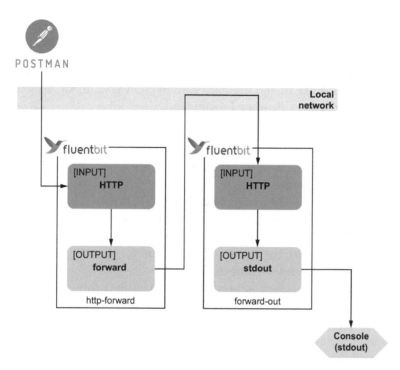

Figure 5.9 The configuration is as we saw in chapter 3, but this time, our focus is on the output (left node).

5.10 *OpenTelemetry*

Fluent Bit can perform two roles when it comes to outputting OpenTelemetry (OTel). We saw in chapter 3 that Fluent Bit can capture OTel data flows. As Fluent Bit may be part of a network of nodes that consolidate logs across multiple sources such as Pods, we need to be able to send data to a downstream node, which may be collecting all the traffic from other nodes capturing data from Pods before filtering and directing traffic to a central solution.

Another common use case is transforming collected sources of metrics, traces, and logs and standardizing them in the OTel format. Data manipulation will make the events between the input and output compliant. We also have the opportunity to take the different signals and associate them with a common subject. For example, we may measure Pod performance metrics and metrics related to error rates and link this data to application logs and trace data. Together, we get a far more holistic view of what a service may be doing and performing. This is part of the reason why OpenTelemetry has worked to unify several disparate standards.

> **NOTE** In v1 and v2 of Fluent Bit, only the HTTP and JSON parts of the Open-Telemetry Protocol (OTLP) specification were supported, not gRPC with HTTP/2 format. OTLP states that the step down is permissible; communication

with gRPC should be used when available. Fluent Bit v3 includes a significant enhancement in the form of introducing support for HTTP/2. The under-the-hood changes needed to introduce support for HTTP/2 are part of the reason we've seen a major version revision. Given that it will be a while before v3 deployments overtake v2 and the step down to JSON is valid, we've focused on the JSON approach to illustrate functionality.

To do this, Fluent Bit can send data using JSON over HTTP(S) to the relevant destination, which should follow the defined URI conventions but can be changed to accommodate updated nonstandard endpoints, such as a proxy server affecting paths. To address this, we need to define the `logs_uri`, `traces_uri`, and `metrics_uri` (excluding the host, which is identified as a separate attribute). We can also label the data to provide more meaning and associate the different signals with a common theme. We can attach labels to the signal by repeating the `add_label` attribute as many times as needed. In our example, we've added two. The value for the `add_label` attribute is constructed by a space-separated name-value pair.

The last consideration is how important it is to get an active confirmation being logged by Fluent Bit. Setting the `log_response_payload` to `true` will result in the response being logged, which will create some additional I/O workload, so it is best only set when configuring and verifying that the Fluent Bit configuration is correct. We're not trying to send the data to a nonexistent endpoint. If we need assurance and absolute traceability that the signals have been received, we can enable this. We can control the logging of the responses to more than just the console by adding an attribute to the `[SERVICE]` section of the configuration in the form of `log_file`, which points to the file to which Fluent Bit will log its logs, as we have done in this configuration.

To make things as compact as possible, we're using the `dummy` input plugin to generate log events. The `fluentbit_metrics` input plugin will generate metrics data. The `event_type` input plugin will create trace events for us. Not shown in the following listing but included in the provided file (`chapter5/fluentbit/otel-output.conf`) are `opentelemetry` input plugins, so we have the option to use our Postman operations from chapter 3. To make it easy to see what is happening, I include an output for stdout.

Listing 5.12   OpenTelemetry output: `otel-output.conf`

```
[SERVICE]
    flush 1
    log_level info
    log_file  fluent-bit.log

[INPUT]
    name fluentbit_metrics
    tag node_metrics
    scrape_interval 300

[INPUT]
    name dummy
    tag dummy.log
```

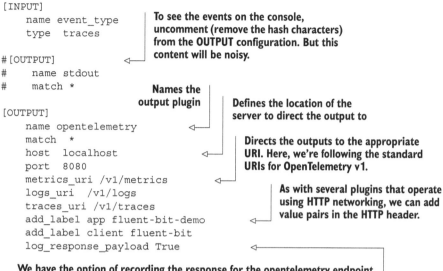

```
[INPUT]
    name event_type
    type   traces
```
To see the events on the console, uncomment (remove the hash characters) from the OUTPUT configuration. But this content will be noisy.
```
#[OUTPUT]
#   name stdout
#   match *
```
Names the output plugin

Defines the location of the server to direct the output to
```
[OUTPUT]
    name opentelemetry
    match  *
    host   localhost
    port   8080
    metrics_uri /v1/metrics
    logs_uri   /v1/logs
    traces_uri /v1/traces
    add_label app fluent-bit-demo
    add_label client fluent-bit
    log_response_payload True
```
Directs the outputs to the appropriate URI. Here, we're following the standard URIs for OpenTelemetry v1.

As with several plugins that operate using HTTP networking, we can add value pairs in the HTTP header.

We have the option of recording the response for the opentelemetry endpoint into Fluent Bit's logging. If we experience any problems passing on the OTel signal(s), we have a record of why. The server may be down and not responding, or it may be overloaded by problems such as authentication errors.

With our configuration ready, we need to handle the output from Fluent Bit. To do this, we're going to use the WireMock container. We've provided the configuration and simplified the task of mapping our configuration by incorporating it into a command-line script. This script needs to be run in the chapter5 folder, as it uses relative paths to map the folders. To start WireMock, we need to run the command

```
./start-wiremock.[sh|bat]
```

and then start Fluent Bit with the command

```
fluent-bit -c fluentbit/otel-output.conf
```

Fluent Bit will be generating events. If we've uncommented the stdout output, this shows content scrolling through. Ideally, we want to see what is being sent by the opentelemetry plugin. We can do this by interrogating WireMock with some HTTP GET calls. Within the chapter 5 Postman collection, we've provided two operations called WireMock mappings and WireMock requests. When used, the WireMock mappings will retrieve the WireMock configuration. To see what WireMock is receiving, we want to use the WireMock requests. With the operation selected (configuration visible in the tool's main panel), click the tool's Send button. As a result, we'll receive an HTTP response in which we can expect to see a message body returned (figure 5.10).

As we can see in figure 5.10, the payload is packed as a Protobuf payload (bodyAs-Base64), but we can also see elements of the payload in the body element of the JSON sufficient to make out that the content reflects what we expect to see. We can use the

Body   Cookies   Headers (2)   Test Results   200 OK   27 ms   145.07 KB   💾 Save as example   •••

Pretty   Raw   Preview   Visualize   JSON ∨   ⇥   ⧉   Q

```
 1  [
 2      "requests": [
 3          {
 4              "id": "05d2b36d-0ce7-407a-b069-c9eda882232e",
 5              "request": {
 6                  "url": "/my/metrics",
 7                  "absoluteUrl": "http://127.0.0.1:8080/my/metrics",
 8                  "method": "POST",
 9                  "clientIp": "172.17.0.1",
10                  "headers": {
11                      "Host": "127.0.0.1:8080",
12                      "Content-Length": "10187",
13                      "Content-Type": "application/x-protobuf",
14                      "User-Agent": "Fluent-Bit"
15                  },
16                  "cookies": {},
17                  "browserProxyRequest": false,
18                  "loggedDate": 1701803516920,
19                  "bodyAsBase64":
                        "CshPEsVPEqgBChBmbHVlbnRiaXRfdXB0aW1lEjNOdW1iZXIgb2Ygc2Vjb25kcyB0aGF0IEZsdWVudCBCaXQg
                        aGFzIGJlZW4gcnVubmluZy46XwpZGXHzy/
                        tHBZ4XIQAAAAAvJJAOhgKA2FwcBIRCg9mbHVlbnQtYml0LWRlbW86FgoGY2xpZW50EgwKCmZsdWVudC1iaXQ
                        6EwoIaG9zdG5hbWUSBwoFV2F0dHMMQAhg8EqABChtmbHVlbnRiaXRfaW5wdXRfYnl0ZXNfdG90YWwwSFk51bWJl
                        ciBvZiBpbnB1dCBieXRlcy46aQpjGX7g3bowBJ4XIQAAAAAAAAAOhgKA2FwcBIRCg9mbHVlbnQtYml0LWRlb
                        W86FgoGY2xpZW50EgwKCmZsdWVudC1iaXQ6HQoEbmFtZRIVChNmbHVlbnRiaXRfbWV0cmljcy4wEAIYARKkAQ
```

Figure 5.10   The Postman view of the output event—in this case, an OpenTelemetry metrics message

search to find the three different types of log events generated by searching for the output URLs (/my/metrics, /my/logs, and /my/traces).

5.11 *Hyperscaler native and SaaS observability*

If we're running solutions on infrastructure providers such as Oracle, AWS, Azure, and Google, to name just a few of the big players, we can use their services to store and visualize metrics, traces, and logs. This raises the question of how Fluent Bit can output these services. A couple of options are available. The long-term answer is that these providers will or do offer OTel-capable endpoints, meaning we can use Fluent Bit as a vendor-agnostic agent and point its output to the relevant cloud service. We're also seeing this pattern of support happening with the specialty observability SaaS/software providers such as Datadog and Splunk.

The short-term answer is that some providers, such as AWS, have created plugins that are built into the Fluent Bit core as outputs. Additionally, the Prometheus API and its associated data definitions have been adopted as a de facto standard. (See the documentation at https://mng.bz/vJPr.) Some services can be sent using the standard HTTP output that we've already looked at.

Summary

- Outputs can be formatted. Fluent Bit provides several formatters that support different ways to format: JSON, MessagePack, and so on.
- Fluent Bit can write to files. This feature has both benefits and challenges. The most notable challenge is that Fluent Bit file output currently doesn't provide native support for log rotation.
- Fluent Bit can direct output to Prometheus in two ways:
  - Prometheus can scrape the data from Fluent Bit using the exporters (ideal if you want Prometheus to control the process).
  - Fluent Bit can remote-write to Prometheus, which is more suitable for dynamic environments in which Fluent Bit instances may be replaced.
- We can direct log events to a Postgres database. The Postgres plugin (`pgsql`), is a good example of an external storage solution that allows users to query data.
- Fluent Bit can work with HTTP endpoints, sending events to a wide range of tools without needing dedicated plugins. This capability includes the option to communicate with other Fluentd and Fluent Bit nodes.
- Fluent Bit can send events to OTLP-compliant destinations using the step-down approach, and since v3, the HTTP/2 with gRPC exchange can be applied.

Parsing to extract more meaning

This chapter covers

- Exploring the relationship between filters, parsers, and decoders
- Examining prebuilt parsers
- Using filters to run parser processes
- Using regular expressions and JSON parsers to extract meaning from log content

In this chapter, we will start working with Fluent Bit's capabilities to examine and manipulate the data it collects and outputs. Parsers are key tools for extracting meaning from unstructured data. Obtaining the meaning of an event allows us to make decisions and transform and route events. To use an old expression, parsing enables us to turn data into information.

6.1 Architectural context

As we can see in figure 6.1, parsers and filters sit in the middle of the pipeline of processing log events after we've ingested the data.

The benefit of separating parsers from the input and output plugins is that we can apply the same parsing processes to different sources. This makes parsers

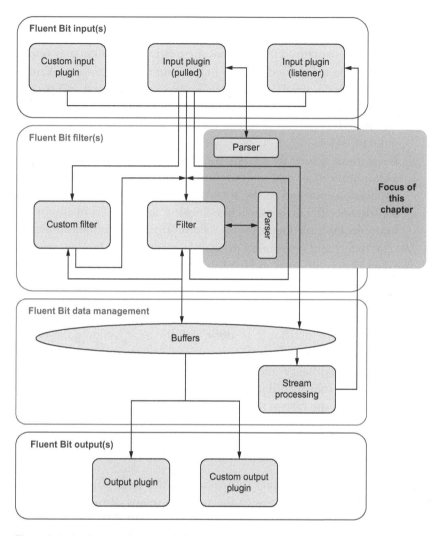

Figure 6.1   Logical architecture of Fluent Bit, with this chapter's focus on parsers highlighted. Parsers are used in special cases with input plugins but primarily through their relationship with filters.

highly reusable, as we'll see. As the figure suggests, we can use parsers with input plugins, but the main relationship parsers have with other components is with filters, as we'll see.

6.2   *The goal of parsing*

Parsers are among the most important tools for extracting meaning from log events, allowing us to find important values. The main reasons for parsing are

- When we've parsed data, we can incorporate the extracted data back into the payload for later use. For example, we can extract the necessary values to incorporate into a structured payload that the destination system may require:
  - We can use the parsed data to help route the events—for example, isolating error codes from a stack trace or the exception type and package, which can help us decide the best path for remediation. In the most advanced situations, parsing could involve processes such as archiving files or clearing old temp data.
  - If the event is security related, such as successful and unsuccessful logins to an application, we may want to route the event to our standard repository for application logs and to the security-monitoring tools. Doing so can add to security-specific analyses, such as looking for patterns of use or misuse, for example, multiple logins for an account from different locations.
- We can detect and implement preventive measures such as ensuring that sensitive data like credit cards and bank account details isn't accidentally included in logs or traces when someone incorporates all the data received into the event without considering the security implications. Ideally, such data is removed or masked before leaving the application, but few frameworks provide such masking or filtering, which has to be done with the logic building the event.

  The value of performing such checks can make a significant difference when addressing compliance audits. The ability to show preventive measures when there is a risk that such data will creep into the logs is a powerful message for the auditor. In the case of the payment card industry (PCI), although our frontline services and servers need to be stringently compliant, downstream servers don't need to demonstrate that they have every control in place. That said, a zero-trust approach to security is always worthwhile.

We can use our ability to extract information from logs, particularly for warnings and errors, to direct notifications to the relevant teams. If we're supporting a multitenant solution, extracting from the logs which tenant the issue is affecting is also key in terms of customer relations. There is great value in showing that we're on top of an issue before customers spot it; it is better than customers raising issues as support tickets.

> **NOTE**   Using regular expressions (*regex*) is a common way to validate or extract text elements from a string. If you're new to regex, it is worth taking a moment to understand better how they work. Appendix B includes resources to help, but we'd suggest starting with https://mng.bz/QVRQ. Multiple flavors of regex exist and are typically influenced by the development languages being used.

6.3   *Relationship between parsers and filters*

Although chapter 7 examines filters in more detail, *parsing* (analyzing the input and extracting meaningful content) is achieved through a specific filter. We're starting with parsing because it can help solve many challenges without requiring more complex filter capabilities. To understand how to incorporate a parser into a use case of capturing log events, parsing them, and outputting the result to a file, we need to take a brief look at filters.

The first important detail is that the parsing configuration lives in a file separate from the definition of the pipeline of events. We identify the file containing the parser configurations in the [SERVICE] part of the configuration, using an attribute called parsers_file, which we supply with the file's location containing one or more parser definitions. In this book, we'll use a relative file path, as the directory structure in which the resources are downloaded will be different for everyone. But for production, consistency, certainty, and clarity about where files are located are important, so we'd recommend using absolute paths.

With the parser file identified (we can identify multiple parser files if necessary by repeating the attribute, sometimes referred to as *chaining parsers*, as one parser's output becomes another parser's input), we need to populate the file with our parser configuration. As with our core configuration files, the classic format starts with a block declaration of [PARSER] for each parser definition in our file. Currently, a YAML configuration will use the same traditional notation for parsers.

Parser definitions use several attributes that depend on the parser implementation, but universally, we need to name the parser with the name attribute, which links to the parser specification to be used in the filter configuration. The name needs to be unique across all the parser definitions we create. Configuration errors may result in the rest of the parser file not being processed. A warning is generated at startup, but lots of unexpected runtime problems may occur if not observed. We also need to tell Fluent Bit what type of parser we want to use with a format attribute. We'll explore more of the attributes as we get further into using parsers. See the following listing and chapter6/fluentbit/parsers.conf.

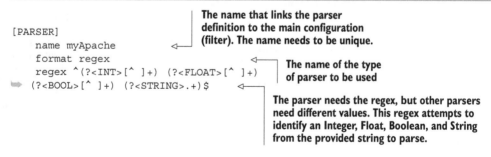

Listing 6.1   Example parser file: parsers.conf

With the parser defined, we can complete the filter definition, which invokes the parser. It should be no surprise that the filter declaration is a lot like an output definition, identified in a classic format with [FILTER] and a dictionary block called filter within the pipeline in YAML.

As we have the option of many kinds of filters, we need to tell Fluent Bit we want a parser filter using the attribute called `name` and the value of the `parser`. We need a `match` attribute, so we filter only the correct data.

The all-important bit is providing the `parser` attribute, which uses the name of the parser definition in the parser file. The final piece of this jigsaw is identifying the attribute `key_name`, which identifies the root element in the log event structure we want to parse.

We don't have to define the entire payload every time. For example, we could produce a parser that extracts the entire error message from a log event. A MySQL database could return to our application the error message "`ERROR 1146 (42S02): Table 'test.no_such_table' doesn't exist`", which may be wrapped up in our application log text. An example log event could be

```
17:13:01.540 [main] ERROR com.foo.Bar - Err from database - ERROR
1146 (42S02): Table 'test.no_such_table' doesn't exist.
```

From this single text, we may want to parse and create an initial set of attributes to hold the log classification, such as `ERROR`; where in the code the error was raised (`com.foo.bar`); and then an attribute to hold the error message

```
Err from the database - ERROR 1146 (42S02): Table
'test.no_such_table'doesn't exist
```

This first parse results in new payload elements, such as `Classification`, `Code-Location`, and `LogMessage`.

Producing a parser that can pass to a subsequent parser the task of parsing the newly extracted `LogMessage` part of the log event and locating the MySQL database error code becomes much simpler and more reusable. See the following listing and `chapter6/fluentbit/apache-log-parser.conf`.

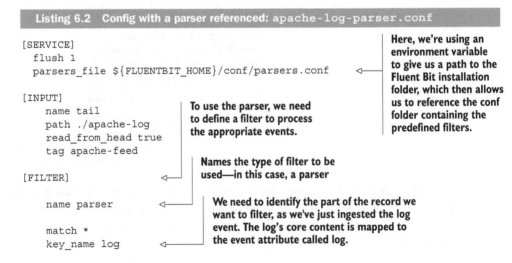

Listing 6.2 **Config with a parser referenced:** `apache-log-parser.conf`

```
[SERVICE]
  flush 1
  parsers_file ${FLUENTBIT_HOME}/conf/parsers.conf

[INPUT]
    name tail
    path ./apache-log
    read_from_head true
    tag apache-feed

[FILTER]

    name parser

    match *
    key_name log
```

Here, we're using an environment variable to give us a path to the Fluent Bit installation folder, which then allows us to reference the conf folder containing the predefined filters.

To use the parser, we need to define a filter to process the appropriate events.

Names the type of filter to be used—in this case, a parser

We need to identify the part of the record we want to filter, as we've just ingested the log event. The log's core content is mapped to the event attribute called log.

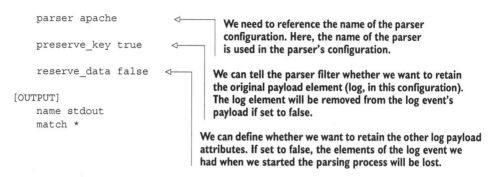

```
    parser apache
    preserve_key true
    reserve_data false
[OUTPUT]
    name stdout
    match *
```

We need to reference the name of the parser configuration. Here, the name of the parser is used in the parser's configuration.

We can tell the parser filter whether we want to retain the original payload element (log, in this configuration). The log element will be removed from the log event's payload if set to false.

We can define whether we want to retain the other log payload attributes. If set to false, the elements of the log event we had when we started the parsing process will be lost.

6.4 Prebuilt parsers

The software industry has a variety of standardized or default log structures, many of which are simply character delimited and ingested as a single string. We need to break them into meaningful parts.

Rather than reinventing the wheel and figuring out the algorithm or regex for these common formats, Fluent Bit incorporates a catalog of parser definitions as part of its installation in a folder called /conf at the root of the Fluent Bit installation. We can copy the parser expressions into our configuration or, better, reference the provided ones directly. The overhead of potentially loading parser configurations we don't need into memory isn't huge unless we're time sensitive to milliseconds or need to optimize memory use to save bytes.

We can implement a simple trick to make it easy to reference these configuration files. Assuming that the path to the Fluent Bit binary is incorporated into the PATH environment variable rather than directly wired into the PATH, declare a separate environment variable with the absolute path to the installation location, refer to that in PATH, and then reference that in our parser file declaration: export FB_PARSERS=" /fluent-bit/conf/". Then we can reference the predefined parsers with parsers_ file ${FB_PARSERS}/ parsers.conf in our configuration file. Change the install location and update the environment variable; we don't need to amend configuration files.

Although the list of predefined parsers will grow slowly, it's worth taking a moment to understand what is already in place and, more important, their names, to prevent any future naming collisions. Appendix B documents the parsers, breaking down the list of possible parsers based on the supplied files and describing each parser's application and attributes.

Services can override default logging behavior

Most applications and services provide the means to tailor or override the default configurations, at which point standard parsers can't help. But foundational technologies like web servers rarely have their logging configurations customized. Appendix B.2 contains tables that describe the provided parsers and identify the attributes provided by the parser's expression.

(continued)

If you review the configuration files, you'll see that they all use the regex parser. We'll explore this parser in more detail shortly. As you'll see, a lot of the provided configurations support Cloud Native Computing Foundation (CNCF)/Kubernetes-related projects, as this is Fluent Bit's natural habitat. But there are other sources for configurations.

If we're interested in a specific part of a standard log, such as the platform hosting a browser recorded in an Apache log, rather than try to create a new parser expression, it will be easier and potentially more reliable to use the standard Apache parser, which will have been proved many times in different environments, and then create a parser to process only the element containing the wanted information.

6.5   *Parsing an Apache log file*

Having worked through the configuration, let's execute this configuration and consume an Apache log file using the example in listing 6.1. To run this scenario, we will use LogSimulator to feed the log data steadily.

> **NOTE** We can run LogSimulator using the Dockerfile provided, as the invocation needs several parameters. We've bundled the Docker command into a shell and batch scripts (with the appropriate .sh and .bat extensions) to simplify this process. If you prefer, you can install LogSimulator and run it locally; details are in appendix A.

LogSimulator expects to be started from the root folder of the downloaded content folder (running from here allows us to share the executable and test data across all the chapters) with the command

```
./SimulatorConfig/apache-log-feed-run.sh
```

When the LogSimulator has started, we can start Fluent Bit within the `chapter6` folder using the command

```
fluent-bit -c fluentbit/apache-log-parser.conf
```

With Fluent Bit running, we should see the log being written to the console with each part of the log record belonging to a JSON, element like this:

```
[0] apache-feed: [[1687345516.000000000, {}], {"host"=>"218.105.111.72",
    "user"=>"-", "method"=>"GET", "path"=>"/scripts/python/wrap/?C=N;O=D",
    "code"=>"200", "size"=>"2631", "referer"=>"-",
    "agent"=>"Mozilla/5.0 (compatible; Ezooms/1.0; help@moz.com)"}]
```

6.6   *Multiline parsing*

Chapter 4 introduced multiline parsing as we explored the capture and processing of Kubernetes logs, but here we dive deeply into the details. We can use the multiline parser with some input plugins (an idea we'll revisit later in the chapter), as illustrated in the Input Plugin (Pulled) in figure 6.1. We can also use the multiline parser via a multiline filter, which works much like the normal parser filter. The parser-specific attributes are prefixed with `multiline`. We identify the field to parser `multiline.key_content` (whereas the simpler single-line filter uses the name `key_content`), and we identify the parser by `multiline.parser`. This parser can be a custom or predefined parser. (See appendix B for the predefined multiline parsers.) Predefined parsers were used in chapter 4; here, we focus on a custom parser, as shown in figure 6.2.

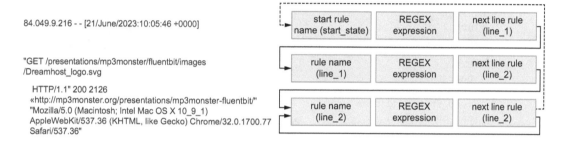

Figure 6.2 Each part of a multiline log (left) can correlate to a parser configuration (right). As long as the regex is valid at the right point, we will keep linking lines into a single event. In the figure, the rule named `line_2` picks up five lines. As the `line_2` rule is cyclical, we can continue consuming many lines into the same event if it isn't expressed well.

Regarding input, we may have managed to ingest an event with newline and/or carriage-return characters into a single event (several lines in a single event). But it is also possible that we've ingested multiple records in a series of events (a single multiline event interpreted as multiple events), in which case we're effectively consolidating records with the same tag in the buffer. We can tell Fluent Bit this with the `buffer` attribute set to `on`. But we need to be confident that events have been consumed in order and/or that we have controls that stop us from accidentally merging many events.

In addition, multiline processing can result in large entries, particularly if the parser process fails to recognize the end of a multiline record, so we have some additional controls over the process of putting the events back into the buffer. These controls come with the `emitter_storage.type`, which defines where the buffer storage is (`memory` or `file`), and the buffer limit, using the attribute `emitter_mem_buf_limit`. This takes a numeric size with the standard Fluent Bit size character (see appendix B), which defaults to 10 MB. We can also force a flush of whatever has been processed into a single record, regardless of whether the correct termination of the multiline event has been identified, by using `flush_ms`, which sets the number of milliseconds (defaulting to `2000` or 2 seconds).

If we consumed event feeds that could be sourced from several input plugins and at least one of these inputs wasn't able to use a multiline parser, we could use the filter with a multiline parser to process the content. To illustrate this behavior, we will read a small text file without a multiline parser configured; it will create a log event in the buffer for each new line. But we know that a new log event starts with a curly bracket ({), and subsequent lines start with a hyphen (-). So, we need the filter to go through the buffer and pull these events back together with a multiline parser. We would have a configuration with a multiline parser in a filter like the following listing and `chapter6/fluentbit/multiline-parser-filter.conf`.

Listing 6.3 A filter that uses a multiline parser: `multiline-parser-filter.conf`

```
[SERVICE]
  flush 2
  parsers_file ./fluentbit/multilineparser.conf    ◁─┤   We reference the
                                                        configuration file with
[INPUT]                                                 the multiline parsers in
    name tail                                           the same way as the
    path ../TestData/multiline-json-small.txt           simple parsers.
    read_from_head true
    tag multi-feed                      We identify the filter as using
                                        the multiline parser rather
[FILTER]                                than the standard parser.
    name multiline           ◁─┘
    match multi-feed
    multiline.parser multiline_Demo     ◁─┐   For all parsers, multiline or
    multiline.key_content log      ◁──────┤   basic, we link the configurations
    buffer on     ◁────┐                      via the parser name.
                       We need to be
[OUTPUT]               explicit that       As we'll be processing a structured
    name stdout        we're looking to    event, we need to define the name of
    match *            process content     the attribute.
                       from the buffer.
```

Unlike in the chapter 4 use case, where we had to support multiple possible log formats, we can still do this here by separating the parser names with a comma. We're applying a custom use case, so the likelihood of needing to identify the best-fit parser is relevant.

The part of multiline filtering that is distinctly different from a conventional parser is how the configuration is expressed in the parser file. Both simple parsers and multiline parsers can coexist in the same configuration file. The question is how to differentiate the two. The simple answer is that the configuration block is denoted by `[MULTILINE_PARSER]` rather than `[PARSER]`. Our example configuration includes a normal parser (`[PARSER]`) definition, which we don't use.

The multiline parser definition has the `name` attribute like a normal parser, linking the configuration to the plugin in our pipeline. Then we identify the parser implementation type using the `type` attribute, which identifies the type of parser that will be used to process the lines. Today, only the `regex` parser can be used. We can also set a `flush_timeout` in the filter and the number of milliseconds. We have multiple `rule` definitions. The rules have three parts, each part bounded by double quotes:

- The state name for this rule. The first state is denoted as `"start_state"`.
- The expression to be applied confirms that the line matches what is expected. This needs to match the entire line's content.
- The next state allows us to define different formats. If the line formatting matches the expression, the parser assumes that it is the end of the multiline.

As previously mentioned, it is possible to provide multiple parsers by having explicit definitions of the log structure. As a result, the parser can more easily fail a parser and try the next one on the list. The tradeoff is that the more advanced the regex is, the more compute effort is needed. Going through multiple parsers to get the right match makes for more work. See the following listing and `chapter6/fluentbit/multilineparser.conf`.

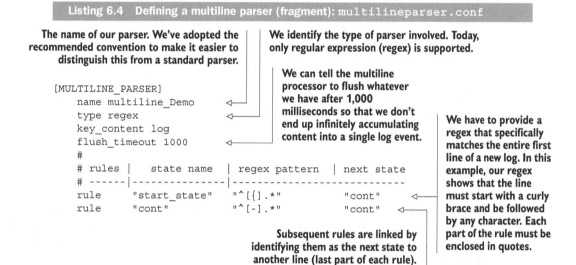

Listing 6.4 Defining a multiline parser (fragment): `multilineparser.conf`

The name of our parser. We've adopted the recommended convention to make it easier to distinguish this from a standard parser.

We identify the type of parser involved. Today, only regular expression (regex) is supported.

We can tell the multiline processor to flush whatever we have after 1,000 milliseconds so that we don't end up infinitely accumulating content into a single log event.

We have to provide a regex that specifically matches the entire first line of a new log. In this example, our regex shows that the line must start with a curly brace and be followed by any character. Each part of the rule must be enclosed in quotes.

```
[MULTILINE_PARSER]
    name multiline_Demo
    type regex
    key_content log
    flush_timeout 1000
    #
    # rules | state name | regex pattern | next state
    # ------|------------|----------------|-----------
    rule    "start_state"  "^[{].*"         "cont"
    rule    "cont"         "^[-].*"         "cont"
```

Subsequent rules are linked by identifying them as the next state to another line (last part of each rule).

Before running this scenario, we might find it useful to temporarily comment out the filter definition. This way, we'll see the events if the filter doesn't apply the necessary changes. From the `chapter6` directory, run the following command:

```
fluent-bit -c fluentbit/multiline-parser-filter.conf
```

The outcome is that every line from the source file generates a single Fluent Bit event, with no consolidation of lines that belong together. It might be worth counting the number of output log events. If we comment on the filter, we can uncomment it and run the scenario again with the same command:

```
fluent-bit -c fluentbit/multiline-parser-filter.conf
```

When we run the scenario, we'll still see carriage-return characters being output, but the recombined lines are single log events. We know this because of the absence of the metadata, such as the timestamp and tag at the start of the line output. Now the outputs look like this:

```
[8] multi-feed: [[1712849159.215674039, {}],
  {"log"=>"{"msg" : "I think my neighbor is stalking me
-  as she has been googling my name on her computer.
-   I saw it through my telescope last night.",
-   "name" : {"firstname": "Slarti", "surname":"Bartfast"},
-  "age": 75}"}]
```

What is clever about this is that in addition to joining the lines, the filter removed the records from the buffer that have been merged. This is the overhead of using a filter rather than the parser on the input.

The nature of regular expressions means it is a lot harder to define a parser that uses a condition to determine when a multiline event has ended. For example, if we assume that all lines are part of a record until a line starting with END is found, it is a lot harder. We can easily see this by modifying our configuration slightly with the following changes to the `multiline-parser-filter.conf`:

- Change the input path from `../TestData/multiline-json-small.txt` to `../TestData/multiline-json-small2.txt`. If we look at this modified file, we see that we've added terminations to the records with the word END.
- Change the multiline parser reference from `multiline_Demo` to `multiline_Demo2`.

The critical difference is that the filter definition is the second rule (the parser expression is `"^(?!END)"`), which essentially means any content as long as it doesn't start with END. So, encountering a line that breaks the regex, we start the filter with `start_state` again. But because our regular expression is not consuming and tokenizing content, we still have the string END, so it ends up remaining an event in the buffer. If we run the configuration, we'll get output like this:

```
[6] multi-feed: [[1712849159.215674039, {}], {"log"=>"
  {"msg" : "Maybe if we start telling people the brain is an
  app they will startusing it.",
  "name" : {"firstname": "Trillian", "surname":"Astra"},
  "age": 25}"}]
[7] multi-feed: [[1712849159.215685992, {}], {"log"=>"END"}]
```

Note that log event 7 exists with the word END. We can apply a second stage of filtering to address this event if necessary. But as we can see, it is more challenging because of the inclusive nature of regex syntax when matching.

6.7 *Custom parsing*

Eventually, we'll encounter a situation where a predefined Fluent Bit parser won't be able to address our needs. When we can't use predefined parser expressions, we need to look elsewhere for our regular expressions or define them ourselves.

NOTE Plenty of published resources exist for predefined regex expressions, such as recognizing credit card numbers and international bank accounts. Using a proven existing regex to process a string is far quicker and more reliable than trying to develop a complex regex on our own. Appendix B provides a list of resources for testing expressions against sample data sets.

When we look at regular expressions, we see subtle variations in implementations, which roughly align with programming languages. However, a standard exists: Perl Compatible Regular Expressions (PCRE; https://www.pcre.org/original/doc/html). Fluent Bit's implementation comes from a library called Onigmo (https://github .com/k-takata/Onigmo), which is the core C library used by Ruby. Therefore, any Ruby regular expression will work with Fluent Bit; any regular expression used for Fluentd also works here.

When constructing a regular expression, we provided a worked illustration in the *Logging in Action* book (https://livebook.manning.com/book/logging-in-action/chapter-3/point-18395-240-252-1), so we're not going to revisit those details, instead concentrating on the behavior of the filter and parser when applied. In many respects, this is far more important. Depending on the settings, the original log content could be lost (addressed in chapter 3 of *Logging in Action*), so if you want to understand the debate, we recommend starting there.

This time, let's use the provided nginx parser, which can break out all the parts of the log event. But the provided nginx retrieves the originating IP address whether it is an IPv4 or IPv6. We don't want to lose that detail, but we want to retrieve IPv4 addresses, which we know are made up of four octets separated by a period. To do this, we want an additional regex on the log event to retrieve the IPv4 address. We also want to know about the agent implementation without the version-related information— Wget or Mozilla, for example. The easiest way to approach this is to have a second parser for the log:

```
172.29.139.108 - - [12/May/2023:08:05:53 +0000]
➡ "GET /downloads/product_1 HTTP/1.1" 304 0 "-"
➡ "Mozilla/5.0  (0.9.7.9)"
```

The parser needs the following:

- To retrieve the IPv4 string (and know that it is v4 and not v6) and obtain the type of agent, the following regex breaks up the string by looking for one to three digits delimited with a dot four times, which forms the IPV4.
- Next, the expression skips the data by looking for the closing (]) square bracket.
- Then the expression looks for the fourth occurrence of a double quote.

The subsequent alphabetic characters become the `agentType`. The regex

```
^(?<IPv4>((\d{1,3}(.))\d{1,3}(.)\d{1,3}(.)\d{1,3}))
➡ (((([^\"]*))\"((((([^\"]*)\")\"){4})(?<agentType>([a-zA-Z]*))
```

results in the creation of elements called IPv4 and agentType. We can verify the regular expression using any tools referenced in appendix B.

With the IPv4 extracted, we can use another parser to retrieve the first octet from it. If this octet value is 192, we know that the web traffic has come from a class C network. To configure this use case, we need to execute three parsers:

- A standard nginx parser to parse the log attribute
- A custom regex parser, which must also be executed against the log element
- A regex, this time executing against one of the extracted IPv4 attributes generated from the second parser expression

We need three filters, with the preserve_key and reserve_data set to true. If these values aren't set, we'll lose data values. After you run the scenario successfully, we recommend experimenting by selectively changing these attributes to off and observing the consequences.

The order in which the filters are defined is important, as there is a dependency between the second and third parsers. The order that is applied is dictated by the order in which they are defined in the configuration file, which we can prove by moving the third filter definition to the first definition in the file chapter6/fluentbit/nginx-log-parser.conf and shown in the following listing.

> ### Listing 6.5 Multiple parsers: nginx-log-parser.conf

```
[SERVICE]
  flush 1
  parsers_file ./fluentbit/parsers2.conf
  parsers_file ${FLUENTBIT_HOME}/conf/parsers.conf

[INPUT]
    name tail
    path ./nginx-log
    read_from_head true
    tag nginx-feed

[FILTER]
    name parser
    match *
    key_name log
    parser nginx
    preserve_key true
    reserve_data true

[FILTER]
    name parser
    match *
    key_name log
    parser myNginxSubset
    preserve_key true
```

The first parsers_file references a custom parser file. The second uses an environment variable to provide the path to our Fluent Bit installation. The remaining path references one of the supplied parser configuration files.

The filter is configured to use a parser. This attribute identifies one specific parser, which is one of the predefined parsers.

Setting the reserve_key and reserve_data to true means we will retain the original data after the filter's processing.

This parser declaration identifies our custom parser configuration rather than a predefined parser.

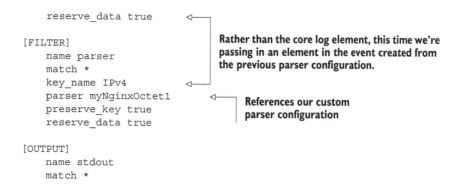

```
        reserve_data true          ◄
    [FILTER]
        name parser
        match *
        key_name IPv4               ◄
        parser myNginxOctet1
        preserve_key true
        reserve_data true

    [OUTPUT]
        name stdout
        match *
```

Rather than the core log element, this time we're passing in an element in the event created from the previous parser configuration.

References our custom parser configuration

Our custom parser file looks like the following listing (`chapter6/fluentbit/parsers2.conf`).

Listing 6.6 Defining multiple parsers in a single file: `parser2.conf`

```
[PARSER]                    ◄──┘    Declaration block start for a parser
    name myNginxSubset        ◄──┐  Defines the name that identifies the parser
    format regex
    regex ^(?<IPv4>((\d{1,3}(.))\d{1,3}(.)\d{1,3}(.)\d{1,3}))
(((["\"]*))\"((((["\"]*)\"){4})(?<agentType>([a-zA-Z]*))

[PARSER]                    ◄───── Start of the next parser
    name myNginxOctet1
    format regex                        The regular expression to be executed,
    regex (?<octet1>\d{1,3})    ◄       with the resulting value put into the
                                        event record with the name octet1
```

To execute our scenario, we need to run LogSimulator with the nginx test data using the command

```
./SimulatorConfig/nginx-log-feed-run.sh
```

When the LogSimulator has started, we can start Fluent Bit within the `chapter6` folder using the command

```
fluent-bit -c fluentbit/nginx-log-parser.conf
```

The resulting console output looks like this:

```
[1030] nginx-feed: [[1683907539.000000000, {}], {"octet1"=>"94",
    "IPv4"=>"94.23.21.169", "agentType"=>"Mozilla",
    "remote"=>"94.23.21.169", "host"=>"-", "user"=>"-", "method"=>"GET",
    "path"=>"/downloads/product_2", "code"=>"404", "size"=>"337",
    "referer"=>"-", "agent"=>"Mozilla/5.0 (0.9.7.9)",
    "log"=>"94.23.21.169 - - [12/May/2023:16:05:39 +0000]
    "GET /downloads/product_2 HTTP/1.1" 404 337 "-"
    "Mozilla/5.0 (0.9.7.9)""}]
```

As we can see, the initial values represent the tag and the internal timestamp, followed by the JSON-formatted log event. The additional JSON elements we created with our second and third parsers—`octet1`, `IPv4`, and `agentType`—appear first, followed by the elements created by the provided nginx parser, followed by the original log element, which we've told the filters to retain.

Sometimes, before we parse an expression, we want to process the element so that the complexity of the regular expression isn't compounded with escape-code characters. If the log was a JSON structure with values that needed escaping, such as quotes, we can enable the string to be preprocessed to resolve the escaped values before we start parsing, making the task simpler. We can control this using the attribute `unescape_key`, which accepts a `true` or `false` Boolean value. As our example doesn't need processing, we can set this to `false` (but could omit it, as its default state is `false`). In addition to escape characters, sometimes our payloads have special character sequences to help encode special meanings. This broader challenge can be addressed by using decoders, which we'll discuss later in this chapter.

6.8 *Processing JSON*

Fortunately, nginx can also generate its logs in JSON format. This makes it easier to understand but comes at the price of consuming some additional resources. As we've seen, when consuming a log file, the ingested log event is treated as a single string. To take advantage of the fact that the log content is formatted for us, we want to use a parser that can translate the payload into meaningful JSON data. To do this, Fluent Bit includes a JSON parser.

The JSON parser can take the log part of the event, process it as a single layer of JSON, and generate attributes in the log event for each element of the first tier of JSON. If the JSON is nested, the nested layer is left as an unprocessed structure. So, it isn't possible to take the JSON output and traverse nested structures using JSON-Path, for example. For cases such as nginx, this isn't a problem, as we can see with this log entry:

```
{"time": "12/May/2023:13:05:17 +0000", "remote_ip": "10.033.133",
➡ "remote_user": "-", "request": "GET /downloads/product_1 HTTP/1.1",
➡ "response": 404, "bytes": 341, "referrer": "-",
➡ "agent": "Mozilla/5.0  (0.8.16~exp12ubuntu10.16)"}
```

If, however, the agent attribute were formatted as

```
"agent": {"agentType": "Mozilla", "agentTypeVer": "5.0",
➡ "agentBuild": "(0.8.16~exp12ubuntu10.16)"}
```

we would need to run the JSON parser on the agent element to decompose the nested elements so that they can be referenced.

Let's build a variation of our previous use case using the JSON parser and then take the output from that to perform the regex to retrieve the first octet again. To do this, we need to define a fresh parser. The declaration for the simplest JSON parser requires only the declaration of the format attribute with the value of `json` and the name, which we can use to reference from the filter definition. We've opted for the name of `myNginxJSONParser`. Therefore, we have a simple parser file (`chapter6/flu-entbit/json-parser.conf`), shown in the following listing.

Listing 6.7   Parser for JSON conversion: `json-parser.conf`

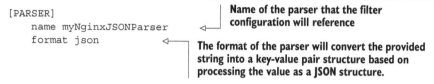

```
[PARSER]
    name myNginxJSONParser
    format json
```

Name of the parser that the filter configuration will reference

The format of the parser will convert the provided string into a key-value pair structure based on processing the value as a JSON structure.

Now we can construct our main Fluent Bit configuration. We want to reuse the `myNginxOctet1` parser, so we need to include both parser files. As sequencing remains important, we need to define the filter, which calls our JSON parser setup, followed by a repeat of the filter configuration, which will reuse the regex parser we defined earlier. As the JSON parser restructures the entire content for us, there is little to gain by retaining any previous attributes like log this time. However, we want to retain the input elements from the previous filter for the output. Our configuration should look like the following listing (`chapter6/fluentbit/nginx-json-log-parser.conf`).

Listing 6.8   Applying a JSON parser: `nginx-json-log-parser.conf`

```
[SERVICE]
  flush 1
  parsers_file ./fluentbit/json-parser.conf
  parsers_file ./fluentbit/parsers2.conf

[INPUT]
    name tail
    path ./nginx.json.log
    read_from_head false
    tag nginx-feed

[FILTER]
    name parser
    match *
    key_name log
    parser myNginxJSONParser
    preserve_key false
    reserve_data false

[FILTER]
    name parser
    match *
    key_name remote_ip
    parser myNginxOctet1
    preserve_key true
    reserve_data true
```

Here, we're referencing a parser that uses the JSON capabilities rather than regex as in our previous examples.

We're telling the filter to parse on the attribute that has been manipulated in the state in which it was received. We're not bothering to pass out the original log event's contents.

We're identifying the element in the log event to be used with the parser. This element comes directly from the JSON conversion of the payload.

Identifies one of our parsers. But this parser expects to pull only the first octet from a string that represents an IP address.

As we're parsing to obtain some additional details, this time we need to retain the data received in the filter.

```
[OUTPUT]
    name stdout
    match *
```

The result of this configuration is almost the same as that of the previous scenarios. The only difference is that LogSimulator needs to reference a different test data file. We can run the scenario with the commands

```
./SimulatorConfig/nginx-json-log-feed-run.sh
fluent-bit -c fluentbit/nginx-json-log-parser.conf
```

With this scenario running, we should see output like this:

```
[0] nginx-feed: [[1695400435.934181800, {}], {"octet1"=>"10",
➡ "time"=>"12/May/2023:08:05:25 +0000",
➡ "remote_ip"=>"10.138.60.101", "remote_user"=>"-",
➡ "request"=>"GET /downloads/product_2 HTTP/1.1", "response"=>304,
➡ "bytes"=>0, "referrer"=>"-", "agent"=>"Mozilla/5.0 (0.9.7.9)"}]
```

Note that the output doesn't contain the original log element. Because the payload is in JSON format, we know converting the payload to its constituent elements will not result in the loss of information. We can see the octet1, which has been generated for us.

6.8.1   Changing the log event timestamp

Modifying the overall log event timestamp is possible with the JSON parser. To do this, we need to extend the parser configuration to name the JSON element that will contain the date and time. In our example, this would be time. Then, we need to tell Fluent Bit how the date and time are laid out using an element called time_format. This attribute uses notation to define where each part of the structure is. Let's try adding these attributes to the configuration and rerunning the scenario. We've provided the correct configuration in a version of the parser file called chapter6/Fluentbit/json-parser.conf.answer.

> **NOTE**   Time format definitions are limited to one. So, if time is expressed in different ways within a Fluent Bit event, multiple parsers need to be applied to address the problem.

6.8.2   *Diagnosing the unhappy paths*

Regular expressions are complex, and it is easy to make an error. What happens if the parser's regular expression is incorrect? Typically, you'll see the Fluent Bit instance terminate as it tries to create the parser that is ready for use. The easiest way to see this is to remove one of the brackets in an expression, such as myNginxOctet1 in the parsers2.conf file, and restart Fluent Bit.

If the log is malformed, the parser will attempt to ingest the content. But if it fails, the parser will typically abort and leave the payload unprocessed. We can see this behavior by running a modified version of the nginx JSON scenario where we have taken a small sample of log entries and deliberately made a single modification (`TestData/nginx.malformed.json.log.txt`) that makes the content invalid. In this source file, we've also modified the dates so the day of the month increments for each record; this will make it easy when running the scenario to trace the output back to the source record. To start this scenario, use the commands

```
./SimulatorConfig/nginx-json-log-feed-run.sh
fluent-bit -c fluentbit/nginx-json-log-parser.conf
```

The `04/May` record is a good example of best endeavors, but it cannot complete the ingestion as the JSON element delimiter (comma) has been omitted after the date. So, the parser stops at that point.

For this reason, it is worth considering retaining the original payload consumed. If there is a risk of ingesting corrupted entries, that may be undesirable. There are options to spot and handle such problems; for example, we could apply the `modify` filter and use its `key_exists` condition or the `expect` filter to check for populated attributes. We'll investigate filters further in chapter 7.

6.9 Other types of parsers

We've seen the two most dominant parsers, but a couple of other parsers are available. Both follow a template similar to what we've seen.

6.9.1 logfmt

The logfmt parser is very much like the JSON parser, taking the payload and transforming the logfmt data into JSON elements. The logfmt structure works with key-value pair expressions using the equal character to separate the key and value; `key=value myLog=myEvent` would result in the Fluent Bit event containing two elements with the keys `key` and `myLog` with corresponding values of `value` and `myEvent`, respectively. Although the format has never been formally ratified, the most authoritative description is at https://brandur.org/logfmt. There are plenty of implementations of the format; for an example, see https://github.com/go-logfmt/logfmt.

6.9.2 LTSV

The Label Tab-Separated Value (LTSV) parser is more like the regex parser as we have had to provide additional information about the layout. An example LTSV string could look like this:

```
line:1 widget:gadget aKey:aValue time:[16/Jun/2024:14:55:01 +0000]
```

As with the JSON parser, we can define the field representing the event date using the attributes `time_key` and `time_format`. But, the heavy lifting comes with the attribute called `types`. Here, we need to define the name of each value (which becomes the key in the JSON internal representation) and the data type, which can be `integer`, `float`, bool, hex, or string. We could process this line with the parser configuration (chapter6/fluentbit/ltsv-parser.conf) shown in the following listing.

Listing 6.9   An LTSV parser configuration: `ltsv-parser.conf`

```
[PARSER]
    name simpleLTSVExample
    format ltsv
    time_key time
    time_format [%d/%b/%Y:%H:%M:%S %z]
    types line:integer widget:string aKey:string
```

> We've identified the value that needs to be processed as a date.

> Defines how to parse the date

> Does the heavy lifting of identifying the keys and their data types

This would result in a record being generated as

```
[[1718549701.000000000, {}], {"line"=>"1",
➡ "widget"=>"gadget", "aKey"=>"aValue"}]
```

You can see for yourself by running the simple `chapter6/Fluentbit/ltsv.conf` configuration in the download pack.

6.10   *Decoders*

Decoders are designed to address the problem of when a log entry needs to contain characters that aren't allowed as part of a name or value. For example, if we want to include a quote character within a JSON payload because the character is reserved, it becomes encoded. But when trying to process the message, encoding can get in the way of the logic. So we need to be able to decode them. For example, to carry the text "Hello\World" to carry it in the log part of a log event, it becomes encoded as "log" : "\"Hello\\World\"". If, along the way, that needs to be wrapped into another JSON structure, things get difficult. To unpick this so we can apply logic to the originally intended value, we can use a decoder. We can apply the decoder to any parser by supplying the attribute `decode_field_as` and the following values:

- Name of the decoder to use
- Payload element that the decoder should process
- Any behavior controls (optional)

If we have the following JSON as our log event where someone had tried to request a path but accidentally swapped forward and back slashes, the details will be encoded with additional slashes. But if we want to store the error in a database correctly, we need to strip back the escape slash characters.

To see how the decoder works at its best, there is a small test payload called `coded-json.txt` in the `TestData` folder. The test contains escaped and Unicode characters:

```
{"time": "1", "coded-msg" : "\\t hello", "coding-type" : "UTF-8"}
{"time": "2", "coded-msg" : "{\"key\":\"value\"}", "coding-type" : "JSON"}
{"time": "3", "coded-msg" : "\\u0077\\u0000\\u004C\\u0069\\u006E\\u0065",
➡ "coding-type" : "escaped Unicode"}
```

The time is set to be simple, so it's easy to correlate the output to the original record. To process this sample data set, we established a new parser file (`parsers3.conf`), which includes parser definitions.

To understand the differences in this scenario, rerun the same scenario multiple times. Each time we run, we will switch which parser is used to observe the difference. The code configuration remains relatively similar to the previous parser configurations (`chapter6/fluentbit/decoding-parser.conf`), as shown in the following listing.

Listing 6.10   Using a decoder with a parser: `decoding-parser.conf`

```
[SERVICE]
    flush 1
    parsers_file ./fluentbit/parsers3.conf        ⟵──┐  A new parser file with variations
                                                      │  in configuration to help us
                                                      │  understand the decoder behavior
[INPUT]
    name  tail
    path ./codedJSON.log
    tag codedFeed

[FILTER]
    name parser
    match *                                           The first parser
    key_name log                                      configuration will be
    parser noDecoder                    ⟵──┘          run against the data set.
    #parser myDecodingUnstructured      ⟵──┐
    #parser myJSONOnly                     │  A commented-out parser. We
    #parser myJSONDecodedUTF               │  want only one uncommented
    preserve_key false                     │  parser per run.
    reserve_data true

[OUTPUT]
    name stdout
    match *
```

With the core configuration defined, referencing different parsers and the associated decoders in a common file, let's look at the parser configuration file (`chapter6/fluentbit/parsers3.conf`), shown in the following listing.

Listing 6.11   Different decoder examples in a parser file: `parsers.conf`

```
                              This is very simple, so we can see that we can ingest
                              the log event as a payload without any implicit
[PARSER]          ⟵──┐        parsing (as occurs if we set the payload as JSON).
    name noDecoder
    format regex              Note that the regex pushes the content to an
    regex (?<NoDecoder>(.*))  attribute called NoDecoder so we can distinguish
                      ⟵──     it from the default attribute called log.
[PARSER]          ⟵──
    name myDecodingUnstructured    This parser continues to treat the
    format regex                   payload as a string structure.
```

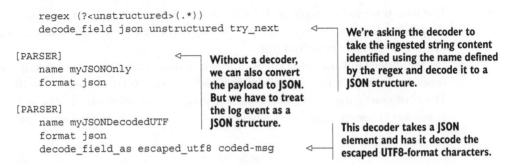

```
    regex (?<unstructured>(.*))
    decode_field json unstructured try_next

[PARSER]
    name myJSONOnly
    format json

[PARSER]
    name myJSONDecodedUTF
    format json
    decode_field_as escaped_utf8 coded-msg
```

We're asking the decoder to take the ingested string content identified using the name defined by the regex and decode it to a JSON structure.

Without a decoder, we can also convert the payload to JSON. But we have to treat the log event as a JSON structure.

This decoder takes a JSON element and has it decode the escaped UTF8-format characters.

Table 6.1 describes the differences that we observe when we run this decoder scenario. The results change as we swap the referenced parsers as previously described. The Parser column traces back to the parser declaration in the configuration file illustrated in listing 6.11 (`chapter6/Fluentbit/parsers3.conf`).

Table 6.1 Effects of different parsers and their decoders in listing 6.11

Parser	Observed differences
noDecoder	The console output looks as though no parser was involved, but rather than the log body's being attributed to a `log=>` in the output, it is `No~Decoder=>`.
myDecodingUnstructured	We'll have larger output with the log content being output to an element called `unstructured` (containing the entire log message). In addition, each JSON element in the event record's root level will be an attribute because we've managed to decode the payload as a JSON object. Because the payload is handled as JSON, the output removes one of the backslashes; it recognizes the content as escaped characters.
myJSONOnly	Because we're telling Fluent Bit to parse the payload as JSON, it includes handling escape characters. But note that the escaped Unicode string (`time =>3`) is not decoded, so the output starts with `\u077`.
myJSONDecodedUTF	When this parser is run, we see the JSON presented correctly and the Unicode string transformed correctly. As a result, the record with a time value of 3 now displays the `coded-msg` as wLine.

Let's run the scenario. It's best to start by running the LogSimulator with the command

```
./SimulatorConfig/encoded-logs-run.sh
```

Then start the Fluent Bit configuration with the command

```
fluent-bit -c fluentbit/decoding-parser.conf
```

When we've seen the logs and events rotate through and observed the described behavior, we stop Fluent Bit, uncomment the next parser (remove the #), comment out the one we've just run (prefix the line with #), and restart Fluent Bit. We've configured LogSimulator to loop slowly through the test data for a considerable duration, so we won't need to keep restarting the simulator. As we've seen, there are several ways to transform source log events to JSON to enable the targeting of specific parts of the payload.

6.11 Parsing shortcut for file inputs

We have been tailing and then parsing our inputs in our demonstration scenarios in this chapter. This means that the input plugin will serialize each log event using MessagePack (https://msgpack.org); then we deserialize them to perform the parse operation. The issue is that the process of serializing and deserializing requires computational effort and therefore can slow event processing. In addition to the serialization effort, the events received are added to and modified in the buffer storage. If the buffer is in memory, this isn't a huge cost, but if the buffer is directed to use file storage, the overhead will be more significant.

We can eliminate this overhead by directing the input to the parser for the `tail` input plugin, bypassing the need to serialize and deserialize the workload. We saw this briefly in chapter 4 when the multiline parser was used to help manage Kubernetes logs. But it should come as no surprise that we can use the basic parser the same way. As a result, we can simplify our previous configuration to become the following listing (`chapter6/fluentbit/decoding-reader.conf`).

Listing 6.12   Input using a parser: `decoding-reader.conf`

```
[SERVICE]
    flush 1
    parsers_file ./fluentbit/parsers3.conf          ⟵─    We continue with the same
                                                           parser file and parsers as in
                                                           the previous example. But this
                                                           configuration has no filter
[INPUT]                                                    definition.
    name  tail
    path ./codedJSON.log
    tag codedFeed
    parser myJSONDecodedUTF          ⟵─    We tell the input plugin
                                           to use the same parser
                                           as before.
[OUTPUT]
    name stdout
    match *
```

Run this configuration using the same LogSimulator and the command

```
./SimulatorConfig/encoded-logs-run.sh
```

Then start the Fluent Bit configuration with the command

```
fluent-bit -c fluentbit/decoding-parser.conf
```

3426686 Parsing to extract more meaning

As we see from the console output, we've successfully ingested the log contents, this time without needing a separate filter, and reducing the overhead.

Summary

- Filters and parsers have an important relationship in Fluent Bit, where parsers can be invoked from a filter definition.
- Fluent Bit has predefined parsers for common log formats such as nginx and Apache web server log files. When a suitable predefined parser isn't available, we can define our own.
- Rather than use a single filter for each parser, Fluent Bit allows us to configure multiple parsers with a single filter, offering many efficiencies.
- We can chain parsers, so the output of one parser can be the input of another. Chaining parsers can make decomposing a problem easier and allows us to reuse parser definitions.
- A JSON parser can convert text input to JSON-structured logs using the parser format option.
- Decoders allow us to handle strings that can carry encoded characters. Using a decoder makes it easy to extract characters that aren't legal within a regular JSON payload.
- Parsers aren't restricted to being used only by filters. Some input plugins allow the use of parsers during input plugin execution.

Filtering and transforming events 7

Chapter 6 looked at parsers and the filter that enables them. This chapter looks at the rest of the filters available to us. We will look carefully at filters that can manipulate the tag value, as this is central to how we route logs, metrics, and traces to different output destinations.

7.1   *Architectural context*

Figure 7.1 shows how filters fit into our logical Fluent Bit architecture.

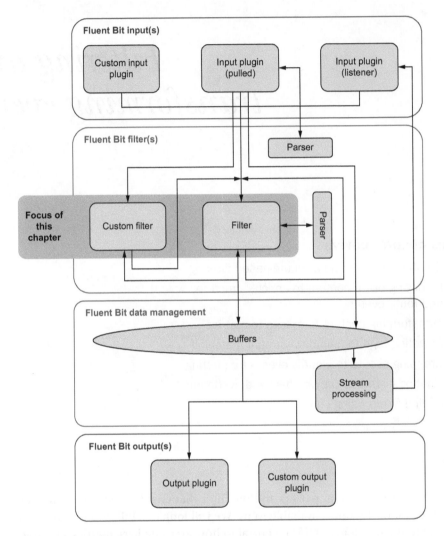

Figure 7.1   The application of filters we're going to consider in this chapter is highlighted in our logical architecture.

We can group filters in the following ways:

- *Integrate and enrich*—These filters allow the use of third-party sources to enrich or examine event data. The filters differ from input and output plugins; the data adds to an existing event, and the values it adds are predicated on existing events. Examples include these:

- *Kubernetes*—This filter accesses the Kubernetes control plane to retrieve additional information about the environment or application execution context, such as metadata about the Pod and container (an area that we took a high-level look at in chapter 4).
- *AWS Metadata*—Filters like the AWS Metadata filter can retrieve additional information from Amazon Web Services (AWS), such as instance ID and availability zone information based on the provision of data from the log event.
- *GeoIP2*—This filter can take IP addresses and interrogate a published repository to provide the geographic location associated with an IP.
- *Nightfall*—This filter uses a third-party service to evaluate the log event for any possibly sensitive data, such as credit cards and personally identifiable information (PII).
- *TensorFlow*—This filter uses machine learning to classify events based on what has been observed before.
- *CheckList*—This filter supplies a configuration data set and checks whether a value exists.
- *Extend and amend*—We extend the value of an event by using filters to extract more meaning from the event payload using parsers, as we saw in chapter 6, and using filters such as
  - `modify`—Allows us to conditionally rename, copy, and remove attributes
  - `record_modifier`—Attributes for defining black- and whitelisting of elements in the payload, as well as defining new elements
  - `nest`—Provides the means to reorganize the hierarchy of elements within the payload
- *Route and control*—These filters allow us to configure data manipulation beyond the use of parsers or control Fluent Bit performance. Filters in this group include
  - `throttle`—Controlling the throughput so we don't swamp a backend with load
  - `rewrite_tag`—Changing tags allows us to dynamically change routing
  - `log_to_metrics`—Converting payload
- *Custom*—These filters allow us to build custom logic to process the event or incorporate custom-built logic through Go, WebAssembly (WASM), and Lua. Although these filters can be used for integration purposes, we've separated them because they involve coding effort rather than configuration. We'll look at extending other aspects of Fluent Bit more in chapter 9.

Previous chapters discussed how Fluent Bit differentiates and handles the different signals (logs, metrics, and traces). It is worth noting that the filters, particularly those in the integrate and enrich group, focus on supporting log signals.

7.2 Integrating and enriching with filters

This group of filters should be handled carefully, as a slow external service could affect Fluent Bit's pipeline. Before using it, consider the performance and volumes such a service can handle, along with the resultant latency that may be introduced. We can mitigate such risks in a couple of ways:

- Implement services like TensorFlow and GeoIP downstream by having a Fluent Bit instance capture the events from the source and then pass them to a second Fluent Bit deployment. The second instance of Fluent Bit should not be competing for CPU, memory, and other resources with other services, such as a business application (which is more likely to be the case in a noncontainerized deployment). Having the dedicated resource ensures that we can configure the second instance of Fluent Bit with plenty of capacity to buffer events if the filter is not keeping up with the volume of events being received. We could implement increased caching by having more memory or caching to disk with high-performance storage. All this means that the event pipeline won't cause problems such as backpressure and that it has the capacity for more intensive processes.
- Filter out data before enrichment so we're enriching only the data from external services that will benefit from enrichment. We should enrich earlier only if the additional information helps further decision making, such as filtering and routing. Often, we look to enrichment to provide more context and support for problem resolution.

7.2.1 Directing and securing logs with GeoIP

Let's look at an example of how enrichment helps us. GeoIP translates our IP address to a physical location by taking information published by organizations such as ISPs, declaring where IPs connect to public networks. We can see this information at work when we visit the Google home page or services like MaxMind (https://maxmind.com) and IPLocation.net (https://iplocation.net), among others. We can see MaxMind demonstrating GeoIP functionality in figure 7.2.

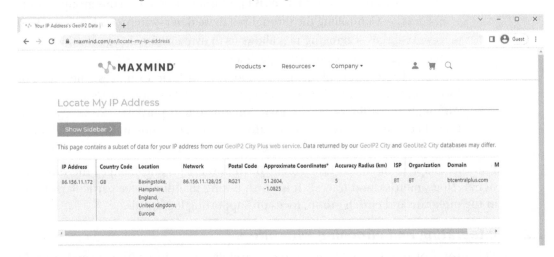

Figure 7.2   MaxMind GeoIP screenshot showing how an IP can be attributed to a physical location (in this case, a postal code or zip code)

NOTE Depending on the provider, the GeoIP data, if offered as software as a service (SaaS), may be subject to a license or subscription fee. Pricing of the data or service can be influenced by factors like location precision (such as mapping an IP to a postal code or, less precisely, to a country), how the data is being used, and the frequency of updates to the provided GeoIP data.

How does GeoIP awareness help with monitoring? We can use it in several ways:

- If our logs must handle PII data, we must respect data sovereignty. Consequently, we have to ensure that we route log events so that they remain within the rules imposed by different countries.
- IPs from unexpected locations indicate network masking through services such as virtual private networks (VPNs) and Tor (The Onion Routing). Although our firewalls may stop such traffic from hitting our applications, we still need to understand where traffic is coming from, particularly if we want to push back on what may be an attempt at denial of service.
- We can also apply the principle to internal networks as, ultimately, the process is a lookup mechanism. Unexpected IPs can indicate that internal malware is in action.
- A global organization may want to direct support activities to a specific team aligned with geography, as the support team will likely speak the local language(s) and be sensitive to local time zones and working practices. (Some countries don't define a work week as Monday through Friday, for example.)
- Some cloud services charge for data egress between cloud regions, so determining the cloud region using an IP creates opportunities to manage such data flows.

The GeoIP2 plugin uses a local database made available by MaxMind. Using a local database gives us control of performance considerations.

7.2.2 Using the CheckList filter

Although the GeoIP2 filter takes data from a commercially managed source, we can implement a similar internal control using the CheckList filter. Like the implementation of the GeoIP2 filter, this implementation uses a local file, which is loaded into memory by Fluent Bit and then queried. Both plugins have similar controls, with the CheckList filter providing additional attributes to support a more generalized use case by supporting exact or partial matching (using the mode attribute) and deciding whether to support case sensitivity of the key during lookup (ignore_case). Being mindful of the performance consideration, we can also get the query time output (print_query_time).

Let's implement a simple check against an expected list of partial or full IPv4 addresses that match those of the remote requests from our JSON nginx feed. First, we need a file containing the partial or full IPs we want to check; by allowing partial IPs, we can specify just subnets rather than every IP permutation that might be allowed. We do this by setting the mode attribute to partial. We've provided this in a file called ip-checklist.data. We need to point the filter to this file using the file attribute. The file's contents are presented by each CheckList option on an individual line, so if the checklist needs to consider whitespace, this isn't an issue, and no quotes are required.

To perform a comparison, we need to identify the event attribute to look for in the list provided. As we've already parsed the payload to JSON, we name the element from the payload, called `remote_ip`, which needs to be identified by the `lookup_key`. When the checklist gets a match, it will generate an additional payload element defined by the `record` attribute. We do this by providing the key and value in the declaration; for example, we record the key value. It is worth noting that the record value being added will be treated as JSON. As a result, a numeric value or values, true or false, need to be quoted; otherwise, they won't be handled as strings. Although this may be desirable, if we want to apply subsequent logic to the new element, we're likely to need a regex expression, which demands a string value. Doing this results in a configuration that contains a CheckList filter like the following listing (`chapter7/fluentbit/ip-checklisted.conf`).

Listing 7.1   CheckList filter: `ip-checklisted.conf`

```
[SERVICE]
  flush 1
  parsers_file ${FLUENTBIT_HOME}/conf/parsers.conf

[INPUT]
    name tail
    path ./nginx.json.log
    read_from_head true
    tag nginx-feed
    parser json

[FILTER]
    name checklist
    match nginx-feed
    file ./fluentbit/ip-checklist.data
    lookup_key remote_ip
    ignore_case false
    mode partial
    record known_origin yes
    print_query_time true

[OUTPUT]
    name stdout
    match *
```

References one of the prebuilt parsers that ensure the records that are read are converted to a JSON payload, eliminating the need for a separate filter declaration

Identifies the CheckList filter

To compare a value to a checklist, we must provide the list. This points to the file containing the values; if identified, it will trigger the addition of a new element to the log event.

If an entry in the checklist matches the contents of this element named by this attribute, the defined record is added to the event.

We can control whether the checking is case sensitive; here, we are asking that it be.

This record is added if the match succeeds. Because we've used a value of yes, we won't have any issues building further logic later.

To run this scenario, we need to run our LogSimulator from the `chapter 6` folder with the command

```
./SimulatorConfig/nginx-json-log-feed-run.sh
```

We also need to start Fluent Bit with the command

```
fluent-bit -c fluentbit/ip-checklisted.conf
```

We'll see Fluent Bit push the log events to the console as they're received and processed. We'll see output like this:

```
[12] nginx-feed: [[1683878714.000000000, {}], {"remote_ip"=>"10.033.133",
➡ "remote_user"=>"-", "request"=>"GET /downloads/product_1 HTTP/1.1",
➡ "response"=>304, "bytes"=>0, "referrer"=>"-",
➡ "agent"=>"Mozilla/5.0 (0.8.16~exp12ubuntu10.16)"}]
[13] nginx-feed: [[1683878745.000000000, {}], {"remote_ip"=>"10.4.66.76",
➡ "remote_user"=>"-", "request"=>"GET /downloads/product_1 HTTP/1.1",
➡ "response"=>404, "bytes"=>318, "referrer"=>"-",
➡ "agent"=>"Mozilla/5.0 (1.0.1ubuntu2)", "known_origin"=>"yes"}]
```

Note that the first entry (with the `remote_ip` of `10.033.133`) doesn't have an element for `known_origin`. Our checklist checks only for IPs in the range `10.4` and `10.239.186.133`. Our second example does match because its `remote_ip` value of `10.4.766.76` is a partial match with the checklist entry of `10.4`. As a result, the end of the JSON structure includes `"known_origin"=>"yes"`. As we've set the `print_query_time` to `true`, we'll also see messages on the console reporting the lookup time like this:

```
[2023/10/03 20:19:00] [ info] [filter:checklist:checklist.0]
➡ query time (sec.ns): 0.500 : '10.4.66.76'
```

To see how performance is affected, try changing the filter configuration to use the `ip-checklist-long.data` file and rerun the scenario.

> **TIP** If you have any trouble running the configuration, check whether you still have the environment variable `FLUENTBIT_HOME` set correctly and you're running the configuration from within the `chapter7` folder.

Although we've used the `checklist` filter to apply an IP-based filter that will work for internal networks, we can use it for a broad range of use cases, such as applying it to logged class paths in code for libraries or subsystems that demand particular attention. The checklist can be used to filter out log entries because they contain expected log values indicating that all is well.

7.3 *Extending and amending with filters*

There are a range of possible reasons for manipulating log events. We've already seen how to extract more meaning by breaking an unstructured text block into more meaningful content using various parsers. Although we can achieve a lot with parsers, they aren't the most efficient solutions when we have a JSON payload. Other reasons for manipulating the payload include the following:

- We need to apply attribute naming conventions so that the JSON payloads coming from different sources are consumed consistently. As a result, logic for data analysis of logs doesn't have to differentiate between sources, for example, recording log events from nginx and Apache web servers in the same way.

- Similarly, when calling a web service, we need to provide the same attributes regardless of whether the call content is being built from different sources.
- If the log entries are lengthy, we may not want to transmit all the content for each record, particularly if we're transmitting between data centers or clouds because of the data egress and network costs that could occur. So, we need to remove the unnecessary elements.

Several filters can help with these goals:

- `record_modifier`—Allows us to define a list of elements (`keys`, defined with the attribute `allowlist_key`) that the event can have. We can target removing one or more elements (`remove_key` attribute). Elements can be added using the `record` attribute, which takes a key-value pair. The filter can also be used to add a unique ID (UUID) with an attribute `uuid_key`, which takes the element's name to hold the generated UUID. The abilities to add the UUID and define a whitelisting of elements in the payload that are allowed are most valuable, as the `modify` filter can match the other capabilities.
- `modify`—Doesn't define whitelists of elements of the event but offers conditionality, `add`, `set` (add or replace), `rename`, `copy`, `remove`, and reorder (`move_to_start` or `move_to_end`) attributes. The copy and rename operations have versions (the attributes prefixed with `hard_`) that can force the operation regardless of whether the target element named already exists.

  The filter has the option of using an attribute called `condition`, which allows us to name a condition and the name of an element. If the `condition` is defined, it must resolve to a Boolean, and the filter will only execute if the result is positive. These operations include

  - `key_exists`, `key_does_not_exist`—Determines the existence or absence of a named element (key).
  - `a_key_matches`—Allows us to verify whether the key (element) exists based on the provided regular expression.
  - `key_value_equals`, `key_values_does_not_equal`—Allow us to test whether the value of the named key (element) equals an explicit value.
  - `key_value_matches`, `key_value_does_not_match`—Variations on `key_matches` that allow us to locate a key based on a regular expression and test its value against an explicit value for equality.
- `matching_keys_have_matching_values`, `matching_keys_do_not_have_matching_value`—Variations on `key_value_matches` that use a regex to identify the key's value to test. Rather than use an explicit value, we test it with another regex to determine whether there is a match.
- `nest`—Allows us to modify the payload structure easily by using an element (key) name that can be combined with a wildcard, placing the matching attributes in a subelement that will use the provided key. The `nest` filter can also implement the reverse process, taking a nested object and promoting the elements to sit under

the parent. We define whether we're demoting (nest) or promoting (lift) using the operation attribute.

7.3.1 Taking a brief look at the nest filter

The nest filter's primary use case is to help group attributes—grouping the additional metadata retrieved from Kubernetes, for example, or flattening unnecessarily complex object hierarchies. Let's look at a simple application. When demoting, we need to define the wildcard attribute, which we use to provide the name(s) of the record's attribute(s) that need demoting. Note that the wildcard character (*) can be used only in a postfix position. Then we need to provide the parent element's name, which can be a new element, such as nest_under newElementName. Typically, when we group related elements, they're likely to have a common name prefix, which may become redundant as the prefix is likely to be the parent element name. So, we can ask the filter to strip the prefixes, as in remove_prefix user_.

Going the other way, the operation attribute is set to lift. We need to identify the element whose child elements will be promoted, using a nested_under request. We can impose a prefix on the elements using the attribute add_prefix.

We've provided a simple example of promoting (lift) and demoting (nest) that uses a dummy-input-created JSON payload, which can be run with

```
fluent-bit -c fluentbit/nest-example.conf.
```

Running this example illustrates how we nest user-related attributes and promote the contents of the request child elements. As the output is to the console, we may find it useful to parse the content with a JSON beautifier; several options are suggested in appendix B. After running the initial configuration, try promoting just the path child elements.

7.3.2 Illustrating the record_modifier filter

We could fill this entire chapter by covering all the possibilities of the record_modifier and modify filters. To demonstrate the behavior of these filters, this chapter extends the scenario. We want to add a UUID to the log event in an element called myUUID. We're also going to extend the log event with the hostname. Having UUIDs can help us in several ways:

- If we see logs from multiple instances of the same application or service generating the same logs, the UUID can make it easy to differentiate the log event occurrences and to track back through a log history to a specific event, as the UUID is unique to a single log generated.
- When we send logs to multiple locations or across our IT infrastructure, we can perform reconciliation and identify the same log in different systems. UUIDs can be used as token substitution for sensitive data.

- If an application logs PII data, we could attach a UUID to that log event, record the PII data and the UUID in a single secure location, and then shed the PII attributes. If necessary, we can track back to the sensitive data by looking up the UUID.

As the modify filter allows us to set elements in the log events based on environmental values, we'll add to the log events the hostname where the log event was captured. This means setting the attribute record with the values hostname ${HOSTNAME}.

7.3.3   *Illustrating the modify filter*

We will use the modify filter to remove and rename some of the log event elements if we've previously been able to link and associate the remote_ip to one in our checklist. We need to define a condition attribute that will use the key_exists check previously described. Then, we need to define the remove attribute to identify what elements to remove from the payload, plus a rename. To add an element, we could use the add or set attributes. Given that we want to be certain that our value is set, we'll use the set operation, as the add will fail if the attribute already exists.

7.3.4   *Bringing it together*

Having identified what we need to implement in terms of the checklist, modify, and record_modifier filters, let's bring them together. The following configuration shows two new filters that were introduced (record_modifier and modify). We've opted to use record_modifier first, as we want to add additional information to all log events before we start introducing conditional operations. Then we've implemented modify with its condition, which means we remove details like the request for the IP addresses we know about, as we're interested only in whether the network traffic is flowing and how much traffic could be flowing through. See the following listing and chapter7/fluentbit/ip-checklisted-modifying-filter.conf.

> **Listing 7.2   CheckList and modify: `ip-checklisted-modifying-filter.conf`**

```
[SERVICE]
  flush 1
  parsers_file ${FLUENTBIT_HOME}/conf/parsers.conf

[INPUT]
    name tail
    path ./nginx.json.log
    read_from_head true
    tag nginx-feed
    parser json

[FILTER]
    name checklist
    match nginx-feed
    file ./fluentbit/ip-checklist.data
    lookup_key remote_ip
    ignore_case false
```

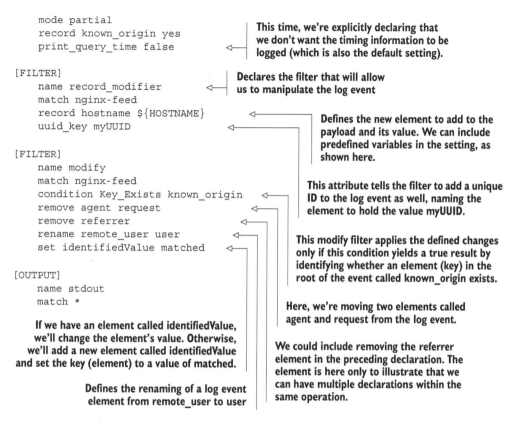

```
        mode partial
        record known_origin yes
        print_query_time false
```
This time, we're explicitly declaring that we don't want the timing information to be logged (which is also the default setting).

```
[FILTER]
    name record_modifier
    match nginx-feed
    record hostname ${HOSTNAME}
    uuid_key myUUID
```
Declares the filter that will allow us to manipulate the log event

Defines the new element to add to the payload and its value. We can include predefined variables in the setting, as shown here.

```
[FILTER]
    name modify
    match nginx-feed
    condition Key_Exists known_origin
    remove agent request
    remove referrer
    rename remote_user user
    set identifiedValue matched
```
This attribute tells the filter to add a unique ID to the log event as well, naming the element to hold the value myUUID.

This modify filter applies the defined changes only if this condition yields a true result by identifying whether an element (key) in the root of the event called known_origin exists.

```
[OUTPUT]
    name stdout
    match *
```
Here, we're moving two elements called agent and request from the log event.

If we have an element called identifiedValue, we'll change the element's value. Otherwise, we'll add a new element called identifiedValue and set the key (element) to a value of matched.

We could include removing the referrer element in the preceding declaration. The element is here only to illustrate that we can have multiple declarations within the same operation.

Defines the renaming of a log event element from remote_user to user

When we run the scenario, we should expect several new elements in each event, representing the added elements from the `modify_record`. Some log events will be far shorter where we previously matched the IP to our list, as we can see next. (To improve readability, we've replaced some values, such as `"Mozilla/5.0 (0.9.7.9)"` with X and `"Mozilla/5.0 (1.0.1ubuntu2)"` with Y.)

```
[0] nginx-feed: [[1683878748.0, {}],
⇒ {"remote_ip"=>"10.138.60.101", "remote_user"=>"-",
⇒ "request"=>"GET /downloads/product_2 HTTP/1.1",
⇒ "response"=>304, "bytes"=>0, "referrer"=>"-", "agent"=>"X",
⇒ "hostname"=>"Watts", "myUUID"=>"33667302-ee7b-4b30-90c8-795d2f68d02e"}]
[0] nginx-feed: [[1683878702.0, {}], {"remote_ip"=>"10.4.66.76",
⇒ "user"=>"-",
⇒ "request"=>"GET /downloads/product_1 HTTP/1.1",
⇒ "response"=>304, "bytes"=>0, "referrer"=>"-",
⇒ "agent"=>"Y", "known_origin"=>"yes",
⇒ "hostname"=>"Watts",
⇒ "myUUID"=>"3246d472-dab6-4d6c-ab12-29cb336de339",
⇒ " identifiedValue"=>"matched"}]
[0] nginx-feed: [[1683878725.0, {}],
⇒ {"remote_ip"=>"10.57.209.92","remote_user"=>"-",
⇒ "request"=>"GET /downloads/product_1 HTTP/1.1",
```
Note the presence of the hostname attribute and myUUID on every log event.

```
➥ "response"=>304, "bytes"=>0, "referrer"=>"-",
➥ "agent"=>"X", "hostname"=>"Watts",
➥ "myUUID"=>"b9756bbf-fe6f-4e93-ad29-6c2175fef271"}]
[0] nginx-feed: [[1683878704.0, {}],
➥ {"remote_ip"=>"10.239.186.133", "user"=>"-",        Note that the entries
➥ "request"=>"GET /downloads/product_2 HTTP/1.1",     with a remote_ip that
➥ "response"=>304, "bytes"=>0, "referrer"=>"-",        got a partial match have
➥ "agent"=>"X", "known_origin"=>"yes",                 the additional element
➥ "hostname"=>"Watts",                                 "identifiedValue"=>"matched".
➥ "myUUID"=>"f7031553-8dbe-4620-bb8c-088765de434b",
➥ "identifiedValue"=>"matched"}]
[0] nginx-feed: [[1683878708.0, {}], {"remote_ip"=>"172.29.139.108",
➥ "remote_user"=>"-", "request"=>"GET /downloads/product_1 HTTP/1.1",
➥ "response"=>304, "bytes"=>0, "referrer"=>"-", "agent"=>"X",
➥ "hostname"=>"Watts", "myUUID"=>"ebeeb4cc-ff23-4c0e-b38d-0001b2d53ce0"}]
[0] nginx-feed: [[1683878704.0, {}], {"remote_ip"=>"10.033.133.001",
➥ "remote_user"=>"-", "request"=>"GET /downloads/product_1 HTTP/1.1",
➥ "response"=>304, "bytes"=>0, "referrer"=>"-", "agent"=>"Y",
➥ "hostname"=>"Watts", "myUUID"=>"777c144d-1073-4092-bd3d-3caa5d89e6c5"}]
➥ [0] nginx-feed: [[1683878757.0, {}], {"remote_ip"=>"10.234.194.89",
➥ "remote_user"=>"-", "request"=>"GET /downloads/product_2 HTTP/1.1",
➥ "response"=>304, "bytes"=>0, "referrer"=>"-", "agent"=>"X",
➥ "hostname"=>"Watts", "myUUID"=>"192f1129-ef92-4b9a-844d-3a5c415b7df0"}]
➥ [0] nginx-feed: [[1683878720.0, {}], {"remote_ip"=>"10.4.72.163",
➥ "user"=>"-", "request"=>"GET /downloads/product_1 HTTP/1.1",
➥ "response"=>304, "bytes"=>0, "referrer"=>"-", "agent"=>"X",
➥ "known_origin"=>"yes", "hostname"=>"Watts", "myUUID"=>"91251b7b-5623-
➥ 4bd7-9f89-33cb961a9b43", " identifiedValue "=>"matched"}]
```

To run this scenario, we need to run the LogSimulator (from the chapter 6 folder) to play the log events using the commands (assuming that the LogSimulator has ended its previous execution):

```
./SimulatorConfig/nginx-json-log-feed-run.sh
```

Then we start Fluent Bit in the process with the command

```
fluent-bit -c fluentbit/ip-checklisted-modifying-filter.conf
```

7.3.5   *Testing filters*

Even with the subset features covered, we have the potential to significantly change and affect the content of events. Because some filters support performing actions based on conditions, now the events can take many more paths in processing, which means we should implement a testing regime on our Fluent Bit configurations. As the conditionality of the event increases, more strenuous testing is necessary beyond confirming that log events go from source to destination.

We've previously mentioned the value of (re)playing events through our configuration, allowing us to (re)examine how our logging configuration behaves. But we also want to verify that the event data exists and is as expected. This can be implemented using the expect filter. This filter allows us to define an action attribute that logs warnings (with a value of `warn`), results in messages (with a value of `result_key`), or even terminates (with a value of `exit`) Fluent Bit's execution. With the `action`, we can determine which element (key) in the event is the cause of the issue (`result_key` attribute). The checks that we can configure include

- `key_exists`, `key_not_exists`—Determines whether the named element (key) is within the log event
- `key_val_is_null`, `key_val_is_not_null`—Evaluates whether the named key (element) has a `null` value
- `key_val_eq`—Determines whether the value of the named key (element) matches a provided literal value

As you can see, this is like a subset of the `modify` filter in many respects. The difference is that the filter treats the event as essentially immutable.

Although the obvious use case is to help validate our logging configuration, we could also use it in production. If an application suddenly changes the way it is creating log events, we can use the `expect` filter to verify that the events are structured as expected, and take action if they're not; as a result, we avoid the adage "Garbage in, garbage out."

If you choose to include `expect` in production, we recommend that the element name provided by the attribute `result_key` be unique and ideally incorporate an error code. Doing so makes it easy to trace the issue back to a specific point, as we would like to think that application errors also carry an error code.

As previously discussed, adding new filters like `expect` adds an element of overhead. We need to allow for the additional effort or exclude this filter from production. If we don't want to use `expect` in production, then we can comment out the filter definition (a little clumsy) or, in a classic configuration, use the include feature (see section 2.4) to hold the `expect` filter and then swap the file for a stub version when deploying to production. Although YAML provides for includes, it doesn't allow us to target and position the `expect` filters. We've included an annotated example of using `expect` in the download pack called `chapter7/fluentbit/ip-checklist-modifying-filter-expected.conf`.

7.4   Routing and controlling

As previously mentioned, using the tag combined with matching is the principal means to route events to specific destinations. We may be clever with the design of our tags so that we can use tag hierarchies and wildcards. Sooner or later, we need to manipulate the tag to direct the event as it flows through Fluent Bit. The solution is the `rewrite_tag` filter. As rewriting every event would be pointless, this filter must support the means to define a condition, which is done using the `rule` attribute.

7.4.1   Using the record accessor

Often, we want to set the tag to reflect the characteristics of the log event we're processing. We may have to convert the payload to be handled as JSON structure within the log event first. This means potentially adding another parser and filter stage to our pipeline. Fortunately, some of our filters support the record accessor (record_accessor), which means we don't need to go through the process.

record_accessor allows us to reference reserved values, such as a log event's tag, along with log event data. The value being referenced is prefixed by the dollar ($) character, so the $tag would retrieve the current log event's tag. It can also be used to reference the root elements of the log payload (assuming that it is in JSON format). Then we can traverse the structure using JSONPath-style syntax. Traversing subelements is done by using the subelement name or index within square brackets ([]). In multiple levels of nesting, each nested layer is addressed by an additional set of square brackets.

The easiest way to follow this is to see how we can apply the syntax to an example log event payload. Using the following JSON, let's pull out some values:

```
{
  "time": "12/May/2023:08:05:52 +0000",
  "remote_ip": "10.4.72.163",
  "remote_user": "-",
  "request": {
    "verb": "GET",
    "path": " /downloads/product_2",
    "protocol": "HTTP",
    "version": "1.1"
  },
  "response": 304,
  "bytes": 0,
  "referrer": "-",
  "agent": "Mozilla/5.0  (0.9.7.9)"
}
```

If we used the expression $remote_ip, the record_accessor would return the value 10.4.72.163 because it accesses a root-level element. If we wanted to retrieve the value GET, we'd use the expression $request['verb'] because the request is a root element. Then we need to access the child element called verb, so it needs to be quoted inside square brackets (i.e., using the child element's name as the index to the request list of elements.

If the expression references an element that doesn't exist, no value is returned, and the logic will not work. Rather than breaking the pipeline for the event(s) being processed or worse, causing Fluent Bit to terminate the current occurrence of the logic will result in no action being taken; the record will remain unmodified, and the step process in the pipeline will be performed, creating the risk of a cascade of errors. The record_accessor capability is available in a subset of all plugins, detailed in appendix B.

> **TIP** The syntax for referencing environment variables and referencing elements within the JSON payload with record_accessor are similar. Both start with the dollar symbol ($), and both use brackets, but the environment

variable uses curly braces ({}), and the `record_accessor` uses square ones ([]). If you get these the wrong way around, you're likely to end up with the reference resolving to an empty string (unless you have a matching declaration with the same name), and then the plugin behaves erroneously.

7.4.2 Rewriting the tag filter example

Let's look at how the `rewrite_tag` filter helps us change a tag. To rewrite the tag, we first need to determine whether the tag needs to be rewritten. This is achieved through the `rule` attribute of the filter, where we provide the element to use (allowing us to use the `record_accessor`) followed by the regular expression, which should result in a Boolean result, which will determine whether to run the tag rewrite.

After the regular expression, we need to provide the replacement tag. We can also use the `record_accessor` syntax to construct the new tag. The value resulting from this expression has to be a string; therefore, we can't reference a non-string element with the accessor.

The final part of the `rule` attribute is a Boolean value indicating whether the filter should create a clone of the event with the new tag and emit (or keep) the original event as well. If we allowed this value to be `true`, we would see the event with both the original tag and the new tag; if we set the value to `false`, the event would have its tag name changed.

Let's look at an example of the definition of the new tag, as we can combine literal values with the use of `record_accessor`. Suppose that we want a new tag that starts with the existing tag (`Apps`) and extends with a dot, followed by the request's verb, the literal `.onSvr`, and the host's name—which, let's say, is `Watts`. Following the JSON example used to explain `record_accessor`, we should have a new tag that looks like `Apps.GET.onSvr.Watts`. To achieve this result, the expression should be `$TAG.$request['verb'].onSrv.$Hostname`.

As our flow becomes more complex, it's worth seeing it laid out logically. Figure 7.3 includes some flows that are not in the example configuration. These operations have black labels to help convey the value of structured tag names.

We have also altered our current IP checklist example so that the log events we route to one output will have some of the attributes removed and those on the other path are kept. To minimize setup effort rather than use PagerDuty and OpenSearch, as the figure illustrates, we will use the console for PagerDuty and a file for OpenSearch. We'll be able to recognize which is which because the console includes outputting the tag. In the real world, such a configuration is plausible, as we want to share enough information in our alerting channels to give the recipient a sense of the problem they need to attend to. However, for operational postmortems and deeper problem analysis, we need to provide a richer level of information. See listing 7.3 and `chapter7/fluentbit/ip-checklist-modified-routed-filter.conf`.

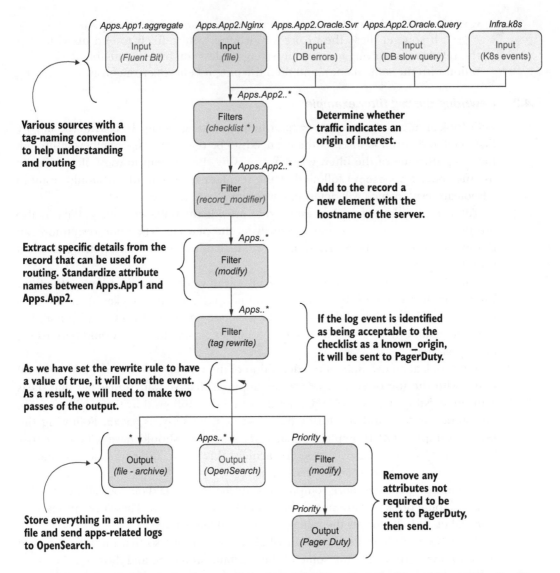

Figure 7.3 A visualization of our route-controlled output as it follows the logical flow of the configuration. The tag names applied or matched are in italics above the process. The process step includes the type and the plugin.

Listing 7.3   Tag rewriting: `ip-checklist-modified-routed-filter.conf`

```
[SERVICE]
  flush 1
  parsers_file ${FLUENTBIT_HOME}/conf/parsers.conf

[INPUT]
    name tail
    path ./nginx.json.log
```

Reuses our log feed to drive the log event processing

```
        read_from_head true
        tag Apps.App2.Nginx
        parser json
```

Adapts a more structured tag
naming that correlates with
figure 7.3 (visualization of our
route-controlled output)

```
[FILTER]
    name checklist
    match Apps.App2.*
    file ./fluentbit/ip-checklist.data
    lookup_key remote_ip
    ignore_case false
    mode partial
    record known_origin yes
```

Enriches the locally
captured log events with our
hostname and unique ID

```
[FILTER]
    name record_modifier
    match Apps.App2.*
    record hostname ${HOSTNAME}
    uuid_key myUUID
```

Renames attributes that have been
sourced from the file and from other
systems, as shown in figure 7.3
(visualization of our route-
controlled output)

```
[FILTER]
    name modify
    match Apps.*
    rename remote_user user
    rename widget gadget
```

Renames an element that doesn't exist,
which helps us see how the filter handles
such problems

```
#[FILTER]
#    name stdout
#    match Apps.*
```

Uses the stdout plugin as a filter to help
with debugging a configuration, but we
don't want this feature in production

```
[FILTER]
    name rewrite_tag
    match Apps.*
    rule known_origin ^(yes) priority true
    log_level debug
```

If the element known_origin is found
and has the value of yes, we'll change
the tag to priority. But we also want
to retain an original copy of the
event, so we set the keep to true.

```
[FILTER]
    name modify
    match priority
    remove agent
    remove request
    remove referrer
    set known_origin matched
```

The log level doesn't have to be
configuration-wide. We can
target a specific operation.

Only for the log events with the tag
priority, as this filter is about tuning
the payload for the destination

```
[OUTPUT]
    name stdout
    match priority
```

Removes several unwanted elements
from the payload

```
[OUTPUT]
    name file
    match Apps.*
    path .
    file Apps-all.txt
```

The value yes isn't best for the reader, so let's
change the value. If it doesn't exist, it will be added.

Replaces OpenSearch, as shown in figure 7.3
(visualization of our route-controlled output)

Replaces the PagerDuty shown in figure 7.3
(visualization of our route-controlled output)

7.4.3 *Explicitly including and excluding events with grep*

The approaches to defining conditions we've seen so far have been constrained to single expressions. The grep filter allows us to define multiple conditions to filter out events from the pipeline. When we define multiple conditions (available since Fluent Bit v2.1), we also need to define how the result of each condition is combined:

- A logical and operation (all values need to be a positive result for the filter to be applied).
- A logical or (any of the values need to have a positive result for the filter to apply).
- A third way to combine the results, known as legacy. The logical operator depends on whether the expression is inclusive (resulting in a logical and) or excluding (resulting in a logical or).

The expressions are defined with the attribute regex (for inclusive expressions) followed by the element name to apply a defined regular expression. The excluding expression is defined using the attribute exclude combined with the named element and a regular expression against that element's value. We can define the logical operation with the attribute logical_op with the values and, or, or legacy as long as we don't mix regex and exclude attributes. If regex and exclude are used together, the attribute logical_op can't be used, as the logical operation implicitly uses the and behavior.

We've provided a file called chapter7/Fluentbit/grep-examples.conf, which is made up of six dummy inputs generating the same JSON log event, each using a different tag, followed by a grep filter being matched to one of the inputs. Each filter provides a different combination of regex and exclude attributes. Try reviewing the complete configuration and determining which tagged logs will reach the console. A fragment of the configuration follows.

> **Listing 7.4 The grep filter: grep-examples.conf (fragment)**

```
[SERVICE]
  flush 1
  parsers_file ${FLUENTBIT_HOME}/conf/parsers.conf

[INPUT]
    name dummy
    dummy {    "time": "12/May/2023:08:05:52 +0000",
➥ "remote_ip": "10.4.72.163",
➥ "remote_user": "-",
➥ "request": {"verb": "GET",
➥ "path": "/downloads/product_2",
➥ "protocol": "HTTP",
➥ "version": "1.1" },
➥ "response": 304}
    tag dummy1
```

```
#
# Additional dummy declarations with the same payload but with
# different tags can be seen in the full configuration
#

[FILTER]
  name grep
  match dummy1
  regex request['protocol'] ^(HTTP)
  regex remote_ip (11)
  logical_op or
#
# Additional filters with various combinations of regex, exclude, and
# logical_op can be seen in the configuration file - each filter only
# acts on a single input
#

[OUTPUT]
    name stdout
    match *
```

Testing a nested element called protocol, which is a child element to request to determine whether it contains the string HTTP

As all our conditions are the same type (regex), we can define which logical operator will combine the condition results.

After reviewing the full configuration, we need to find out which tagged inputs will pass through the filters. Run the configuration using the command

```
fluent-bit -c fluentbit/grep-examples.conf,
```

We see that the input log events with tags dummy1, dummy4, and dummy6 reach the console. The other dummy sources will have been filtered out. Let's look at how the results produced an outcome:

- dummy1—Succeeds, as it needs the protocol to be HTTP (true) or the remote_ip to contain the value 11 (false). Combining these two values with a logical or, we get a positive outcome.
- dummy2—Fails, as the protocol needs to have a value of HTTP (true), and the remote_ip must include the value 11 within it (false). However, the remote_ip does not have such a value; the operation is a logical and, requiring both to be true to pass the filter.
- dummy3—Fails. as it requires the protocol to be HTTP (true) or the remote_ip to include the number 11 (false), and we are using a logical or. As one of the regex expressions is true, the overall outcome of the regex stage is true. But we have to consider that the expressions have the exclude declaration, which in effect is a logical not operation, thereby eliminating the response.
- dummy4—Succeeds, as it requires the protocol to be HTTP (true) and the remote_ip to include the number 11 (false). We are using a logical or operation, resulting in a false result. But we must consider that the expressions use exclude, which in effect is a logical not operation. As a result, the false from the and becomes true.

- dummy5—Fails, as the `protocol` is `HTTP` (true) and `remote_ip` contains `11` (false). We need to consider the `exclude`, which affects only the `protocol`'s result, making it `false`. With no explicit logical operation defined, an implied and should be used, producing a `false` result.
- dummy6—Succeeds, as the `protocol` is `HTTP` (true) and `remote_ip` contains `11` (false). But this time, we apply `exclude` to the `remote_ip`, which was already `false`, so it is now `true`. As we have a logical and implied with both values positive, we get an overall positive outcome.

If you'd like to test yourself, see what happens if the `remote_ip`'s first octet changes to `11`.

7.5 Controlling events

We've seen how we can manipulate and direct the log events. The remaining option for controlling behavior is throttling the log throughput so that we don't experience errors, or worse, the destination accepts and dumps data.

7.5.1 throttle

Throttling allows us to control the rate at which log events are released from Fluent Bit. Throttling is controlled by defining the number of events per period (`rate`). The input is calculated as an average set by the `window` attribute with the number of `intervals`. (Chapter 8 looks more deeply into time windows.) When throttling kicks in, events start being dropped to ensure that the rate set is not exceeded. Let's look at a simple scenario in which a `dummy` input generates events at a rate of five per second. But we will throttle the throughput at two events (`rate`) every two seconds (`interval`), with the message dropping being dictated by the average over a 6-second period (`window`). We'll see the consequences of throttling immediately. We can also switch on `print_status`, which will tell us what is being calculated. Our configuration should look like the following listing and is available in `chapter7/fluentbit/throttle-demo.conf`.

Listing 7.5 Example of throttling: `throttle-demo.conf`

```
[SERVICE]
  flush 10

[INPUT]
    name dummy
    copies 5          ⟵  Defines the number of
    rate 1                 copies per second to send
    dummy {"message":"dummy"}
    tag throttle_demo

[FILTER]
    name throttle     Defines the number of events
    match *           per interval to allow
    rate 2        ⟵
    window 3      ⟵  Defines how many intervals to
                       calculate the average over
```

```
        interval 2s
        print_status true

[OUTPUT]
        name stdout
        match *
```

The length of the interval using
standard Fluent Bit time notation

Switches print status on so we can
see whether throttling is affected

We can run this scenario with the command

```
fluent-bit -c fluentbit/throttle-demo.conf
```

Setting the `print_status` flag tells Fluent Bit to output messages like this:

```
[ info] [filter:throttle:throttle.0] 1718567870:
⇒ limit is 2.00 per 2s with window size of 3,
⇒ current rate is: 2 per interval
```

As the `dummy` plugin doesn't include an incremental counter, we can't see which events are being dropped. Throttling prevents backend systems from being overwhelmed by events, but there are some limitations. The most significant is that no rules govern which events are dropped and which ones are kept. Given the arbitrary nature of the throttle, we could lose important error logs. We can do a couple of things to limit this risk or at least know when potential risk exists:

- Fluent Bit's logging is captured, and we filter the logs to capture when Fluent Bit reports we're sending the maximum allowed messages (rate is `x per interval`). This tells us there is a distinct risk at play.
- Separate log events are based on the log level they're reporting. Consider first filtering or throttling logs classified at lower levels in the log hierarchy, such as trace and debug and then info.
- If log loss is a sensitive subject, write all logs to a simple high-performance file store and protect the analytics platform with throttling. (Analytical platforms are likely to need rate limits.) If events are missing, we can reingest the log file's contents when things are slower.

In addition to the `throttle` plugin, Fluent Bit recently added `throttle_size`. It applies windowing techniques, but eviction is based on the size of the message or the size of an element of a message.

7.5.2 *log_to_metrics*

Applications may generate metrics-related data but emit these signals through logs. This could happen because when the application was built, it was the only practical way to emit application-monitoring values, or associating a Prometheus node exporter as a sidecar was considered undesirable. Regardless of the reason, generating metrics for Prometheus from log events is desirable.

To address this need, Fluent Bit has a plugin called `log_to_metrics`, which allows us to map or calculate values from JSON log data to provide Prometheus metrics (counter, gauge, and histogram; for details, see https://prometheus.io/docs/concepts/metric_types).

To illustrate, we'll use two `dummy` inputs to provide simulated log inputs. We'll also extract values for the gauge and histogram metric types. The counter will count the occurrences of the matched events. Each metric needs a name (`metric_name`) and description (`metric_description`). Each metric also needs a filter to be defined, which provides the `metric_mode` attribute that defines the Prometheus metric type (`counter`, `gauge`, or `histogram`). We can also include a label in the values, based on an attribute of the log message that is identified by the `label_field` attribute. The metric type dictates the additional attributes needed. For histograms and gauges, we need to identify the numeric value in the log event to use with the `value_field` attribute. For a histogram, we also need to provide a `bucket` attribute that provides a sample value size.

The plugin includes some advanced capabilities, such as defining a regular expression that includes or (`regex`) or excludes (`exclude`) log events from the measurement based on whether the element in the log matches the regular expression. The plugin can also be used in conjunction with the Kubernetes Filter plugin, which, when combined, adds labels for `pod_id`, `pod_name`, `namespace_name`, `docker_id`, and `container_name`. For the combination to be applied, the `kubernetes_mode` attribute needs to be provided. The configuration in the following listing illustrates the generation of each of the metric types, available in `chapter7/fluentbit/log-to-metrics.conf`.

Listing 7.6   Generating Prometheus metrics: `log-to-metrics.conf`

```
[SERVICE]
  flush 1

[INPUT]
  name dummy
  dummy {"greeting ":"hello", "gauge_value":"1"}
  tag dummy.hello

[INPUT]
  name dummy
  dummy {" greeting":"bonjour", "gauge_value":"7"}
  tag dummy.hello

[INPUT]
  name dummy
  dummy {"greeting":"goodbye", "gauge_value":"3"}
  tag dummy.goodbye

[FILTER]
  name log_to_metrics
  match dummy.*
  tag test_metric_all
  metric_mode counter
  label_field greeting
```

Uses a JSON element called gauge_value for the gauge and histogram metric types. Although the figure is hardwired, the value is different for each dummy input.

We have two dummy inputs with the dummy.hello tag. But we'll use the greeting as the label to see how it affects the result of the count and histogram.

A different tag so we can see the differences in events

Identifies the metric type. In this example, we're creating a counter.

To have the count dimensioned by the greeting type, we need to identify the JSON element to use.

```
    metric_name count_all_dummy_messages
    metric_description count of messages by greeting

[FILTER]
    name log_to_metrics              ◄──┐   This counter doesn't have a label_field
    match dummy.*                        │   identified but remains a count so we can see
    tag test_metric_all                      the effect of not dimensioning the counts.
    metric_mode counter
    metric_name count_all_dummy_messages    ◄──────┐   Each metric needs
    metric_description count of ALL messages  ◄────┤   a unique name.

[FILTER]                                              The description is incorporated
    name log_to_metrics                               into the # HELP output.
    match dummy.goodbye                   ◄─────
    tag goodbye_gauge                                 We're using the tag name to
    metric_mode gauge                     ◄───        filter what is being calculated
    metric_name goodbye_gauge                         rather than a regex or exclude
    value_field gauge_value           ◄───            attribute.
    metric_description A gauge from dummy.goodbye
                                                      Defines a Prometheus
[FILTER]                          Identifies the      gauge metric type
    name log_to_metrics           metric-type
    match dummy.hello             histogram, so       For a gauge or histogram metric,
    tag hello_test_histogram      we also need        we need to identify the attribute in
    metric_mode histogram     ◄── to provide the      the log event to use, which needs
    metric_name hello_histogram   value_field         to be numeric.
    label_field greeting
    bucket 0.4                            ◄───        Histograms also
    value_field gauge_value           ◄───┐          need a bucket value
    metric_description A histogram for dummy.hello events   to control the
                                                      sample size.
[OUTPUT]
    name prometheus_exporter                          Identifies the numeric
    match *                                           field in the log event to
    host 0.0.0.0                                      be used in the histogram
    port 9885
```

To run the scenario and see the results, we can start Fluent Bit with the command

```
fluent-bit -c fluentbit/logs-to-metrics.conf
```

Then we can use the `PrometheusGet` configuration in the `chapter 7` collection provided in the Postman configurations or the following curl command:

```
curl -s http://127.0.0.1:9885/metrics
```

The result appears something like this (depending on how quickly we execute the command):

```
# HELP log_metric_counter_count_dimensioned count of messages by greeting
# TYPE log_metric_counter_count_dimensioned counter
log_metric_counter_count_dimensioned{greeting="bonjour"} 12
log_metric_counter_count_dimensioned{greeting="goodbye"} 13
```

```
log_metric_counter_count_dimensioned{greeting="hello"} 12
# HELP log_metric_counter_count_all_messages count of ALL messages
# TYPE log_metric_counter_count_all_messages counter
log_metric_counter_count_all_messages 37
# HELP log_metric_gauge_goodbye_gauge A gauge from dummy.goodbye
# TYPE log_metric_gauge_goodbye_gauge gauge
log_metric_gauge_goodbye_gauge 3
# HELP log_metric_histogram_hello_histogram A histogram
➡ for dummy.hello events
# TYPE log_metric_histogram_hello_histogram histogram
log_metric_histogram_hello_histogram_bucket{le="0.4",greeting="bonjour"} 0
log_metric_histogram_hello_histogram_bucket
➡ {le="+Inf",greeting="bonjour"} 12
log_metric_histogram_hello_histogram_sum{greeting="bonjour"} 84
log_metric_histogram_hello_histogram_count{greeting="bonjour"} 12
log_metric_histogram_hello_histogram_bucket{le="0.4",greeting="hello"} 0
log_metric_histogram_hello_histogram_bucket{le="+Inf",greeting="hello"} 13
log_metric_histogram_hello_histogram_sum{greeting="hello"} 13
log_metric_histogram_hello_histogram_count{greeting="hello"} 13
```

As we can see from this output, the various metrics are generated and dimensioned by the greeting value from the log event.

> **WARNING** There are recommended practices for developing and defining metrics for Prometheus. But, the number of dimensions (also referred to as *cardinality*) of the metrics is most critical, as it can affect Fluent Bit's behavior as a Prometheus exporter. Each dimension will result in additional values being collected and calculated. Be careful about the number of possible values that could appear in the JSON element identified with the `label_field` attribute.

7.5.3 *Advanced use of matching*

The use of the match attributes in all the plugins isn't strictly part of the filter plugins but is sufficiently related to discuss here. We explored typical uses of the `match` attribute when looking at the output plugins. As we've seen, we can use absolute or partial tag names with wildcards to filter which events are processed by a plugin. The most advanced possibility for a match incorporates regular expressions. In this context, we can look at regex as an advanced form of wildcarding insofar as we can bound the match more precisely but still allow some variety.

Considerations when using regex

When using regex, we need to consider the performance implications. A regular expression can be computationally demanding to execute. As we're effectively applying the expression against all events in the pipeline, it can have a detrimental effect on performance. Therefore, we should be cautious with their use. The more complex the expression is, the greater the compute effort. In the worst case, it may be worth considering a wildcard use case in a `rewrite_tag` filter. The website https://www.regular-expressions.info highlights some pitfalls that make expressions particularly horrible.

In addition, regular expressions that become complex can be difficult to understand and maintain. It would be easy to assert that log structures rarely change, so maintenance needs are low. But remember that someone may introduce something to a log that we never expected, and this something can break the expression. We may be processing a JSON-like log event, and someone adds a log reporting that some JSON they received is malformed and including the JSON, which could easily break our expression. Although regex is created for its brevity, as with all things, we're trading the ability to manage unexpected/unhappy scenarios with coding the processing. We're not suggesting not using regex. We're saying you should imagine how well a less-experienced colleague might react if they must make a change. If the right answer is complex, describe how you expect the regex to achieve a match, or any specific constraints or assumptions the regex has, or break the expressions into several steps.

To use a regular expression for matching, rather than the normal `match` attribute, we use the attribute `match_regex` and then provide a regular expression. Let's take a hypothetical situation to see this in action. Development teams have agreed they'll postfix the value that will be treated as the tag with the error level. In the Fluent Bit pipeline, we're interested only in errors and warnings. The problem is complicated by the fact that some developers have interpreted the log level as a numeric value, with error being 1, warning being 2, and so on.

We could address this by having an output plugin for each log level we're interested in, but that could present ongoing maintenance problems as we need to apply configuration changes to multiple outputs. Using the `match_regex`, we can explicitly target outputs that are postfixed with the log levels wanted, which we've done in the following example. We have multiple `dummy` input plugins generating events with tags that have log level postfixes that differ by using both word and numbered levels. Some of these events aren't wanted. We see the error and warning log level events when we run this listing (`chapter7/fluentbit/regex-match.conf`).

Listing 7.7 Matching using regex: `regex-match.conf` (fragment)

```
[SERVICE]
  flush 1

[INPUT]
  name dummy
  dummy {"message":"an ERROR message using a numeric code"}
  tag myTag.1

[INPUT]
  name dummy
  dummy {"message":"an ERROR message"}
  tag myTag.error

[INPUT]
  name dummy
```

> **We've omitted additional combinations of dummy outputs, but the GitHub/download-pack version of this configuration contains additional combinations that exclude or include them.**

```
   dummy {"message":"a warning message using numeric code"}
   tag myTag.2

[INPUT]
   name dummy
   dummy {"message":"an info message using numeric code"}
   tag myTag.3
```

◁── We've omitted additional combinations of dummy outputs, but the GitHub/download-pack version of this configuration contains additional combinations that exclude or include them.

```
[OUTPUT]
   match_regex myTag.(error|warn|1|2)
   name stdout
   format json
```

◁── Our regular expression that will permit tagged events starting with myTag with the value error, warn, 1, or 2

Let's run the configuration with the command

```
fluent-bit -c fluentbit/regex-match.conf
```

We can expect to see output like this:

```
[{"date":1702639498.957197,"message":
   "an ERROR message using a numeric code"}]
[{"date":1702639498.95723,"message":"an ERROR message"}]
[{"date":1702639498.957239,"message":
   "a warning message using numeric code"}]
```

Experiment with this configuration further by changing the dummy inputs to generate other variations, such as events tagged with .err, .warning, debug, and 5. Then tune the regular expression to get a subset of logs going to the console as before. We've provided an example configuration in chapter7/fluentbit/regex-max-answer.conf.

7.6   *Custom filtering with Lua*

The filters we've examined are potent and easy to work with because they're entirely configuration driven. The downside is that there are limits to what problems they can solve. Sometimes, we need to drop into a coding approach to our log event processing. Examples where Lua can really help are

- When performance is critical, and the plugin approach to manipulating the event uses multiple filters or a single filter with multiple parsers, we can implement the transformation using a single Lua filter more efficiently.
- Performing additional computational logic that existing filters can't address, such as transforming date formats, considering whether they're using a time zone or shifting for daylight saving time.
- Implementing data masking so sensitive values can be safely hidden. This is particularly helpful for uncommon data formats where we can't simply use a predefined utility.

7.6.1 Background of Lua

To understand how Lua can help us, the possible drawbacks of using it, where we can see its use, and how we can understand the syntax more, it's worth looking at the background of the language. Lua is a language that looks a bit like a blend of C (relative simplicity) and Ruby (syntax) that is easy to incorporate into other language runtimes, such as those written with C. Lua can be run as a purely interpreted language or with the use of a just-in-time (JIT) compiler (LuaJIT; https://luajit.org), converting the code to a binary on the fly as needed. Fluent Bit uses the JIT compiler to run Lua scripts. An efficient language, a good JIT compiler, and a well-written script can produce good performance, although not as fast as code already compiled to a native binary, and the JIT will always represent overhead. This makes it ideal for custom logic for context-specific filtering expressions that should be aligned to a configuration, not the core Fluent Bit codebase.

> **NOTE** Lua (Portuguese for *moon*) has been around since 1993 due to work by the Department of Computer Graphics Technology Group at Pontifical Catholic University in Rio (PUC-Rio). The governance and upkeep of the language are now performed by the Lua Lab research laboratory, which still has connections to PUC-Rio.

Using Lua as part of Fluent Bit may seem out of place, as it isn't the best-known language. The TIOBE language index (https://www.tiobe.com/tiobe-index) currently has it sitting in 26th place, behind languages such as Lisp. Although it may not be a well-known language, it does pop up regularly in the cloud-native community. Lua is supported as a plugin option for Apache APISIX (https://mng.bz/XVqp) and Envoy for HTTP filtering. Outside the Cloud Native Computing Foundation (CNCF) ecosystem, the well-known Kong API gateway (https://mng.bz/yoZy) supports Lua. Nginx has a Lua module (https://mng.bz/M19o) used by OpenResty, and Vector (https://mng.bz/aVmo) from Datadog as another tool for running observability and monitoring pipelines.

Given these examples, Lua's early associations with graphics appear in some big-name games, such as *World of Warcraft* as a scripting tool, and the game *Angry Birds* is implemented primarily with Lua. It shouldn't be a surprise to hear that Lua is easy to embed in C-based applications, and despite its use, JIT compilation is performant.

Lua and the JIT compiler are provided as open source, so their use is unrestricted. In the unlikely event that you need to run the solution on a less common OS or chipset, such as Tizen and FreeRTOS, you can do so as long as you have a C compiler build your specific binaries.

> **TIP** To learn more about Lua and its history, try https://www.lua.org/history .html. For more on Lua's gaming success, see https://mng.bz/gA7x.

7.6.2   Implementing a Lua filter

The best way to see Lua work is to implement a simple script. Fluent Bit includes some basic samples in the master branch of its GitHub repository (https://mng.bz/5OoZ), although these samples are minimal. We will produce a script that counts the number of root elements in the log event and adds the result back into the log event. We will also print the element names (keys) to see what data Lua can access.

Lua is typically and best handled as a separate script, similar to how parsers are handled. Fluent Bit invokes the Lua script with the three parts of a log event—timestamp, core record, and tag—and expects a code, timestamp, and record back. Note that we can't return the tag because manipulating the tag would affect the internal structures of the events managed by Fluent Bit. The code returned tells Fluent Bit about the effect of changes that occurred within the Lua script. The code is numeric (table 7.1).

Table 7.1   Response-code values and their meanings

Code	Meaning
−1	The record needs deleting.
0	All values are unmodified.
1	Both timestamp and record structures have changed, and the Fluent Bit record needs to be updated.
2	Only the record has changed, and the timestamp remains unmodified.

The timestamp follows Fluent Bit's convention of handling the value as a double (decimal) data type representing `seconds.nanoseconds`. The record is passed as a Lua table structure (name-value pairs), and if the element contains subelements, they are represented as a table, so we can use iteration and recurse through the structure. Lua tables can be indexed using the key name or a numeric value, which makes it easy to traverse and manipulate the content.

To illustrate adding values and manipulating existing ones if they can be found, we'll add the count of elements and change the attribute `remote_user` if it can be found. As a result, our Lua script looks like this listing (`chapter7/fluentbit/attribute-count.lua`).

Listing 7.8   Lua attribute counter: `attribute-count.lua`

```
local function elementCounter (record)          ◁
    -- this function can be used recursively so we can count nested elements
    counter = 0
    for key,value in pairs(record) do
        if (type(value) == "table") then         ◁
```

A local function separated from the main function called by Fluent Bit so that it can be recursively invoked to handle nested elements in the event

Lua allows us to interrogate the data structure's types. As we know, nested elements are handled as tables, so if we find something of the type Table, we should examine it recursively.

```
      counter = counter + elementCounter(value)      ⟵───┐  Performs recursion
    else
      counter=counter+1
      print(string.format("-->[%d] %s --> %s",counter, key, value))
    end
  end
  return counter                                          ┐  The function
end                                                       │  declaration that we
                                                          │  have to configure
                                                          │  Fluent Bit to invoke
function cb_addElementCount(tag, timestamp, record)  ⟵───┘
  -- we need to indicate back to Fluent Bit that the
⟹ record will have changed, but not the timestamp         ┐  Shows whether an
  local code = 2;                                         │  element exists in
                                                          │  the record
  if (record['remote_user'] ~= nil) then             ⟵───┘
    -- if the remote_user attribute exists let's change it to be Lua
    record ['remote_user'] = "Lua"        ⟵───┐  We've found an element,
  end                                         │  and we'll modify its value.

  -- add a new element with the count of elements in the structure passed
  record["element_count"] = (elementCounter(record) + 1)   ⟵──┐
                                                               Adds the count
                                                               element. As you
  return code, timestamp, record   ⟵──┐  The returned values.  can see, this is no
                                         We're not going to    different from
  end                                    manipulate the        the creation.
                                         timestamp we've set up.
```

Ideally, we would build some unit testing for our script with a framework such as LuaUnit (https://luaunit.readthedocs.io/en/latest), which is the Lua implementation of the xUnit framework. Appendix B provides details on retrieving and running LuaUnit.

With a script produced, we need to configure the filter, which results in the function's being invoked. To do that, we need to provide Fluent Bit the script's location using the `script` attribute and then the name of the correct function with the `call` attribute. By providing both details, we can combine multiple functions to use within a single script file. Combined with the `name` and `match` attributes, we have the minimum footprint to invoke a Lua script.

This minimum set of configurations is enough to run the script, but if the script encounters an error, Fluent Bit will terminate. During development, this is helpful, but in production, it represents a real problem. We can overcome it with the `protected_mode` attribute, which protects Fluent Bit from crashing if Lua experiences a problem when set to `true`. It is worth considering configuring this attribute using an environment variable. This way, we're not toggling the value back and forth when committing changes to Git—something that is easy to overlook. See the following listing and `chapter7/fluentbit/lua-filter-example.conf`.

Listing 7.9 Lua invocation config: `lua-filter-example.conf`

```
[SERVICE]
  flush 1

[INPUT]
    name dummy
    dummy {"time": "12/May/2023:08:05:52 +0000",
"remote_ip": "10.4.72.163",
"remoteuser": "-",
"request": {"verb": "GET",
"path": "/downloads/product_2",
"protocol": "HTTP","version": "1.1"},
"response": 304}
    tag dummy1
```

Note the difference in how we named the remote user element in dummy1 and dummy2. This has consequences for the execution of Lua code.

```
[INPUT]
    Name dummy
    dummy {"time": "12/June/2023:08:05:52 +0000",
"remote_ip": "10.4.72.163", "remote_user": "-",
"request": {"verb": "GET",
"path": " /downloads/product_2",
"protocol": "HTTP", "version": "1.1"},
"response": 304,
"another_root_element" : "horrah",
"why" : "just so the counter varies"}
    tag dummy2
```

```
[INPUT]
    name fluentbit_metrics
    tag fluentbitmetrics
    scrape_interval 15
    scrape_on_start true
```

Despite collecting the metrics today, it isn't possible to use this data within Lua.

```
[FILTER]
    name lua
    match *
    script ./attribute-count.lua
    call cb_addElementCount
    protected_mode true
```

Identifies the Lua filter

When the Lua code is kept as an external script, we need to name the script's location.

As our Lua script may contain multiple functions, we need to define the name of the correct function to invoke. The named function must comply with the definition required.

```
[OUTPUT]
    name stdout
    match *
```

Tells Fluent Bit to control the effect of any script errors. During development, it is worth switching this off.

As we're using Fluent Bit–generated data for the inputs, we can run this configuration easily with the command

```
fluent-bit -c fluentbit/lua-filter-example.conf
```

With Fluent Bit running, we see the following fragments on the console:

```
[0] dummy1: [[1696619883.228085400, {}],
 {"request"=>{"path"=>" /downloads/product_2",
```

```
        "verb"=>"GET", "version"=>"1.1", "protocol"=>"HTTP"},
        "remoteuser"=>"-", "element_count"=>9,
        "time"=>"12/May/2023:08:05:52 +0000",
        "remote_ip"=>"10.4.72.163", "response"=>304}]
-->[1] path -->  /downloads/product_2
-->[2] verb --> GET
-->[3] version --> 1.1
-->[4] protocol --> HTTP
-->[5] remoteuser --> -
-->[6] time --> 12/May/2023:08:05:52 +0000
-->[7] remote_ip --> 10.4.72.163
-->[8] response --> 304
[0] dummy2: [[1696619883.227222300, {}],
    {"remote_user"=>"-", "element_count"=>11,
    "why"-->[1] remote_user --> -
-->[2] why --> just so the counter varies
-->[3] time --> 12/June/2023:08:05:52 +0000
-->[4] another_root_element --> horrah
-->[5] remote_ip --> 10.4.72.163
-->[1] path -->  /downloads/product_2
-->[2] verb --> GET
-->[3] version --> 1.1
-->[4] protocol --> HTTP
-->[10] response --> 304

[0] dummy2: [[1696634412.729062200, {}],
    {"remote_user"=>"Lua", "request"=>{"version"=>"1.1",
    "protocol"=>"HTTP", "verb"=>"GET",
    "path"=>" /downloads/product_2"},
    "time"=>"12/June/2023:08:05:52 +0000",
    "element_count"=>11, "another_root_element"=>"horrah",
    "remote_ip"=>"10.4.72.163", "why"=>"just so the counter varies",
    "response"=>304}]
```

The remote user value hasn't been overridden. The attribute element_count has been added to the log event.

We can see the content of each of the elements (key and value).

We have the element_count attribute in the log event again, but note that the remote_user attribute has also been modified to Lua.

Looking beyond the basic invocation, Fluent Bit includes several configuration attributes for 1.x versions of Fluent Bit (predating our baseline):

- `type_int_key`
- `type_array_key`

In addition, we have two advanced options. The attribute `time_as_table` addresses the possibility of small shifts in the timestamp. The timestamp is, by default, passed to Lua as a floating-point number. However, the type conversion can result in minor rounding errors, resulting in nanosecond shifts in the timestamp. We can mitigate this by telling Fluent Bit to pass the value as a table with two key values called `sec` and `nsec`. We've illustrated this with the `chapter7/fluentbit/lua-filter-types-example` `.conf` and associated Lua code `chapter7/fluentbit/attribute-types.lua`.

The remaining significant attribute is `code`. This attribute provides an alternative way to provide Fluent Bit the Lua script to execute by passing the code rather than a reference to a script file. This makes it easy to configure Fluent Bit when using a containerized deployment, as configuring mount points or custom containers for Fluent Bit is not required. The one challenge is that we are mixing different notations, making maintaining the code a lot messier. So we always recommend developing Lua scripts and passing them using the `script` attribute, copying the script to the code option only when everything has been shaken down and proven.

The configuration in the following listing and `chapter7/fluentbit/lua-filter-types-embedded.yaml` adapts the previous example so we can see how an array is handled and the alternative approach to passing the timestamp. This time, we've replaced the `script` attribute for the use of code, allowing us to embed our script in our configuration file. Note that we've included the YAML version of the configuration here. The classic configuration syntax would require all the code to be on a single line, making it unintelligible or unprintable.

Listing 7.10 Embedding Lua: `lua-filter-types-embedded.yaml`

```
flush: 1
daemon: off
log_level: info

pipeline:
  inputs:
    - name: dummy
      tag: dummy1
      dummy: '{"time": "12/May/2023:08:05:52 +0000",
"remote_ip": "10.4.72.163", "remoteuser": "-",
"request": {"verb": "GET",
"path": "/downloads/product_2",
"protocol": "HTTP", "version": "1.1"   },"response": 304}'

    - name: dummy
      tag: dummy2
      dummy: '{"time": "12/June/2023:08:05:52 +0000",
"remote_ip": "10.4.72.163", "remote_user": "-",
"request": {"verb": "GET",
"path": "/downloads/product_2",
"protocol": "HTTP", "version": "1.1"},
"response": 304,
"another_root_element" :
"horrah", "why" :
["just"," so", " the counter"," varies"]}'

  filters:
    - name: lua
      match: "*"
      call: cb_displayDataAndTypes
      time_as_table: true
      code: |
        local function printDetails(record, indent)
          local counter = 0
          for key, value in pairs(record) do
            local elementType = type(value)
```

The last element in this dummy output is tweaked to provide an array of strings so we can see how it is passed to Lua.

Asks Fluent Bit to pass the timestamp part of the event record as a table. In doing so, we avoid any possible rounding errors due to passing numbers as floating-point values.

The code attribute, with the YAML notation indicating the use of multiple lines and making the code easier to read

```
            if (elementType == "table") then
              print(string.format("%s { %s = ", indent, key))
              printDetails(value, indent .. " ")
              print("}")
            else
              print(string.format("%s %s = %s --> %s",
indent,
key,
tostring(value), elementType))
            end
          end
        end


      function cb_displayDataAndTypes(tag, timestamp, record)
        local code = 0
        if (type(timestamp) == "table") then
          print(tag, ":", timestamp['sec'], " . ", timestamp['nsec'])   ◁
        else
          print(tag, "  ", timestamp)
        end
        printDetails(record, "")
        return code, timestamp, record
      end
```

If the timestamp is of type table, we retrieve the two elements making up the timestamp.

```
  outputs:
    - name: null       ◁
      match: "*"
```

As the Lua script is printing all the content and we're not doing anything else with the log events, we can direct all the outputs to null to be neat and tidy.

Running this configuration can be done simply with the command `fluent-bit -c fluentbit/lua-filter-types-embedded.yaml`. As the output is being sent to the `null` output plugin, the only output we'll see this time is from Lua. We should see Lua displaying the different attributes, their values, and their Lua data type. Additionally, as we're passing the date as a table, we see the timestamp being displayed as two attributes. Here is an illustrative fragment of the output that will be generated:

```
dummy1  :        1696776394        .        848984498     ◁
 remote_ip = 10.4.72.163 --> string
 remoteuser = - --> string
 response = 304 --> number     ◁
{ request =
 path =  /downloads/product_2 --> string     ◁
 protocol = HTTP --> string
 verb = GET --> string
 version = 1.1 --> string
}
 time = 12/May/2023:08:05:52 +0000 --> string
dummy2  :        1696776394        .        849111579
 remote_ip = 10.4.72.163 --> string
 another_root_element = horrah --> string
{ why =
 1 = just --> string     ◁
 2 =  so --> string
```

The first difference is that the timestamp is output as two separate parts, and we've concatenated the two values as a string with a dot between the values.

Numeric data in the JSON structure is being passed through as a numeric value.

As we recurse down the table content, we're indenting the output with additional whitespace characters.

When we pass data as an array, the elements become numerically indexed.

```
  3 =   the counter --> string
  4 =   varies --> string
}
 response = 304 --> number
 { request =
 path =  /downloads/product_2 --> string
 protocol = HTTP --> string
 verb = GET --> string
 version = 1.1 --> string
}
```

The script determines how to display the timestamp depending on setting the attribute time_as_table value to false and rerunning. See whether you can see occurrences of rounding; you need to understand how Fluent Bit sees the timestamp to do this. You can introduce an additional filter before the Lua filter that uses stdout as in an earlier example. We've provided an implementation called lua-filter-types-embedded-answer.yaml.

Summary

- Fluent Bit has a wide range of available filters covering integration and enriching, extending and amending payloads, routing and control, and custom filtering.
- Fluent Bit supports plugins that can use third-party services to enrich log events, such as obtaining a geolocation for an IP address (GeoIP) and using TensorFlow.
- Fluent Bit provides filters that allow us to manipulate events such as nesting or flattening the event data structure, renaming event attributes, and changing their values.
- The tag_rewrite filter allows us to manipulate the event tag and alter the routing of events with the match attributes. The filter supports the ability to define rules to control which events have their tags changed.
- We can manipulate the events to change their signal type, such as generating metrics from logs.
- Filters like throttle can ensure that backend systems aren't overwhelmed.
- Fluent Bit supports the development of custom filter through the use of Lua. Using Lua allows us to achieve custom filter processes without resorting to full plugin development.

Part 3

Plugins and queries

Part 3 explores Fluent Bit's advanced capabilities. Chapter 8 covers stream processing, showing how it allows us to perform queries on events and time series calculations as events pass through Fluent Bit. This gives Fluent Bit a Kafkaesque ability to perform time series calculations. We'll explore the limits of what can be queried and turn our query answers into new events.

Chapter 9 examines the idea behind processors, a feature of input and output plugins that allows us to incorporate advanced manipulation of logs, traces, and metrics. If this feature isn't sufficient to solve our input and output needs, we have the option of creating custom plugins. Each approach has pros and cons, so we'll suggest the right one for different needs.

This leads us neatly into chapter 10, which takes us through the process of building custom plugins. We apply only one of the options in chapter 9, but it is the easiest to follow and fits most of the needs we're likely to encounter. By the end of this chapter, we'll build one input and one output plugin that can work with databases such as MySQL and can be easily extended to work with other databases.

This part closes by looking at an enterprise use case in chapter 11. Although the enterprise is hypothetical, the needs and circumstances are drawn from real-world organizations. As we go through the use case, we'll explain how Fluent Bit can be applied and iteratively refine its use. We'll also link to pertinent chapters of the book so you can connect what you see to a realistic environment.

Stream processors for time series calculations and filtering

This chapter covers

- Learning some core ideas about stream analytics
- Querying data streams created by Fluent Bit
- Exploring the SQL-like syntax provided for streaming analytics
- Creating new outputs based on Fluent Bit inputs

Let's start by orienting ourselves in the Fluent Bit landscape, seeing how this chapter fits into our technology landscape.

8.1 Architectural context

Figure 8.1 gives us some immediate insights into what we can do with streaming, with the flow going back to an input. Similarly, we can output stream-processing results to the relevant output plugins. Before we can look at that, however, we need to understand the key ideas involved.

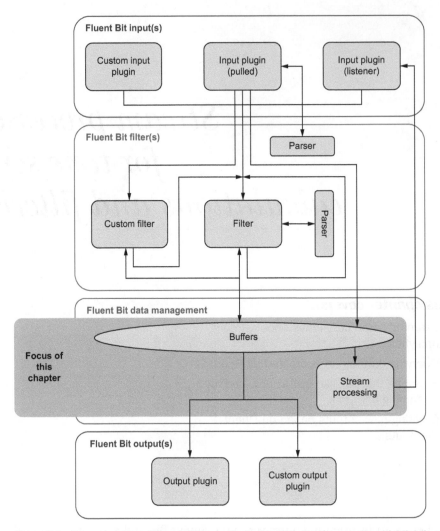

Figure 8.1   Representation of Fluent Bit from a logical architecture perspective, highlighting the aspects of Fluent Bit that this chapter will address. Here, we're particularly interested in the buffer and the stream processing that depends on the buffer's capabilities.

8.2   *Key ideas*

To understand how streaming works, we need to come to grips with a few new ideas:

- We express the logic to be applied using SQL-style syntax.
- Although the syntax is SQL-based, no database is involved. The only data pool available is the buffer.
- Our analogy for tables in the SQL syntax is a stream or a tag, and columns in a relational table are analogous to the log event attributes in the Fluent Bit event.
- We can execute our expressions against streams and tags.

As things progress and the application of streams advances, this understanding will help us appreciate the nuances. The key is that the stream processor operates as a separate subsystem triggered by data interacting through the storage interface, which is part of the buffer and abstracts whether the buffer may be configured to use the filesystem or only memory. It is important to recognize that buffering plays a role at every stage after an event has been accepted. Even if our configuration pipeline was defined as an input plugin passing to a filter and to an output plugin, the events(s) will be sent to the buffer before leaving the input plugin, and as the filter does its work, it also maintains the buffer contents. Then the output stream gets data from the buffer for processing and holds that data in its own private buffer to process.

If figure 8.1 does not accurately portray the underlying code, why not change the figure? The short answer is that the figure would become far more complex and make it visually less apparent how we should work with Fluent Bit. When we define our Fluent Bit configuration files, we define the buffer behavior as part of the `server` configuration block. Otherwise, it is transparent to the configuration pipeline with one exception: using the stream processor, as its actions are triggered from the buffer's interface.

8.3   *Basic query*

Let's start with a simple query introducing the basics of Fluent Bit's stream processing. We'll use the `random` input plugin, which operates the same way as `dummy`, but rather than allowing us to define a payload, it generates a predefined JSON structure with a random integer value like `{"rand_value"=>9130800433333918836}`, in which `9130800433333918836` is the randomly generated number. We'll set the `random` plugin to use the tag `random-num` and generate a value every second, and we'll set the flush statement to every 5 seconds. That way, we know that the buffer will have multiple values.

We'll select the random value from the tag for the expression itself. From a structural perspective, the SQL is defined in a separate configuration file and then referenced by the main Fluent Bit configuration file. If this sounds familiar, it should; it's the same approach as the one for incorporating parsers.

The stream-processing configuration defines each referenceable expression by starting with `[STREAM_TASK]`, followed by a `name` attribute used to reference the expression and then an `exec` for defining the SQL-like expression, which must end with a semicolon. If we wrote our SQL expression by selecting a column from a table, we write `SELECT myColumn FROM myTable;`, which is close to what we need for our streaming logic. Rather than a column, we want an attribute, which we know will be called `rand_value`. (the output from the `random` input plugin). Then our table is either a stream or a tag. We need to identify which type of source to use, so we need to prefix the table name with `TAG` or `STREAM`, and the name needs to be quoted (to deal with any unusual characters in the tag). As a result, our complete expression is `SELECT rand_value FROM TAG:'random-num'`. Now we have the essential elements for a configuration file that looks like the following listing; see `chapter8/fluentbit/query.conf`.

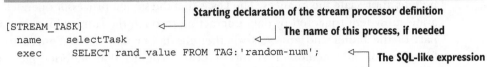

Listing 8.1   Query stream processor definition: `query.conf`

```
[STREAM_TASK]
  name      selectTask
  exec      SELECT rand_value FROM TAG:'random-num';
```

Starting declaration of the stream processor definition

The name of this process, if needed

The SQL-like expression

Now we need to bring in the main configuration file. To start, we're going to direct all
output to the `null` output plugin. Any initial output generated can come only from the
stream processor. When we define a basic `SELECT` statement, the result of the select
gets directed to stdout. So, with this configuration, the only output we can expect to
see will come from the processor. See the following listing and `chapter8/fluentbit/`
`query-streamer.conf`.

Listing 8.2   Config using query stream process: `query-streamer.con`

```
[SERVICE]
  flush 5
  log_level info
  streams_file ./query.conf

[INPUT]
  name random
  interval_sec 1
  tag random-num

[OUTPUT]
  match *
  name null

#[OUTPUT]
#  match *
#  name stdout
#  json_date_format iso8601
```

Brings the stream processor
configuration file into the scope
of the Fluent Bit configuration

This random plugin generates a log event with the
element rand_value, which has a random integer value.

As we don't want to output any of our
events to stdout, let's use the null plugin.

If we want to confirm that the stdout content is
coming from the stream processor, we can see the
values generated by uncommenting this output.

Before running this configuration, notice that we've referenced the stream processor
configuration file. There is no direct reference to the expression itself in the same way
that we linked the use of parsers. In analyzing the expression, we can derive the relationship with our buffer(s) by using the `FROM` part of the clause. Let's run the configuration.
Because we're generating the data within Fluent Bit, we only need to start the following:

```
fluent-bit -c fluentbit/query-streamer.conf
```

The output looks something like this:

```
[2023/12/18 21:25:24] [ info] [input:random:random.0]
  initializing
  [2023/12/18 21:25:24] [ info] [input:random:random.0]
  storage_strategy='memory' (memory only)
[2023/12/18 21:25:24] [ info]
  [output:null:null.0] worker #0 started
```

Startup of the console
output for the stream
processor

```
[2023/12/18 21:25:24] [ info] [sp] stream processor started
[2023/12/18 21:25:24] [ info]
[sp] registered task: selectTask
[0] [1702934725.024952265, {}, {"rand_value"=>14541635925168437956}]
[0] [1702934726.024890593, {}, {"rand_value"=>7178464768418648777}]
[0] [1702934727.024900018, {}, {"rand_value"=>7073757049224596515}]
```

Startup of the stream processor expression is logged.

The preceding output shows the creation of the `random` input, and the `output:null`: `null` handles our `SELECT` statement console output. Then (and most important) we see that the stream processor—identified in the logs as `[sp]`—has started and registered a task, which aligns with our task `name` attribute of the task definition (`registered task: selectTask`).

The behavior we see may not be what we expected. The output doesn't occur every 5 seconds in line with the flush declaration but at the same frequency as an event created by the `random` input plugin. A standard stream processor `SELECT` statement writes its result to stdout as it calculates its results. This helps us because the `SELECT` statement is a key part of the larger statement where we can create new data streams, as we'll see in section 8.7. Using only a `SELECT` statement is a convenient way to understand what is happening when we're developing our stream processors. The output looks like this:

```
[0] [1702896844.182314550, {}, {"rand_value"=>15668481522459365240}]
[0] [1702896845.182015611, {}, {"rand_value"=>10201632310136221749}]
[0] [1702896846.181963688, {}, {"rand_value"=>15632835645568553858}]
[0] [1702896847.181958820, {}, {"rand_value"=>8912068240649376789}]
```

We can confirm that the correct output behavior is unaffected by uncommenting (removing #) from the final `output` definition in the configuration file and rerunning the scenario. This time, we see that additional outputs are sent to the console in batches and formatted differently, as we can inform the output formatting used.

> **NOTE** To understand syntax, we can benefit from the Extended Backus Naur Form (EBNF) notation and railroad diagrams. The EBNF representation for the syntax is available at https://mng.bz/6YnZ. We can also use railroad diagrams (https://mng.bz/o0r2) that were built from the EBNF.

Before we move on from the constraints of the `SELECT` statement, let's explore more of what's possible to do with it, given its role in the other operations. As with most SQL implementations, several functions are available, such as `count`. Appendix B describes the available functions. We can also support using a `WHERE` clause, which can reference values in the event. Given these capabilities, let's define several new stream-processing tasks using a new file, which we can call `query2.conf`. In the configuration, we include three `SELECT` statements:

- `SELECT record_tag(), rand_value FROM TAG:'random-num';`—Extends our original `SELECT` statement so that we can see the tag name incorporated into the output as a result of selecting the function `record_tag`. So that we can refer to it easily, let's name this task `selectTaskWithTag`.

- SELECT now(), sum(rand_value) FROM TAG:'random-num';—Adds the timestamp in human-readable format to the output record. But we're also asking the query to sum the random numbers. Let's name this task selectSumTask.
- SELECT unix_timestamp(), count(rand_value) FROM TAG:'random-num' WHERE rand_value > 0;—Provides a record with a timestamp using seconds in a nanoseconds format and a count of the number of records where the random number is greater than zero. Let's name this one selectWhereTask.

Taking these expressions together, we should have a configuration file that looks like the following listing; see chapter8/fluentbit/query2.conf.

Listing 8.3   Multiple stream processor definitions: query2.conf

```
[STREAM_TASK]
  name selectTaskWithTag
  exec SELECT record_tag(), rand_value
➥ FROM TAG:'random-num';
```
Retrieves the tag value using the record_tag() function and the random value from any stream tagged as random-num because we're not using a wildcard in the tag name. The use of the record_tag is redundant, but it shows the application of the function.

```
[STREAM_TASK]
  name selectSumTask
  exec SELECT now(), sum(rand_value)
➥ FROM TAG:'random-num';
```
Retrieves the date and time when the processor is executed and applies the aggregate function sum, adding all the values in the processor's scope

```
[STREAM_TASK]
  name selectWhereTask
  exec SELECT unix_timestamp(),
➥ count(rand_value) FROM TAG:'random-num'
➥ WHERE rand_value > 0;
```
To help differentiate Now and Unix Timestamp from the result of now(), we included the UnixTimeStamp in this task. We're also counting the number of records with an element called rand_value. We're considering only events where the rand_value is greater than 0.

For these processor definitions to work, we need to amend the query-streamer .conf file to reference this configuration file rather than the original one by changing the streams_file ./query.conf statement in the SERVICE section of the configuration. In the provided configuration file, we've included the other streamer configuration files, commented out. If you uncomment the stdout plugin configuration, we recommend commenting it out again. With that change made, we can rerun the scenario using the command

```
fluent-bit -c fluentbit/query-streamer.conf
```

This time, the output looks like this:

```
[0] [1702943626.020400561, {},
➥ {"RECORD_TAG()"=>"random-num",
➥ "rand_value"=>4668199473915963542}]
[0] [(ext:0)"e\x80\xdb\x8a\x018c\xc1",
➥ {"NOW()"=>"2023-12-18 23:53:46", "SUM(rand_value)"=>4668199473915963542}]
[0] [(ext:0)"e\x80\xdb\x8a\x018\xdd\x8d",
➥ {"UNIX_TIMESTAMP()"=>1702943626, "COUNT(rand_value)"=>1}]
[0] [1702943627.020404263, {},
```

```
⮞  {"RECORD_TAG()"=>"random-num",
⮞  "rand_value"=>11887209388767628999}]
[0]  [(ext:0)"e\x80\xdb\x8b\x018\x80&",
⮞  {"NOW()"=>"2023-12-18 23:53:47", "SUM(rand_value)"=>-6559534684941922617}]
[0]  [1702943628.020396409, {}, {"RECORD_TAG()"=>"random-num",
⮞  "rand_value"=>14491574902839362681}]
[0]  [(ext:0)"e\x80\xdb\x8c\x018M\x00",
⮞  {"NOW()"=>"2023-12-18 23:53:48",
⮞  "SUM(rand_value)"=>-3955169170870188935}]
[0]  [1702943629.020415689, {},
⮞  {"RECORD_TAG()"=>"random-num",
⮞  "rand_value"=>15567006026439619077}]
```

Several things in the output are of interest:

- Where we used the `record_tag()`, `now()`, and `unix_timestamp()` functions, the values are in the JSON response, with the function as the name and the appropriate value.
- Where the `rand_value` is greater than 0, we see three lines of output, one for each of the `stream_task` declarations. But if the value is 0 or lower, we don't get an output for the `selectWhereTask`. We see a behavior more like a logical `and`.
- The `count` always returns a result of 1, not a number up to 5, which is how big the buffer should be. Unlike in SQL, which returns a count based on the entire table, the logic applies only to the current events being recorded. To overcome this, we need a window of events. We'll come back to this topic shortly.
- The `count` behavior also explains the result of the `sum`; it returns the same value as the `rand_value` because the natural scope is not the entire buffer.

It's clear from these observations that for the WHERE clause and any aggregation clauses to work, we must calculate data against more than a single event, so we need to define windows. With respect to real-world applications of `now` and `unix_timestamp`, these functions are partners, with `now` providing a reader-friendly view and `unix_timestamp` providing the same information in a format that makes it easy to perform calculations. The first and simplest use case for these functions allows us to record into the stream when events have been created or manipulated. With `unix_timestamp`, we can use comparative logic, such as the time between the first occurrence of the event or the timestamp of an important milestone in the data life cycle, such as when an order was placed. When compared with `now`, we have a sense of latency in the system, which may well be material, measuring performance against service-level agreements.

8.4 Stream-processing windows

The best way to explain the concept of windows is to use a visual analogy. Suppose that you're sitting on a moving train. The landscape you see out the window is limited or framed by the window. As you move, the landscape you see comes and goes out of sight as you pass by. What you see is never reordered or sorted; you see things as they happen in a moment of time as you pass by. Now imagine data instead of a landscape. If we tried to express this concept in a traditional relational database, we might create a query along the lines of

```
select * FROM timeSeriesTable WHERE eventTime > now()-5 AND
➥ eventTime < now() ORDERBY eventTime
```

How our window is refreshed or when our query is reexecuted depends on the kind of window being used. Fluent Bit supports hopping windows and tumbling windows.

8.4.1   Hopping windows

A *hopping window* is the easiest to appreciate; it effectively gets the window of data updated at a time frequency (hop). This type of window is sometimes referred to as a *sliding window,* as the effects can appear similar, particularly when the hops are small. The difference is that the time events that enter or leave the window can vary, making execution far more computationally intensive.

Let's look at things in terms of our analogy. Suppose your window is a projected image of the landscape, and what you see is refreshed 24 times a second. Something in the first frame will have moved in the opposite direction of your movement when you hop to the next frame and will appear to be sliding through the frame. Changes in aggregated calculations are likely to be smoother, as some preceding frame data points influence the current frame's data points (figure 8.2).

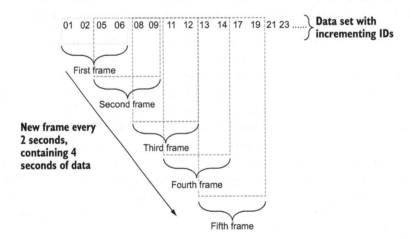

Figure 8.2   Visualization of a sliding or hopping window in terms of how it sees the data

We can express this in the stream task by adding this code after the `where` statement:

```
WINDOW HOPPING (<window size in seconds as an integer> SECONDS, ADVANCE
BY <hop duration as an integer> SECONDS).
```

Let's take our `selectSumTask` and `selectWithTag` forward to a new `stream_task` file (`query3.conf`) and extend the `selectSumTask` to add a hopping window that looks at an interval of 4 seconds and advances every 2 seconds. The resulting configuration looks like the following listing; see `chapter8/fluentbit/query3.conf`.

Listing 8.4   Stream processor with hopping window: `query3.conf`

```
[STREAM_TASK]                                      The query we carried forward
  name selectTaskWithTag                           from the previous section
  exec SELECT record_tag(), rand_value FROM TAG:'random-num';

[STREAM_TASK]
  name selectSumTask
  exec SELECT now(), sum(rand_value) FROM TAG:'random-num'
  WINDOW HOPPING (4 SECOND, ADVANCE BY 2 SECOND);
```

> Incorporates the aggregation function sum, which means we need to use a window. Here, we've used a hopping window, which recalculates every 2 seconds, looking at 4 seconds of data.

To make it easy to observe the behavior of the window, we're also going to modify the `query-streamer`. Rather than use random values, we'll use the `dummy` plugin to generate the message that always gives the `rand_value` attribute a value of 2 and triggers once per second. Again, we need to update the `query-streamer-1.conf`'s attribute `streams_file` to reference our new configuration file. As a result, our main configuration will look like the following listing; see `chapter8/fluentbit/query-streamer-1.conf`.

Listing 8.5   A dummied value fed to our stream processor: `query-streamer-1.conf`

```
[SERVICE]
  flush 5                                          We've updated our configuration
  log_level info                                   to reference the new query
  streams_file ./query3.conf                       processor configuration.

[INPUT]
  name dummy                                       We've replaced the random number
  interval_sec 1                                   plugin with the dummy plugin, but the
  dummy {"rand_value":"2"}                         payload generated will look the same.
  tag random-num
                                                   We're using the same tag as before, so
[OUTPUT]                                           the change to the processor statement
  match *                                          has only the window change.
  name null
```

With this configuration, we should expect a predictable result, and as we're using a small figure, we avoid the risk that the calculation will yield an unexpected negative value. The `random` plugin–generating numbers that are large positive numbers, when added together, can result in an integer overflow error (https://mng.bz/n0Ie) and produce a negative value. When the changes have been applied, we can rerun the configuration with the command

```
fluent-bit -c fluentbit/query-streamer-1.conf
```

As a result of this configuration, we see output a bit like the following. For readability, We've replaced the `dummy` tag outputs `"RECORD_TAG()"=>"random-num"` with `"TAG()"=>"XX ")`:

```
[0][1709583296.798773500,{},{"TAG()"=>"XX","rand_value"=>"2"}]
[0][1709583297.792872900,{},{"TAG()"=>"XX","rand_value"=>"2"}]
[0][1709583298.778259300,{},{"TAG()"=>"XX","rand_value"=>"2"}]
[0][1709583299.806917000,{},{"TAG()"=>"XX","rand_value"=>"2"}]
[0][(ext: 0)"e\xe6+\xc30\"\x0e|",
    {"NOW()"=>"2024-03-04 20:14:59",
    "SUM(rand_value)"=>8}]
[0][1709583300.804949800,{},{"TAG()"=>"XX","rand_value"=>"2"}]
[0][1709583301.804049600,{},{"TAG()"=>"XX","rand_value"=>"2"}]
[0][1709583302.801290100, {},{"TAG()"=>"XX","rand_value"=>"2"}]
[0][(ext:0)"e\xe6+\xc7/\xb1\x9b\xc4",
    {"NOW()"=>"2024-03-04 20:15:03",
    "SUM(rand_value)"=>12}]
[0][1709583303.801065200, {},{"TAG()"=>"XX","rand_value"=>"2"}]
[0][1709583304.802936700, {},{"TAG()"=>"XX","rand_value"=>"2"}]
[0][1709583305.798320300, {},{"TAG()"=>"XX","rand_value"=>"2"}]
[0][1709583306.795026500, {},{"TAG()"=>"XX","rand_value"=>"2"}]
[0][(ext:0)"e\xe6+\xcb/L\x0dT",
    {"NOW()"=>"2024-03-04 20:15:07",
    "SUM(rand_value)"=>14}]
```

Reflects the window of every 4 seconds and shows the value we expect (4 x 2)

The second 4-second interval. We expect it to yield 4 x 2, but its value is derived from 8 + (2 x 2). The SELECT statement results in the calculated value going back into the buffer, and we're calculating every 2 seconds the values in the buffer over the past 4 seconds.

On the third trigger, we expect the last calculated value (12) plus another 2 x 2, but that isn't what we have. The reason is nanosecond precision. If the time in which the value reaches the buffer is a nanosecond out, it won't be included in the calculation. So the number makes sense if one value falls just outside the 4-second window. If we review the timestamps on the logs, we see that they're not perfectly sequential because of the nature of threading and I/O operations.

The output generated doesn't yield the results we expected: a reading of 8 with a fluctuation of plus or minus 2 due to millisecond precision. There are two reasons for this result:

- The window is a direct multiple of the event frequency. If there is any slight variation in the timestamping of when the event is added to the buffer, it will be excluded if it falls outside the window. This can be further affected by the fact that Fluent Bit is multithreaded. Depending on how the threads are allocated to CPUs, a nanosecond or two of latency is introduced. We need to be mindful of this problem when choosing our windowing intervals compared with the event frequency.
- The SELECT statement results in the calculated value being added to the buffer. Given our window and recalculation intervals, the previously calculated value is included in the next calculation. We can ensure that the calculated values get a separate tag and, as a result, don't go back into the same buffer.

We should keep some other behavioral characteristics in mind:

- If we set the window period to be more than the flush period, the data will continue to flush at the right interval but be retained in the buffer. We need to be conscious of what our query expressions can do to buffer sizing.

- If we set the advance duration larger than the data period, we move into the domain of sampling rather than calculating on a continual flow. As a result, the outcomes are less predictable. Today, this is allowed, but sampling doesn't line up conceptually with a sliding window, as we no longer perform calculations against the full data set. There is always a chance that enhanced validation may prevent this result in the future.

- Despite having a uniform time-based rate of event generation, and although our windows are defined by time as well, we may see small fluctuations in the number of events in each window due to nanosecond timestamping and whether the event generation adds another event into the buffer quickly enough to fall inside or outside a window. As a result, we see variations of one event more or less in a window calculation. In a real use case, this change can be more volatile (such as CPU use measurements on a server executing batch jobs), and if we're working against data buffered to disk, the I/O operations have the potential to affect data that falls inside or outside the window.

8.4.2 Tumbling windows

Tumbling (sometimes called *cascading*) *windows* differ from hopping windows in one key aspect: there is no potential for data overlap in each window. Put another way, the hop duration is the same as the window duration. Here, we set a window of a certain duration, and the next window starts immediately after the last one is completed (figure 8.3).

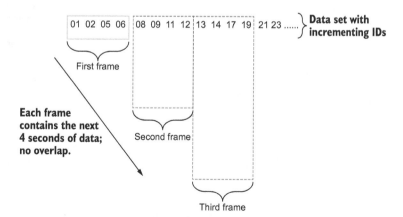

Figure 8.3   Visualization of a tumbling window in terms of how it sees the data. Note that there is no overlap of the window periods.

The easiest way to relate to this figure is to imagine you're rolling (or tumbling) down a corridor with windows at intervals in the wall. Each time you get to look out the window, you see a different landscape.

Let's put this into action by adapting our windowing dummy use case again. We'll copy our query3.conf file to query4.conf so we keep our example of a hopping configuration. Now we can replace the selectSumTask's exec attribute value, so instead of WINDOW HOPPING (4 SECOND, ADVANCE BY 2 SECOND), we have WINDOW TUMBLING 4 SECOND. See the following listing and chapter8/fluentbit/query4.conf.

Listing 8.6 Stream processor with tumbling window: `query4.conf`

```
[STREAM_TASK]
  name selectTaskWithTag
  exec SELECT record_tag(), rand_value FROM TAG:'random-num';

[STREAM_TASK]
  name selectSumTask
  exec SELECT now(), sum(rand_value) FROM TAG:'random-num'
➥ WINDOW TUMBLING (4 SECOND);                              ◀─
```

We've swapped the hopping window for the simpler tumbling window, which evaluates each consecutive block of 4 seconds of data.

We need to update the query-streamer-1.conf file so that the service attribute references this new file. Let's run the scenario again:

```
fluent-bit -c fluentbit/query-streamer-1.conf
```

This time, we see far more predictable outcomes because we're not recalculating data within our window. We've applied the same readability modifications as before by replacing the dummy tag outputs "RECORD_TAG()"=>"random-num" with "TAG()"=>"XX"):

```
[0][1709586021.421976700,{},{"TAG()"=>"XX","rand_value"=>"2"}]
[0][1709586022.419766400,{},{"TAG()"=>"XX","rand_value"=>"2"}]
[0][1709586023.418403000,{},{"TAG()"=>"XX","rand_value"=>"2"}]
[0][1709586024.429872900,{},{"TAG()"=>"XX","rand_value"=>"2"}]
[0][(ext:0)"e\xe66h\x19\xaa\xc7\xec",
➥  {"NOW()"=>"2024-03-04 21:00:24", "SUM(rand_value)"=>8}]   ◀─
[0][1709586025.430094600,{},{"TAG()"=>"XX","rand_value"=>"2"}]
[0][1709586026.423181800,{},{"TAG()"=>"XX","rand_value"=>"2"}]
[0][1709586027.420841300,{},{"TAG()"=>"XX","rand_value"=>"2"}]
[0][1709586028.417736700,{},{"TAG()"=>"XX","rand_value"=>"2"}]
[0][(ext:0)"e\xe661\x18\xefd\xd4",
➥  {"NOW()"=>"2024-03-04 21:00:28", "SUM(rand_value)"=>8}]   ◀─
```

Now the previously calculated number doesn't affect the calculation because we're not recalculating at any time before the end of the window duration, so the result is consistent.

We're not recalculating until the end of the next window, so the previous calculation doesn't fall into the scope of the calculation of the window (where it was because we recalculated every 2 seconds). It is possible to reintroduce uncertainty if the window length is the same as the event input length, at which point we risk the nanosecond precision problem again. We can prove that by adjusting the calculation window in this configuration to 1 second.

8.4.3 Setting window durations

All of our examples to date have been in seconds, but Fluent Bit's stream processor also supports the use of Hour, Minute, and Second keywords. We need to be mindful of how much data is being buffered to support the duration of the processor. If we have too little, we'll end up processing empty windows; if we have too much, we could need more memory than is available. When considering the duration, we may go long as we don't see too many events in normal operations. But when things go wrong, we often see huge surges in events, particularly logs, so we need to ensure that Fluent Bit won't fail and lose data.

If we use stream-processing windows, it is essential that the data sources don't shift their timestamps to accommodate daylight saving time adjustments (clocks moving back or forward one hour twice a year). We also want all the sources to report against the same time zone to eliminate confusion. In some business cases, we want to know the local time. We'd advise managing those time values as part of the event payload and naming them clearly as local time to prevent confusion.

8.4.4 Deciding which window to use

From an application perspective, hopping windows are best suited to use cases in which we need to smooth out the data to see true anomalies and minimize false positives in events such as these:

- Spikes or drops in network traffic
- Fluctuations in application workload

The key to hopping windows is to use them for near-real-time detection. Tumbling windows are better for looking at trends rather than real time, such as answering the following questions about our events:

- What is the trend or pattern for our system use during the day?
- Is the number of experienced hardware faults increasing?
- Can we forecast a likely failure point?

Looking at these questions from a computational perspective is straightforward. Assuming that we are processing data for 1 minute, we have a window of 10 seconds, and a hop interval is 5 seconds. If we use a tumbling window, we'll analyze the data 6 times, but if we use a hopping window, we'll perform 11 calculations ([60s / 5s] –1).

Although these points can be helpful in deciding whether to use tumbling or hopping windows, validating the windowing configuration is in the realm of data science, particularly for optimizing the window configurations. We don't want to smooth the data so much that we eliminate the effect of true outliers; neither do we want trends to span so long a period that it's hard to derive any value from the measurement.

8.5   *Selecting multiple attributes and naming*

As we create a new record structure, we may want to change the element names in the JSON output, particularly because the names used from derived values are the expressions themselves, such as NOW(). We can achieve this using the reserved word AS, which works like SQL; we can select a value and use AS to give the selected value a different name (such as SELECT columnElementName AS myMeaningfulElementName).

We can also retrieve multiple elements from the log event we're processing by separating elements to be selected with a comma. If we receive a JSON structure with nested elements, we may also want to take an element from that nested structure by naming the root element within square brackets.

Let's put that example in practical terms. We could use a new set of sources, so we created a new base configuration called query-streamer-2.conf, which uses the dummy plugin to generate different JSON events. See the following listing and chapter8/fluentbit/query-streamer-2.conf.

Listing 8.7   Generating JSON to process: `query-streamer-2.conf`

```
[SERVICE]
  flush 5
  log_level info
  streams_file ./query-naming.conf

[INPUT]
  name dummy
  samples 10
  dummy {"myData":{"innerNo":"1",
  "innerText1" : "blah", "innerText2" : "more blah"},
  "outerNo": "10", "outerTextA" : "widget",
  "outerTextB" : "gadget"}
  tag complexMsg

[INPUT]
  name dummy
  samples 10
  dummy {"myMessage":"Im simple", "really" : "I am"}
  tag simpleMsg

[INPUT]
  name dummy
  samples 10
  dummy {"myMessage":"I dont know what to say"}
  tag simpleMsg

[OUTPUT]
  match *
  name null

# [OUTPUT]
#   match *
#   name stdout
#   json_date_format iso8601
```

The inclusion of our stream processor configuration file. When included, it identifies the streams against which processors need to be linked.

So we don't get an endless output of the same content, we've used the samples attribute to limit the plugin activity to creating 10 events.

So we don't get an endless output of the same content, we've used the samples attribute to limit the plugin activity to creating 10 events.

Although the output messages are different, these input plugins use the same tag.

Because we're looking at the logging generated, we're applying only a SELECT statement. It is good practice to direct the events to null to show that we're not trying to do anything with them downstream.

To see the raw tagged data, uncomment the output plugin configuration.

Taking the JSON that is generated and tagged `complexMsg`, let's formulate a query that retrieves the following values and creates the output as follows:

- Take `tag` and output it as `myTag`.
- Take `outerTextA` and rename it `myThingType`.
- Take `innerText` from the nested JSON structure and call it `myComment`.

As mentioned, the elements in the root need to be referenced directly, and we use the `AS` keyword to provide the new name. For the `innerText`, we need to use the parent attribute name and then reference the inner value by quoting it within square brackets. The resulting configuration should look like the following listing and `chapter8/fluentbit/query-naming.conf`.

Listing 8.8 Stream processor outputting JSON: `query-naming.conf`

```
[STREAM_TASK]
  name selectTaskWithRenaming
  exec SELECT record_tag() AS myTag, outerTextA AS
  myThingType, myData['innerText1']
  AS myComment FROM TAG:'complexMsg';
```

> Here, we're accessing data that is nested within the event's JSON structure and creating a new payload event with the value myComment.

As our configuration is generating its own data, we can run the example using the command

```
fluent-bit -c fluentbit/query-streamer-2.conf
```

The resulting output isn't exciting because the `dummy` doesn't have any randomization, but we'll see 10 entries—and only 10, as we've restricted the `dummy` plugin using the `samples` attribute to trigger only 10 times. But the tags are as defined, and we retrieved part of the nested JSON:

```
[0] [1703190995.687085814, {}, {"myTag"=>"complexMsg",
 "myThingType"=>"widget", "myComment"=>"blah"}]
```

Extend the stream processor to retrieve the `innerNo` element from the JSON, and make the `tag` element the last part of the output JSON with the name `originalTag`. If you want to see an implementation, we've provided the stream processor (`query-naming-answer.conf`) with the modified algorithm. If you want to run it, you'll need to amend `query-streamer-2.conf` to reference this file.

8.6 Streams vs. tags

Before we can look at the use of a stream, we need to understand the differences between streams and tags. A *stream* is a single unique source that can be an input or the result of a stream processor's output. We can set the stream name on inputs using the attribute name `alias`. Once set, the stream name is immutable.

We can align a tag to a single source or multiple sources. We can also use filters to manipulate a tag. If we look at the output from the startup of Fluent Bit with the `query-streamer` configuration, we see the following output:

```
[2023/12/29 16:31:19] [ info] [fluent bit] version=2.2.1,
⮡ commit=, pid=4406
[2023/12/29 16:31:19] [ info] [storage] ver=1.5.1,
⮡ type=memory, sync=normal, checksum=off, max_chunks_up=128
[2023/12/29 16:31:19] [ info] [cmetrics] version=0.6.6
[2023/12/29 16:31:19] [ info] [ctraces ] version=0.4.0
[2023/12/29 16:31:19] [ info] [input:random:random.0] initializing
[2023/12/29 16:31:19] [ info] [input:random:random.0]
⮡ storage_strategy='memory' (memory only)
[2023/12/29 16:31:19] [ info] [sp] stream processor started
```

Notice that the fifth line reports the `initializing` of the `random` plugin—specifically, the name between the second set of square brackets, which shows us the plugin type (input, output, and so on) followed by a colon, the plugin name (such as `random`), followed by the default plugin name, which is the plugin name followed by a dot and the occurrence number of that plugin starting at `0` (such as `random.0`).

Copy `query-streamer.conf` (use the name `query-streamer-multiple.conf`), and create a copy of the `dummy` input within the configuration. Then rerun the configuration with the command

```
fluent-bit -c fluentbit/query-streamer-multiple.conf
```

We've provided a version of the file if you want to use it. The resulting output includes the following:

```
[2023/12/29 16:47:37] [ info] [input:random:random.0]
⮡ storage_strategy='memory' (memory only)
[2023/12/29 16:47:37] [ info] [input:random:random.1] initializing
[2023/12/29 16:47:37] [ info] [input:random:random.1]
⮡ storage_strategy='memory' (memory only)
```

This output shows two inputs being initialized with postfixes of `.0` and `.1`. Let's take this one step further and add the alias declaration of the first input (`alias myRandom`) and run things again (provided as `query-streamer-multiple-alias.conf`). Now we'll see the following output in the startup:

```
[2023/12/29 16:53:44] [ info] [input:random:myRandom] initializing
[2023/12/29 16:53:44] [ info] [input:random:myRandom]
⮡ storage_strategy='memory' (memory only)
[2023/12/29 16:53:44] [ info] [input:random:random.1] initializing
[2023/12/29 16:53:44] [ info] [input:random:random.1]
⮡ storage_strategy='memory' (memory only)
```

Part of the name has become the stream name, but the counter has still been incremented. Also, because the stream processor is using the tag, not the stream name, it continues to perform the queries. Let's make a final change by modifying the query2.conf stream task definition and align the task to the STREAM instead of the tag. We need to replace the TAG:'random-num' part of the statement with STREAM:random.0. Notice that we no longer need to include the quotes, as wildcards are no longer possible. Let's copy query2.conf to query2-stream-name.conf and apply the change. We can also amend the names to reflect the fact that we're using a STREAM by modifying the last part of the name. As a result, our configuration looks like the following listing and chapter8/fluentbit/query2-stream-name.conf.

Listing 8.9 Using the STREAM keyword: query2-stream-name.conf

```
[STREAM_TASK]
  name selectTaskWithStream          ◄──  We've modified the name to reflect the fact
  exec SELECT record_tag(), rand_value    that we're using a stream rather than a tag.
⟿ FROM STREAM:random.0;           ◄──┐

[STREAM_TASK]
  name selectSumStream            ◄──
  exec SELECT now(), sum(rand_value)       The expression
⟿ FROM STREAM:random.0;           ◄──    identifies a
                                          specific stream
[STREAM_TASK]                             rather than a tag.
  name selectWhereStream          ◄──┘
  exec SELECT unix_timestamp(), count(rand_value)
⟿ FROM STREAM:random.0 where rand_value > 0;   ◄──┘
```

We need to modify the query-streamer.conf configuration to use the modified version of the streams file by changing the streams_file attribute to streams_file ./query2-stream-name.conf. When we rerun our configuration with the command

```
fluent-bit -c fluentbit/query-streamer.conf
```

the resulting output is the same as before. Although this example is not hugely impressive, it enables us to create streams and attach downstream processors to preceding stream tasks.

8.7 Creating streams

We've focused on the query aspect of the stream processor because the CREATE STREAM option largely depends on the SELECT statement. Let's extend our existing queries to create a new stream and output that new stream.

We'll continue using random as our source of input, as we did for our query-streamer.conf examples. This time, we'll create a stream called createTaskWithStream, which should be tagged as myStream.select. Then the new log event should contain the following:

- rand_value from the random plugin
- The current time in pretty format (the output from the now() function), which we'll call dtg (often used as shorthand for Date Time Group)

- The UNIX timestamp value from the corresponding function, which we'll call `unixTime`

We'll use our `random-num` tag as the source. This is built on our `selectTaskWithTag` query. To build this expression, we use the template `CREATE STREAM <streamName> WITH (tag='<tag>') SELECT <value>, <value> AS <name> FROM TAG: '<tag>' ;`. The stream name has to be provided as there isn't an easy way to default the value. The `WITH` allows us to perform name-value pair assignments within the brackets for the properties used as metadata, such as the tag. We can assign only literal values here and can't use functions such as `now()` and `unix_timestamp()`. Typically, we use the `WITH (tag='<tag>')` only to set a tag value. We connect this to a `SELECT` statement with the keyword `AS`. After that, this is no different from SQL. As a result, our `create.conf` file will look like the following listing; see `chapter8/fluentbit/create.conf`.

Listing 8.10   Creating a new stream with a tag: `create.conf`

```
[STREAM_TASK]
  name createTaskWithTag
  exec CREATE STREAM createTaskWithStream          ◁──── We've used a different name
                                                         here because we're exploiting
⇒ WITH (tag='myStream.Select')                          the CREATE STREAM syntax.
⇒ AS SELECT record_tag(),
⇒ rand_value, now() AS dtg,            This expression is like the SELECT syntax but leads with
⇒ unix_timestamp() as unixTime         a CREATE STREAM that names a new stream and uses
⇒ FROM TAG:'random-num';        ◁───── the WITH syntax to set the tag name of the event.
```

Let's briefly look at our parent configuration file with its `random` input plugin and an output plugin for the tagged stream in the following listing; see `chapter8/fluent-bit/create-streamer.conf`.

Listing 8.11   Config using our stream: `create-streamer.conf`

```
[SERVICE]
  flush 5                      We include the new
  log_level info               stream processor
  streams_file ./create.conf   ◁── configuration file.

[INPUT]
  name random
  interval_sec 1
  tag random-num    ◁──┐
                       │  The source tag is random-num, but
[OUTPUT]                │  because of the stream processor, we'll
  match myStream.*  ◁──┘  be outputting with a different tag.
  name stdout
```

The listing illustrates the `match` statement, ensuring that the output we'll see comes only from our stream processor. Because we tag the stream's output, logically, we should see the stream processor flow feeding back as an input, although we don't have to define the input within the main configuration (figure 8.4).

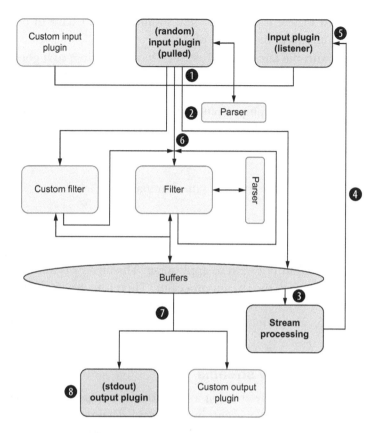

Figure 8.4 Overlay of our architecture view with the sequence of actions our events pass through. The numbering shows the path the events take through the components. The numbering indicates the sequence.

Figure 8.4 shows how the events pass through our logical representation of the architecture. We can follow the flow in numeric order:

1 The `random` plugin creates an event with the tag `random-num` every second.
2 The input plugin passes the created event to the buffer without any parsing. As no filtering is associated with the pipeline, we don't need to consider triggering such an activity when the event is secured in the buffer.
3 The event reaching the buffer triggers as it comes into contact with the storage interface. As a result, we evaluate whether a processor is attached. For this tag, we have an attached processor, so the event needs to be handed off to the stream processor. The event is not part of a window but is processed immediately, resulting in the creation of a new event with the tag `myStream.Select`.
4 The result of the stream processor is a new event in the stream with a tag, which logically needs to be reingested into the pipeline.

5 Because this is a logical input of the new event, we don't have to declare an input plugin configuration; this is implicit.

6 The new event with the tag `myStream.Select` has no parsing, so it goes directly to the buffer again. This time, no processor is attached, so no stream processing is required.

7 The event is routed to an output plugin because there is a valid match definition in line with the flush scheduling.

8 The output plugin consumes the events that are flushed, resulting in the output's being written to the console.

With that detail, let's run the scenario using the command

```
fluent-bit -c fluentbit/create-streamer.conf
```

Applying a tag to the stream is an optional step. You may wonder what happens to the stream and why we might not want to apply a tag. The answer is that we can still address the new stream within the stream processor. Therefore, we can chain stream processes without the event going through the input pipeline. If there were a wildcard filter at stages 2 and 6, the events would be processed. Without the tag, the event remains unmodified.

8.8   *Chaining and creating new streams*

Let's explore chaining streams by creating a variation on our previous SELECT statement, which counted the number of events in an interval. That stream processor won't be tagged. But we'll take the result into a separate stream processor, which will generate an event only where the count is greater than a certain value. Let's count how many occurrences of the random value are more than 20,000,000,000,000,000,000. (Our random numbers are 20 digits long, so we need a reasonably large number to create an element of exclusion.) Then we'll put the result of the count and the current time into our output record in a stream called `createCountStream`. We won't see any output from this stream, which has no associated tag to match against. Because we want to create an aggregated value, we need to use a window. In this scenario, we'll use a tumbling window of 5 seconds.

We'll consume the `createCountStream` events with two processors that create an event depending on whether the count element produced in the previous (`createCountStream`) stream has a value of more than 2 or a value equal to or less than 2. Both streams include the `counted` and `countTime` elements from the previous stream but use different tags: `MyStream.more` and `myStream.lessEqual`, respectively. As a result, the output will be from one of the two streams and tagged as `MyStream.more` or `myStream.lessEqual`. Figure 8.5 shows this configuration.

Taking what we saw in previous examples, we should arrive at a configuration that looks like the following listing; see `chapter8/fluentbit/create2.conf`.

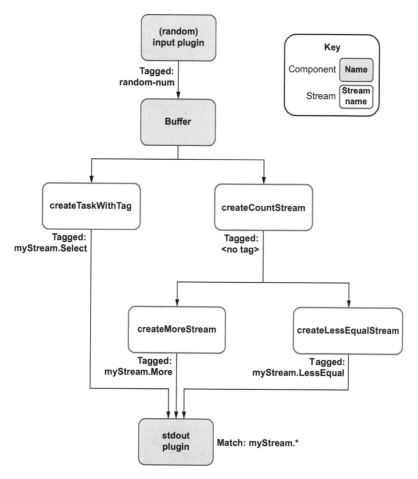

Figure 8.5   Sequence and tagging of plugins and stream processors. The stream processor tasks in the middle of the flow are shaded to distinguish them. Note that `createCountStream` doesn't tag its output.

Listing 8.12   Chained streams example: create2.conf

```
[STREAM_TASK]
  name createTaskWithTag
  exec CREATE STREAM createTaskWithTagTag WITH
  (tag='myStream.Select') AS SELECT record_tag(),
  rand_value, now() as dtg,
  unix_timestamp() as unixTime FROM TAG:'random-num';

[STREAM_TASK]
  name createCountStream
  exec CREATE STREAM createCountStream
  AS SELECT unix_timestamp(), count(rand_value)
  as counted, now() as countTime
```

Reuses the simple select to create a stream that enriches the event with different representations of the time

```
⇥ FROM TAG:'random-num'
⇥ WINDOW TUMBLING (5 SECOND) where
⇥ rand_value > 20000000000000000000;

[STREAM_TASK]
  name createCountMoreStream
  exec CREATE STREAM createMoreStream WITH
⇥ (tag='myStream.More') AS
⇥ SELECT countTime, counted FROM
⇥ STREAM:createCountStream where counted > 2;

[STREAM_TASK]
  name createCountLessEqualStream
  exec CREATE STREAM createLessEqStream
⇥ WITH (tag='myStream.lessEqual')
⇥ AS SELECT countTime, counted FROM
⇥ STREAM:createCountStream where counted <= 2;
```

Using the same source, we use a tumbling window to count the number of occurrences where the random number is of a certain size. The output stream is untagged, and each event every 5 seconds contains the number of events identified and the time the event was created.

These streams are chained to use the createCountStream content. The results of these streams are tagged. We've filtered the streams so that only one of these two streams will create an event for onward processing.

For this example to work, we need to update the streams_file attribute to reference our new streams2.conf file. Then we can run our scenario with the command

```
fluent-bit -c fluentbit/create-streamer.conf
```

We can expect to see three types of output:

- The result of our stream createTaskWithTag, which is tagged myStream.Select, shows every generated event, and looks like this:

  ```
  [0] myStream.Select: [[1703955995.504518444, {}],
  ⇥ {"RECORD_TAG()"=>"random-num", "rand_value"=>18186270176722129669,
  ⇥ "dtg"=>"2023-12-30 17:06:35", "unixTime"=>1703955995}]
  ```

- The result of our stream createMoreStream, which is tagged myStream.More and may appear at the end of the window period only if counted is greater than 2:

  ```
  [0] myStream.More: [[1703955999.504615067, {}],
  ⇥ {"countTime"=>"2023-12-30 17:06:39", "counted"=>3}]
  ```

- The result of our stream createLessEqStream, which is tagged myStream.lessEqual and may appear at the end of the window period only if counted is less than or equal to 2:

  ```
  [0] myStream.lessEqual: [[1703956019.504577312, {}],
  ⇥ {"countTime"=>"2023-12-30 17:06:59", "counted"=>1}]
  ```

As we can see, we can chain stream processors to create more sophisticated operations.

> **Demonstrating untagged stream flow behavior**
>
> As previously mentioned, without a tag, the flow of the events would not reach a plugin. Using our completed example, we can easily demonstrate the flow by introducing the `stdout` filter (chapter 7). Simply introducing this filter with a wildcard `match` results in any event flowing through the pipeline being written to the console. As a result, we'll continue to see only the output of tagged events. If you'd like to confirm this, run `chapter8/fluentbit/filtered-create-streamer.conf;`, which includes the additional filter.

8.9 Typical use cases for streaming

Now that we have a handle on the capabilities of streaming, let's explore some common applications of the stream processor and address some constraints compared with dedicated stream-processing services.

8.9.1 Forecasting

With a window of data, it is possible to extrapolate likely future values from a trend. If we have data on storage use, we can forecast possible problems such as reaching use levels in storage at which I/O performance will degrade. As a result, we can implement actions proactively. To use the forecast capability, we can use a function called `timeseries_forecast`, which takes the element name or key from the events in the window and a number of seconds forward from now to forecast.

> **NOTE** There are multiple mathematical approaches to forecasting; you can find explanations of some at https://mng.bz/vJP1. The Fluent Bit implementation uses a simple linear regression. Put in simple terms, it takes the data points over time and calculates the average change over time. Then that calculated change over time is used to predict forward in a linear path. This approach doesn't take historical patterns into account.

8.9.2 Intermittent error tolerance

Good applications tolerate a level of errors through techniques such as catch and retry mechanisms. So, any transient problems that occur, such as network connections timing out, can be managed easily. At the same time, applications will likely report an error, so if we need to examine error logs, we can isolate the initial occurrence of a fault. We don't want these managed intermittent error events to trigger alerts if the application is handling them on a retry unless they're happening at a frequency that indicates a more serious problem that could cause backpressure problems. We can deal with this by looking at the average number of errors generated during a period. Below a threshold, we can suppress triggering a problem; above a threshold, we should initiate an intervention.

8.9.3   *Spurious data values*

Occasionally, we receive metrics with an anomaly. This problem is common in industrial Internet of Things (IoT) environments where a sensor may be subject to conditions that can cause a misread or corruption of the signal or a sensor fault. A temperature sensor on a computer motherboard reports a temperature, and within a second, the temperature leaps 20 degrees. In normal operations, we wouldn't expect to see such violent temperature changes. As a result, we may want to eliminate the data value unless it continues to remain high.

8.9.4   *Absence of events*

Some applications generate heartbeat events so that we know things are functioning as expected. We no longer need to poll the application to determine whether it's alive or rely on a log being generated when an application crashes or terminates. But proving the absence of an event over a time frame can be difficult. Using windowing with the stream processor makes this incredibly simple to achieve. If we know that an application generates a heartbeat event every minute, we can count the number of events over 2 minutes to provide some tolerance for process scheduling. If we count the events in that window, there should be at least one event in the window; if not, we can reasonably assume that the application died and that some intervention is needed (manual or automated).

8.9.5   *Cross-referencing streams*

Feature-rich specialist stream processors such as Apache Spark (https://mng.bz/ 4p6D) and Kafka's ksqlDB (https://mng.bz/QVRR) enable streams to pull data from other streams. This capability is interesting in Fluent Bit; it allows us to create and establish alerts only when these two separate event streams are alerting. If a database's performance drops and the number of users spikes, for example, these alerts are important individually but not catastrophic; together, they indicate that the system may crash.

> **TIP**   To learn more about Apache Spark and Kafka for streaming queries, check out https://www.scaler.com/topics/kafka-vs-spark. If you want to go deeper into this area, you can find additional resources in appendix B.

Another use case is correlating logs, traces, and metrics data, so a metric from a compute node could be referenced by a log generated on the same node in real time. As a result, we could start to establish cause and effect in real time. The alternative would be to collect the events in a database and then perform relational joins or nested SQL actions on the events. Unfortunately, Fluent Bit's stream processor currently doesn't support this capability.

Although it isn't possible to perform cross-stream enrichment of individual events, we can still perform some correlation activities. By running a stream processor against a tag, we can feed multiple sources into the stream via tag rewriting with a filter. Better, if the sources use a clever tag-naming convention, we can use wildcards in the naming. The common stream runs a small window, and we aggregate and group records in the window to produce a composite record.

If absolute precision of event stream record joining is necessary, a better option is to outsource the work to Kafka, where Fluent Bit has input and output connectors. The last option is to use Lua to perform the enrichment by connecting to a caching solution such as Redis (https://github.com/nrk/redis-lua) or a database with memory-caching capabilities for performance and Open Database Connectivity (ODBC) capabilities, which the LuaSQL (https://github.com/lunarmodules/luasql) library can work with. A word of caution on the Lua approach: using additional libraries is going to complicate your deployment, as only the standard Lua libraries are bundled by default. Enrichment of this nature is likely to be resource intensive.

Summary

- The stream processor's SQL-based `SELECT` syntax is central to all the uses of Fluent Bit's stream processor. The `SELECT` allows us to identify specific occurrences of events currently buffered, such as to determine whether a process has been executed.

- Fluent Bit's stream processor includes aggregation functions such as `count` and `average`. When using aggregations, we need to use Windows. This allows us to perform tasks such as translating event occurrences into metrics or generating new events, such as recognizing if something occurs too few or too many times.

- We can use stream processors to filter out the events that are important to a calculation.

- Fluent Bit's stream processor supports two types of windows: hopping and tumbling. These window types have different cost/performance implications. Hopping windows are more computationally expensive but less likely to miss fluctuations and more granular in data analysis.

- Stream processors can consume streams or tags. The difference between a `STREAM` and a `tag` relates to the fact that one or more sources are available in a tag, but a stream is always a single source with an immutable identifier.

- Streams without tags can only be handled by other streams and won't trigger other plugins. But when we attribute a tag to the stream, it has the behavior of an (implied) input plugin.

- An untagged stream can only be handled by `STREAMS`, which can be chained together to create more sophisticated processing.

- Fluent Bit's stream processors provide a powerful mechanism but should not be confused with a pure streaming technology such as Apache Spark and Kafka. For example, it isn't possible for data from one stream to be used to inform another.

Building processors and Fluent Bit extension options

This chapter covers

- Applying processors to interact and manipulate metrics, traces, and logs
- Using SQL-like expressions to work with signals using a processor
- Exploring the need for a custom plugin
- Reviewing the technology options for creating custom plugins
- Understanding of the technologies involved in custom plugins

This chapter looks at different approaches to extending Fluent Bit logic. Using Lua, we'll look at new feature processors that allow us to extend logic around the input and output of all signal types (logs, traces, and metrics). If this isn't sufficient, we can consider developing our own plugins. We can build new plugins by forking or contributing to the Fluent Bit project or using the technologies provided to create independent plugins. In this chapter, we'll examine what is involved in the options and their pros and cons.

9.1 Architectural context

Processors provide the opportunity to enhance input and output plugin behavior in several ways without resorting to custom plugins. However, processors allow us to go only so far; sometimes, we must consider developing custom plugins to extend Fluent Bit. To support this, we'll explore the design decisions when selecting a strategy to develop an extension. Figure 9.1 highlights where the choice of strategy can affect Fluent Bit. In chapter 10, we will apply one of these custom plugin strategies.

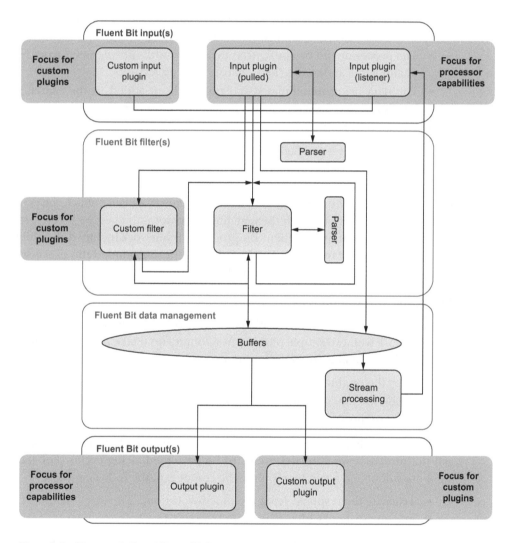

Figure 9.1 Representation of Fluent Bit from a logical architecture, showing where custom plugins can be used, along with the processor feature that allows us to change the behavior of existing plugins

9.2   Fluent Bit processor: Changing the behavior of existing plugins

Fluent Bit v2.1.2 introduced additional customization logic for input and output plugins called processors (not to be confused with the stream processor). It has a similar feel to using Lua as a custom filter in many respects, but there are some notable differences:

- The processor can be viewed as being an inline piece of logic. The logic implemented can directly affect the performance of the input or output plugin. As a result, we can significantly affect the plugin's behavior and performance, such as its ability to ingest data, so it should be treated with care.
- The processor can be configured to interact with the telemetry types Fluent Bit v2 and later can handle (logs, metrics, and traces).
- The data being manipulated has not yet been added to the buffer, and this logic's actions could potentially prevent that from occurring.
- We can only configure the processor feature using YAML.

As a result, this isn't a full-fledged custom plugin capability (as we'll see later in the chapter), but it can have a greater potential effect. We're not yet interacting with the buffer, so we get more performance as we're not serializing and deserializing the event with MessagePack. The downside is that reuse is limited; we can't attach the processor to multiple event sources through the matching behavior.

The introduction of the Fluent Bit processor framework included the ability to use Lua in the processor to manipulate logs. Fluent Bit v3 extended the processor's capability to support working with traces and metrics.

9.2.1   Processor with Lua for logs

So that we can easily separate the effect of the processor from that of the plugin, we're going to work with two simple plugins. As a source, we'll take the `random` input plugin, which we'll manipulate in the following ways:

- Copy the original random value to a new event attribute.
- Divide the random value by 2, truncating any fractional parts.
- Capture the response from pinging Google.com.

As the `random` plugin generates log events rather than traces or metrics, we'll need to tell the processor we want the events to be presented as log events. For the output, we'll use stdout and again manipulate the contents in the following ways:

- Truncate the response from the ping invocation.
- Add an attribute with a value to the log event.

To use the processor, we need to introduce a new declaration block for the processor (called `processors`) and use it first to name the type of event we want to interact with (in our case, `logs`, but with the ability to interact with signals and traces, too). When we identify the filter using the `name` attribute, we use the same parameters that we'd use to define a custom filter. For a Lua filter, we need to define the method's name to invoke in the code (`call` attribute). This example (`chapter9/fluentbit/processor-demo.yaml`) uses the YAML facility to inline the code into the configuration with the `code` attribute.

Listing 9.1 Using processors in input and output plugins: `processor-demo.yaml`

In this YAML configuration, we've set the random-number generator input to run every 5 seconds to give us time to evaluate the output.

We start the configuration for the processor.

Tells Fluent Bit we're interested in the log-based inputs. (The other options are traces and metrics.)

We tell the processor we want to use the Lua plugin. (We could use other plugins here as well.)

As with using Lua as a custom filter, we need to identify the method to invoke.

Rather than reference a separate file, we can embed the script in the YAML configuration. But be aware that any errors from LuaJIT will report line numbers based on the start of the Lua code, not the actual line number in the configuration file, so we need to know how many lines precede the code in the configuration file.

For a deeper look at how Lua is invoked, such as the parameters and return values, see chapter 7.

Copies the rand_value in the event to another element of the event's record called original_val

Gets the random number divided by 2 and applied back to the data structure

Pings Google.com once with a short delay

We have this commented-out filter, so if necessary, we can look at the final input.

Inside the output plugin configuration, we declare another processor.

```yaml
service:
  log_level: info
  http_server: on
  flush: 1

pipeline:
  inputs:
    - name: random
      tag: test-tag
      interval_sec: 5
      processors:
        logs:
          - name: lua
            call: modify
            code: |
              function modify(tag, timestamp, record)
                new_record = record
                new_record["original_val"] =
                    record["rand_value"]
                local num = tonumber(record["rand_value"])
                local newNum = string.format("%d", num/2)
                new_record["rand_value"] = newNum
                new_record["tag"] = tag
                local handler =
                    io.popen(
                    "ping -c 1 -i 0.1 google.com")
                new_record["ping"] = handler:read("*a")
                return 1, timestamp, new_record
              end
#filters:
#  - name: stdout
#    match: "*"
  outputs:
    - name: stdout
      match: "*"
      processors:
        logs:
          - name: lua
            call: modify_out
            code: |
              function modify_out(tag, timestamp, record)
                new_record = record
```

```
            local search = record["ping"]
            local start = string.find(search, " ms")
          new_record["ping"] = string.sub(search, 0, start + 2)
            new_record["output"] = "new data"
            return 1, timestamp, new_record
        end
```

The output from pinging Google.com is lengthy, so we'll truncate the response string and update the attribute.

We can run this scenario easily with the command

```
fluent-bit -c fluentbit/processor-demo.yaml
```

Fluent Bit generates output like this:

As a result of our processor, we see additional elements, including the result of pinging Google.com.

```
[0] test-tag: [[1707683937.869194269, {}],
 {"rand_value"=>"3468270981094447104",
 "ping"=>"PING google.com(142.250.178.14) 56(84) bytes of data.
 64 bytes from lhr48s27-in-f14.1e100.net (142.250.178.14):
 icmp_seq=1 ttl=116 time=2.82 ms", "output"=>"new data",
 "tag"=>"test-tag", "original_val"=>6936541962188894208}]
[0] test-tag: [[1707683942.869093656, {}],
 {"rand_value"=>"718867304183793408",
 "ping"=>"PING google.com (142.250.178.14) 56(84) bytes of data.
 64 bytes from lhr48s27-in-f14.1e100.net (142.250.178.14):
 icmp_seq=1 ttl=116 time=3.41 ms", "output"=>"new data",
 "tag"=>"test-tag", "original_val"=>1437734608367586816}]
[0] test-tag: [[1707683947.869064092, {}],
 {"rand_value"=>"-4611686018427387904",
 "ping"=>"PING google.com (142.250.178.14) 56(84) bytes of data.
 64 bytes from lhr48s27-in-f14.1e100.net (142.250.178.14):
 icmp_seq=1 ttl=116 time=3.78 ms", "output"=>"new data",
 "tag"=>"test-tag", "original_val"=>-9223372036854775808}]
```

The text that is normally produced as a result of using ping was changed before the output operation was complete.

The random number from the original plugin has been copied to a new attribute, and the original rand_value tag has had its value modified.

Note from this console output sample that we have two different generated numbers: the random one and the result of dividing it by 2. We can also use the shortened output from the ping command.

9.2.2 *Content modifier processor*

We saw the `modifier` filter in chapter 7. The processor has a similar capability called the `content_modifier`, but there are some notable differences. The `content_filter` applies only a single change, such as adding or removing an attribute in a single invocation. Between filter invocations, the data is serialized and amended in the buffer before being deserialized for the next filter to process. But within the processor, we can make multiple calls to the processor logic without the back-and-forth of serializing and deserialization, making the process easier to follow in the configuration as well.

The modifier processor uses the `action` to tell the processor what to do. We need a `key` and, depending on the action value, a `value` and `pattern`. The `key` attribute usually identifies the event element to interact with, except `insert`, which names the new element. The `value` attribute, when used, is usually the new value for the attribute except for `rename`, which provides the new name to use. The supported actions include the following:

- `insert`—Adds a new value.
- `upsert`—Inserts a value if it doesn't exist; if it does, the value is replaced.
- `delete`—Removes the element identified by the `key`.
- `rename`—Takes the event's element identified by the `key` and renames it to the `value` identified by the `value` attribute.
- `extract`—Uses a `pattern` attribute to apply a regular expression to the value identified by the `key` attribute. The regular expression results in a `key` and `value`.
- `hash`—Converts the named (`key`) element to a hashed value.
- `convert`—Converts the data type of the identified (named by `key`) element. This requires an additional attribute called `converted_type` to provide the new data type. The accepted values are `string`, `boolean`, `int`, and `double`.

Let's put this processor to work. We'll use the `dummy` input, and on the input, we'll use the `content_modifier` processor to add an element to the payload. So that we can see what occurred, we'll include a filter to `stdout`. Then we'll direct the event to `stdout` but add multiple processors to the output that `delete` an event element called `recipient`, add new elements called `message` and `rename`, and `hash` an element called `noName`. Our configuration will be like the following listing; see `chapter9/fluentbit/processor-modifier.yaml`.

```
service:
  log_level: info
  http_server: on
  flush: 1

pipeline:
  inputs:
    - name: dummy
      tag: dummy-input
      dummy: '{ "message": "hello my world",
 "recipient" : "no one", "noName" : "nameless" }'
      interval_sec: 10
      processors:
        logs:
          - name: content_modifier
            action: insert
            key: "ImNew"
            value: "cool value"
```

The start state for our log event, which will be generated and passed to the processor before reaching the buffer

Declares the use of the content_modifier processor

Identifies the action to apply. In this case, we'll add a new element called ImNew with the value "cool value".

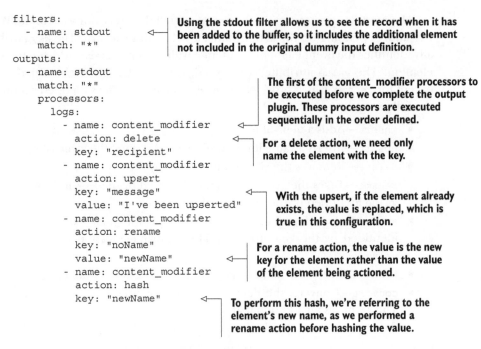

```
filters:
  - name: stdout
    match: "*"
outputs:
  - name: stdout
    match: "*"
    processors:
      logs:
        - name: content_modifier
          action: delete
          key: "recipient"
        - name: content_modifier
          action: upsert
          key: "message"
          value: "I've been upserted"
        - name: content_modifier
          action: rename
          key: "noName"
          value: "newName"
        - name: content_modifier
          action: hash
          key: "newName"
```

Using the stdout filter allows us to see the record when it has been added to the buffer, so it includes the additional element not included in the original dummy input definition.

The first of the content_modifier processors to be executed before we complete the output plugin. These processors are executed sequentially in the order defined.

For a delete action, we need only name the element with the key.

With the upsert, if the element already exists, the value is replaced, which is true in this configuration.

For a rename action, the value is the new key for the element rather than the value of the element being actioned.

To perform this hash, we're referring to the element's new name, as we performed a rename action before hashing the value.

We can run this scenario with the command

```
fluent-bit -c fluentbit/processor-modifier.yaml
```

When we run this command, we'll see output like this:

```
[0] dummy-input: [1714239548.467153200, {},
  {"message"=>"hello my world", "recipient"=>"no one",
  "noName"=>"nameless", "ImNew"=>"cool value"}]
[0] dummy-input: [[1714239548.467153200, {}],
  {"newName"=>"17d72fdf1868464ade4f11f794ecd73b655d
  b1e8eed322d2f66bdcba5bcfdad5", "ImNew"=>"cool value",
  "message"=>"I've been upserted"}]
```

The first line of output reflects the effect of the stdout filter. The second line is the output plugin at work after it executes the processors. Note that the element newName didn't exist in the filter's output but does in the final output, illustrating the effect of the processor on the output plugin. To modify the metadata, we need to add an attribute called context, which defaults to the value body but can be switched to attributes.

9.2.3   *Processor for traces*

The content_modifier doesn't work only for logs; it can also be applied to traces. To apply the content_modifier to a trace, we need to be explicit about the processor type in the pipeline's processors declaration, changing it from logs to traces. The second critical element is the attribute context. To preserve the trace structure, the context identifies which part of a trace we want the modifier to apply to. Therefore, the context must be one of the following:

- `span_name`—Name attributed to the span.
- `span_kind`—Client, server, producer, consumer, or internal. The value depends on the way the span has been triggered (synchronous, asynchronous, remote in, or remote out).
- `span_status`—Should be `Unset`, `Ok`, or `Error`.
- `span_attributes`—The values associated with the attribute.

Let's see how the input looks when we use the `content_modifier` to alter a span's attributes. See the following listing and `chapter9/fluentbit/processor-trace-modifier.yaml`.

Listing 9.3   Trace-modifying configuration: `processor-trace-modifier.yaml`

```
pipeline:
  inputs:
    - name: opentelemetry
      listen: 127.0.0.1
      port: 4317
      processors:
        traces:
          - name: content_modifier
            action: upsert
            context: span_attributes
            key: "BIGkey"
            value: "Modified"
```

Note that we've switched from logs to traces.

We've explicitly set the context to define which part of the trace to apply the action to.

Defines the key and its new value

As Fluent Bit v3 can handle the gRPC invocations, the easiest way to invoke Fluent Bit this way is via the `telemetrygen` (from the OpenTelemetry project) utility. We can run the utility directly with the Go install command to download and compile the code or via a container. To make it easy to (re)use, we've adopted the container approach here, using a `docker-compose` file to override the default container settings. To run the scenario, let's start Fluent Bit with the command

```
fluent-bit -c fluentbit/processor-trace-modifier.yaml
```

Then we can start our Docker container using `docker-compose`, which tells `telemetrygen` to send a single trace event to Fluent Bit. When successful, the container will stop. We can do this with the command

```
docker compose -f compose.yaml up
```

The output should look like this:

```
|------------------- RESOURCE SPAN -------------------|
  resource:
    - attributes:
          - service.name: 'telemetrygen'
    - dropped_attributes_count: 0
  schema_url: https://opentelemetry.io/schemas/1.4.0
  [scope_span]
    instrumentation scope:
        - name                   : telemetrygen
        - version                :
        - dropped_attributes_count: 0
        - attributes:
```

**The start of each span data structure,
which details when the span was executed
and whether the span has a parent**

```
  schema_url:
  [spans]
      [span 'okey-dokey-0']    ◄┘
          - trace_id                : 11fd2ace7d8a9b8591bd65dab9c85737
          - span_id                 : fdc707e5bd13341c
          - parent_span_id          : 6055c353fcd7e95c
          - kind                    : 2 (server)
          - start_time              : 1714503268725436216
          - end_time                : 1714503268725559216
          - dropped_attributes_count: 0
          - dropped_events_count    : 0
          - status:
              - code        : 0
          - attributes:         ◄┘
              - net.peer.ip: '1.2.3.4'
              - peer.service: 'telemetrygen-client'
              - BIGKey: 'Modified'
          - events: none
          - [links]
      [span 'lets-go']         ◄┘
          - trace_id                : 11fd2ace7d8a9b8591bd65dab9c85737
          - span_id                 : 6055c353fcd7e95c
          - parent_span_id          : undefined
          - kind                    : 3 (client)
          - start_time              : 1714503268725436216
          - end_time                : 1714503268725559216
          - dropped_attributes_count: 0
          - dropped_events_count    : 0
          - status:
              - code        : 0
          - attributes:         ◄┘
              - net.peer.ip: '1.2.3.4'
              - peer.service: 'telemetrygen-server'
              - BIGKey: 'Modified'
          - events: none
          - [links]
```

**The start of the attributes associated with
the span. As we've asked the processor to
add to the span attributes, we expect to
see a new key-value pair here.**

**The start of each span data structure,
which details when the span was executed
and whether the span has a parent**

**The start of the attributes associated with
the span. As we've asked the processor to
add to the span attributes, we expect to
see a new key-value pair here.**

**Our new attribute added to the
attributes of the span construct**

Our trace structure contains the additional elements. Removing the processor configuration and rerunning Fluent Bit and `telemetrygen` confirms that they normally aren't there.

> **NOTE** `telemetrygen` parameters allow us to tailor which OpenTelemetry Protocol (OTLP) events are generated. The tool is relatively simple. The options for its configuration are described at https://mng.bz/WVEl.

> **TIP** If the configuration doesn't produce any output, there is a problem with the Docker network configuration. For this configuration to work, both Fluent Bit and our Docker container must be visible on the same host network. If you're uncertain, we recommend replacing the reference to `host.docker` `.internal` in the `docker.compose` file with the IP of the host machine with Fluent Bit running.

9.2.4 *Processor to metrics*

Unlike logs and traces, metrics are simple. At their simplest, they are key-value pairs, so the number of things we may want to do is a lot simpler. One challenge is that a substantial number of metric values can be generated out of the box; if we need to supply only a subset of such metrics, we need to reduce the data volume involved. The new v3 processor includes a `metrics_selector` processor that can define a filter, so we can retain metrics or exclude specific metrics. We can set the behavior using an `action` attribute; this attribute, when set to `include`, allows only metrics whose name matches the filter expressed by the metric `name_attribute`. We can exclude by setting the attribute to be excluded. Strictly speaking, the code currently treats anything but `include` as meaning exclude.

The filter is defined using the `metric_name`, which can be a regular expression (inferred if the value starts with a forward slash) or the actual metric name (such as matching a literal value). We can also be explicit by using the attribute `operation_type`, which accepts the values `prefix` or `substring`, treats the metric as a literal value, and matches the start of the metric name or searches the full name.

Let's create a simple example using the `node_exporter_metrics` input plugin. We want the `node_cpu` metrics that start with the string `node_cpu`, not the hundreds of measures that can be provided. We need a configuration like the following listing; see `chapter9/fluentbit/processor-metrics.yaml`.

> **Listing 9.4   Using processors to filter our metrics: `processor-metrics.yaml`**

```
service:
  log_level: info
  http_server: on
  flush: 1

pipeline:
  inputs:
    - name: node_exporter_metrics
```

We've defined the use of the
node_exporter_metrics
plugin as normal.

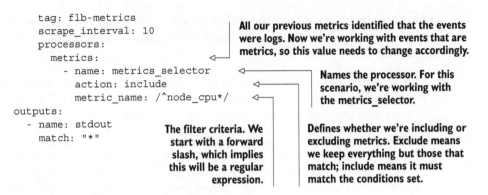

```
        tag: flb-metrics
        scrape_interval: 10
        processors:
          metrics:
            - name: metrics_selector
              action: include
              metric_name: /^node_cpu*/
    outputs:
      - name: stdout
        match: "*"
```

All our previous metrics identified that the events were logs. Now we're working with events that are metrics, so this value needs to change accordingly.

Names the processor. For this scenario, we're working with the metrics_selector.

The filter criteria. We start with a forward slash, which implies this will be a regular expression.

Defines whether we're including or excluding metrics. Exclude means we keep everything but those that match; include means it must match the conditions set.

We can run this scenario with the command

```
fluent-bit -c fluentbit/processor-metrics.yaml
```

As a result, we'll see metrics being output that look like this (only a subset, as the output will be influenced by how many CPUs are available, and we've stripped the date timestamp from the front of the output to aid readability):

```
node_cpu_seconds_total{cpu="0",mode="idle"} = 201493.66
node_cpu_seconds_total{cpu="0",mode="iowait"} = 821.74000000000001
node_cpu_seconds_total{cpu="0",mode="irq"} = 0
node_cpu_seconds_total{cpu="0",mode="nice"} = 1.8500000000000001
node_cpu_seconds_total{cpu="0",mode="softirq"} = 5053.6599999999999
node_cpu_seconds_total{cpu="0",mode="steal"} = 0
node_cpu_seconds_total{cpu="0",mode="system"} = 3754.0300000000002
node_cpu_seconds_total{cpu="0",mode="user"} = 10724.059999999999
```

When we looked at the configuration options, we've highlighted the fact that we can declare how to handle the `metrics_name` value, for example, by declaring that the metric name must start with `node_cpu`, which is what our regular expression declares. A regular expression is computationally more demanding than checking a string prefix. Why not try changing the configurations to use this alternative approach? We've supplied the answer in the configuration file `processor-metrics-answer.yaml`.

9.2.5   *Processor using SQL*

The Fluent Bit team has been working to ease and simplify the ways we interact with events. An approach adopted for stream processors (chapter 8) uses a SQL-based syntax as most people will have some familiarity with the syntax. Although the syntax that can be used here and with the stream processor is similar, there are constraints when we apply the principle to these processors, as we're not interacting with the buffer. As the data we can apply the SQL to is within the scope of the input or output plugin, we can interact only with streams, not tags. It is also fair to assume that not all the operators, such as the windowing operators, will be available. But we can use the syntax to filter, apply simple transforms, and rename, as we illustrated in chapter 8.

To see this in action, let's use the `dummy` plugins to generate several inputs and then use SQL to filter out events and select the event elements to be output. We need to formulate a suitable SQL statement, which must be terminated with a semicolon. This is supplied by referencing the SQL process with the `name` attribute set to `sql`. Then we have to provide the `query` attribute to the SQL expression, as the following code illustrates; see `chapter9/fluentbit/processor-sql.yaml`.

Listing 9.5 Using a SQL processor to control output: `processor-sql.yaml`

```
service:
  log_level: info
  http_server: on
  flush: 1

pipeline:
  inputs:
    - name: dummy                                    ⊲─────────┐
      tag: dummy-input                                         │    We have two inputs
      dummy: '{ "message": "hello my world",                   │    using the dummy plugin
➥ "recipient" : "notMe", "noName" : "nameless" }'             │    generating slightly
      interval_sec: 1                                          │    different messages.
    - name: dummy                                    ⊲─────────┘
      tag: dummy-input2
      dummy: '{ "message": "bye bye cruel world",
➥ "recipient" : "Pink Floyd", "noName" : "Im not a number"}'
      interval_sec: 1
  outputs:
    - name: stdout
      match: "*"
      processors:              Identifies the        The SQL statement that includes
        logs:                  SQL processor         the names of the attributes we
          - name: sql    ⊲─┘                         want to retain (the select clause)
            query: "SELECT message, noName           and then the filtration through the
➥ FROM STREAM WHERE recipient = 'notMe';"   ⊲─┘     WHERE part of the statement
```

We can easily run this example with the command

```
fluent-bit -c fluentbit/processor-sql.yaml
```

Our SQL expression is going to exclude some of the elements in the payload from the output and block the events created by `dummy-input2` because the payload it generates sets its `recipient` value to a value other than `notMe`. The result is output like this:

```
[0] dummy-input: [[1714326098.658997100, {}],
➥ {"message"=>"hello my world", "noName"=>"nameless"}]
[0] dummy-input: [[1714326099.648579300, {}],
➥ {"message"=>"hello my world", "noName"=>"nameless"}]
```

9.3   *Why we need to extend Fluent Bit*

As we've seen in previous chapters, Fluent Bit is flexible, with multiple protocols that can interact with source and target systems. We have Lua for writing custom scripts. So why do we need more extensibility options? The answer to this question involves several factors:

- To allow Fluent Bit to provide common behavioral characteristics, we need the plugins to interact with the core of Fluent Bit consistently. The easiest way is to provide a set of standard interfaces and means to build the plugins for the committers of Fluent Bit, most clearly visible in the C extension option.
- There will always be special cases where existing plugins can't support our needs. They might use an unusual authentication mechanism, encryption algorithm, serialization, or compression logic. Sometimes, APIs work by providing predefined objects; to use them, we have to generate code, as in the case of gRPC and Protobuf APIs.
- We could achieve connectivity using an existing plugin, but we'd make performance compromises, such as by using several filters. This will work, but it has a performance cost. Implementing the logic as a native binary plugin means we can optimize the performance while benefitting from Fluent Bit's other features.

Fluent Bit offers several ways to build native binary extensions:

- C
- Go language (often written as Golang)
- WebAssembly (WASM)

We'll take a high-level look at these options and why we might choose to use such an approach to build a Fluent Bit extension. We'll also identify where to get more details. This will set us up for chapter 10, where we will walk through building an extension.

Using C is the only option if you want plugins to be incorporated into a standard Fluent Bit deployment. Still, the Go and WASM approaches help enforce lower coupling through the interfacing controls, which can be easier to bypass if the plugin is compiled into the same binary.

9.4   *C language*

When we talk about building extensions with C, we mean building functionality directly into the core of Fluent Bit. We could approach this by permanently forking the code base and maintaining the downstream version. This approach creates a lot of additional effort in the long term, as we'll take on the challenge of merging and retesting the changes to ensure that they don't affect our own forked code base. Typically, we adopt this approach only if we want to provide a managed, supported version of Fluent Bit, so if our customer encounters a bug, we have the means to fix and release it outside the cadence of the open source project. Typically, this involves feeding the change back into the core open source, so code divergence is minimized. The alternative to code forking is contributing directly to the open source project. This approach is the one we're going to consider here.

9.4.1 Considerations

We need to make a wider set of design and implementation decisions before adopting this approach to building extensions. These problems have practical, technical, and potentially commercial implications. These considerations include:

- *Licensing*—Fluent Bit, like nearly every Cloud Native Computing Foundation (CNCF) project, has adopted the Apache 2 open source license (https://www .apache.org/licenses/LICENSE-2.0). Without going into the deep details of the license, it essentially allows anyone to do whatever they like with the provided code, including creating extensions or building solutions or services that use it. If the plugin needs to contain proprietary code or intellectual property, we'll be giving it away.
- *Development standards and processes*—To support consistency and maintainability of the source code, any contributions need to be made by following Fluent Bit's development processes, coding styles, and tools, which could be at odds with the tools and processes adopted within our organizations. A bit of effort is certainly required to become familiar with these styles and tools. If C isn't used regularly in our organization, there is going to be a notable learning curve.
- *Development and release cycles*—These Fluent Bit cycles may not match our commercial needs in terms of timelines. If we've provided a plugin that works with our product and want to align a release launch to the availability of the plugin, we'll need to align to Fluent Bit, not the other way around.

> ### Contribution is not a guarantee for becoming a committer
>
> Developing a feature or enhancement doesn't automatically grant the right to become a committer. Contributions of any size come by raising pull requests, which are reviewed by project committers, so the acceptance of a contribution is gated. Although key considerations include code quality and compliance, there is a chance that if our contribution functionally is niche or at odds with the norms of the wider capabilities, the committers may decline to accept the pull request. I recommend discussing a proposed submission with the community, including committers, and explaining how you would implement the solution before starting any code.
>
> Becoming a committer entails time and effort in terms of contributions through pull requests. Approval to become a committer is granted only when the other committers in the community feel that you have proved your knowledge, understanding, and alignment with the project and its expectations.

9.4.2 Benefits

By adopting C, we can take advantage of Fluent Bit's internal structures and interfaces as with any out-of-the-box plugin. From a commercial perspective, this has several advantages:

- The benefits of open source solutions are likely to be maximized, given Fluent Bit's high profile as a leading CNCF project. These benefits include the following:
  - Effort in maintaining the code is potentially spread across a wider community.
  - Security benefits from Linus' law ("Many eyes make all bugs shallow") are not to be confused with a guarantee of being secure. We only have to see the Log4j shell vulnerability to confirm that.
  - Licensing is easier, as the Apache license is widely used and understood.
  - Support and knowledge of using a plugin are more widely distributed.

From a more technical perspective, we'll see benefits such as these:

- *Performance*—As the code is directly integrated into the Fluent Bit core, there are no additional interfacing or abstraction layers. Given C's low-level nature, it is possible to highly optimize a plugin's resource use and performance (at the cost of requiring the development process to test for memory leaks).
- *Code reuse*—Because we're working directly with the core code it will be easier to use and reuse existing code to support the plugin. As a result, the amount of development may be smaller than implementing the plugin outside the core code base.
- *Easier plugin use*—There are no additional steps for deploying and configuring the additional deployment of resources. The process is deploy and go.
- *Promotion and collaboration*—If the plugin supports our service, it will help draw attention to that service.

> **NOTE** Resources for C-based development are available at https://mng.bz/ 86w5, which covers the relevant internal APIs for plugin contexts, enabling plugins, and so on. In addition, documentation on core development practices, such as how memory management is implemented, is available at https:// mng.bz/EOZX and https://mng.bz/NBRv. Also, appendix B lists information and tools that can help with C-based development for Fluent Bit.

9.4.3 Drawbacks

Unless our development tooling and processes neatly align with those of the Fluent Bit project, we'll need to establish additional development environments, tooling, quality controls, and so on, effectively increasing time and effort. The libraries Fluent Bit uses have been established, and introducing new dependencies is likely to attract a lot of due diligence to ensure that it doesn't introduce new license constraints on Fluent Bit, duplicate capabilities, or introduce new vulnerabilities to Fluent Bit. We must ensure that the new dependency is suitably supported and maintained so that it doesn't create additional overhead.

For input and/or output plugins, we must manage any changes we make in the solution being connected to so that it doesn't create periods of incompatibility, such as releasing changes and deprecating the old interfaces before an update to the Fluent Bit plugin can be produced, released, and adopted.

> **NOTE** Fluent Bit's use of semantic versioning (https://semver.org/) means that Fluent Bit has minor releases every six months, and patch-level revisions every two or three weeks, regularly including minor improvements. So far, we've seen only three major revisions: v1.0.0 in 2018, v2.0.0 in 2022, and v3.0.0 in 2024. The major version changes occur when significant feature changes are made. Version 2 had an internal data structure change, for example, and v3 saw the web server upgraded to support HTTP/2 and support gRPC.

It is possible to create and offer a forked version of Fluent Bit, which isn't unusual. Amazon Web Services (AWS) provides its own distribution of Fluent Bit (https://github .com/aws/aws-for-fluent-bit). Typically, organizations do this to fit their support processes and incorporate custom extensions. They can incorporate their plugin into the core of Fluent Bit and use proprietary code without developers getting visibility. Merging and regression-testing changes are a lot of work, however. We also have to consider whether our users will be comfortable not using the common builds.

It may be necessary to extend the build process with feature flags so that if the plugin is unavailable on a particular platform, there is no attempt to compile the plugin to the code base. This task involves additional effort and means that custom builds can remove the plugin.

With Go, it is possible to create proprietary extensions and keep the code secure, but this requires deploying additional binary files and requires the user to configure the dependencies. Certain combinations of technology with WASM may also be able to keep the source code hidden, but WASM currently has restrictions on how it can be used.

9.4.4 *Tools for the job*

If building directly into Fluent Bit is the approach that meets our needs, we'll need to be aware of several resources.

CONTINUOUS INTEGRATION AND DELIVERY

Fluent Bit includes a script library that runs a continuous integration process to allow development to be regression- and integration-tested. This library has been set up to be as light as possible, using the lightweight Kind packaging of Kubernetes, but it uses OpenSearch, which needs a reasonable number of resources allocated to it.

By default, the tests pull the Fluent Bit image tagged as latest from GitHub, so localized testing needs to modify the configuration of where the `FLUENTBIT_IMAGE_RESPOSITORY` is defined in `run-tests.sh`. The relevant repository is at https://github .com/fluent/fluent-bit-ci.

TERRAFORM ENVIRONMENTS

As Fluent Bit is a CNCF project, it makes sense that there is infrastructure as code to spin up environments to support the development and testing of Fluent Bit. In the fluent-bit-infra GitHub repository (https://github.com/fluent/fluent-bit-infra/tree/main), we find Terraform configurations for spinning up environments in the Google cloud.

9.5   Go language

Go (https://go.dev) is the most dominant language for CNCF projects (https://gloutnikov.com/post/cncf-language-stats), bringing the benefits of native binary performance while retaining features of languages such as Java in the form of memory management and abstractions and ease of development. It helps that the originators of Kubernetes (Google) are the driving force behind the development of Go.

The emphasis on native binary performance benefits for cloud solutions, particularly at hyperscale, makes easy direct integration between C/C++ and Go important as the Linux Kernel is written with C/C++, and it is second after Go in terms of native binary languages used by CNCF projects.

The Go plugins interact with the Fluent Bit framework through the Goproxy module (https://mng.bz/DpdA) in Fluent Bit. At this writing, the Goproxy and the associated Go binding code expose only input and output plugins, not the filter method interfaces.

9.5.1   Benefits

Using Go and configuring the addition of Go plugins into Fluent Bit provides a range of organizational and technical benefits:

- The open source project does not dictate release cycles and development processes.
- Because the result is delivered as a native binary, the plugin can be offered without exposing proprietary code or intellectual property.
- Specialist use cases are ideal for niche use cases that reflect specific organizational needs or niche requirements. These kinds of use cases often have a level of intellectual property rights (even if it is indirect when it comes to support functionality). For example, in the case of a plugin that handles errors from a video transcoder, the number of organizations using video transcoders is relatively small, and the number using a specific transcoder with a custom means to generate logs and events is even smaller.
- Plugins can be implemented to meet specific internal needs without giving due consideration to the community. If our organization has a specific standard for naming conventions, we can hardwire it into the plugin without concern about whether it meets wider community needs.

The technical benefits of using Go to build the plugin are

- Go retains the performance of native binary executables without losing the benefits of memory management being performed by a language runtime.
- The Go language provides binding to C applications as standard (https://pkg .go.dev/cmd/cgo), and Fluent Bit includes a library (https://github.com/fluent/ fluent-bit-go) that further helps with interfacing.
- Development approaches, particularly for closed source or private solution implementation, can be aligned to internal principles and practices without considering the wider community.

9.5.2   *Drawbacks*

The drawbacks are more operational than specific to code development itself. These challenges include the following:

- At this writing, the filter interfaces are not available.
- If the development team(s) don't work with Go, overhead remains in implementing and maintaining processes such as continuous integration. We need to include regression testing for major and minor revisions.
- If we intend to make the plugin open source, it is not as likely to get the same level of attention as the core Fluent Bit repositories. As a result, more of the maintenance burden will be on the plugin provider.
- Users have additional deployment effort when deploying our plugin in their existing environments, which could be problematic if customers use prepackaged platforms like OpenShift.
- The scope of paid support services can be ambiguous, as third-party support offerings typically don't cover third-party plugins.
- The plugin needs to be subject to ongoing periodic updates, even if the solution is stable and mature, to prevent the possible perception that the plugin is stale.
- Additional development effort is needed to translate between C- and Go-native data types. We will have to use other Go language libraries and frameworks.
- We may have to rebuild Fluent Bit with Go support enabled (`cmake -DFLB_DEBUG=On -DFLB_PROXY_GO=On`) depending on the build of Fluent Bit we use. Note that the images provided by the Fluent Bit project have this build flag enabled by default.

NOTE Resources for Go-based development are available at https://github .com/fluent/fluent-bit-go, including example implementations and a Go utility library to ease the workaround for the Go–C interface.

9.6   WebAssembly

WASM and the associated WebAssembly System Interface (WASI) represent the most flexible approaches to building custom plugins because they allow for greater freedom in development languages. At the same time, WASM has an increased learning curve. We need to master how to define and build the assemblies and the means through which we can debug our code.

> ### WebAssembly background
>
> WASM is designed to be invocable and contains discrete local executables, so it is ideal for Fluent Bit; it helps enforce the low coupling between the core and extensions. Although using WASM forces developers to adopt a more stringent framework, it allows a rich choice of languages for developing the logic within WASM, covering C, Rust, Python, C#, Go, and JVM-based languages.
>
> WASM started its journey in 2017 as an evolution of Java's Applet concept, delivering executable solutions that can be run safely within the browser. The problem with Java's applets (and Flash) is that a runtime engine must be installed on the client before the application can be run. Furthermore, the client-side execution container is dictated by the language used.
>
> WASM addresses this problem by allowing a binary to be deployed and run securely by the browser. WASM provides all the necessary packaging to protect the browser from needing anything preinstalled. To communicate with anything external, WASM needs WASI, which provides a controlled layer, conceptually similar to Java's sandboxing of applets.
>
> WASM has yet to take off as expected to enable in-browser extensions, possibly due to continued development with JavaScript frameworks and factors such as portability concerns. However, it has found a new, unexpected use case: packaging and deploying server-side functionality, particularly in cloud-native use cases. WASM's security controls required to work with a web browser created a tightly controlled relationship with the outside world, making it more secure than containers by default. Also, WASM needs a smaller footprint than a container but can still execute applications. As a result, it can start up and run more efficiently. This secure, small, quick startup aligns neatly with Fluent Bit's guiding principles.

Because WASM was built with the intent to be used within the browser, security is a big aspect of its design but also a limiting factor. WASM was intended to communicate with the browser via stdin and stdout; all other channels are blocked. In principle, WASM does the hard work and shares the results with the browser for the purpose of rendering. For a Fluent Bit plugin, other than for implementing parsers and filters, this is going to be rather restrictive. After all, the ideal reason to build a plugin is to integrate neatly with the source or destination. As WASM progresses into backend adoption, work is being done to address the problem, but this effort is still in progress at this writing.

9.6.1   *Benefits*

Like the Go benefits, we can divide these into more commercial/organizational factors and purely technical ones. From a technical standpoint, the WASM benefits are

- Configuring a WASM plugin is no more complex than that of a Go plugin from
  the perspective of Fluent Bit configuration.
- WASM, like containers, makes the boundaries between components more
  robust for better separation of concerns, particularly because WASI is designed
  to support accessing resources outside the assembly in one of the most security-
  aware scenarios running in a browser.
- WASM provides far greater freedom of choice of development languages for
  the logic needed, which can potentially accelerate the development process. By
  using WASM, it is possible to develop the logic with JavaScript, Java, PHP,
  Python, and Rust, to name a few options (https://mng.bz/lrMd).

Following are some commercial and organizational benefits:

- Because the artifact produced is binary, WASM allows us to offer commercial
  plugins and adopt a closed-source approach to the code if we want. When we
  provide the WASM, we have no obligation to provide the source code.
- Build and release cycles are not tied to the Fluent Bit project. If we want to
  release a WASM that can manipulate a Fluent Bit event to a structure that Fluent Bit can carry along with our application, we can release it and subsequent
  changes that meet our timeframe, as the deployment is not bound to Fluent Bit.
- WASM emphasizes providing and securing the code within the assembly, so it is
  a difficult attack vector to exploit. Deploying third-party plugins will make
  accessing any of our environments difficult.

9.6.2   *Drawbacks*

The drawbacks of using WASM and WASI are technical, particularly given that this
technology is relatively young. The most significant points are

- A significant additional learning curve is involved unless the organization is
  already working with WASM. Conceptually, WASM has ideas similar to containers, but it isn't a straightforward skills transfer, which may be part of the reason
  why we're not seeing WASM adopted as quickly as many people expected.
- The additional abstraction and ability for WASM to support interpreted and virtual machine (VM) languages can make the development process more removed
  from performance considerations. Building a Python WASM as a plugin used
  for a high-volume pipeline within Fluent Bit will have significant performance
  implications.
- Each layer of abstraction adds a small amount of overhead. WASM has the
  greatest level of abstraction from Fluent Bit and, therefore, comparatively, the
  largest overhead.

- The chances of maximizing the benefits from an open source community are significantly lower because the plugin isn't linked to the Fluent Bit code base. The community needs to make a conscious decision to investigate other sources of plugins.
- As the code is wrapped in an assembly, debugging the code can be much harder, just as debugging code within a container is harder.
- WASM's security strength is also a constraint, as today, the model is very difficult to use to allow a plugin to access services such as the network for HTTP and TCP interfaces. However, we believe that some of these challenges will be addressed over time.

Learning more about WASM

Reference documentation is available at https://webassembly.org (for WASM) and https://wasi.dev (for WASI). Books such as *WebAssembly in Action* (https://www .manning.com/books/webassembly-in-action) and liveProjects such as Simple App with WebAssembly (https://www.manning.com/liveproject/simple-app-with-webassembly) are also available. If you like to learn from examples, examples of WebAssemblies are freely available; https://wasmbyexample.dev shows the same WASM using different languages. There are plans to establish a registry to hold WebAssemblies through the development of a standard (so established registries can be extended to support this new type of object). This standard is known as WebAssembly Registry (Warg); details are at https://warg.io and https://github.com/ bytecodealliance/ registry.

9.7   Selecting an extension strategy

Table 9.1 is a decision matrix (sometimes referred to as a *stress test*). It works by providing a series of factors that are key to deciding which technology best suits your requirements or preferred approach. The table shows how well each extension option meets each factor. If a factor is important, choose the columns with a Y result. When you've evaluated all the rows, count the columns in which you've selected an answer. The column with the most responses selected reflects the most suitable option. For more about this approach to decision making, check out https://mng.bz/Bgdw.

Table 9.1   Decision matrix to help determine the most suitable plugin technology

Factor	C (part of Fluent Bit)	Go	WASM
Code is kept proprietary (for considerations such as protecting intellectual property).	N	Y	Y
Code mustn't be subject to Apache licensing.	N	Y	Y
The change and release process is controlled by the Fluent Bit community.	Y	N	N

Table 9.1   Decision matrix to help determine the most suitable plugin technology *(continued)*

Factor	C (part of Fluent Bit)	Go	WASM
Build and development needs to work with the existing build process.	Y	N	N
You can use your own development and testing standards and tools.	N	Y	Y
Code reuse and behavior consistency are maximized.	Y	-	-
The plugin supports niche use cases in which extensions must be implemented without forking the Fluent Bit core.	N	Y	Y
The plugin offers value to a wider community, and the value and cost of maintaining the code is shared within the community.	Y	-	-
The language has inbuilt memory management, eliminating the work of managing memory explicitly and the associated risks.	N	Y	Y
The plugin benefits from language-native memory management, allowing it to be highly optimized.	Y	N	N
You have increased programming-language freedom (such as Rust, JavaScript, or Java).	N	N	Y
Abstraction overheads must be minimal.	Y	Y	N

Although the decision matrix will help you arrive at a considered position, as a general rule of thumb, we recommend adopting Go as the default approach for custom plugins. Although this approach ignores the potential commercial benefits of implementing it into the core of Fluent Bit, it allows a great deal of latitude for development and use.

Summary

- The processor capabilities added in v2 of Fluent Bit (Lua scripting) and the significant new capabilities added in v3 (`content_modifier`, `metrics_selector`, and `SQL`) can deliver powerful means to work with all signal types.
- The SQL processor is a quickly relatable way to define the filtering and processing of events.
- We can use an OpenTelemetry project contribution to help test our Fluent Bit configuration.
- The benefits and drawbacks of the approaches to building plugins align with common themes:
  - Control (or lack of) of the delivery approach and tooling being use
  - Choice of development language and people's familiarity with languages
  - Whether the plugin logic should be open or closed source, reflecting the possibility of needing to include proprietary code

- New plugins can be created that compile directly into Fluent Bit using C. This approach has benefits (the plugin becomes core to Fluent Bit if accepted by the committers) and drawbacks (ownership is entirely bound to Fluent Bit's governance).

- Using Go as a technology for building custom plugins has its own pros and cons. Go offers improved decoupling and increased control of the plugin code base. Still, it can be more difficult to deploy and use when Fluent Bit is bundled within an opinionated platform like OpenShift.

- WASM and WASI as plugin technologies offer unique and distinct pros and cons, particularly, increased freedom in terms of development language but significant constraints in how they currently connect to outside services.

- A decision matrix can help you make an informed and transparent decision on the approach to adopt.

Building plugins 10

This chapter covers

- Implementing custom plugins using the Go language
- Using the Fluent Bit–provided Go binding layer
- Consuming Fluent Bit configuration data to control plugin behavior
- Managing data between method calls using the context object
- Seeing how contexts are applied for multiple instances of the same plugin type

So far in the book, we've concentrated on using capabilities entirely within a standard Fluent Bit deployment. Chapter 9 went through the options for building custom plugins. In this chapter, we will implement input and output plugins using Go.

10.1 Architectural context

We've reviewed the options and elected to build custom plugins. Now let's revisit our architectural view to see how our development relates to our architectural view, as shown in figure 10.1. Using Go currently allows us to interact only with

271

the input and output plugin frameworks, so we won't see any of the inner workings, such as the buffers.

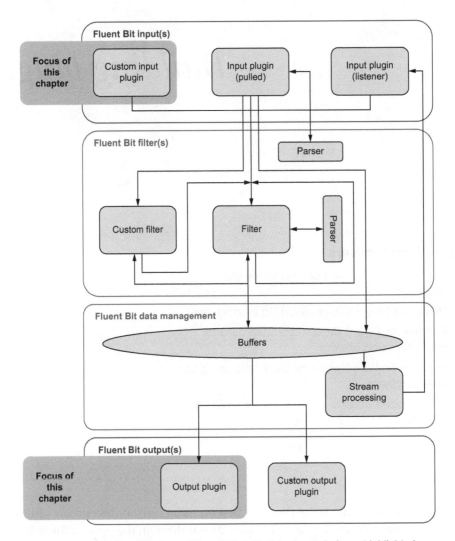

Figure 10.1   Logical architecture of Fluent Bit, with this chapter's focus highlighted

To understand the development of a Go plugin, we need to look more closely at a few technical areas:

- Understanding the structure of our code and dependencies
- Understanding the plugin life cycles that dictate the implementation
- Understanding the functions we need to implement, what we can do, and what is expected to be done within those functions

- Ensuring the solution can be built and then repeated for the output, paying close attention to the differences in life cycle methods
- Looking at how custom plugins are configured in a Fluent Bit configuration file

10.2   Why Go?

We'll use Go for several reasons:

- We're not bound to the processes and rules expected of us if we produce a C plugin that compiles into the Fluent Bit core. We don't have to recompile the entirety of Fluent Bit.
- Go frees us from worrying about memory resource management without compromising performance considerations.
- Go frees us from the additional complexity of WebAssembly (WASM) and WebAssembly System Interface (WASI) and the constraints for connecting to other services, such as the network.
- Go helps enforce the API layers because the touchpoints are clearly established.

We will focus on input and output plugins as the `filter` plugin implementation uses principles from both types of plugins. When we have a working plugin, we'll deploy and run it before completing the capability, as completing the functionality should reflect more of the technicalities of the service we're going to interface.

> **NOTE**   Go language resources may be necessary, depending on your familiarity with the language. This book isn't about Go, so although it explains what is happening, understanding and appreciating what is happening with the code is necessary. To understand more about the language, we recommend bookmarking the language website https://go.dev. A quick reference to the language structure and style is on the Go website at https://go.dev/doc/effective_go. The Go language website includes lots of additional resources. If you want to dive deeper, we recommend *Go in Action* (https://www.manning.com/books/go-in-action-second-edition).

10.3   Plugin objective

We will implement a relational database plugin that can be used with multiple databases. The rationale is that enterprise applications often keep tables with audit records as to actions completed by users, particularly at the administration level, which could affect end-to-end operations. Some databases, such as Oracle, manage audits and other actions in tables, so we can observe not just an application but also what is happening within the entire database. Operational teams that support databases often run queries to check the database's health, being able to execute these queries and inject the data into the observability pipeline. Likewise, injecting the relevant information into a database with a data model that helps with specific analysis tasks can be significantly labor saving.

To make the plugins as flexible as possible, the input and output plugin configuration will provide attributes to receive the different values needed to build an SQL statement. As observability has a key element of sequencing (either by a timestamp or a proxy such as an increment key), we'll need that information. When the data is ingested, we may want to delete the record from the source. These goals mean the configuration for our plugin should look like this:

```
[INPUT]
    name in_gdb
    tag  db1
    db_host 192.168.1.135
    db_port 3306
    db_user demo
    db_password demo
    ordering_col a_key
    table_name pluginsrc
    db_name demo
    db_type mysql
    pk a_key
    delete false
    query_cols a_key, a_string
```

This approach will be applied to both input and output plugins. Our configuration will have a variable number of parameter attributes. As we're pulling data from a database, we can reasonably expect the Fluent Bit engine to initiate our execution, but for completeness, we'll touch on how a network-driven push can be handled as an input.

Although the provided code includes a lot of functionality, the solution isn't enterprise complete. The GitHub repository (https://mng.bz/vJKa) includes suggestions on how to further develop the plugin.

10.4   *Go plugin approach*

Before we start looking at how the plugins work, let's look at how Go connects to the core Fluent Bit code base without recompiling Fluent Bit itself. The Go language has a framework called *cgo*, which allows us to connect Go and C applications. Through the use of specific types of code comments, cgo enables us to map Go functions to C header definitions and provide code to wrap the handling of memory between raw C code and how Go works with its more type-strict and robust memory management. This mapping means that when we call a wrapped method, the call and the parameter values in memory are passed between the languages.

In addition, cgo can generate shared object binaries (recognized by their file extension .so). Fluent Bit can load these objects at startup if it knows about them.

As well as loading the shared object files at startup, Fluent Bit's hot reload feature will reload these objects as part of the reload process. As a result, we can deploy updates to the plugin without having to restart Fluent Bit fully.

The downside is that if we're developing a plugin for multiple platforms, we have to compile the binaries for each OS (such as Windows and Linux) and CPU chipset (Intel, Arm, and so on). For in-house solutions, the multiplatform problem may not be an issue, but it's certainly a consideration for a service provider. To support multiple platforms, we need to address the demands of more configuration and the existence of the appropriate libraries.

NOTE You can find more on cgo at https://go.dev/blog/cgo and https://pkg .go.dev/cmd/cgo, along with information on how Go handles memory mapping with C via a package called unsafe (https://pkg.go.dev/unsafe).

10.4.1 *Simplifying our build process*

Rather than go through the challenges of configuring Go (which can be onerous if we don't want to use its defaults), we're going to build on top of a Go language Docker image (https://hub.docker.com/_/golang) that has all the necessary details. If we want to take the .so files to be distributed, Docker provides the means to retrieve the generated artifacts.

Building our Docker image will take a little time because it will copy our code into the container and compile it. If we don't want to copy the source code, we could mount the host filesystem. Depending on the machine's performance capabilities, this will still take less than a minute, but any code and debug processes can take longer.

We'll load the container with configuration files so that if the container is successfully built, it will run a simple scenario that can exercise our logic. In a production environment, we would also be creating and building unit tests.

10.4.2 *Code structure*

To ease the development of the code, we've structured things so that the database-related logic of our use case has no dependencies on the cgo layer. As a result, we can run this locally in a more agnostic manner. (The code is in the file run_gdb.go.) This is useful for any extensions or improvements we may want to make. As an additional benefit, we can separate the code that is secondary to what we're trying to understand: how to use the way Fluent Bit can be extended rather than the mechanics of a specific extension.

The database code has many commonalities for an input and output plugin, so rather than separate the logic and duplicate code into each of the plugins, we put the code in a single folder called common, and we copy it into the compilation of each of the plugins.

If you're an experienced Go developer, you'd probably elect to build this code as a separate package and create package dependencies. But, as the amount of code involved is small and keeping all the code together and the build process easy to follow, we've elected to apply simple copy steps into the build. Figure 10.2 shows how the code is laid out in the repository and the relationships between the files.

The code that provides the binding between C and the Go code skeleton that we have to flesh out is at https://github.com/fluent/fluent-bit-go, which includes simple examples. The examples also follow a similar strategy of using Docker but do not support the idea of a single container using Go plugins for both input and output. Calyptia (now part of Chronosphere), which has been the primary contributor to Fluent Bit, has a similar implementation (https://github.com/calyptia/plugin). Crucially, the

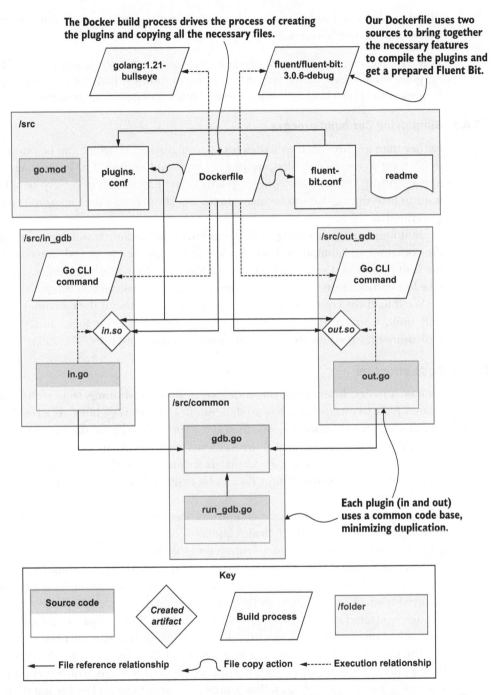

Figure 10.2   The straight lines represent development relationships. The curved lines are execution-related relationships. The dashed lines show what artifacts contribute to the creation of the artifact pointed at. The diamonds represent our generated .so (shared object) files. The Dockerfile drives everything.

Go methods that appear in both the Fluent Bit repository and the Calyptia repository are the same.

The one detail not included in figure 10.2 to prevent it from becoming too cluttered is documentation of the plugin properties. Several folders contain appropriate markdown files that include details such as descriptions of the configuration attributes.

> **NOTE** The Fluent Bit–Go repository has a constraint in the input plugin. We believe that the problem will be resolved in due course, allowing the input plugin to have the dual option of having a context object passed with the operation just as the output plugin provides. For the book, we describe how things work, assuming that the problem is resolved. The `readme` file in GitHub goes into more detail so we can update things inline with the code release of the improvement.

In addition to an example solution, we have provided a skeleton copy of the code in `chapter10/code-baseline`. It has the input and output Go files with methods marked with `TODO`, so you could use them as a starting point rather than review the implementation. If you want the common SQL logic, copy the `common` folder into `code-baseline` or copy the `code-baseline` over the completed implementation provided.

10.4.3 *Fluent Bit feature switches*

If we elect to set everything up or change the Dockerfile and its sourcing of the Fluent Bit image, we may need to confirm that the Go proxy layer within the core Fluent Bit binary is enabled. (The standard builds in the Fluent Bit repository are enabled.) This can be done by looking at the output from the command `fluent-bit --help`. The output will be a list of build flags enabled when Fluent Bit is compiled. We need to confirm the existence of `FLB_HAVE_PROXY_GO`. The output will look something like this:

```
Internal
 Event Loop  = libevent
 Build Flags = FLB_HAVE_IN_STORAGE_BACKLOG FLB_HAVE_CHUNK_TRACE
⇒  FLB_HAVE_PARSER FLB_HAVE_RECORD_ACCESSOR FLB_HAVE_STREAM_PROCESSOR
⇒  JSMN_PARENT_LINKS JSMN_STRICT FLB_HAVE_TLS FLB_HAVE_OPENSSL
⇒  FLB_HAVE_METRICS FLB_HAVE_AWS FLB_HAVE_SIGNV4 FLB_HAVE_SQLDB
⇒  FLB_HAVE_METRICS FLB_HAVE_HTTP_SERVER FLB_HAVE_TIMESPEC_GET
⇒  FLB_HAVE_PROXY_GO FLB_HAVE_REGEX FLB_HAVE_UTF8_ENCODER FLB_HAVE_LUAJIT
```

The flag in the preceding output appears in boldface to make it easier to spot.

> **NOTE** The approach and dependencies in this example assume the use of Fluent Bit v1.9 or later. An implementation of the library can support Fluent v1.4. To benefit from some of the features this book describes, we've assume at least v1.9, ideally v2.1 or later.

10.4.4 *The build process for plugins*

To build a plugin such as our database example, we need a build process, which is embodied within a Makefile. As Dockerfile configures all the necessary Go environment variables, we can exploit defaults and dependencies within the base image. The Dockerfile's build process has retrieved many of the dependencies. The compilation process is simple:

```
go build -buildmode=c-shared -o in_gdb.so
```

10.5 *Understanding the plugin life cycle*

All plugins have to work within the life cycle defined by the Fluent Bit engine, whether we're building a custom plugin for a bespoke business application or want to make it easy to use Fluent Bit with a commercial tool. Each step of the life cycle has a function associated with it. The life cycles of the different plugin types have some common elements. Let's start by examining what these common operations do:

- *Registration* (FLBPluginRegister)—This operation is invoked as Fluent Bit's engine creates an internal catalog of plugins, allowing it to help the user immediately if they use the command-line plugin to list plugins, for example. We must return the proper name and description of this plugin.

- *Initialization* (FLBPluginInit)—When the pipeline is being translated from a configuration file to executable processes, Fluent Bit will invoke our code with the configuration details. Each context-aware plugin has an initialization invocation per configuration file reference, which could include actions such as checking network connectivity or confirming that a file for that context (configuration reference) can be opened.

- *Exit* (FLBPluginExit)—When the Fluent Bit engine wants to shut down gracefully, it issues each plugin a call using this method. In our case, we should use the invocation to release the database connection gracefully. Hence, the database knows we're no longer connected and can release any resource it holds for us.

This list shows that the startup and shutdown behaviors are the same, which makes sense.

10.5.1 *Input life cycle*

Figure 10.3 illustrates the input plugin life cycle. We can see common operations. The core part of the life cycle is iterative, as shown by outputs leading back to inputs. The iteration is driven by Fluent Bit, so these loops pass back through the Fluent Bit core representation.

Let's discuss the role of each method specific to an input plugin, as shown in figure 10.3:

- *Input callback, input callback context*—The Fluent Bit engine triggers this method to collect data. We can put a sleep operation in to create a delay before accessing data again. Otherwise, we end up in a tight loop, which is fine for a fast-moving

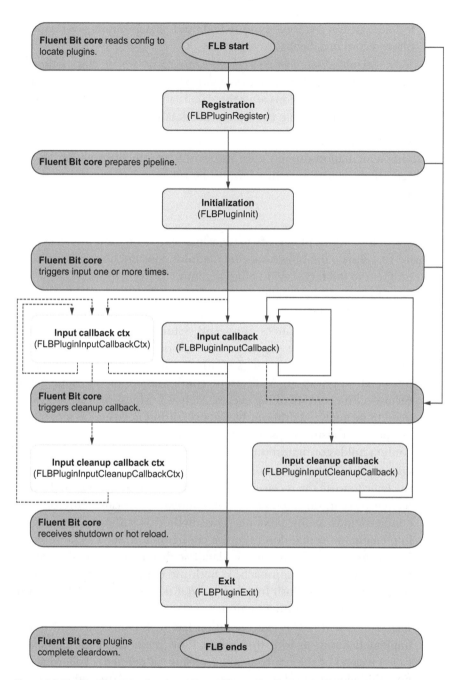

Figure 10.3   The life cycle of an input Fluent Bit plugin. Each solid-filled rectangle block needs a function implemented in the plugin. The unfilled rectangle blocks are the expected methods when the context problem is addressed. The dotted lines show the equivalent invocation flows to the solid ones that exist today. The execution passes back to the Fluent Bit core (diagram-wide shapes) after each invocation; the core's role is illustrated by the shapes. This figure allows us to see the life cycle as a flow and where execution flows.

log file but not for something that should change more slowly, such as a slow query record in a database.

- *Input cleanup callback and input cleanup callback context*—If this method is defined, the engine will call it after the result of the initial callback is returned. The intent is to enable actions after the data is added to the buffer. In our example, we could use it to delete the data in the database after we've read it.

These methods have two versions, one without a context and one with a context. As the Go implementation doesn't have its own cache, any information associated with the plugin, such as attributes that have to be retained between invocations, must be stored in the context.

10.5.2 *Output life cycle*

Let's look at the output plugin life cycle, which has a common initialization and exit. As figure 10.4 shows, the plugin-specific methods consume the contents of the buffer and send them to the target we're plugging into.

Let's walk through the functions:

- *Output flush (with context)*—Having a context-based output allows us to connect to different instances of an end system. We might use the same plugin type to write different events to different database schemas if our DB output plugin was used to record logs relating to user events, such as signing in and out of an application. A different configuration of the same plugin might receive a different set of log events, such as business-process key events, which need to be analyzed differently. Data retention needs to be separate for different people (business-ops users rather than security auditors). As a result, the context holds configuration differences.

- *Output flush*—Like the contextual version of this method, this method contains the logic to write the received buffer data it to the target system. Unlike the contextual version, this method has no context, so we can't differentiate between configurations in the pipeline. This method is sufficient for plugins such as implementations that don't require configuration, such as those using stdout. In our use case, we'll use the Go database driver to write to the database, so we need the contextual approach. If both the contextual and noncontextual versions of the output flush function are defined, the Fluent Bit core will call the contextual version of the function.

- *Exit (with context)*—The exit operation has both contextual and noncontextual implementations, as with the output flush methods, if the context version is called instead of the noncontextual version (if defined). Following our illustration, this allows us to close the connections to a database without affecting other connections using the same plugin. This approach is particularly handy if our connections need to be terminated independently, as with the dummy plugin, which can be told to run a predefined number of times and then stop.

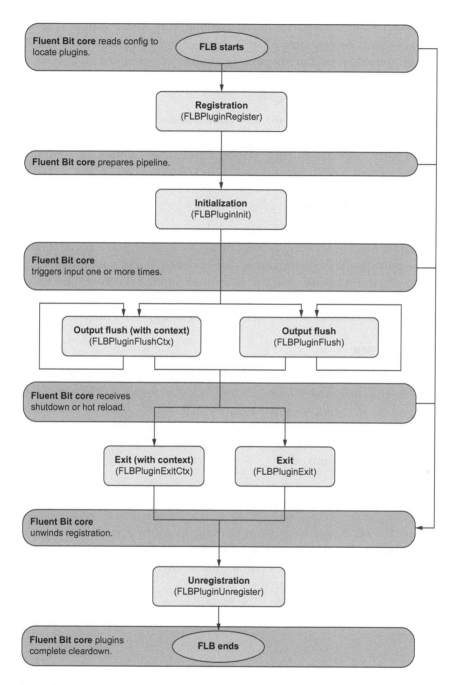

Figure 10.4 The life cycle of a Fluent Bit output plugin. Each rectangle block represents an implementable method. Here, we have output flush with or without a context object and a corresponding exit with or without context. Each method we implement is triggered by the Fluent Bit core, as shown with the full-width shapes. We can see the logical life cycle with clarity on the invocation source.

- *Exit*—This method allows us to wrap things up. If our output is to something like stdout, we can induce the flushing of any I/O buffers that may be necessary. Whether or not the exit is contextual, we need to release any held resources, such as the database connection so that the database can reuse that connection for something else.

In both figures 10.3 and 10.4, for input and output, the Fluent Bit core representations are connected because, at any phase of the life cycle, the core may be forced to jump out of the normal sequence. During startup, for example, the shutdown signal is received.

10.6   *Implementing the plugin*

Let's step down in detail, starting with the development environment and code. The first detail we need to have in place is our database. MySQL is a popular open source database with maintained containers that currently doesn't have its own plugin; it makes for a good database. Postgres is another popular database, and we've already used it; we'll also prove the idea by incorporating the Postgres driver. If you want to go further with the scenario, we recommend trying things with Postgres.

10.6.1   *Setting up MySQL*

The first step is downloading and setting up MySQL. You can use the official Docker image at https://hub.docker.com/_/mysql or install it locally, which is easy with a UI-based installer. To configure and manage MySQL, we recommend installing the Community Edition of the MySQL Workbench or the command-line interface (CLI) tool. The steps are covered in appendix B. To start the MySQL database for the first time, we need to use the command

```
docker run --name mysql -p 3306:3306 -e MYSQL_ROOT_PASSWORD=mySQLRoot -d
➥ mysql:latest
```

When the Docker image is running, we want to connect to the database using the MySQL Workbench. (If you prefer a tool like the MySQL CLI, feel free to use it instead.) We need to create a new connection in the Database menu and complete the details to be like those shown in figure 10.5.

Figure 10.5   The MySQL Workbench as we connect to the containerized instance of the database

When we're connected to the database server, we need to create the database and tables. To do this, select the Query 1 tab in the center of the UI, copy into it the SQL provided in the file `chapter10/sql/initialize_mysql.sql`, and click the lightning bolt icon to execute it. The Output section at the bottom of the screen in figure 10.6 shows the results.

We need to repeat this process for the contents of the SQL files `chapter10/ sql/create_user_mysql.sql` and `populate.sql`, which create a user to test with and a couple of rows of data in the `pluginsrc` table. Now we have a database table ready for use with our plugin.

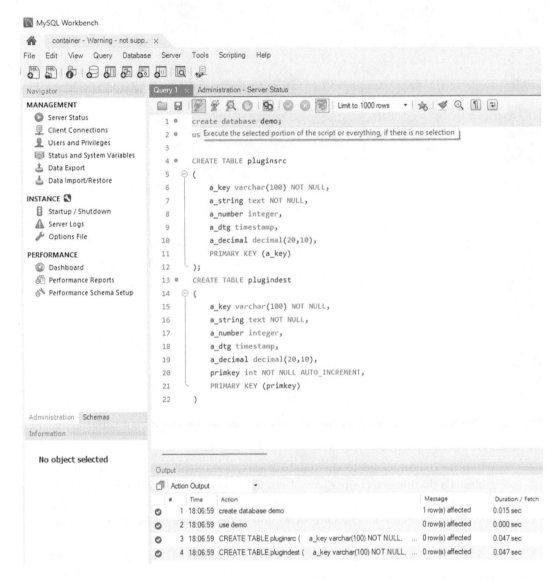

Figure 10.6   MySQL Workbench with SQL is used to create the database and tables for our use. The SQL executed successfully, as we can see in the Output section at the bottom.

10.6.2 *Input plugin*

Let's examine each of the functions we need to implement following the input plugin's life cycle, which we saw in figure 10.3.

INPUT REGISTRATION

Registration is simple. We need to return the plugin's name and a description. This data is added to that of the other available plugins. If command-line help is used to list the available plugins, our plugin will be included in the help information. Further, the name provided links this plugin to the configuration file references. The following listing shows the implementation; see `chapter10/go/src/in_gdb/in.go`.

Listing 10.1 Implementation of the register function: `in.go`

```
//export FLBPluginRegister
func FLBPluginRegister(def unsafe.Pointer) int {
    log.Printf("[%s] Register called", PluginName)
    return input.FLBPluginRegister(def, PluginName,
    "Go plugin for reading content from a database")
}
```

A hint for the cgo process for mapping code

The first of many uses of the unsafe features because we're not isolated from the fact that our code is being initiated by C. To tell the invoking C code whether things have been executed successfully, we need to return an integer value.

Helps our code be a bit chatty during development so we can see our methods being invoked. We defined the plugin name as a constant so we can reference it throughout the code, which makes it easy to repurpose the code.

We need to communicate with the controlling C code whether or not our operation has been successful, and occasionally, we have the option to say, "Please retry." As is typical of C solutions, we do this by passing an integer. The abstraction layer has defined the values as meaningful constants. Table 10.1 lists the names of the constants and their integer values.

Table 10.1 The constants that can be used for return codes in plugin development

Constant name	Value
FLB_OK	1
FLB_ERROR	0
FLB_RETRY	2

INPUT PLUGIN INITIALIZATION

The next step is initialization. Here, we need to interact with the plugin layer to retrieve the configuration values; we call the `FLBPluginConfigKey` method provided by the interface layer. Although the bulk of the configuration values are handled separately, we have retained one invocation within the function to check the log level setting.

With the value gathered, we should validate that all the necessary values are defined and sensible. If any values are missing or unsuitable, we need to tell the user. We've addressed this situation by separating out the validation logic using a method called `validateSqlParams`. This method returns an `error` struct that contains an appropriate message. Unlike all the other logging in which we use the log features, this method's logging is routed directly to the console so the user will see a meaningful message. When defining the configuration attribute names to use, we must be mindful that many reserved attribute names exist. (See appendix B for the reserved names.)

Within this method, we also retrieve the configuration value for `Log_Level`, and if it is set to `debug`, we'll print the configuration. If the values are valid, we'll cache them. Our implementation is, in effect, the orchestration logic of the whole process, as shown in the following listing and `chapter10/go/src/in_gdb/in.go`.

Listing 10.2   Implementation of the initialize function: `in.go`

Here, we're calling a separate function to retrieve all the configuration values. This function executes a series of calls to FLBPluginConfigKey.

If retrieving the configuration values from the Fluent Bit configuration file results in an error, we need to propagate this back to the core of Fluent Bit to handle.

```
//export FLBPluginInit
func FLBPluginInit(plugin unsafe.Pointer) int {
    params, err := getParams(plugin)
    if err != nil {
        return input.FLB_ERROR
    }

    if strings.Contains(strings.ToLower(
 input.FLBPluginConfigKey(plugin, "Log_Level")),
 "debug") {
        log.Printf("%s configured with %v\n",
 params.pluginName, params)
    }

    validateErr := validateSqlParams(params)
    if validateErr == nil {
        cacheParams(params)
        return input.FLB_OK
    } else {
        fmt.Printf("%s - Configuration error - %s \n",
 params.pluginName, validateErr)
        return input.FLB_ERROR
    }
}
```

Retrieves the configuration values using the interface function that communicates back to the core of Fluent Bit. The getParams method is a series of these calls that retrieves all the needed values. In this case, we're looking for the attribute value called Log_Level.

If we're configured to work at a debug log level, we need to log all the configuration values we've aggregated into a convenience structure called MyParams.

With all the data values collected, we use a function to check whether all the mandatory values are populated and meaningful.

If the validation is OK and if we've cached our data structure (making it quicker and easier to use without recasting and validating values later), we can tell Fluent Bit everything is OK.

The `getParams` method is a collection of statements that use the calls to `FLBPluginKey` (such as `input.FLBPluginConfigKey(plugin, "Log_Level")` with appropriate type casting). Listing 10.2 shows an example that interrogates the configuration values to see whether the `Log_Level` has been set and, if so, whether the level is `debug`. The method provides a Go `struct` representing all the values and their correct data types. We pass this structure around to make the code somewhat tidier. We pass back an error code if key configuration values are missing or wrong. To ensure consistency between input and output, we've named the configuration attributes as constants in the common code.

INPUT CALLBACK
The real work takes place as we interact with the source and translate the retrieved values into an appropriate structure and payload format. We have decoupled the logic of

formulating and pulling the database from the database; when invoked, it returns an array of map values. Then we map each record to a structure that holds the current timestamp and values retrieved, using their column names as the key.

When we have the correct structure (note that we aren't pinning a tag to the structure because it's implied and understood by Fluent Bit's core process management), we use an encoder that encodes the payload using the MessagePack library. Finally, as we're passing the data by using memory references provided in the invocation, we apply the Go transformation so that the C binary understands the data. Only the success or error flag is provided as a return value.

The final step is calculating how long to idle, as described by the configuration. Strictly speaking, the sleep time should be calculated from the time when the callback is invoked. Still, for simplicity, we're assuming that the latency of calling the database and processing the results is small enough not to count because we're not allowing triggers faster than once per second. See the following listing and `chapter10/go/src/in_gdb/in.go`.

We need to associate the log entry with a timestamp, so let's get the date and time as we ingest the event.

```
//export FLBPluginInputCallback
func FLBPluginInputCallback(data *unsafe.Pointer, size *C.size_t) int {
    //log.Printf("FLBPluginInputCallback - START -------------")
    now := time.Now()
    flbTime := input.FLBTime{now}
    params := retrieveParams()
    dataSet, sequenceId := dynamicQuery(params)

    if dataSet != nil && len(dataSet) > 0 {
        dataCtr := len(dataSet)

        if len(sequenceId) > 0 {
            params.LatestSequencerId = sequenceId
            cacheParams(params)
        }

        var entry []interface{} = nil
        if dataCtr > 0 {
            for dataLine := 0; dataLine < dataCtr; dataLine++ {
                recd := dataLineToStrMap(dataSet[dataLine])
                entry = []interface{}{flbTime, recd}
            }
        }
    }
```

Retrieves the cached configuration of the configuration values for this plugin instance. As we have a lot of values, it is easier to pull a complete data structure.

If we have some data to send, we process it. Otherwise, we push back a null pointer and zero length.

We need to manage the value used to track the event ordering so that the next time we query the database, we don't select data we've already retrieved. Instead, we get the next values in order. If the tracking value needs updating, we ensure that we update our cached data. Note that if we delete records after they're read, we don't need this tracking.

We need to give the record we received from the SQL logic (a key-value map) the structure expected by Fluent Bit. As we saw in chapter 1, we have metadata (including the tag), a timestamp, and the log event. The metadata is handled for us. But we're entirely responsible for building the event's record.

```
    enc := input.NewEncoder()
    packed, err := enc.Encode(entry)
    if err != nil {
        log.Printf("[%s] error:
%s,\n Can't convert to msgpack: %v\n",
PluginName, err, entry)
        return input.FLB_ERROR
    }

length := len(packed)
*data = C.CBytes(packed)
*size = C.size_t(length)
} else {
  length := 0
  *data = nil
  *size = C.size_t(length)
  time.Sleep(time.Second *
time.Duration(params.QueryFrequency))
  }

  return input.FLB_OK
}
```

Fluent Bit handles the events in the msgpack format. We need to perform the conversion before setting the pointers to reference these values using data *unsafe.Pointer, size *C.size_t.

Takes the msgpack data and wraps it up so it can be handled and safely passed across the Go–C boundary

If our query resulted in no records, we need to delay the next iteration, as the chance of getting a zero-row result is high.

You may have noticed in the code that we use {interface} heavily. This Go language feature allows us to pass around constructs of varying types. Using an interface permits a derived mapping to operations for different data types.

When we've passed the data back to the core of Fluent Bit, the data provided is incorporated into the buffer mechanism and managed through the pipeline for us. We could consider using the context structure to cache the database connector object, but this can become complex for a couple of reasons:

- *The server can time out connections.* We need to reopen the connection. If not handled carefully, this approach leaks resources. Therefore, for simplicity, we're going to instantiate a new connection. If the database is pooling its connections, the overhead is not much more than authenticating HTTP requests.
- *We don't know (and shouldn't care) what data may be inside a connection structure.* As a result, we are handling it as a data structure using the C-related utilities. Rather than getting buried in these details, we can keep things simple by caching only the data structures that we control. The server can time out connections.

CLEANUP CALLBACK

This operation is simple. When it's invoked, we retrieve any contextual values that hold resources and release them. If any errors occur, they're passed back to the callback and logged, and we report an error back to the Fluent Bit core. At this level, we need to release only resources specific to this callback cycle.

Depending on the type of connection being managed, we may want to close the connection to the source. We may want to exploit the context to determine whether it is worth cleaning up. If the context yielded no data in the query, we might want to clean it up because we might be waiting a long time. Then we might as well clean up everything rather than discover that the DB timed out our connection. The outcome of the callback and the cleanup actions could be passed through the context. See the following listing and `chapter10/go/src/in_gdb/in.go`.

Listing 10.4   Implementation of the cleanup callback function: `in.go`

Calls the internal function to release any resources we use. Releasing resources at this stage, although clean and tidy, can have performance implications as we'll need to open resources again in future uses of the plugin instance. Unless a significant risk exists, it's better to leave this for the exit.

```
//export FLBPluginInputCleanupCallback
func FLBPluginInputCleanupCallback(data unsafe.Pointer) int {
  // err := releaseResources(data)
  // if err != nil {
  //  log.Printf("%s had an error during cleanup, error is %s\n",
  //     Plugin_Name, err)
  //  return input.FLB_ERROR
  //}
  return input.FLB_OK
}
```

If we experience a problem clearing down, returns an error; otherwise, returns OK. This may be important because it could result in leaking memory.

INPUT EXIT

This callback is often only used when we need to handle open connections for the entire operating period of Fluent Bit. We're closing things down quickly, which means that the plugin is less efficient, but it makes for simpler code. We can get away with acknowledging via an OK response. See the following listing and `chapter10/go/src/in_gdb/in.go`.

Listing 10.5   Implementation of the exit callback: `in.go`

```
//export FLBPluginExit
func FLBPluginExit() int {
    return input.FLB_OK
}
```

As with all the code samples, the cgo comment helps us understand the methods' need for exposure.

We want to return an error message only when a genuine error occurs. Calling a method when nothing needs to be done isn't an error.

As our functions operate within the standard Fluent Bit framework, if the user has configured a `grace` value in the service part of the configuration, Fluent Bit will be afforded some time for resources to close.

10.6.3 Building the code

With the plugin code in place, we want to see whether it will compile and generate the binary statically linkable file. We can do this by asking Docker to create the image; the Dockerfile includes the steps to pull the code from the local development environment and build and deploy the plugin. As we saw in figure 10.2, the Dockerfile drives the whole process. Let's review it in the following listing; see `chapter10/go/src/Dockerfile`.

Listing 10.6   Configuration that will build the plugin and container: Dockerfile

As mentioned earlier, this container image builds
on top of an official Go image, so we know that
all the necessary utilities are in place.

Declares the folder that will form the
base of all the code and resources

```
FROM golang:1.14 as gobuilder

WORKDIR /root

ENV GOOS=linux\
    GOARCH=amd64

COPY / /root/
COPY /common/* /root/out/
COPY /common/* /root/in/

COPY /out_gdb/* /root/out
COPY /in_gdb/* /root/in

RUN go mod edit -replace
➥ github.com/fluent/fluent-bit-go=
➥ github.com/fluent/fluent-bit-go@master
RUN go mod download & make -C out all
RUN go mod download & make -C in all

FROM fluent/fluent-bit:2.2

COPY --from=gobuilder /root/out/out_gdb.so
➥ /fluent-bit/bin/
COPY --from=gobuilder /root/in/in_gdb.so /fluent-bit/bin/
COPY --from=gobuilder /root/fluent-bit.conf /fluent-bit/etc/
COPY --from=gobuilder /root/plugins.conf /fluent-bit/etc/

EXPOSE 2020

CMD ["/fluent-bit/bin/fluent-bit", "--config",
➥ "/fluent-bit/etc/fluent-bit.conf"]
```

For cgo, we can rely on many
defaults, such as where libraries
will be downloaded. But we still
need to declare explicitly which OS
and chipset we're building for.

Copies the configuration files and source code for the
plugin into the container. Note that we're copying the
common code into both plugin folders rather than
building a package and then declaring a dependency.

Makes sure we have
the latest Fluent Bit
Go source

We use Go to retrieve the
dependencies for the module
(defined in the go.mod file)
and then execute the
Makefile in one of the plugin
folders. This step is repeated
for the second plugin.

Defines a dependency on the Fluent Bit
container image, which results in Fluent
Bit executables being put in place

Copies our
generated code
to the right place

The container execution instructions.
Note that it uses a default. If we want
to introduce alternative configurations,
the Dockerfile must be changed.

To help with running the plugins, in addition to the default configuration, we included additional configurations in the chapter10/fluentbit folder that can be swapped in, which allows the input or output plugins to be exercised.

10.6.4 *Output plugin*

As we've already seen, the input and output plugins have many similar definitions, such as the registration and initialization phases. We've also implemented a lot of core logic in a common code base. We don't need to examine FLBPluginRegister and FLBPluginInit. Things diverge when we handle the plugin flush. As we want to have differences and track states, we'll implement FLBPluginFlushCtx.

OUTPUT FLUSH

As we saw when reviewing the plugin life cycle, this functionality is given a chunk of data and pushes it to the destination—the database for which we have the configuration. Like the input callback, the data is exchanged using C pointers with the payload serialized with MessagePack. To make the data meaningful, we decode the payload. We also need to handle some quirks of how data can be represented. A string can be passed as a series of unsigned integers, for example. Before sending the data anywhere, we convert the data to more appropriate Go types.

When this problem has been addressed, we can hand off the work of injecting the data into the database. This time, we use the configuration values to inform the insert behavior. See the following listing and `chapter10/go/src/out_gdb/out.go`.

Listing 10.7   Implementation of the flush callback: `out.go`

```go
//export FLBPluginFlushCtx
func FLBPluginFlushCtx(ctx, data unsafe.Pointer,
length C.int,
tag *C.char) int {

  params := NewSqlParams()
  myContext := output.FLBPluginGetContext(ctx)
  if myContext != nil {
    strContext := myContext.(*string)
    params = JSONToParams(*strContext, PluginName)
  } else {
    params = envToParams(PluginName)
    if params == nil {
      return output.FLB_ERROR
    }
  }

  if params == nil {
  return output.FLB_ERROR
  }

  dec := output.NewDecoder(data, int(length))

  count := 0
  for {
    ret, ts, record := output.GetRecord(dec)
    if ret != 0 {
      break
    }

    var timestamp time.Time
    switch t := ts.(type) {
      case output.FLBTime:
        timestamp = ts.(output.FLBTime).Time
    case uint64:
      timestamp = time.Unix(int64(t), 0)
    default:
```

The data payload comes through C-wrapped data structures and uses Go's unsafe feature.

Here, we see the call to the plugin to get the actual context for this instance of the plugin.

Unwraps the context and prepares to use it. Out of an abundance of caution, because we're passing across the Go–C boundary, we've marshaled our config to JSON and back again.

We need to decode the data we've been provided, as it will be in msgpack format.

Starts an infinite loop of processing data. (We may receive multiple records from the buffer to store.)

Makes sure we have the correct representation for the timestamp

```
      timestamp = time.Now()
  }

  count++
  insertErr := execInsert(params, record)
  if insertErr != nil {
    return output.FLB_ERROR
  }
}

return output.FLB_OK
}
```

We have a record. Let's invoke the logic to load the record into the DB.

As with all the callbacks, we need to provide a status in the response.

The context (ctx) can be any data you want, but it has to be handled via a pointer. Therefore, we need to use the cgo C functions to ensure that data is handled correctly for passing back and forth.

EXIT AND UNREGISTER FUNCTIONS

As with the input plugins, we're keeping things simple, not caching the database connection object or any other resources that must be explicitly resource managed. We can handle these method invocations with a simple logging action and returning FLB_OK.

10.7 *Deploying the custom plugin*

When the plugin is built, we want to deploy and use it. We need to tell Fluent Bit about the additional plugin files. This process is similar to including parsers (chapter 6) and Lua scripts (chapter 7). We need a file to reference the plugin .so files. The file format is the same as the parser-inclusion configuration, as shown in the following listing; see chapter10/go/src/plugins.conf.

Listing 10.8   Configuration identifying the custom plugins: plugins.conf

```
[PLUGINS]
  path /fluent-bit/bin/out_gdb.so
  path /fluent-bit/bin/in_gdb.so
```

The identifier tells us that the following configuration will identify the location of plugin binaries.

Each plugin is referenced by an attribute of the path and then an absolute file path.

The conventional location for custom plugins is a /bin folder of the folder containing Fluent Bit. But this location is not mandatory. We could argue that referencing the folder that contains the build objects in our container would be better, as it can simplify the Dockerfile. But as we're copying other resources in place, consolidating helps, particularly if someone wants to export a copy of the Fluent Bit part of the filesystem. Wherever the plugin file resides, we identify each one with the attribute path and then an absolute path. To clarify the configuration file's purpose, we start with a declaration block of [PLUGINS].

With the plugin's configuration established, we add a reference to it in the Fluent Bit configuration file. As we did with the parsers, we add an attribute to the

[SERVICE] block of the configuration, an attribute called `plugins_file`, and the file's location:

```
plugins_file plugins.conf
```

When Fluent Bit starts and parses the configuration file, it loads the identified plugins, even if they're not used.

10.8 Configuring our scenario

Now that we've walked through all the Fluent Bit core callbacks that drive the plugin, we've developed our own version or examined the plugin code base deeply. Either way, we need to exercise the plugins. We've included a couple of extra configurations in addition to the primary one that the Docker image will pick up in `chapter10/fluentbit`:

- A configuration that uses the `random` input plugin and a filter to generate a synthetic source to test the output plugin (`output-only-test.conf`).
- A configuration that reads from a database source and sends the received events to stdout.
- A configuration with two outputs using the same input, which helps demonstrate the application of context. As the plugin supports giving each instance of the plugin configuration a unique name, it is possible to see in the logs when each instance is triggered.

All these configurations work with the MySQL database we set up at the start of this chapter and should also work with the Postgres versions because the provided code keeps to American National Standards Institute (ANSI) SQL. To deploy these configurations, we need to use them to replace the contents of `chapter10/go/src/fluent-bit.conf`.

Let's examine the full end-to-end configuration, which uses both the input and output plugins. Many of the configuration values affect how the SQL is generated and executed rather than the plugin. All the attributes are detailed in the file `chapter10/go/src/README.md` with example values. See the following listing and `chapter10/go/src/plugins.conf`.

> **Listing 10.9 Configuration identifying the custom plugins: `plugins.conf`**

```
[SERVICE]
    flush          5
    daemon         Off
    log_level      info
    parsers_file parsers.conf
    plugins_file plugins.conf          ◁──  Directs Fluent Bit to
    HTTP_Server    Off                        read the file that tells it
    HTTP_Listen    0.0.0.0                     where the plugin objects
    HTTP_Port      2020                         to load are located

[INPUT]
    name in_gdb          ◁──
```

Directs Fluent Bit to
read the file that tells it
where the plugin objects
to load are located

The name of our plugin has to tie up with the name
in the name provided by the FLBPluginRegister
method (listing 10.1: PluginName).

```
    tag  db1
    db_host 127.0.0.1
    db_port 3306
    db_type mysql
    db_user demo
    db_password demo
    ordering_col a_key
    db_name demo
    table_name pluginsrc
    pk a_key
    delete false
    query_cols a_key, a_string
    #where_expression
    #log_level debug

[OUTPUT]
    name  out_gdb
    match *
    db_host 127.0.0.1
    db_port 3306
    db_type mysql
    db_name demo
    db_user demo
    db_password demo
    table_name plugindest
    pk a_key
    log_level debug

[OUTPUT]
    match *
    name stdout
```

We need to provide the details necessary to connect to the DB server for input and output plugins. Depending on the network configuration, it may be necessary to change this to the IP for the host of the database. Depending on how your local networking is configured, you may want to replace this address with the IP of your host machine.

We need to know which DB type so we can use the correct driver and construct the connection URL appropriately.

As a DB server can support multiple schemas and tables, we need to know which one.

In our configuration, we're not deleting records after they're read by the plugin.

Identifies the names of the table columns we want to send

We need to provide the details necessary to connect to the DB server for input and output plugins. Depending on the network configuration, it may be necessary to change this to the IP for the host of the database. Depending on how your local networking is configured, you may want to replace this address with the IP of your host machine.

Ideally, we inject these values into the configuration so that the DB credentials aren't in clear text. Further, in a production environment, we want to use a set of credentials that are limited in terms of what can be seen and done.

TIP Depending on how your Docker and host network are set up, you may need to modify the IP configuration to explicitly be the IP of the machine running the database. We like to wire this to a Domain Name System (DNS) address or the IP of our host machine.

10.9 *Executing the build*

As described earlier in the chapter, we've incorporated into the Docker image build the steps to invoke Makefiles for each plugin. If we want to build only one of the plugins, we need to comment out the entries in the Dockerfile that calls the Makefile and copy the resulting file to the target folder where Fluent Bit is installed. Don't forget to amend the `plugins.conf` file as well. The build command run from the `chapter10/go/src` folder for the Docker image is

```
docker build . -t fluent-bit-gdb -f Dockerfile
```

If the build fails, we see the compilation errors displayed as an outcome. But failing to build the first plugin won't prevent the build process for the second plugin.

Keep in mind that if we run the build process multiple times, we'll accumulate copies of some layers from the Dockerfile—specifically the layers associated with building the plugins because they're generated every time. Therefore, it is worthwhile to purge (or prune) them periodically using the command

```
docker builder prune -f
```

If you want to distribute the built plugins, you can use Docker commands to retrieve the generated shared object files.

10.10 *Running the custom plugins*

Before we run our Docker image, remember to ensure that the MySQL container is running. With everything in place, we start our container with the command

```
docker run -it --rm fluent-bit-gdb
```

This command starts the container, triggering the Dockerfile's RUN statement to execute Fluent Bit. The console output from our Docker image shows details such as the plugin methods being invoked. But the real proof is to query the tables in the MySQL database periodically. The simplest way is to run the SQL statement select * from plugindest, as we did when setting up the tables (using a SQL tab in the center of the MySQL Workbench and clicking the lightning bolt icon to execute the SQL statement). Notice that to ensure that the destination table (plugindest) can consume our events, we set up a separate primary key, which is autoincrementing. Every time we send data across, we're guaranteed to get a new row.

Summary

- Fluent Bit's core directs the plugin execution logic through a series of interfaces that support a life cycle. For each phase of the life cycle, a Go function needs to be implemented.
- The code is structured, and our approach to having common logic has been to copy the common code to the right place for the build process rather than the more mature approach of using packaging to keep things simple.
- Building Go extensions involves the use of cgo. Cgo tools and commands to enable Go code to be bound to C applications have been explored, where cgo is necessary to enable our code to be called from the Fluent Bit core when necessary.
- Plugins can access the configuration attributes to tailor plugin behavior as defined in a standard Fluent Bit configuration file.
- Fluent Bit has constraints on the naming of configuration values (which appear in the configuration file).

11

Putting Fluent Bit into action: An enterprise use case

This chapter covers

- Reviewing an enterprise use case's needs
- Seeing why adopting Fluent Bit can be evolutionary
- Looking at multicloud observability
- Connecting what we've learned with the real world

To understand how to use different features of Fluent Bit in a real-world context, we'll link our examples to a hypothetical use case in this chapter. Although the use case is for a hypothetical company, many aspects of the example are based on real-world needs. As we work through the use case and see how Fluent Bit can be applied to deliver value, we'll refer to specific chapters that cover the relevant concepts and capabilities.

11.1 Use case

Media Management Solutions (MMS) provides media content management as a service, covering tasks such as cataloging media, streaming, and transcoding formats for content such as audio and video. The product is a specialized form of headless content management system in many respects. Enterprise customers will incorporate and extend the core product into their own services. Customers are typically large corporations that need to provide videos, such as instructional videos, for their staff or customers.

The MMS team often describes its business as a blend of the brains of YouTube and Netflix, with APIs that allow customers to build a user experience like Netflix and with strong, easy-to-use content organization, curation, and analytics for providing content features such as those that YouTube offers.

The internet enabled a new generation of technology titans, companies that can flex and scale like never before and are cloud born, free of heritage challenges. Many businesses today don't have those benefits. MMS is part of the latter group, having started at a time when application solutions had to be deployed to a company's own hardware.

11.2 Deployment needs

The MMS product was originally developed and deployed with J2EE application servers installed in customer data centers. With the maturation and acceptance of cloud services, MMS has many customers running the product in various clouds. To take advantage of this fact, MMS developed a road map to transition its business model from a license offering with the option of a managed service or (primarily) a Software as a Service (SaaS) offering.

Cloud adoption increased pressure on cost management by making resource use as elastic as possible and increasing service availability (such as removing maintenance downtime). As a result, MMS incrementally refactors or rewrites its core application to run on Kubernetes.

These goals led to the decision that the core solution must stick with core Cloud Native Computing Foundation (CNCF) solutions rather than cloud-vendor-specific services. Customers want to use the product with their own preferred cloud provider to minimize latency between the application and their extensions and to lower the possible cost of data-egress charges from the cloud vendor. The solution must operate across Google Cloud Platform (GCP), Amazon Web Services (AWS), Microsoft Azure, and Oracle Cloud Infrastructure (OCI) as a design principle, as illustrated in figure 11.1. Cloud vendors provide native functionality that is compliant with the CNCF stack, which they should take advantage of to minimize their IT operations effort. Using managed Kubernetes is acceptable, but monitoring visualization through a cloud vendor's tools is not.

MMS could have adopted a strategy of connecting the different components directly to their observability toolset, but this was seen as restrictive. It would create a complex web of many-to-many connections. It would also mean there was no option to improve incrementally and it would be constrained by what could be done with current implementation technologies. As we saw in chapter 1, adopting Fluent Bit provides a small vendor-neutral footprint that offers options for extension when necessary. Fluent Bit can be deployed almost anywhere, including all the major hyperscalers and OSes for on-premises deployments to support license-based customers.

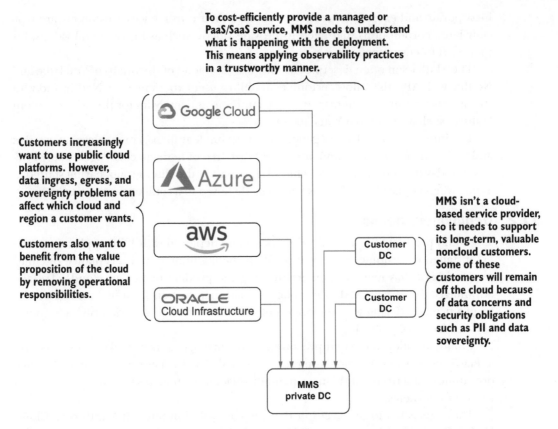

Figure 11.1 Multiple cloud vendors are supported as part of a managed service, along with some cases of customer data center (DC) managed services, although this business is contracting.

MMS considered Fluentd, but Fluent Bit supports OpenTelemetry, which is on its road map and the more efficient footprint. In addition, Fluent Bit does not need to address the deployment and patching of Ruby or in-house Ruby development skills, which makes Fluent Bit a far more attractive option.

11.3   Customer dashboards

The customer's management console serves static content, such as CSS and HTML, from a web server. The console is used mainly for understanding and managing content permissions, content curation, and business-process-related controls. In addition to serving static content, the web server acts as a load balancer, cache, and proxy.

Although Apache did its job well, it is being replaced by nginx as part of the technology changes being made. Nginx offers better performance without sacrificing capabilities. Apache's greater flexibility was not being fully used.

The software logic for the dashboards is implemented like the core application technologies, using Java in J2EE (now called Jakarta EE) with Eclipse Glassfish (https://github.com/eclipse-ee4j/glassfish) implementation. The database used for managed and licensed deployments has been customer-choice relational DB in the form of Oracle, MySQL, or Postgres, which they had to license to get the necessary support and assurances on patching.

The JavaScript UI part of the dashboards interacts RESTfully with the backend via an API gateway. The technology road map is to continue with Java as the principal programming language; the organization has considerable expertise in Java, with a code base that can be refactored to move quickly from J2EE to MicroProfile architecture (https://microprofile.io). Helidon (https://helidon.io) is also being adopted because it is perceived to be leading the way with MicroProfile-compliant frameworks and is maximizing Java's evolution. The transition to MicroProfile and microservices is intended to be iterative, with the Glassfish servers decomposed to a MicroProfile architecture. Subsequent iterations will adopt GraalVM (https://www.graalvm.org), which translates Java into native binaries. Further enhancements will be made using OpenTelemetry solutions, such as code instrumentation for tracing.

11.3.1 Customer dashboards with Fluent Bit

Fluent Bit deployment will use a sidecar pattern for the Pods created, given that their code base is already established with a logging framework (chapter 4). Initially, the sidecar will access commonly mounted folders for the containers, so some benefits of using Fluent Bit can be obtained without changing the application.

These first iterations of deploying Fluent Bit tapped into the Log4j outputs, using Fluent Bit's file-handling plugin (chapter 3) and the parser (chapter 6), reflecting the traditional log file approach. As a result, some benefits of using Fluent Bit could be obtained without changing the application.

The team quickly recognized that shifting to the Log4j HTTP appender would simplify things, eliminating the challenges of processing multiline log events and managing file mount points (chapters 3 and 4). It also removes the challenge of storage in Kubernetes (chapter 4) and allows the team to quickly improve and tune event processing, extracting essential events and filtering out successful housekeeping events.

This was seen as a good intermediate state until the team understood how to get the most out of OpenTelemetry and transition Fluent Bit to be an OpenTelemetry Protocol (OTLP) Collector, able to receive and send OpenTelemetry standardized events (chapter 3). Adopting the OpenTelemetry models requires the team to master automated code instrumentation and add explicit OpenTelemetry calls, identifying the start and end of spans that might reflect business transactions, for example.

11.3.2 Customer dashboard containers

The precise way to connect Kubernetes to Fluent Bit monitoring depends on the cloud being used; what is visible in these managed services differs. Oracle's fully managed Kubernetes means that OCI will look after and operate the master and worker nodes, which does not prevent the customer from using the Kubernetes filter to enrich the captured events. The Fluent Operator and Helm charts (chapter 4) will be starting points for automating the deployment of Fluent Bit to the Kubernetes environments where node monitoring is required.

11.3.3 Customer dashboard innovation

MMS is taking full responsibility for the dashboard experience in the SaaS deployments, being able to measure user experience (UX) performance. OpenTelemetry provides a framework that allows client-side traces to be sent back to Fluent Bit (https://mng.bz/dZ6g) via an API gateway that understands the OTLP protocol, ensuring that it can't be used as an attack vector. It also exploits the OpenTelemetry capabilities discussed in chapter 3. The Fluent But deployment can easily be addressed by deploying a standard Fluent Bit container (chapter 4).

11.4 Development pipelines

Docker will support developing and testing microservices. The Docker configuration will use the Fluent Bit log driver so that logs don't get routed via the Log4k configuration and are picked up and flagged. Chapter 4 describes the logging-driver model.

In addition to developing and testing MMS's products, the team will use Fluent Bit to monitor continuous integration/continuous development (CI/CD) and the development toolchain. These logs will be captured directly in the security tooling to ensure no attempts are made to poison deployable artifacts with malicious code.

11.5 Core services

The core services of MMS are written in a mix of Java and C/C++. Java is used for everything other than transcoding services; the transcoders were developed and built using C/C++ so that hardware optimizations could be used. Java development follows the same model as the dashboard features. The Java solutions have been deployed to separate Glassfish servers on separate networks to provide additional security isolation. The C/C++ transcoding functionality uses journald; because the logic is closer to the OS and hardware, journald makes it easier to see what the transcoders report as errors, alongside OS and hardware logs.

Strategically, the transcoding is largely seen as recompiling and deploying the services. Transcoding is a computationally intensive process, so these components will be developed to exploit the increasing power of GPUs.

Streaming operations focus on auditing who streams media, what they stream, and when they stream it. Sending media down socket connections is much easier. These services are written in Java and mix Glassfish-developed functionality with custom-threaded applications. Media streaming is a sensitive area regarding product perception and can be heavily influenced by performance and application stability.

The data collected from the streaming services is expected to become the primary revenue driver because it is the most customer-relatable service use. In the future, the backend will have to help calculate and optimize the use of storage tiers. Also, the transcoding service will charge based on media length (duration) and resolution, so getting insights into resource use will be an avenue for improving service margins.

The current MMS solution is a managed service. The customer had to pay for resource use. As long as MMS's forecasts for customers were within a certain tolerance, customers tended to accept a resource-generous approach to these services, with plenty of spare capacity and redundancy. MMS managed the services without tending to every aspect of the deployments around the clock. However, as customers using the managed service shift to the cloud, this approach has led to pushback.

For the core services, MMS will use the `systemd` plugin, which provides access to journald along with plugins for memory, CPU, disk, and network (chapter 3). In addition, any existing scripts in place can be instrumented with Fluent Bit so that their outputs can be captured in the logs, providing full visibility and audit trailing to environment processes. Chapter 2 shows how to use the Fluent Bit command-line interface (CLI) directly; chapter 3 shows how to capture the stdout. This not only gives MMS an audit record of what happened but also enables it to perform analysis of the corrective actions.

The Java functionality will evolve similarly to the customer dashboards. Whereas the dashboards' use of Helidon provides good integration with OpenTelemetry, the team will need to use the OTel instrumentation tooling.

11.6 Central accounting needs

MMS has operated an enterprise resource planning (ERP) solution to manage core processes such as accounting, human resources, and budgets. These processes haven't been particularly demanding because they've worked on a licensing model, and managed services have been licensed, plus standardized support packages and consulting services on configuration, deployment, and integration are available. As a result, the on-premises deployment of the ERP has been standard and predictable work. The product has been well maintained as on-premises deployment. The move toward SaaS, however, is expected to drive more real-time interactions by users who want to see their service-use data, creating more work. Strategically, MMS wants to switch to a SaaS ERP but also wants to sweat the existing assets as long as possible so it can focus on the product.

The logs from the ERP will be collected with Fluent Bit to monitor its well being along with the supporting database (chapters 3 and 5). Additional custom metrics will be built using Go's extension capability (chapters 9 and 10) so that the ERP can be monitored in terms of the lag between billing events for service consumption and how up to date the ERP is. Combined with other measures, this data can be used to forecast whether ERP performance is likely to become a problem earlier than expected.

Each virtual machine (VM) or physical server has its own Fluent Bit node to monitor resource use, capturing OS logs such as journald and core performance metrics, which will be shared with Prometheus via the remote write exporter. When a SaaS solution eventually replaces the ERP, several SaaS selection criteria will support operational needs, and several potentially custom plugins will be needed. The requirements are

- The ability to retrieve from the application audit information that can be incorporated into security operations so that the SaaS capability can be monitored and combined to create a more comprehensive security picture
- APIs that retrieve key measures to help with holistic monitoring, such as detecting lag between service consumption and billing
- APIs that measure the ERP to reconcile service charges from the service provider and forecast demand, aligning with budget

Fluent Bit may need some customized plugins to implement the automation of such operational support (chapters 9 and 10). However, these features can be implemented with Lua scripts rather than Go plugins.

11.7   *Operational processes*

Current operational processes are driven by wiring applications to the company's Slack or email to trigger alerts for major problems, such as service failures detected by pinging various nodes. Additionally, problems have come from customers raising support requests.

Operational health has been driven primarily by the ops team performing routine health checks as a result of experience and the use of runbooks and checklists. The additional capacity created a fair bit of redundancy in the deployments, so the existing automation is sufficient. With large enterprise clients, the fees involved enable the company to manage a head count–to-customer ratio of 1:10. If resources are stretched, engineering (which is expected to take periodic rotations in ops) helps out.

Correction is achieved by using localized scripts and simple tools in the managed environment. An occasional log incorporating sensitive data isn't a problem, but the team recognizes that the situation could be better. Adopting Kubernetes and microservices will demand better tooling, and the SaaS offering is likely (and wanted) to help grow the customer base in smaller organizations.

To increase engineering productivity and help the product transition to at least its initial version, the team needs to spot operational problems sooner and gain diagnostic insights that will improve the product. The team decided to focus on metrics to understand existing deployments better because raw measures like the number of processes running, CPU, and storage loads won't reveal sensitive data. Strategically, each supported cloud vendor for the SaaS offering will have an operational monitoring backend. For the first customers of the new microservices-built implementation, the operational processes will run on the current on-premises spare capacity.

A Fluent Bit node will be used in each MMS deployment as a controlled point of egress from the application. Egress is tightly controlled, and the Fluent Bit node can be configured with filters to apply parsers that can be used for the following:

- Filtering out or masking logs with sensitive data values.
- Filtering out data identified as not needing to be centralized. This data will be stored with the application deployment for up to 14 days so it can be retrieved and examined if necessary.
- Enriching passed-on events with deployment information to determine the origin, including a managed token based on random-number generation.
- Using a stream processor (chapter 8) to count the number of warnings received within a 5-minute window and determine whether a heartbeat was received from the upstream sidecar Fluent Bit instances.

These egress controls will use filters, including the record modifier filter and custom parsers (chapter 6), to spot sensitive data in the events received. The egress Fluent Bit node will use the Prometheus remote write plugin (chapter 5) to send its local metrics to the central node. The count of remote nodes will indicate whether contact with a managed or SaaS instance has been lost.

Central operations will use a Prometheus server and corresponding Grafana instance to visualize the received metric and alert on upper or lower thresholds. The central Fluent Bit will consist of several separate deployments covering the following tasks:

- Handling data receipt from the distributed MMS deployments. Although most communications are expected to use the OpenTelemetry protocol, OTLP edge cases will be handled using the `forward` protocol. Transport Layer Security (TLS) will be applied to these communications, and when the infrastructure to roll out certificates quickly is in place, it will be extended to mutual TLS (mTLS; see chapters 3 and 5).

  Operations will monitor the Grafana, Prometheus, OpenSearch, and Tempo infrastructure and receive traffic from other nodes. The `checklist` plugin from chapter 7 will be used to validate the identifying token.
- Applying stream processing to derive overall measures for all the MMS product deployments.

The aggregating central nodes are expected to receive a lot of data eventually. To address this, the plan is to include deployment IDs within the tag names. Then workloads can be split up by using worker threads, regular expressions, and wildcards in the match definitions (chapter 5).

Figure 11.2 illustrates the deployment architecture between MMS and a single location. We assumed that the management node in Kubernetes is a managed service.

This will depend on the cloud provider. In Oracle's Cloud Infrastructure (OCI), for example, the management node is part of the managed service. For customer deployments, additional configuration is needed to monitor the management node.

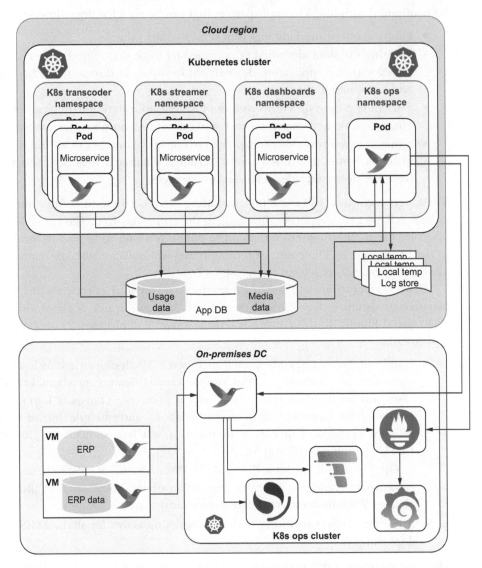

Figure 11.2   Architecture of our use case, made up of modern cloud-native technologies and private data center deployments using virtualization and private Kubernetes clusters

Dashboards work particularly well with metrics and provide great visual cues about what is happening operationally. But they present several challenges:

- Remote work means that many organizations no longer need a dedicated large display showing all the indicators.
- Conveying critical log events on a dashboard effectively can be difficult.
- Latency exists between events and dashboards, visually indicating a problem as the data is collected. With automated scaling, there is a risk of making things worse because the scaling mechanism could increase the compute load and accelerate the problem.

MMS recognizes this challenge and will test and develop notifications through social channels, such as Microsoft Teams and Slack, linked to their dashboards, which will mitigate the risk of not detecting a situation that needs attention during metrics and dashboard processing. MMS has also developed a set of filters and streams that can detect import events and send them through social channels as alerts.

MMS uses a ticketing system that allows customers to raise requests and show where and when correction is needed, as well as a log of the decision processes. Tickets associated with standard problems are linked to a copy of the standard runbook. Automated notifications from Fluent Bit that are perceived to deliver value will also raise tickets.

11.8 Tool choices

A range of tools support the analysis and actioning of signal types. In this use case, MMS has adopted the following:

- *Prometheus* (https://prometheus.io)—One of the most dominant open source solutions for capturing and storing time series data. Prometheus holds its data in a time-ordered structure. The data is handled as key-value pairs and processed as counter, gauge, histogram, or summary metrics.
- *Tempo* (https://grafana.com/oss/tempo)—Part of the Grafana Labs open source solutions, providing analytical insights on trace data. Jaeger (https://www.jaegertracing.io) is often the default option, but historically, extra work has been required to secure it.
- *OpenSearch* (https://opensearch.org)—A fork of Elasticsearch (https://www.elastic.co/elasticsearch) and interface compatible with Elasticsearch APIs without the more restrictive license and offered as a managed service by some cloud providers.
- *Grafana* (https://grafana.com/oss/grafana)—A visualization tool commonly used with Prometheus.

11.9 Conclusion

MMS developed a road map that exploits Fluent Bit's fundamental features, using Fluent Bit's core functionality to capture and drive insights in a distributed model. The company also identified actions that will exploit the advanced features, such as streaming, to help with special use cases. Fluent Bit's application clearly lends itself to modern Kubernetes-centered use cases and more traditional deployments.

MMS recognizes that observability is an important part of ensuring the health of its build processes as they become increasingly automated to ensure that the pipelines are operating correctly (not failing because they can't store built artifacts due to storage capacity). The organization recognizes that the transition and changes are significant and that the challenges and Fluent Bit adoption ultimately need to support business goals. Revenue will be much more dynamic under a consumption pricing model. Therefore, operational awareness and the ability to control costs must be far more reactive and, if possible, proactive.

Summary

- Fluent Bit is platform- and vendor-agnostic, so it can support multicloud and filter what is needed for the centralized views.
- Fluent Bit supports modern Kubernetes-style deployments and more traditional VM deployments.
- Both monolithic application technology stacks and microservices are supported by Fluent Bit.
- Monitoring isn't just for production software. Tools such as Fluent Bit can retrieve data and create metrics on SaaS services to ensure that suppliers are true to their quality-of-service commitments.
- Fluent Bit enables the incremental adoption of new technologies and standards in the observability space.
- Observability isn't only for business production services. Development pipelines need care to keep operating efficiently, so outputs are crucial as development processes become increasingly automated.

appendix A
Installations

This book uses components and tools in addition to those necessary to run Fluent Bit v2.x and later. This appendix addresses the setup of the tools. There is a strong focus on working with the Kubernetes ecosystem, which is dominated by Linux containers. As a result, the instructions focus on configuring Linux and using containers. We'll use Docker to run our containers and Docker Compose to simplify parameterizing our execution of Docker containers.

A.1 Tool installation overview

Because the use of Linux dominates the Kubernetes ecosystem and containers, we'll focus on using Linux, but where practical, we'll also provide reference information for the Windows equivalent. If you're working with a Windows environment, we recommend that you adopt one of the following options:

- *Use Windows Subsystem for Linux 2 (WSL2).* For more information on installing this free solution, we recommend starting at https://mng.bz/r1Vx.
- *Use VirtualBox to run a Linux Virtual machine.* we recommend using a virtual machine (VM) with a graphical UI for simplicity. VirtualBox (https://www.virtualbox.org) is an open source solution. It is better to download an OS image and create the VM, which eliminates the problem of using an out-of-date instance configured so that it's harder to work with.
- *Adopt Windows Docker desktop.* The benefit is that it includes a Kubernetes deployment and can work with WSL2 or Hyper-V virtualization.
- *Add Linux capacity with a free cloud account.* Some cloud hyperscalers, such as Oracle Cloud, provide free computing resources, offering a way to start a Linux server to run processes.

We will use tools like Fluent Bit outside containers, which makes it easier to understand what is going on and how we can drive Fluent Bit when creating or extending containers that run Fluent Bit.

The following sections provide enough detail for you to install the tools that support the examples in this book. If an installation value isn't stated, use the default value. We've included details on installing utilities locally so you can try things out, such as using the Fluent Bit command line in a console rather than configuring the container environment for all Fluent Bit scenarios. Installing services in Linux can be messy because different flavors handle details such as package management differently—Advanced Packaging Tool (APT), Yellowdog Updater Modified (Yum), and Snap, to name a few.

A.2 Downloading book resources

All the example configurations, scenario solutions, test data, and Docker container files needed for this book can be retrieved from https://www.manning.com/books/logs-and-telemetry or https://mng.bz/vJKa. Before we do anything else, let's get that content in place. The repository is structured so that each chapter has its own folder. The test data, as well as the code and configurations to create a container for Log-Simulator, gets its own folders, which are used across chapters.

We assume that you'll set up an environment variable called `flbBookRootDir`, referencing the root folder where you've downloaded and unpacked the book's resources. The following sections provide guidance on setting up such a variable. The environment variable might reference `/home/Phil/Fluent-Bit-with-Kubernetes`, for example.

> **WARNING** The downloads include several shell scripts, so you may need to set permissions explicitly to allow their execution. The root directory contains a script called `linux-set-permissions.sh` that recurses through the directories and corrects permissions (when run with permissions and has execute privileges itself). This is particularly important for the container build processes.

We have assumed that when you run the provided scenarios, you'll run them from within the relevant chapter folder, such as `$flbBookRootDir/chapter3`.

A.3 Prepping Linux

If your Linux instance is connected to a repository manager, you should update the metadata using the appropriate command. Depending on your privileges, you may need to prefix these commands with `sudo`:

- `yum update`
- `apt-get update`
- `snap refresh`

If the Linux setup doesn't include any of the services, you have the choice to configure your Linux instance to a repository, and you'll need to look at the instructions associated with the relevant tool or download the installation package (easier).

A.4   Fluent Bit

The book assumes an installation of Fluent Bit v2.1 or later. Most of the content will work in earlier versions, but some features may not. You can confirm the Fluent Bit version with the command `fluent-bit --version`.

Fluent Bit provides the details and means you need to build the binaries yourself. We've assumed that your environment is supported by one of the prebuilt images, but if that is not the case, we recommend that you follow the guidance in the Fluent Bit official manual at https://mng.bz/V2xN. All the prebuilt installation downloads are at https://packages.fluentbit.io.

A.4.1   Linux Installs

Most package managers have versions of Fluent Bit, and you can follow this approach if you choose. Sometimes, however, these package managers don't support the latest version, particularly if you're trying to install in an environment where package management is directed to a privately managed repository. The guaranteed approach is to use the following command in Linux environments:

```
curl https://raw.githubusercontent.com/fluent/
➥ fluent-bit/master/install.sh | sh
```

Update the environment variable `$PATH` to include the folder path in the Fluent Bit binary folder. To find out how, see https://mng.bz/x627.

Depending on your OS and its environment, Fluent Bit can be added as a daemon service. You can see the configuration at https://mng.bz/Aade.

A.4.2   macOS

Fluent Bit can be installed using the Homebrew package manager, which is much like the Linux approach. Homebrew supports both Intel and Arm CPUs. For more information on Homebrew, see https://brew.sh. To install Homebrew, use the command

```
/bin/bash -c "$(curl -fsSL
➥ https://raw.githubusercontent.com/Homebrew/install/HEAD/install.sh)"
```

Then install Fluent Bit with Homebrew using the command

```
brew install fluent-bit
```

If you use this approach, you must update the environment variable `$PATH` to include the path to the Fluent Bit binary folder. Changing `$PATH` in macOS is described at https://mng.bz/ZVEN.

Official Intel images are available at https://packages.fluentbit.io/macos in `.pkg` format. Our recommendation is to use Homebrew.

A.4.3 Windows installs

Prebuilt binaries are available for Windows in an installer package or a zip bundle. For maximum control of the environment, download the zip file and unpack it to a preferred location. Both download types are available at https://packages.fluentbit.io/windows, which contains folders for each release. Navigate to the preferred version folder in a browser and then download the correct file (right-click Save). Configure the PATH environment variable to point to the bin folder within the unzipped folder structure. You can find guidance on changing the PATH variable at https://mng.bz/RNZR.

> **TIP** If you want to reference the location of your Fluent Bit installation in other scripts or swap between versions of Fluent Bit, consider defining an environment variable with the Fluent Bit bin folder (such as FLUENT_BIT_HOME) and reference it in the PATH environment variable. Then change the value of FLUENT_BIT_HOME, which is easier than finding and modifying the right part of the PATH, particularly from the command line.

A.5 Docker

You can introduce Docker in several ways:

- Using Docker Desktop
- Using the vanilla Docker command-line interface (CLI) with its utilities
- In older environments, using Docker within tools such as VirtualBox
- Using a cloud provider's free tier to instantiate a Linux machine with Docker preinstalled (such as Oracle's Developer Image)

We recommend using Docker Community Edition or Docker Desktop. Larger organizations may prevent Docker Desktop, which can attract a license fee. If you're a Linux user who can use Docker Desktop, replace the references to docker-ce with docker-desktop. An alternative to Docker is Rancher (https://www.rancher.com), but this book focuses on Docker, which is better recognized.

A.5.1 Windows

For Windows installations, you can download an installation executable at https://docs.docker.com/get-docker, which guides you through the installation. You need to enable Hyper-V, which may incur a BIOS change, or Windows Subsystem for Linux (WSL) on your machine. We recommend adopting WSL.

A.5.2 Verifying the installation

When the Docker installation is complete, confirm that Docker and Docker Compose are usable by running the command docker info. Then confirm Docker Compose with the command docker compose version. These commands work on all platforms.

A.5.3   Linux (including macOS)

When your environment is ready with up-to-date metadata from your package manager, run the command, possibly with the `sudo` prefix (such as `sudo apt-get <package name>`). Examples are

- `yum install docker-ce docker-ce-cli containerd.io`
    - ⤷ `docker-buildx-plugin docker-compose-plugin`
- `apt-get install docker-ce docker-ce-cli containerd.io`
    - ⤷ `docker-buildx-plugin docker-compose-plugin`
- `snap install docker`

> **NOTE** Depending on your Linux configuration, you may first have to configure the OS to reference the correct repository. Docker provides the details at https://mng.bz/2ggo.

You may want to create a Docker group and attribute your user account(s) to it so that you don't require elevated privileges to run the Docker commands. Docker provides guidance on this topic at https://mng.bz/2ggo, but whether such configurations are necessary will depend upon how you have configured your environment.

The alternative is to download the relevant package directly from https://docs.docker.com/get-docker. Unless you're a proficient Docker user or your environment doesn't include a GUI, using Docker Desktop will be convenient because it makes seeing and clearing the containers after use easier.

A.5.4   macOS

If you prefer to execute installations on macOS using the Homebrew package manager, you can install Docker this way. Assuming that you have Homebrew installed as described for the Fluent Bit installation, the command is

```
brew install docker
```

If you prefer to have a Docker Desktop deployment, you can download an Apple Disk Image (`.dmg`) package at https://www.docker.com/products/docker-desktop. Regardless of the installation process, make sure that the Fluent Bit `bin` folder is in the `$PATH` environment variable.

A.6   Kubernetes

Although this book isn't about Kubernetes and its configuration and administration, it uses Kubernetes. We've been asked what we use so that readers who are less comfortable with administrating Kubernetes will feel more comfortable mirroring what we've done.

We have used the Kubernetes cluster as an option with Docker Desktop (https://docs.docker.com/desktop). Docker Desktop is free for personal use and some commercial use. Professionally, we work with Oracle Container Engine for Kubernetes with its serverless and virtual nodes option.

Docker Desktop is cross-platform (Windows, Linux, and macOS with Intel and Apple chipsets). For Windows users, it integrates with Windows Subsystem for Linux 2 (WSL2). It also comes with features that make it easy to reset your Kubernetes environment if you want. For more details on Docker Desktop and Kubernetes, see https:// docs.docker.com/desktop/kubernetes.

An alternative is Minikube (https://minikube.sigs.k8s.io/docs), which probably is more popular. Like Docker Desktop, Minikube works across Linux, macOS, and Windows. It's easy to install using package managers such as Homebrew, Chocolatey, RPM, and Debian dpkg. Minikube has done a nice job of simplifying actions such as enabling and accessing the Kubernetes dashboard (the command `minikube dashboard` will install the dashboard).

A.7 *LogSimulator*

Several chapters use a custom application that simulates an application generating log events. We can control the content and rate at which log events are played. Log-Simulator provides a host of other features that help test the monitoring of log events (from files, HTTP, and so on). Originally written to help demonstrate Fluentd, it has grown and evolved. You have several ways to deploy and run the LogSimulator to support the book:

- Use an image shared on Docker Hub (https://mng.bz/1aaQ).
- Use the Docker commands in the GitHub repository or the Manning.com download pack (https://www.manning.com/downloads/2686) and build the image locally (our recommendation, which guarantees the image will be up to date and benefit from any improvements made).

NOTE The Dockerfile includes files from the downloads. If they don't have the correct permissions, the image won't work. If you follow this approach and the container fails in Linux, check file permissions.

- Run it as a Java application (requires Maven to generate the Java archive file [JAR]). Although written in Groovy, the code complies with Java, so running it as a Java app with the Groovy JAR is possible.
- Run the utility as a Groovy script (requires Java and Groovy to be installed). This is how the utility was originally intended to be used. It provides the benefits of Java's structure without requiring additional steps to use Maven, making it easy to tweak, tailor, and extend for your own needs.

This book uses the packaging of the LogSimulator with Docker Compose to wrap the mounting process for the configuration to make running the utility as easy as possible. The tool will continue to be improved and made easier to use. The GitHub repository for the LogSimulator (https://mng.bz/PNN8) contains documentation

on the configuration, and additional information and news are available at https://
mng.bz/JNNz.

The following sections cover the native Groovy and Java approach and the container setup. Within the exercises, we've configured things to work as though you're running a built container, but running the scenarios as a local Java or Groovy script is trivial. The utility and all its documentation, including installation guidance, are available at https://github.com/mp3monster/LogGenerator.

A.7.1   *Running as a downloaded image*

To use the prebuilt image, we first need to get the image stored locally with the command

```
docker pull mp3monster/flb-logsim
```

Then tag the image so that it works as though it was built locally with the command

```
docker image tag mp3monster/flb-logsim logsimcontainer-logger:latest
```

A.7.2   *Running as a locally built Docker image*

We've provided a dynamic container in the GitHub repository for the book (https://github.com/mp3monster/Logs-and-Telemetry--Using-Fluent-Bit). All the resources are in the folder called `LogSimContainer`. The container is built from the official Groovy container, so there is no need to worry about Groovy or Java packaging. The container's `RUN` command invokes a script called `run.sh`, which pulls the latest version of the Groovy code from GitHub and runs it. All the necessary resources are in a folder called `LogSimContainer`.

The easiest way to build the container locally is to use the Docker Compose file with the command `docker compose -f docker-compose-logsim.yaml build`. (We've supplied `build.sh` and `build.bat` scripts as a convenience.) If you want to change how the container works, you must modify the `run.sh` file and rebuild the container. Because all the logic is in a single file, only one layer is rebuilt. But the Groovy script is retrieved each time the container is run—ideal if you want to tinker with the LogSimulator code itself. To help you tidy up, we have also provided a simple script called `docker-clean.sh` and a Windows `docker-clean.bat`. To run the LogSimulator, you must provide several parameters to Docker:

- Three volume mounts, which define
  - Mapping the output folder for any created log files, such as when using the LogGenerator to create log files as a Fluent Bit input. This folder must map to `/vol/log`.
  - Mapping the folder containing the simulator configuration files to `/vol/conf`.
  - Mapping the test data sets folder to `/vol/test-data`.

You also need to set several environment variables in the container for

- run_props, to define which configuration file to use. Note that the properties file can also define the location of the test data, but the environment variable will overrule it; the values provided in the configuration file for the LogSimulator assume a native deployment rather than a container one.
- The test data file, to use with the variable data.

Because we provide file paths to Docker, we recommend using absolute paths. As mentioned earlier, to simplify life, you define an environment variable called flbBookRoot-Dir, which points to the root folder of your copy of the downloaded resources. As a result, a command to run the LogSimulator looks like this:

```
docker run -v .:/vol/log -v \
$flbBookRootDir/chapter3/SimulatorConfig/:/vol/conf -v \
$flbBookRootDir/TestData/:/vol/test-data \
--env run_props=basic-log-file.properties \
--env data=medium-source.txt logsimcontainer-logger
```

Because this command is lengthy, we've provided scripts with .sh and .bat extensions in the SimulatorConfig folders for the chapters that use the LogSimulator (such as chapter3/ SimulatorConfig). The filenames are the combination of the configuration filename and -run (e.g., basic-log-file-run.bat), When you run this command, you should see Docker download the relevant container artifacts and the log (figure A.1).

```
logsimcontainer-logger-1 | logToString iterCount=>1< counter=>1< output=>%m< dtgFormat=>HH:mm:ss< log=>offset=1000|INFO
||com.demo|{"time": "12/May/2023:08:05:32 +0000", "remote_ip": "10.180.71.3", "remote_user": "-", "request": "GET /downl
oads/product_1 HTTP/1.1", "response": 304, "bytes": 0, "referrer": "-", "agent": "Mozilla/5.0 (0.8.16~exp12ubuntu10.21)"
}<-
logsimcontainer-logger-1 | logToString - returns:{"time": "12/May/2023:08:05:32 +0000", "remote_ip": "10.180.71.3", "re
mote_user": "-", "request": "GET /downloads/product_1 HTTP/1.1", "response": 304, "bytes": 0, "referrer": "-", "agent":
"Mozilla/5.0 (0.8.16~exp12ubuntu10.21)"}
logsimcontainer-logger-1 | logToString iterCount=>2< counter=>1< output=>%m< dtgFormat=>HH:mm:ss< log=>offset=1000|INFO
||com.demo|{"time": "12/May/2023:08:05:23 +0000", "remote_ip": "10.180.71.3", "remote_user": "-", "request": "GET /downl
oads/product_1 HTTP/1.1", "response": 304, "bytes": 0, "referrer": "-", "agent": "Mozilla/5.0 (0.8.16~exp12ubuntu10.21)"
}<-
```

Figure A.1   Output from running the LogSimulator

> **NOTE**   As with many Linux-related challenges, if any problems occur, it is worth checking file permissions. Although we have not experienced problems, permissions have tripped up other people.

A.7.3   *Java and Groovy*

The LogSimulator uses Java v8 or later. To run the tool with Java without first creating a JAR file, you need Java v11. You can use the latest version of Java. You need the Java Development Kit (JDK), not the Java Runtime Engine (JRE). Alternatively, you can run the tool as a Groovy script, so you can avoid generating a JAR file before JDK v11.

You can install Java and Groovy manually by visiting the following links to get the downloads; follow the OS-specific instructions. Alternatively, install SDKMAN! (https://sdkman.io/install), which will help you install Java and Groovy and enable you to switch between Java versions as necessary:

- Java (https://mng.bz/w55B); follow the links to the installation instructions
- Groovy (https://groovy-lang.org/install.html)

If you want to use the LogSimulator as a Groovy utility, we recommend that you observe the compatibility details with Java, particularly as the Java release cycle is faster.

A.7.4 Post-LogSimulator use

For chapters that create files with the LogSimulator, in the chapter folder, we have also provided a `clean-cX.sh` file, where x represents the chapter number. We've provided a `.bat` version as well.

A.8 WireMock

Chapter 4 uses WireMock to get sight of data sent by Fluent Bit. We adopted the open source version of WireMock. WireMock can be deployed in several ways. For this book, you can run the Docker container image but not in background mode, so you can see what data is being received and what WireMock is doing. Therefore, you can execute the simple command

```
docker pull wiremock/wiremock:latest
```

to retrieve the latest version of the Docker image, ready to be used. We've provided a simple script to start WireMock. If you'd like to start WireMock manually, review https://wiremock.org/docs/standalone/docker. If you prefer to install WireMock locally, download it at https://wiremock.org/docs/standalone/java-jar.

A.9 Postman

Postman is a relatively small, undemanding tool, so trying to run it in a container is more complex work than is warranted. It's best to install Postman in your native environment. You can download it at https://www.postman.com/downloads. The website recommends the binary based on what it can derive from your browser metadata. For Linux, it recommends a gzipped TAR file. For Windows, it provides an installation executable. When the download is unpacked and installed, ensure that the location of the binary is included in the `$PATH` environment variable.

Postman describes groupings of API call collections. Each chapter has its own collection, and the JSON export of each collection is provided in the download material.

A.10   Postgres

With Docker installed, the easiest way to install Postgres is to use a Docker container image, which you can get at https://hub.docker.com/_/postgres or deploy with the command `docker pull postgres`. When you use this approach, Postgres is self-contained, so when the container is stopped, all data will be lost.

This book uses pgAdmin to examine what is happening when we use Postgres. If you're happy using the Postgres CLI and prefer not to have a UI, feel free to use the CLI instead of pgAdmin. You can download the Postgres admin tool at https://www.pgadmin.org/download. Like Postman, this tool is relatively lightweight, and trying to run a containerized option creates unnecessary additional setup, so we recommend that you download the most suitable installer for your environment.

A.11   MySQL

Chapter 10 uses MySQL. There are cloud-managed implementations of MySQL, but for this book, the simplest solution is to use the Docker image. You can download and use the official image at https://hub.docker.com/_/mysql or via the Docker command `docker pull mysql`. If you follow the Docker Hub startup instructions, you must expose the MySQL port (`3306`) by adding the `-p 3306:3306` parameter to the Docker `run` command.

To configure and manage MySQL, use the official MySQL Workbench, which you can download at https://dev.mysql.com/downloads/workbench. This website offers a menu of Linux OS versions and associated release numbers that will link to the correct package manager bundle to download. Install the bundle with the `install` command, such as

```
apt-get install mysql-workbench-community-dbgsym_8.0.36-
1ubuntu23.10_amd64.deb.
```

A.12   Prometheus

Prometheus is a larger installation that generates various files and needs configuring. As a result, it is best to run it locally using a container. We've provided a Docker Compose file to drive the installation process. This file drives both the download and the configuration of the properties for Prometheus. Remember that the Prometheus configuration keeps everything in the container. Stopping the container results in losing previous run data. There are other ways to install Prometheus if you prefer, including

- Downloading the latest installation at https://mng.bz/755V.
- Deploying to Kubernetes with Helm. Install Helm (https://helm.sh/docs/intro/install) before following the instructions on a site such as https://mng.bz/mRRy.

A.13   *Jq*

This book refers to the jq tool. Although jq isn't used in the book, you may want to use it. You can install jq via Yum, APT, and Homebrew. Alternatively, follow the guidance at https://jqlang.github.io/jq/download.

appendix B
Useful resources

B.1 Standard plugins based on platform

The tables in this section describe the plugins available for various platforms, based on v2.1 and v3.0 of Fluent Bit. Version 3.0 is denoted by *Y (3)*. In several cases, plugins appear for one platform earlier than another, so don't be surprised to see Y in one column and Y (3) in another. An empty cell means that the plugin is unavailable for that platform. Each section also identifies the chapter(s) that provide(s) appropriate coverage of the plugin.

B.1.1 Input plugins

Table B.1 covers the input plugins provided as standard in Fluent Bit v2.1. Those available for v3.0 are shown as Y (3).

Table B.1 Input plugins included in Fluent Bit and the platforms they work on

Input plugin	Linux?	macOS (M2)?	Windows?	Descriptions	Chapter(s)
collectd	Y	Y		Accepts data from the collectd service (https://www.collectd.org)	–
cpu	Y			CPU use	3
disk	Y			Disk stats	3
docker	Y			Docker container metrics	4
docker_events	Y			Docker events (such as life cycle)	4
dummy	Y	Y	Y	Generates dummy data	2

Table B.1   Input plugins included in Fluent Bit and the platforms they work on *(continued)*

Input plugin	Linux?	macOS (M2)?	Windows?	Descriptions	Chapter(s)
elasticsearch	Y	Y	Y	Bulk API endpoints for Elasticsearch	–
event_test	Y	Y	Y	Tests input plugins	–
event_type	Y	Y	Y	Tests input plugins	–
exec	Y	Y		Results from executing a shell script	3
exec_wasi	Y	Y		WebAssembly System Interface (WASI) input	3
fluentfbit_metrics	Y	Y	Y	Internal metrics	5
forward	Y	Y	Y	Input using the forward protocol (used primarily by Fluentd and Fluent Bit)	3
head	Y	Y		An inversion of the Tail file reader plugin that behaves like the Linux head command	–
health	Y	Y		Response from health-check URLs	–
http	Y	Y	Y	REST API using HTTP/S	3
kafka	Y	Y (3)	Y (3)	Kafka consumer	–
kmsg	Y			Kernel log buffer	–
kubernetes_events	Y	Y (3)	Y (3)	Kubernetes events (via API server)	4
mem	Y			Memory use	3
mqtt	Y	Y		MQTT messaging input	–
netif	Y			Network Interface use data	3
nginx_metrics	Y	Y	Y(3)	Nginx metrics	–
node_exporter_metrics	Y	Y (3)		Generates metrics as though it were the Prometheus Node Exporter	9
opentelemetry	Y	Y	Y	OpenTelemetry-compliant consumer using HTTP with JSON	3
podman_metrics	Y			Podman container manager metrics	4

Table B.1 Input plugins included in Fluent Bit and the platforms they work on *(continued)*

Input plugin	Linux?	macOS (M2)?	Windows?	Descriptions	Chapter(s)
proc	Y			Checks process health using Linux	–
process_exporter_ metrics	Y (3)			Supports process metrics in Prometheus format	6
prometheus_remote_ write		Y (3)		Integrated with the Prometheus remote write framework	–
prometheus_scrape	Y	Y	Y	Scrapes metric from a Prometheus endpoint	–
random	Y	Y	Y	Generates random values	8
serial	Y	Y		Input from a serial port	–
splunk	Y		Y (3)	Handles messages from the Splunk HTTP Event Collector (HEC; https://mng.bz/QVVR)	–
statsd	Y	Y	Y	Accepts metrics using the StatsD protocol (https://github.com/statsd/statsd#statsd)	–
stdin	Y	Y		Captures stdin	3
syslog	Y	Y	Y	Handles syslog messages over UDP, TCP, or UNIX sockets	–
systemd	Y			Collects log messages from the journald daemon on Linux environments	–
tail	Y	Y	Y	Tracks file input	3
tcp	Y	Y	Y	Receives JSON or raw messages from a TCP port	–
thermal	Y			Hardware temperature data via OS	–
udp	Y	Y	Y	Receives JSON or raw messages from a TCP port	–
windows_exporter_ metrics			Y	Generates metrics as though it were the Prometheus Node Exporter in Windows	3
winevtlog			Y	Reads the Windows Event Log with new API	–

Table B.1 Input plugins included in Fluent Bit and the platforms they work on *(continued)*

Input plugin	Linux?	macOS (M2)?	Windows?	Descriptions	Chapter(s)
winlog			Y	Reads the Windows Event Log	–
winstat			Y	Captures Windows statistics	–

B.1.2 Output plugins

Table B.2 covers the output plugins provided as standard in Fluent Bit v2.1 and v3.0. The latter are denoted by Y (3).

Table B.2 Output plugins included in Fluent Bit and the platforms they work on

Output plugin	Linux?	macOS (M2)?	Windows?	Description	Chapter(s)
azure	Y	Y	Y	Sends events to the Azure Monitor's Log API	–
azure_blob	Y	Y	Y	Outputs events to Azure Blog Storage	–
azure_kusto	Y (3)	Y (3)	Y (3)	Sends event to Azure's Data Explorer (kusto)	–
azure_logs_ingestion	Y	Y (3)		Uses the Azure Log Analytics APIs to send log events	–
bigquery	Y	Y		Sends log events to Google Cloud Big Query Service (still considered experimental in Fluent Bit v2.2)	–
chronicle	Y		Y (3)	Sends unstructured (security) log to the Google Chronicle service	–
cloudwatch_logs	Y	Y	Y	Sends logs and metrics (using Embedded Metric Format) to Amazon CloudWatch	–
counter	Y	Y	Y	Outputs the number of events output since Fluent Bit started	–
datadog	Y	Y	Y	Sends events to the Datadog service	–
es (Elasticsearch)	Y	Y	Y	Sends events to Elasticsearch and OpenSearch	–

Table B.2   Output plugins included in Fluent Bit and the platforms they work on *(continued)*

Output plugin	Linux?	macOS (M2)?	Windows?	Description	Chapter(s)
exit	Y	Y		Stops Fluent Bit after the number of flushes and helps with testing	–
file	Y	Y	Y	Outputs to a defined file	5
flowcounter	Y	Y	Y	Outputs the number of events and their size based on a time unit	–
forward	Y	Y	Y	Sends log events to Fluentd (can also be used by Fluent Bit and other services)	5
gelf	Y	Y	Y	Sends Gelf (Graylog Extended Log Format) events to an endpoint over TCP or UDP; can include TLS	–
http	Y	Y	Y	Uses HTTP POST to send events to an endpoint in MessagePack or JSON format; includes optional extensions to support Amazon Web Services (AWS) endpoints and TLS	5
influxdb	Y	Y	Y	Sends events to an Influx time-series database	–
kinesis_firehose	Y	Y	Y	Sends events to Amazon Kinesis Firehose service	–
kinesis_streams	Y	Y	Y	Sends events to Amazon Kinesis Streams service	–
logdna	Y (3)	Y	Y	Sends logs to LogDNA cloud service	–
loki	Y (3)	Y	Y	Sends logs to a Grafana Loki server	–
kafka	Y	Y (3)		Sends events to the Apache Kafka service using the provided Kafka library	–
kafka-rest	Y	Y		Sends events to Kafka using the Apache Kafka REST proxy	–
nats	Y	Y		Sends log events to a NATs messaging server	–

Table B.2 Output plugins included in Fluent Bit and the platforms they work on *(continued)*

Output plugin	Linux?	macOS (M2)?	Windows?	Description	Chapter(s)
nrlogs	Y	Y	Y	Sends events to a New Relic (nr) service	–
null	Y	Y	Y	Disposes of any events	5
opensearch	Y	Y	Y	Sends events to an Open-Search database	–
opentelemetry	Y	Y	Y	Sends OpenTelemetry-compliant (OTLP) events to another OTel-compliant endpoint	5
oracle_log_analytics	Y	Y (3)	Y (3)	Sends events to Oracle's Log Analytics service	–
pgsql	Y			Sends events to a Postgres database	5
plot	Y	Y		Generates data file for GNU Plot	–
prometheus_exporter	Y	Y	Y	Provides an endpoint that allows Prometheus to scrape from the Fluent Bit instance as it would for an agent	5
prometheus_remote_writer	Y	Y	Y	Pushes events to Prometheus using Prometheus' remote write mechanism	5
skywalking	Y	Y	Y	Sends events to a deployment of Apache Skywalking	–
slack	Y	Y	Y	Sends log events to the Slack collaboration platform	–
splunk	Y	Y	Y	Sends events to Splunk deployments	–
stackdriver	Y	Y	Y	Sends events to Google's Stackdriver service	–
stdout	Y	Y	Y	Sends events to stdout	5
s3	Y	Y	Y	Stores log events in Amazon's S3 object store	–
syslog	Y	Y	Y	Sends events to a syslog server supporting RFC3164 and RFC5424	–

Table B.2 Output plugins included in Fluent Bit and the platforms they work on *(continued)*

Output plugin	Linux?	macOS (M2)?	Windows?	Description	Chapter(s)
tcp	Y	Y	Y	Sends events to a TCP server with different payload formats	–
td	Y	Y		Send events to a Treasure Data cloud service	–
udp	Y	Y	Y	UDP broadcast	–
vivo_exporter	Y	Y	Y	Sends logs, metrics, and traces over HTTP to a Vivo endpoint (visualization solution)	–
websocket	Y	Y	Y	Establishes an HTTP connection via GET and sends events in JSON or Message-Pack format	–

B.1.3 Filter plugins

Table B.3 covers the filter plugins provided as standard in Fluent Bit v2.1 and v3.0.

Table B.3 Filter plugins included in Fluent Bit and the platforms they work on

Output plugin	Linux?	macOS (M2)?	Windows?	Description	Chapter(s)
alter_size	Y	Y	Y	Alters incoming chunk size	–
aws	Y	Y	Y	Adds AWS metadata	–
checklist	Y	Y	Y	Checks record attributes against a list of configured values	7
ecs	Y	Y	Y	Adds AWS ECS metadata	–
expect	Y	Y	Y	Validates keys and their values	7
geoip2	Y	Y	Y	Adds geolocation data based on IP to location-mapping data	7
grep	Y	Y	Y	Applies grep to specific event attributes	7
kubernetes	Y	Y	Y	Appends Kubernetes metadata to the events	7
log_to_metrics	Y	Y	Y	Generates metrics from logs	7

Table B.3 Filter plugins included in Fluent Bit and the platforms they work on *(continued)*

Output plugin	Linux?	macOS (M2)?	Windows?	Description	Chapter(s)
lua	Y	Y	Y	Executes Lua scripts	7
modify	Y	Y	Y	Modifies records using rules	7
multiline	Y	Y	Y	Combines logs that span multiple lines to a single event	7
nest	Y	Y	Y	Alters the nesting of attributes in an event	7
nightfall	Y	Y	Y	External solution; scans an event for sensitive data such as PII- and PCS-related data	–
parser	Y	Y	Y	Uses different types of parsers to extract data from events	7
record_modifier	Y	Y	Y	Modifies records	7
rewrite_tag	Y	Y	Y	Changes the event's tag	7
stdout	Y	Y	Y	Copies events to stdout	7
sysinfo	Y	Y	Y	Filters for system info	–
throttle		Y	Y	Throttles using a sliding-window algorithm	7
throttle_size	Y		Y	Throttles messages by size using a sliding-window algorithm	7
type_converter	Y	Y	Y	Converts the data types of record attributes	–
wasm	Y	Y		Provides WASM support for custom filters	–

B.1.4 Processors

Table B.4 covers the processor capability introduced after v2.1 and doesn't differentiate among versions.

Table B.4   Filters supported with processor

Output plugin	Linux?	macOS (M2)?	Windows?	Description	Chapter(s)
content_modifier	Y	Y	Y	Modifies contents of logs, metrics, and traces	9
labels	Y	Y	Y	Modifies metrics labels	9
metrics_selector	Y	Y	Y	Selects metrics by name	9
sql	Y	Y	Y	Allows events to be manipulated with a SQL-like syntax	9

B.2   Predefined parsers

The following tables describe additional parser configurations. The Parser column shows the parser name, which can be referenced from plugins capable of using a parser, and the filter definitions. The Description column explains the purpose of the parser and supplies available links for more detailed information. The Output Attributes column reflects the values the parser will produce, making it easier than looking through the regular expression.

B.2.1   parser.conf file

Table B.5 describes the main parser file (parser.conf) in the installation bundle and supports many common log formats used by technologies such as Apache and nginx.

Table B.5   The main parser.conf file bundled

Parser	Description	Output attributes
apache, apache2	As a web server, Apache is incredibly pervasive, even if nginx is slowly displacing it. Having prebuilt for the standard configurations of Apache log files is of great value.	▪ hosts ▪ user ▪ time ▪ method ▪ path ▪ code ▪ size ▪ referer
apache_error	For parsing Apache's own error logs.	▪ time ▪ level ▪ pid ▪ client ▪ message

Table B.5 The main `parser.conf` file bundled *(continued)*

Parser	Description	Output attributes
Cri	The Container Runtime Interface (CRI) provides the layer between container engines such as Docker and CRI-O. Container logs are directed out through the logging aspect of CRI. The logging is described at https://mng.bz/gAA8. This parser makes it possible to ingest the log format.	• `time` • `stream` • `logtag` • `message`
docker	This parser allows the Docker logs to be parsed. It's needed only for Fluent Bit versions earlier than v1.2.	These attributes reflect the payload. The definition includes correct date and time formatting.
docker-daemon		• `time` • `level` • `msg`
Envoy	Envoy is a Layer 7 proxy service typically used in Kubernetes-based deployments and often used as a foundation for other Kubernetes components, such as Istio. The access logs are described at https://mng.bz/M11D.	• `start_time` • `method` • `path` • `protocol` • `code` • `response_flags` • `bytes_received` • `bytes_sent` • `duration` • `x_envy_upstream_service_time` • `x_forwarded_for` • `user_agent` • `request_id` • `authority` • `upstream_host`

Table B.5   The main `parser.conf` file bundled (*continued*)

Parser	Description	Output attributes
`istio-envoy-proxy`	Istio provides a service mesh and gateway capabilities for Kubernetes. Built on top of Envoy, the log formatting is at https://mng.bz/aVV9 and provides the parser for standard logs.	▪ `start_time` ▪ `method` ▪ `path` ▪ `protocol` ▪ `response_code` ▪ `response_flags` ▪ `response_code_details` ▪ `connection_termination_details` ▪ `upstream_transport_failure_reason` ▪ `bytes_received` ▪ `bytes_sent` ▪ `duration` ▪ `x_envoy_upstream_service_time` ▪ `x_forwarded_for` ▪ `user_agent` ▪ `x_request_id` ▪ `authority` ▪ `upstream_host` ▪ `upstream_cluster` ▪ `upstream_local_address` ▪ `downstream_local_address` ▪ `downstream_remote_address` ▪ `requested_server_name` ▪ `route_name`
`Json`	This convenience definition means we don't need to declare a JSON parser to use the built-in parser mechanism. We can refer to it directly from the filter.	These attributes reflect the payload. The definition includes correct date and time formatting.
`K8s_nginx_Ingress`	Nginx is often used as a Kubernetes Ingress controller.	▪ `host` ▪ `user` ▪ `time` ▪ `method` ▪ `path` ▪ `code` ▪ `size` ▪ `referrer` ▪ `agent` ▪ `request_length` ▪ `request_time` ▪ `proxy_upstream_name` ▪ `proxy_alternative_upstream_name` ▪ `upstream_addr` ▪ `upstream_response_length` ▪ `upstream_response_time` ▪ `upstream_status` ▪ `reg_id`

Table B.5 The main `parser.conf` file bundled *(continued)*

Parser	Description	Output attributes
`kube_custom`	Parser to extract details from a Kubernetes logging output using Docker as the container runtime engine. This is included in the Fluent Operator deployment.	▪ `tag` ▪ `pod_name` ▪ `namespace_name` ▪ `container_name` ▪ `docker_id`
`mongodb`	The parser handles the NoSQL MongoDB logs. See https://mng.bz/yooo.	▪ `time` ▪ `severity` ▪ `component` ▪ `context` ▪ `message` ▪ `ms`
`Nginx`	Defines the mapping of the non-JSON-formatted nginx web server access log elements. For more information, see https://mng.bz/XVV1.	▪ `remote` ▪ `host` ▪ `user` ▪ `time` ▪ `method` ▪ `path` ▪ `code` ▪ `size` ▪ `referrer` ▪ `agent`
`syslog-rfc3164`	This parser configuration addresses the IETF-defined RFC standards for syslog-formatted log messages and differs from local by having the `host` attribute. See https://www.rfc-editor.org/rfc/rfc6134.html.	▪ `pri` ▪ `time` ▪ `host` ▪ `ident` ▪ `pid` ▪ `message`
`syslog-rfc3164-local`	This parser configuration addresses the IETF-defined RFC standards for Syslog-formatted log messages. See https://www.rfc-editor.org/rfc/rfc6134.html.	▪ `pri` ▪ `time` ▪ `ident` ▪ `pid` ▪ `message`
`syslog-rfc5424,`	This parser configuration addresses the IETF-defined RFC standards for syslog- formatted log messages, as defined by the first syslog RFC. See https://www.rfc-editor.org/rfc/rfc5424.html and https://www.rfc-editor.org/rfc/rfc6134.html.	▪ `pri` ▪ `time` ▪ `host` ▪ `ident` ▪ `pid` ▪ `msgid` ▪ `extradata` ▪ `message`

B.2.2   *parsers_ambassador file*

The `parsers_ambassador` file (table B.6) focuses on parsers to support the Cloud Native Computing Foundation (CNCF) Emissary API gateway led by Ambassador Labs. For more information on the API gateway, see https://www.getambassador.io/products/api-gateway. For information on other Ambassador solutions, see https://www.getambassador.io.

Table B.6   Parser configurations for the `parsers_ambassador.conf` file

Parser	Description	Output attributes
`ambassador`	CNCF's API Gateway log-file-reading regular expression (https://www.getambassador.io)	<ul><li>`type`</li><li>`time`</li><li>`method`</li><li>`path`</li><li>`protocol`</li><li>`response_code`</li><li>`response_flags`</li><li>`bytes_received`</li><li>`bytes_sent`</li><li>`duration`</li><li>`x_envoy_upstream_service_time`</li><li>`x_forwarded_for`</li><li>`user_agent`</li><li>`x_request_id`</li><li>`aurthority`</li><li>`upstream_host`</li></ul>

B.2.3   *parsers_cinder file*

Cinder is part of OpenStack, providing block storage and using Ceph. Table B.7 describes the parser for `parserss_cinder.conf`.

Table B.7   Parser for the `parsers_cinder.conf` file

Parser	Description	Output attributes
`ceph`	Ceph (https://ceph.io) is a distributed filesystem solution. This regular expression reads its log file. It can be used with OpenStack.	`log_time` `message`

B.2.4   *parsers_extra*

Table B.8 describes a catchall file for other common parsers, such as the Chief client and MySQL.

Table B.8   Parser configurations for the `parsers_extra.conf` file

Parser	Description	Output attributes
Chef client	Chef (https://www.chef.io) is a configuration management tool (often compared with Ansible). The Chef client is an agent deployed to nodes to deliver and execute configuration management actions. This configuration supports Chef agent logging.	▪ `log_time` ▪ `severity` ▪ `message`
`couchbase_erlang _multiline`	Some parts of Couchbase, such as the cluster manager, use Erlang, which can generate multiline logs. This parser handles those logs.	▪ `logger` ▪ `level` ▪ `timestamp` ▪ `message`
`couchbase_http`	Couchbase's configuration for Apache differs slightly from standard Apache, so this parser accommodates those modifications.	▪ `host` ▪ `user` ▪ `timestamp` ▪ `method` ▪ `path` ▪ `code` ▪ `size` ▪ `client`
`couchbase_java _multiline`	The Couchbase SDK supports Java development. Because Java logging libraries can generate multiline logs, this parser configuration addresses that requirement.	▪ `timestamp` ▪ `level` ▪ `class` ▪ `thread` ▪ `message`
`couchbase_json_ log_nanoseconds couchbase_rebalance_ report`	Couchbase is an open source distributed NoSQL database (https://mng.bz/o0OD). These logs are formatted as JSON, so the fields depend on the log content. The configuration includes the definition of how dates are formatted.	Depend on the JSON payload
`couchbase_simple _log_space_separated couchbase_simple_log, couchbase_simple _log_utc couchbase_simple _log_mixed`	Because Couchbase's logs differ in purpose and structure, we have multiple parser definitions. These parsers produce the same output and need to be selected depending on subtle variations in the log formatting, such as space separation, and date and timestamp formatting. See https://mng.bz/o0OD.	▪ `timestamp` ▪ `message`
Crowbar	Crowbar is an environment tool used with OpenStack (https://crowbar.github.io).	▪ `log_time` ▪ `message`
`http_statement`	This parser extracts details from a record of HTTP traffic.	▪ `req_method` ▪ `req_path` ▪ `alnum` ▪ `req_protocol` ▪ `req_status` ▪ `req_len` ▪ `req_log_time` ▪ `req_mver`

Table B.8   Parser configurations for the `parsers_extra.conf` file (continued)

Parser	Description	Output attributes
`iptables`	This parser is for processing the logs that can be generated through the Linux IPTables service.	■ `rule_chain` ■ `rule_name` ■ `accept_or_drop` ■ `in_interface` ■ `out_interface` ■ `mac_address` ■ `source` ■ `dest` ■ `len` ■ `pkt_tos` ■ `pkt_prec` ■ `pkt_ttl` ■ `pkt_id` ■ `pkg_frg` ■ `protocol` ■ `source_port` ■ `dest_port` ■ `proto_kpt_len` ■ `proto_window_size` ■ `pkt_res` ■ `pkt_type` ■ `pkt_flag` ■ `pkg_urgency` ■ `pkt_icmp_type` ■ `pkt_icmp_code` ■ `pkt_icmp_id` ■ `pkt_icmp_seq`
`mysql_error`	This parser is for self-managed logs from MySQL database deployments (https://mng.bz/5OO7). It includes MySQL database server diagnostic information.	■ `log_time` ■ `myId` ■ `severity` ■ `subsystem` ■ `message`
`mysql_slow`	The `mysql_slow` log provides details on slow SQL operations, usually queries that can be used to help turn databases. For details, see https://mng.bz/6YYR.	■ user ■ dbhost ■ dbhost_address ■ message
`pacemaker`	Pacemaker (https://clusterlabs.org/pacemaker) is a cluster resource manager from ClusterLabs.	■ `log_time` ■ `pid` ■ `node` ■ `component` ■ `severity` ■ `message`

Table B.8   Parser configurations for the `parsers_extra.conf` **file** *(continued)*

Parser	Description	Output attributes
`rabbitmq`	RabbitMQ (https://www.rabbitmq.com/logging.html) is one of the dominant open source messaging services, allowing logs to be consumed and broken into their constituent parts. Fluent Bit's support can help because message brokers can be distributed and clustered, so routing logs together provides end-to-end insight.	■ `severity` ■ `log_time` ■ `message`
Universal	This parser is ideal for capturing everything in a simple message field and for serving as a placeholder to incorporate a parser into a pipeline.	■ `message`
Uuid	This parser looks for a universally unique identifier (UUID) made up of a series of hexadecimal values separated by hyphens.	■ `uuid`

B.2.5   *parsers_java file*

This `parsers_java` file (table B.9) is for Java log files that use standard language logging configuration.

Table B.9   Parser definitions for the `parsers_java.conf` **file**

Parser	Description	Output attributes
`java_multiline`	Java logs can generate multiline logs. The most common scenario is logging a stack trace as a result of trapping an exception. Fluent Bit typically treats a log entry as a single line. This parser addresses that situation.	■ `time` ■ `thread` ■ `level` ■ `message`

B.2.6   *parsers_kafka file*

Kafka uses a range of components and technologies. Some of these components use standardized log formats, and some don't; logging frameworks like SLF4J support extensive configuration. The `parsers_kafka` file (table B.10) provides parsers to handle the variations from default.

Table B.10   Parser definitions for the `parsers_kafka.conf` file and Kafka technologies

Parser	Description	Output attributes

`confluent-schema-`
`registry`
`confluent-schema-`
`registry-prefixed`
	Most of Kafka's logging is implemented with the Java SLF4J logging framework. The pre-fixed version of the parser produces a version of the `schema_registry` output. The only difference is that the output elements have a prefix to the name `_sr_` and an additional catchall field, `_sr_extra_info`.	▪ `time`
		▪ `level`
		▪ `src`
		▪ `date`
		▪ `method`
		▪ `path`
		▪ `http_version`
		▪ `code`
		▪ `size`
		▪ `_sr_exrta_info`

B.2.7   *parsers_openstack file*

Table B.11 describes OpenStack technologies and their log formats. These configurations are for the standard OpenStack configuration. As with many platform solutions, you can change the configuration of parts, particularly if the platform is being deployed to an environment that expects services to operate in a particular way.

Table B.11   Parsers for the `parsers_openstack.conf` file and OpenStack log configurations

Parser	Description	Output attributes

`cinder`
`glance`
`Heath`
`keystone`
`neutron`
`nova`
	These parsers represent open source components within OpenStack, generate the same log format, and are declared separately to reduce divergence:
	
	▪ Glance provides an image management service (https://docs.openstack.org/glance).
	▪ Heat provides service orchestration, like Kubernetes itself (https://docs.openstack.org/heat).
	▪ Keystone supports authentication and several API management services (https://docs.openstack.org/keystone).
	▪ Neutron provides virtual networking, comparable to Falco and Flannel in a Kubernetes deployment (https://docs.openstack.org/neutron).
	▪ Nova provides the compute abstraction layer, just as Docker or CRI-O can for Kubernetes (https://docs.openstack.org/nova).
		▪ `log_time`
		▪ `pid`
		▪ `severity`
		▪ `component`
		▪ `req_id`
		▪ `req_user`
		▪ `req_project`
		▪ `req_domain`
		▪ `req_user_domain`
		▪ `req_project_domain`
		▪ `message`

B.3   *Multiline parsers*

Fluent Bit provides several prebuilt multiline parsers, described in table B.12.

Table B.12 Prebuilt multiline parsers

Parser	Description
`cri`	Supports the recombining of multiline logs generated inline with CRI, as illustrated by CRI-O
`docker`	Concatenates multiline logs generated by a Docker engine
`go`	Supports the concatenation of log entries created by the Go programming language
`Java`	Supports the concatenation of log entries created by Google Cloud's Java application framework
`python`	Supports the concatenation of log entries created by the Python programming language

B.4 *Sources of predefined regular expressions*

Creating regular expressions (regex) for known data formats can be time consuming, but several websites publish predefined regex. Table B.13 describes sources that will work with the Fluent Bit regex library.

Table B.13 Sources of predefined regular expressions

Name	Description	URL
AutoRegex	AI tool that takes an English description and generates a regex	https://www.autoregex.xyz
Multinational Postal Codes	Regular expression to identify a country's postal codes	https://mng.bz/vJJa
IBAN/BBAN Regular Expression Patterns	Tool for getting regular expressions specific to different countries or regions	http://mng.bz/n0q2
iHateRegex	Tool and some predefined expressions; includes nice expression visualization	https://ihateregex.io
Regex Hub	Collated community-driven regex patterns	https://projects.lukehaas.me/regexhub
Regex Planet	A testing tool with a small cookbook	https://www.regexplanet.com/cookbook/index.html
RegExLib	Catalogs several thousand community-provided expressions	https://regexlib.com/Search.aspx
Regular Expressions 101	Has a community-provided set of patterns	https://regex101.com/library
Regular-Expressions info	A website dedicated to regular expressions. It covers implementation differences and regular expressions for common use cases.	https://www.regular-expressions.info

B.5   Plugins supporting record accessor

Chapter 7 looks at routing and control of Fluent Bit events. One way is to use record_accessor, which allows plugins that support it to use the record_accessor to retrieve event data values from the Fluent Bit event. The feature is not available with all plugins. See table B.14.

Table B.14   Plugins and filters supporting the record_accessor

Name	Type
azure	Outputs
checklist	Filter
expect	Filter
forward	Outputs
grep	Filter
http	Outputs
kubernetes_events	Inputs
log_to_metrics	Filter
loki	Outputs
modify	Filter
opensearch	Outputs
oracle_log_analytics	Outputs
rewrite_tag	Filter
splunk	Outputs
stackdriver	Outputs
tcp	Outputs
udp	Outputs

B.6   Stream processor functions

Fluent Bit's stream processor capabilities include functions that we typically expect to have, given its similarity to SQL. In table B.15, <key> represents the name of a JSON element.

Table B.15   Functions available in the stream processor

Function	Description
avg(<key>)	Returns the average value for the identified key
count(<key> | *)	Returns the number of occurrences of a key or can be used with an asterisk as a wildcard (or all)

Table B.15   Functions available in the stream processor *(continued)*

Function	Description
max(<key>)	Returns the largest value of a given key for the selected events
min(<key>)	Returns the smallest value of a given key for the selected events
now()	Returns the current time and date expressed as a string in the format %YYYY-%mm-%dd %HH:%MM:%SS
record_tag()	Returns the tag value for the log event
record_time()	Returns the timestamp of the event in the format <seconds>.<milliseconds>
sum <<key>)	Returns the total of the values selected for the identified key
timeseries_forecasst (<key>, <seconds from now>)	Returns the forecast value of a key a defined number of seconds into the future
unix_timestamp()	Returns the current datetime as the number of seconds from epoch (midnight, January 1, 1970) in the format <seconds>.<nanoseconds>

B.7 Reserved attribute names

Table B.16 describes the attribute names that are effectively reserved and can't be used by a custom plugin. It identifies the reserved attribute names, explaining what they're used for, and the plugin types that use attributes, including families of configuration values. These values follow a namespace-style naming convention in a path to identify subpaths. tls.ca_path, for example, is a child of the tls namespace. If you want to define a custom attribute because you're using a different Transport Layer Security (TLS) framework, you could use tls_ but not tls. These constraints reflect where functionality within the core can be used or reused by a plugin.

Table B.16   Tags that are reserved and have special meanings

Attribute name	Explanation	Input?	Output?	Filter?
alias	Provides the ability to define an alternative value for the tag	Y	Y	Y
dns.*	Is reserved for Fluent Bit's dns configuration, such as dns.mode	Y	Y	
host	Provides the address of a source or target service	Y	Y	
ipv6	Is reserved for supporting network configurations using IP v6	Y	Y	
listen	Defines the port on which to listen to HTTP traffic	Y		
log_level	Defines the overall logging level or the logging level for a specific plugin	Y	Y	Y

Table B.16   Tags that are reserved and have special meanings *(continued)*

Attribute name	Explanation	Input?	Output?	Filter?
log_suppress_ interval	Defines any logging from Fluent Bit that can be suppressed temporarily	Y	Y	Y
match	Defines which tagged event to process		Y	Y
match_regex	As an alternative to a standard tag match, matches using regular expressions		Y	Y
Mem_buf_limit	Defines the maximum size of the memory buffer	Y	Y	
port	Defines the port on the host to listen to or communicate on	Y	Y	
retry_limit	When a plugin indicates that a retry is possible, defines the maximum number of retries allowed	Y		
routable	Is reserved for internal logic to manage data routing	Y	Y	
scheduler.*	Defines any attribute that can control the behavior of the scheduling within Fluent Bit	Y	Y	
storage.*	Is reserved for configuration behavior related to the file and memory buffer configuration	Y	Y	
tag	Identifies the pipeline of events	Y	Y	Y
threaded	Used internally to manage thread control	Y	Y	
tls	Indicates whether TLS should be used	Y	Y	
tls.*	Is reserved for the TLS functionality provided by Fluent Bit	Y	Y	
workers	Defines the number of worker threads that Fluent Bit can use to boost performance	Y		

B.8   Expressing time

Some output plugins allow you to define how date information is displayed. Table B.17 lists the options and uses the following abbreviations:

- YYYY—Four-digit year
- MM—Month as a two-digit representation (1–12)
- DD—Day of the month as a two-digit representation (1–31)
- hh—Hour of the day in a twenty-four-hour clock (0–23)
- mm—Minute of hour (0–59)
- f—Fraction of a second, with number of characters denoting precision (ffffff is to six decimal places)

Table B.17 Data formats that Fluent Bit allows you to request

Format name	Appearance	Description
Double	`1701127927.958472`	`Seconds.NanoSeconds`
ISO 8601	`2018-05-30T09:39:52.000681Z`	`YYYY-MM-DDThh.mm.ffffffZ`
Epoch	`1701127928`	Seconds from January 1, 1970
`java_sql_timestamp`	`2018-05-30 09:39:52.000681`	`YYYY-MM-DD hh:mm.ss.ffffff`

B.9 Expressing data sizes

Some attributes allow you to express data sizes in terms of bytes up to terabytes, but terabyte sizing is not recommended. See table B.18.

Table B.18 Describing data volumes in attributes

Size	Character options	Examples
Bytes	–	100 represents 100 bytes.
Kilobytes	k, K, kb, KB	12k represents 12 kilobytes (Kb).
Megabytes	m, M, mb, MB	5m represents 5 megabytes (MB).
Gigabytes	g, G, gb, GB	3g represents 3 gigabytes (GB).

B.10 Fluent Bit formatters

Formatters are prebuilt pieces of logic that some plugins can use to output Fluent Bit payloads in different ways. Table B.19 lists built-in formatters and the output plugins that support them.

Table B.19 Predefined formatters available to output plugins

Formatter	Outputs that use it
MessagePack	HTTP, Observe, Kafka, stdout
Json_lines	HTTP, Observe, Kafka, stdout
Json_stream	HTTP, stdout
Gelf	HTTP

B.11 Useful third-party tools

Good logging is the key to effective log use. Table B.20 lists tools outside the Fluent Project that can be helpful for working with Fluent Bit.

Table B.20   Helpful tools to use with Fluent Bit

Tool	Description	URL
Calyptia	Calyptia provides much of the development effort and expertise behind Fluent Bit and Fluentd. It includes a supported version of Fluent Bit and additional plugins.	https://calyptia.com
Docker	Containerization platform that enables containers to be run, containers to be packaged and orchestrated together (Docker Compose).	https://www.docker.com
Docker Desktop	This tool provides a desktop management layer and Kubernetes deployment using Docker Core capability. The solution is multiplatform-capable.	https://www.docker.com/products/docker-desktop
EpochConverter	This tool provides different ways of presenting dates.	https://www.epochconverter.com
Fluentular	This tool is a Fluentd (and Bit) regex editor.	https://fluentular.herokuapp.com
Grafana	This metrics visualization tool is open source and available to deploy wherever you want.	https://grafana.com/oss/grafana
Grafana Cloud	Cloud SaaS combines several open source services (Prometheus, Loki, Thanos, Grafana) as a managed service.	https://grafana.com/products/cloud
Jq	This JSON query tool can be used from the command line.	https://jqlang.github.io/jq
jqplay	This tool is the web version of jq.	https://jqplay.org
JSON Beautifier	This tool formats an unformatted JSON string to be readable.	https://jsonbeautifier.org
JSONPath Beautifier	This tool allows you to beautify JSON with several representations.	https://jsonpath.com
MessagePack converter	This tool is for compressing and decompressing MessagePack payloads manually.	https://msgpack.solder.party
pgAdmin	This admin console can be used with Postgres (https://www.postgresql.org).	https://www.pgadmin.org
Regex validator	This online utility develops and validates regex that complies with the Ruby flavor.	https://rubular.com
Regexp Explain	This Visual Studio (VS) Code plugin is for visualizing regex.	https://mng.bz/4ppQ
RegExr	This online tool is for regex development and visualization.	https://regexr.com

Table B.20   Helpful tools to use with Fluent Bit *(continued)*

Tool	Description	URL
Regulex	This tool provides open source regex visualization.	https://jex.im/regulex
Tracee	This tool can send eBPF events to Fluent Bit using the `forward` protocol.	https://github.com/aquasecurity/tracee
UNIX timestamp-Converter	This website converts UNIX timestamps (time from epoch) to a more easily readable format.	https://www.unixtimestamp.com
VS Code	This IDE has a wealth of plugins covering all the technologies used in this book.	https://code.visualstudio.com
VS Code plugin for Fluent Bit	This syntax plugin for VS Code supports classic format configuration files.	https://mng.bz/QVV4
WireMock	This potent, easy-to-use tool provides simulated web endpoints. It can capture web-service calls and return dummy results.	https://wiremock.org
YAML plugin for VS Code	This tool is a YAML syntax checker and highlighter.	https://mng.bz/XVVE
Ytt (YAML templating tool)	YAML templating allows us to define common configurations and then inject contextual-specific values. The greatest benefit is that we can use the same context file to ensure that multiple configuration files are consistent, as when setting ports to use in Istio, Kubernetes, and application configuration files.	https://carvel.dev/ytt

B.12   Observability

A great deal of observability content is available these days. Table B.21 lists suggested resources that will help not just with technical details but also with foundational thinking.

Table B.21   Recommended reading on observability

Title	Description	URL
Cloud Observability in Action	This book looks at broad observability perspectives.	https://www.manning.com/books/cloud-observability-in-action
OpenTelemetry	OpenTelemetry is rapidly becoming the standard for communicating telemetry data (logs, metrics, and traces) and falls under CNCF.	https://opentelemetry.io
"The Four Golden Signals"	Part of Google's SRE guide and embodies ideas around monitoring and observability.	https://sre.google/sre-book/monitoring-distributed-systems

Table B.21 Recommended reading on observability *(continued)*

Title	Description	URL
O11ynews!	This blog is by Michael Hausenblas (Manning author).	https://o11y.news

B.13 *Helpful logging practices and resources*

The key to the effective use of logs is good logging. Table B.22 lists sources of additional information on logging practices.

Table B.22 Resources on logging good practices

Description	URL
Logging best practices from Logz.io	https://logz.io/blog/logging-best-practices
Ultimate Guide to Logging (covers multiple language perspectives)	https://www.loggly.com/ultimate-guide
The Pragmatic Logging Handbook	https://mng.bz/M118
National Institute of Standards and Technology (NIST) Guide to Computer Security Log Management	https://mng.bz/aVVX
Definition of Syslog standard; also contains good ideas for logging practices	https://tools.ietf.org/html/rfc5424
OpenObservability Talks YouTube channel	http://www.youtube.com/@OpenObservabilityTalks

B.14 *Additional reading*

Table B.23 lists resources that provide additional insight into the technologies used in this book, related to logging, traces, and metrics.

Table B.23 Further reading on technologies in this book

Title	Description	URL
Core Kubernetes	This book and *Kubernetes in Action* cover much of what you'll need for Kubernetes.	https://www.manning.com/books/core-kubernetes
Docker in Action, Second Edition	Docker is the typical technology for implementing a container. When we do not need the sophistication of Kubernetes, we use Docker more directly. This book covers the core of building and running containers.	https://www.manning.com/books/docker-in-action-second-edition
Operations Anti-Patterns, DevOps Solutions	Operational processes and logging are integral to achieving a DevOps way of working. This book looks at the pitfalls (or antipatterns) you could face.	https://www.manning.com/books/operations-anti-patterns-devops-solutions

Table B.23 **Further reading on technologies in this book** *(continued)*

Title	Description	URL
Software Telemetry	This book is about getting metrics, logging, and using certain types of business application state data to get a health perspective. Fluent Bit can be a crucial part of a telemetry solution.	https://www.manning.com/books/software-telemetry
Linux in Action	This book covers the use of Linux, including log management with syslogd.	https://www.manning.com/books/linux-in-action
Cloud Observability in Action	This book explores the ideas behind metrics, traces, and logs (aka signals). It takes into account aspects of signal management such as correlation.	https://www.manning.com/books/cloud-observability-in-action
Learn Kubernetes in a Month of Lunches	The book focuses on Fluentd rather than Fluent Bit but also includes content on Prometheus.	https://www.manning.com/books/learn-kubernetes-in-a-month-of-lunches
Securing DevOps	This book includes sections on log analytics and stream processing.	https://www.manning.com/books/securing-devops
WebAssembly In Action	This book is a comprehensive guide to WASM.	https://www.manning.com/books/webassembly-in-action
Logging In Action	This book focuses on Fluentd and logging frameworks.	https://www.manning.com/books/logging-in-action
Monitoring with Prometheus	The book takes a top-to-bottom look at Prometheus.	https://www.prometheusbook.com
Spark in Action, 2nd ed.	This book covers the Apache event-based distributed data processing platform.	https://www.manning.com/books/spark-in-action-second-edition
Gnuplot in Action, 2nd ed.	This guide to Gnuplot is helpful if you choose to use the `plot` output plugin.	https://www.manning.com/books/gnuplot-in-action-second-edition

B.15 Web resources

These helpful online documentation resources provide details on a range of subjects that influence logging and using Fluent Bit. They cover standards (de facto or formal), such as logging formats and ways to format log attributes (such as dates), and offer guidance on common problems.

B.15.1 Formal and de facto standards

Table B.24 lists online resources that support formal and de facto standards.

Table B.24   Information related to Fluent Bit standards

Title	Description	URL
Apache Kafka	Kafka has several variants (additional features from Confluent, managed services, and API-compatible alternate implementations). This documentation is the core Apache solution.	https://kafka.apache.org
Apache SkyWalking	This application performance monitoring solution is ideally suited to Kubernetes and other container-based solutions.	https://skywalking.apache.org
Conmon	This OCI container runtime monitor is used by CRI-O and other container runtimes.	https://github.com/containers/conmon
containerd	This container runtime is drawn from the core of Docker.	https://containerd.io
CRI-O	CRI-O is a container runtime for Kubernetes.	https://cri-o.io
Escape Sequence in C	This tutorial provides information on character escape sequences.	www.geeksforgeeks.org/escape-sequence-in-c/
"11 Fluent Bit Examples, Tips & Tricks for Log Forwarding with Couchbase"	Couchbase is a popular open source database product. This article describes how best to monitor Couchbase using Fluent Bit.	https://mng.bz/gAAG
Date formatting (ISO 8601)	This documentation explains the ISO 8601 date-format standard.	Part 1: https://mng.bz/eVVq Part 2: https://mng.bz/pxxw
Helm	Helm is a leading Kubernetes package manager.	https://helm.sh
journald	journald is a Linux system service for collecting log data.	https://mng.bz/Omma
Introducing JSON	This web page provides the official definition of JSON format and includes a nice railway diagram.	https://www.json.org/json-en.html
Kubernetes	Kubernetes is the container orchestration platform.	https://kubernetes.io/docs
"Rotate and archive logs with the Linux `logrotate` command"	This article is about log rotation.	https://mng.bz/YVVa
Labeled Tab-Separated Values (LTSV)	LTSV is a way of formatting data that Fluent Bit's parser can handle.	http://ltsv.org
NATS	NATS is a messaging service designed to support microservice use cases and is part of the CNCF.	https://nats.io

Table B.24   Information related to Fluent Bit standards *(continued)*

Title	Description	URL
Open source version of Loki	Grafana offers Loki as a managed service in addition to the open source version. This web page is the open source product page.	https://grafana.com/oss/loki
Prometheus Metrics Exposition format	Prometheus' approach to communicating metrics in a text format doesn't follow conventions such as YAML and JSON. This content explains how the formatting works.	https://mng.bz/GNNJ
Vivo	Vivo is an open source visualization service for logs, events, and traces,	https://github.com/calyptia/vivo
YAML	The official YAML site includes details on its syntax. A reader-friendly explanation of YAML provides references to more content (https://yaml.com).	https://yaml.org
systemd	systemd performs a variety of tasks at the heart of Linux. The primary interest from an observability perspective is events and interaction with journald.	https://mng.bz/znnA

B.15.2   *Additional web resources*

Table B.25 lists sources of additional information.

Table B.25   Additional resources

Title	Description	URL
"Creating a Self-Signed Certificate with OpenSSL"	There are a variety of ways to create certificates. The simplest is to use self-signed certificates.	https://www.baeldung.com/openssl-self-signed-cert
Automated certificate management	Rotating certificates regularly is good practice. This task can be complex, but several organizations have developed technologies for it, Let's Encrypt being the trailblazer.	• https://letsencrypt.org • https://certbot.eff.org
Docker CLI Cheat Sheet	Docker provides a convenient cheat sheet for command-line interface (CLI) commands. Unlike CLI help, it provides answers to common questions.	https://mng.bz/0MMv
"Linux Directory Structure and Important Files Paths Explained"	This article provides an overview of the typical layout of Linux filesystems. It helps you understand where to install components in production deployments and where logs should go.	https://mng.bz/KDDO

Table B.25   Additional resources *(continued)*

Title	Description	URL
sysfs	This Linux kernel service exports information about various kernel subsystems, hardware devices, and associated devices.	▪ https://linuxhint.com/linux-sysfs-file-system ▪ https://man7.org/linux/man-pages/man5/sysfs.5.html
Proc	This filesystem service in Linux operating systems can be used to expose information about processes.	▪ https://linuxhint.com/use-proc-filesystem-linux ▪ https://man7.org/linux/man-pages/man5/proc.5.html
"Run a private online TLS certificate authority in a Docker container"	Just as we can configure an OS to know about a private certificate authority, we can do the same for a container.	https://mng.bz/9oor
"Sidecar Containers"	The sidecar pattern is a common approach to deploying containerized support services, such as Fluent Bit, within a Pod.	https://mng.bz/j00e
Apache Spark	This stream-based processing engine supports data science and machine learning.	https://spark.apache.org

B.16   *Fluent Bit resources*

Table B.26 lists resources that provide additional insights into the technologies that Fluent Bit uses and its users are exposed to.

Table B.26   Fluent Bit technologies

Title	Description	URL
MessagePack	This compression library is implemented in multiple languages that Fluent Bit can use and is used when the `forward` plugin is sending or receiving events.	https://msgpack.org
gRPC	This website provides documentation, libraries, and tools for the gRPC messaging standard.	https://grpc.io
Protobuf	Protocol Buffers (Protobuf) is a key technology in the way gRPC works, which is the preferred way to communicate between OpenTelemetry components.	https://protobuf.dev
HTTP/2	HTTP/2 is the next version of HTTP. The specification is governed by the IETF.	https://http2.github.io
SQLite	SQLite is a lightweight embeddable database.	https://sqlite.org
Go implementation of `forward` protocol	Fluent Bit and Fluentd use the `forward` protocol. This repository has a Go implementation of the protocol.	https://github.com/IBM/fluent-forward-go

Table B.26 Fluent Bit technologies *(continued)*

Title	Description	URL
Kustomize	Kustomize is a configuration templating tool. Fluent Bit uses it to manage the Operator configuration files.	https://kustomize.io
cAdvisor	cAdvisor (Container Advisor) enables you to export metrics from Docker.	https://github.com/google/cadvisor

B.17 Lua

Lua allows us to write custom filters without building a full plugin extension. Table B.27 lists tools and documentation sources that are helpful for developing custom filters with Lua.

Table B.27 Tools and information for Lua

Title	Description	URL
Lua language guide	The bible of the Lua language	https://www.lua.org
LuaUnit	An xUnit-based testing framework for Lua	https://luaunit.readthedocs.io/en/latest
Lua sandbox	A utility that allows you to see how input events will look when processed by a Lua script	https://fluent.github.io/lua-sandbox
Lua Language Server for VS Code	Plugin for VS Code to support Lua development	▪ https://mng.bz/WVVW ▪ https://luals.github.io
Istio in Action	Covers the application of Lua in Istio	https://www.manning.com/books/istio-in-action
Redis in Action	Describes using Lua in Redis scripting	https://www.manning.com/books/redis-in-action
Mozilla Firefox tool Hindsight	Analyzes traffic	https://github.com/mozilla-services/hindsight
Rosetta Code (programming chrestomathy)	Code to solve common problems, such as validating international banking codes	https://rosettacode.org/wiki/Category:Lua

B.18 WASM and WASI

Fluent Bit supports WebAssembly (WASM) and WebAssembly System Interface (WASI) for building extensions. WASM and WASI are big fields in their own right. Table B.28 lists resources to help you understand these technologies better.

Table B.28   Information on WASM and WASI

Title	Description	URL
WebAssembly Community Group	Home of the WASM standards	https://www.w3.org/community/webassembly
WebAssembly.org	Primary website for information on and links to the standards	https://webassembly.org
WebAssembly	Mozilla's developer resources for WASM	https://mng.bz/866D
WASM by Example	Guide to WASM development, supporting Rust, AssemblyScript (TypeScript-like language), Emscripten (C/C++), and TinyGo	https://wasmbyexample.dev/home.en-us.html
Rust and WebAssembly	GitHub-based e-book on using Rust and WASM	https://rustwasm.github.io/book
WASI	Web page listing the relevant resources for the standard	https://wasi.dev
Regex Explain	Regex visualization generation tool for VS Code	https://mng.bz/EOaR

B.19   C development resources

Table B.29 lists resources for developing and compiling C.

Table B.29   Resources for C development

Resource	Description	URL
Mastering CMake	Tool for building Fluent Bit	https://mng.bz/NB1d
VS Code C plugin	Plugin that provides C/C++ intellisense and debugging	https://mng.bz/DpMV
GitHub CLI	Command-line tool for GitHub	https://cli.github.com
Vagrant	Tool for creating development environments	https://www.vagrantup.com/
Chocolatey	Tool used in Windows continuous integration processes	https://chocolatey.org
Windows Flex and Bison	Windows port of Flex lexical analyzer and GNU Bison parser generator	https://github.com/lexxmark/winflexbison
Valgrind	Dynamic analysis tool	https://valgrind.org

B.20   Logging format definitions

Table B.30 identifies common technologies and associated approaches to generating logged events. This information can help you understand how to process events with these tools.

Table B.30   Logging formats

Name	Description	URL
CMetrics	A variation on the Prometheus format for communicating metrics	https://github.com/fluent/cmetrics
Common Event Format (CEF)	A common format developed by ArcSight	https://mng.bz/x6KX
Embedded metric format	A standard Amazon has proposed to incorporate metrics into log events	https://mng.bz/AaQx
Graylog Extended Log Format (GELF)	Commonly supported log format that can be sent using UDP	https://mng.bz/V2VG
Kubernetes logging (klog)	How Kubernetes logging is generated and structured	https://mng.bz/dZXw
logfmt	A common log format, still the most authoritative definition despite the existence of a formal standard	https://brandur.org/logfmt
MySQL error logs	Details on how MySQL error logs are constructed	https://mng.bz/lrYo
MySQL slow queries	Details on how MySQL slow query logs are structured	https://mng.bz/BgX2
Prometheus	The format for sharing metrics data with Prometheus	https://mng.bz/ZVIA
statsd	A network daemon that runs as part of the Node.js platform to capture and emit stats	https://github.com/statsd/statsd
syslog-rfc3164	More recent specification for the standard used by syslog	https://datatracker.ietf.org/doc/html/rfc3164
syslog-rfc5424	The initial version of the syslog definition	https://datatracker.ietf.org/doc/html/rfc5424
Windows Event Logs	Definition of Windows logs	https://mng.bz/vJq4

appendix C
Comparing Fluent Bit and Fluentd

This appendix highlights the differences between Fluent Bit and Fluentd. Fluent Bit is far more than a simple reimplementation of Fluentd using C. Although the goals and ideas at the heart of both solutions are essentially the same, there are also many differences. Some differences are subtle but important, such as the YAML Ain't Markup Language (YAML) configuration structure, and others are minor, such as additional attributes for a plugin. They are noticeable in other areas, such as how custom plugins can be built.

We're not going to describe the Fluentd features here beyond naming them. If you want more in-depth understanding of how the Fluentd features work, we recommend reading *Logging in Action*.

C.1 Technology differences

Chapter 1, and to some extent chapter 2, looked at the implementation and deployment differences between Fluentd and Fluent Bit. We'll summarize them in bullet points rather than repeat the details:

- Implementation technologies, with Fluent Bit using C and supporting extensions with C, Go, Lua, and WebAssembly (WASM), compared with Ruby for Fluentd
- Smaller, more compact, platform-native binary for Fluent Bit and a platform-agnostic runtime for Fluentd
- A basic management UI in Fluentd if needed; no such capability in Fluent Bit

- Support for HTTP/2 (introduced in Fluent Bit v3); no use of HTTP/2 in Fluentd yet

C.2   Configuration capabilities

As we saw in chapter 2, the Fluentd and Fluent Bit configurations have similarities but are not the same. Fluent Bit leads the way by enabling configuration with YAML (which Fluentd has also adopted), making it easier to embed Fluent Bit in a Kubernetes environment and read, although the YAML structures used differ. The configuration features that vary between Fluentd and Fluent Bit are

- Inclusion files are more flexible in Fluentd than in Fluent Bit, particularly in Fluent Bit YAML format.
- The way that parsers are configured in Fluent Bit is rich and lends itself to better reuse, with the ability to import multiple parser configurations from separate configuration files, including canned configurations. This idea extends to Lua and stream processing.
- Fluentd's support for validating configuration files using the Dry Run feature seems much more comprehensive than Fluent Bit's. The fact that YAML is more sensitive to layout probably doesn't help.
- The ability to set global (service-level) configuration values, such as `log_level`, and then override them in specific plugins in Fluent Bit is helpful, allowing us to focus logging on where we're introducing new configurations, not the entire pipeline.

C.3   Inputs and outputs

Plugins, particularly input and output plugins for specific product and technology endpoints, are freely available. But this free availability is offset by the rapid adoption of OpenTelemetry for technologies and products that support cloud-native solutions.

C.3.1   Support for logging frameworks

The support for logging frameworks is a little bit of a dummy. The documentation for Fluentd and logging frameworks is more substantial than the documentation for Fluent Bit. But taking that to mean that Fluentd is better with logging frameworks is an error. Most logging frameworks, when not writing to files or using a tailored adapter for a specific service such as a database, use basic RESTful web services or support the `forward` protocol. Chapter 5 states that Fluentd and Fluent Bit are interchangeable in this regard. If you're looking for extensions to a logging framework that will interact with Fluent Bit, your best bet is to research Fluentd-compatible solutions.

C.3.2 *Plugin choice*

When you consider the wider ecosystem and the fact that until a few years ago, Fluentd was more dominant than Fluent Bit, it's no surprise that the portfolio of plugins is much larger. But standards (de facto and formal) have developed, matured, and been embraced by many vendors. This situation has reduced the need for plugins, particularly downstream, where we're more likely to use an off-the-shelf solution.

The ability to develop plugins for Fluentd is far more mature, although you can build plugins for Fluent Bit. Having created plugins for both Fluent Bit and Fluentd, we find the Fluentd framework a bit easier to use. Large organizations have opted to implement solutions directly into the core of Fluent Bit using C. As a result, the pressure to mature the plugin layer hasn't been as great, with the additional benefit of not having to deploy additional Ruby gems.

C.3.3 *Secondary/fallback output options*

Some of Fluentd's core plugins support defining a secondary output, so if you experience problems connecting with an output, the plugin will use a secondary plugin. This means it is possible to monitor events written to a local filesystem if you can't connect with a remote service. Fluent Bit doesn't provide this capability. The closest equivalent is a second output, such as a local log file, with all events going to both destinations. It is up to an ops team to determine which events have been dropped and to retrieve them from the file.

C.3.4 *OpenTelemetry*

The influence of OpenTelemetry has been substantial. It has taken some time for the OpenTelemetry Protocol (OTLP) specification to be declared stable, reflecting how standards are developed these days, emphasizing securing functioning, usable code before ratifying the specification.

Fluent Bit has a clear narrative for supporting OpenTelemetry, and the major version-number changes are in the internal structural changes made to support OpenTelemetry and even operate as an OTel-compliant collector. Fluentd doesn't have such a clear narrative. It is possible to work with OTLP by taking advantage of the step down from gRPC on HTTP/2 to JSON on HTTP, then Fluentd can treat the payload like any other log event. However, the OTLP schema isn't trivial, and we've not seen plugins referencing OTLP support, so creating compliant payloads or working with the payloads requires more configuration effort.

C.3.5 *Customization with embedded code*

Both Fluentd and Fluent Bit allow code fragments, but the approaches are notably different. With Fluentd, we can invoke simple Ruby statements to return values for any attribute in the configuration. By contrast, Fluent Bit allows Lua, which is declared as a discrete script and invoked, along with predefined configuration, by processors and filters.

The ability to embed a Ruby statement lends itself to creating a more dynamic runtime configuration, such as working out the absolute path to a file based on where Fluentd is installed. By contrast, using Lua filters in Fluent Bit allows us to perform sophisticated, efficient event processing. Stream processing brings SQL capabilities to the buffered events, and processors offer the chance to implement advanced parsing logic.

C.4 *Routing*

One key internal difference between Fluentd and Fluent Bit is the approach to sending the same events to multiple destinations. In Fluentd, to send a log event to multiple destinations, we need to copy the log event explicitly. In Fluent Bit, it's not necessary to define or even consider the problem of copying, making configuration much simpler.

Figure C.1 (from *Logging in Action*) illustrates the relationship between Fluentd's core engine, which includes the buffer and output plugins, followed by a Fluent Bit perspective. At first glance, they look alike. The key is that as each output plugin is called, no return path hands the event back to be tried with the next plugin if it wasn't consumed.

Another difference between Fluent Bit and Fluentd routing is the label feature in Fluentd. This feature allows us to group plugins to form a pipeline; a single configuration file can contain multiple label groupings or pipelines. Although Fluent Bit's YAML configuration has an ideal pipeline structure, a Fluent Bit YAML configuration file can contain only a single pipeline, and the classic format doesn't have such a construct.

C.5 *Buffering and internal data structure*

The approaches to buffering in Fluentd and Fluent Bit allow using memory or the filesystem, and the data is handled in chunks. There are notable differences, however. First, the data is serialized using MessagePack for efficiency, but Fluentd uses simpler zip compression.

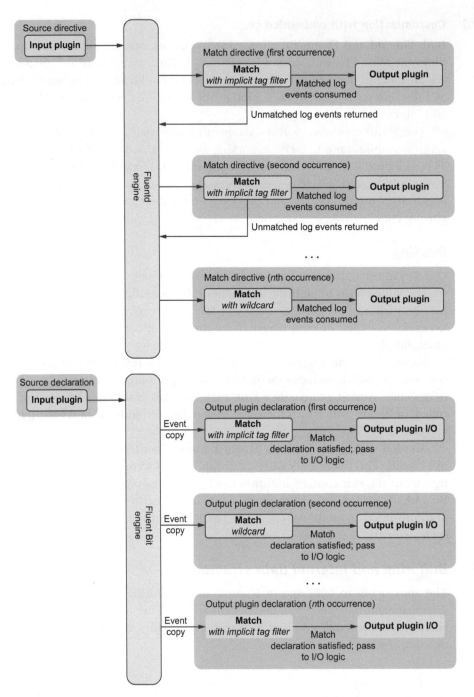

Figure C.1   The difference between Fluent Bit and Fluentd's handling of buffered events and the output plugin. Fluentd offers the event to each output plugin in the pipeline until a match occurs. Fluent Bit offers the event to all the output plugins in the pipeline without regard to whether it is consumed elsewhere.

Fluent Bit's internal data structure started in v1 with the same structure as Fluentd, but from v2 on, Fluent Bit adjusted its internal model slightly to make it easier to manage logs, traces, and metrics (figure C.2).

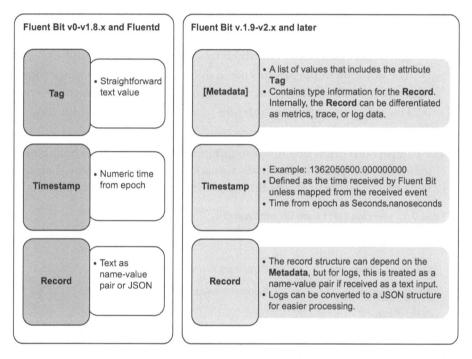

Figure C.2 Comparing the internal data structure of an event. The key difference between the two structures is the Tag (Fluentd on the left) and the Metadata (Fluent Bit on the right) as an array of values that includes the tag value.

Fluentd's approach to threading with its workers construct gave configuration developers a great deal of control, enabling them to group different input and output plugins in a thread, as well as configure threading for the buffer. By comparison, Fluent Bit offers some thread control, but it isn't as direct and explicit. More important, the buffer doesn't have direct thread controls. This situation is not so much a constraint as a reflection of how the relationship between buffers and inputs is implemented.

C.6 *Streaming processing*

Streaming (or streaming analytics, to use the more common term) is a notable difference. Fluent Bit has it, and Fluentd does not. The feature allows Fluent Bit to generate more real-time analytical data, such as the volume of types of data processed per minute. We shouldn't expect the stream processor to be as feature-rich as Apache Spark in processing observability events (at least at the moment). Several constraints must be overcome before the possibility can even be considered.

C.7 Conclusion

Several websites compare Fluent Bit and Fluentd. The level of detail varies, but typically, the comparison boils down to several basic points:

- Fluent Bit's execution footprint is much smaller than Fluentd's.
- The portfolio of plugins specific to different services is far greater for Fluentd.
- Available features align Fluent Bit more closely to the Kubernetes ecosystem.
- Fluentd, in our opinion, scales up more easily, and Fluent Bit is easier to scale down.

The comparisons often boil down to differences in use cases, as both Fluent Bit and Fluentd can be applied to almost any scenario. Some scenarios lend themselves better to Fluentd and others to Fluent Bit (table C.1).

Table C.1 Use cases for Fluent Bit and Fluentd

Fluent Bit	Fluentd
Cloud-native/Kubernetes	Containers and VMs
Internet of Things	Monolithic and traditional applications
Logs and metrics	Logs

Perhaps the most valuable factor to consider is the rate of development. Fluent Bit is evolving and adding significant new capabilities faster than Fluentd, which continues to develop at a more measured pace.

index

L

latency
  between events and
      dashboards 305
  in getting logs 101
  in the system 229
  minimizing 297
  of calling the database 287
  of important metrics 148
  of storage devices 69
  resultant 190
  timestamping and 232
legacy 204
lines 171
Linux 311
  Fluent Bit installations 309
  prepping 308
  sockets 78
log events 4
  generating metrics from
      207–210
  sending to console 135–138
log files, capturing 62–69
logfmt parser 181
logging
  application direct to Fluent
      Bit 101–111
  format definitions 348
  frameworks 13, 51, 57, 61, 67,
      69, 111, 351
  helpful practices and
      resources 342
logging driver 51, 76, 100–101,
    111, 300
Logging in Action, book 20, 58,
    69–70, 85, 135, 158, 175,
    343, 350, 353
logical architecture 8–10
Logrotate 67
logs 330
  configuring Fluent Bit 22
  container log drivers
      100–101
  file-based log events 61
  filtering and transforming
      events 190–199
  Kubernetes and containers,
      architectural context 91
  OpenStack 330, 334
  parsing 164, 169, 178–181,
      330

processors with Lua for 250
stream processors, creating
    streams 239–242
LogSimulator 19, 58–59, 62–64,
    66, 308, 312–314
  Java and Groovy 314–315
  post-LogSimulator use 315
  running as downloaded
      image 313
  running as locally built
      Docker image 313
  running containerized 58–60
Loki 11, 125, 312, 336, 340, 345
LTSV (Label Tab-Separated
    Value) parser 181
ltsv (label tab-separated values)
    format 139
Lua 212–220, 347, 350–351, 353
  background 213
  filters 189, 212, 214–216, 220
  processors with, for logs
      250–252
  processors with for logs 250
  scripts 9, 15, 115–116, 214,
      260, 302

M

macOS 52–53, 151, 308–316
  Fluent Bit installations 309
matching 210–212
  seeing at work 138
  wildcards 27, 53, 110, 135–
      136, 138, 194, 210, 239,
      247, 303
MessagePack 7, 28, 76, 83, 137,
    185
  msgpack format 139–140,
      288, 291
metadata 7
metrics
  capturing 52–54
  capturing from Docker
      containers 96–97
  defined 4, 80
  DockerMetrics plugin 96–97
  environment 23
  generating from log events 4,
      207–210
  local 12
  log_to_metrics 207
  memory metrics 50

network metrics 55, 100, 121,
    135, 142, 292
OS-based 55
processors to 257
pulling back 99
sending and receiving 7, 86
system metrics 50, 145
minikube 104, 106, 312
Modify filter 42, 194, 196–198
modify operation 196
MongoDB 329
monitoring Fluent Bit 42–45,
    131–133
mTLS (mutual TLS) 303
multiline
  content 121
  filtering 172
  log events/logs 101, 171, 299,
      331, 335
  outputs 117
  parsers 115–117, 170–174,
      185, 334–335
  processing 171
  use cases 110
multiline parsers 334
MySQL 316
  setting up 282

N

naming, selecting multiple
    attributes 236–237
native executables 52–55
Nest filter 195
.Net 82
netif plugin 52–53, 133, 319
network controls 129
network metrics 55, 100, 121,
    135, 142, 292
Nginx 329
Node Explorer 52, 56, 97–98,
    142–143, 145–146, 148, 207,
    257, 319–320
null output 131
  configuring 133

O

observability
  hyperscaler native and SaaS
      observability 162
  resources 341